# At the Edges of Thought

D1614504

# At the Edges of Thought

Deleuze and Post-Kantian Philosophy

Edited by Craig Lundy and Daniela Voss

EDINBURGH
University Press

© editorial matter and organisation Craig Lundy and Daniela Voss, 2015
© the chapters their several authors, 2015

Edinburgh University Press Ltd
The Tun – Holyrood Road, 12(2f) Jackson's Entry, Edinburgh EH8 8PJ

www.euppublishing.com

Typeset in 10.5/13 pt Sabon by
Servis Filmsetting Ltd, Stockport, Cheshire,
and printed and bound in Great Britain by
CPI Group (UK) Ltd, Croydon CR0 4YY

A CIP record for this book is available from the British Library

ISBN 978 0 7486 9462 4 (hardback)
ISBN 978 0 7486 9464 8 (webready PDF)
ISBN 978 0 7486 9463 1 (paperback)
ISBN 978 0 7486 9465 5 (epub)

The right of Craig Lundy and Daniela Voss to be identified as Editor of this work
has been asserted in accordance with the Copyright, Designs and Patents Act 1988,
and the Copyright and Related Rights Regulations 2003 (SI No. 2498).

# Contents

# Acknowledgements

First thanks must go to Sean Bowden, whose outstanding symposium *Deleuze, Pragmatism and Post-Kantian Thought*, held at Deakin University (Melbourne) in December 2012, this collection first emerged from. Much that is good about this book is due to his early efforts and vision. An affiliated event, *Continental Philosophy and Social Transformation*, was also held at the University of New South Wales in late 2012, which provided a further forum for the development of several papers contained herein. For this we are grateful to the School of Humanities and Languages at the University of New South Wales and the Institute for Social Transformation Research at the University of Wollongong, who co-hosted this workshop.

We have been blessed and honoured to work with an unquestionably first-rate cast of contributors on this project. Engaging with them and their ideas has been immensely rewarding, for which we would like to express our heartfelt thanks. Other academic colleagues/friends who are most deserving of our gratitude are Jon Roffe and Gregg Flaxman, for their astute intellectual guidance. Jorinde Voigt, whose work features on the cover, has been enormously generous in allowing us to associate her artistic brilliance with the Idea of this book. And of course, copious thanks must be extended to Carol Macdonald and the team at EUP for being so professional and such a pleasure to work with.

Finally, the editors would like to thank Camden House for granting permission to reprint Frederick Amrine's chapter '"The magic formula we all seek": Spinoza + Fichte = x', in Elisabeth Krimmer and Patricia Simpson (eds), *Religion, Reason and Culture in the Age of Goethe* (Rochester: Camden House, 2013). The same thanks are due to Wiley-Blackwell for granting permission to reprint Gregg Lambert's piece 'Kant's Bastards: Deleuze and Lyotard', *Philosophical Forum*, 43.3, (2012), pp. 345–56. In both cases there have been modifications made to the text.

# List of Contributors

**Brent Adkins** is Associate Professor of Philosophy at Roanoke College in Salem, VA. He is the author of several books on Deleuze including *Death and Desire in Hegel, Heidegger and Deleuze* (2008), *Rethinking Philosophy and Theology with Deleuze* (2013), and *Deleuze and Guattari's* A Thousand Plateaus: *An Introduction and Guide* (2015).

**Frederick Amrine** is Arthur F. Thurnau Professor in German Studies at the University of Michigan, Ann Arbor. His major publications include *Goethe and the Sciences: A Reconsideration* (1987) and *Goethe in the History of Science* (2 vols, 1996); recent studies have been devoted to aesthetics, Goethe's *Faust*, and Rudolf Steiner.

**Sean Bowden** is Lecturer in Philosophy at Deakin University, Australia. He is the author of *The Priority of Events: Deleuze's* Logic of Sense (Edinburgh University Press, 2011), and the co-editor of *Badiou and Philosophy* (Edinburgh University Press, 2012) and *Deleuze and Pragmatism* (Routledge, 2014).

**Gregory Flaxman** is an Associate Professor in the Department of English and Comparative Literature and the Director of Global Cinema Studies at the University of North Carolina, Chapel Hill. The editor of *The Brain is the Screen* and the author of *Gilles Deleuze and the Fabulation of Philosophy*, his latest book (co-authored with Robert Sinnerbrink and Lisa Trahair) on 'cinematic thinking' will be published in 2014.

**Joe Hughes** is a Lecturer in English and Theatre Studies at the University of Melbourne. He has written widely on Deleuze. His most recent work is *Philosophy After Deleuze*.

**Gregg Lambert** is Dean's Professor of the Humanities at Syracuse University, New York, and author of many books on the philosophy of Deleuze and on Continental Philosophy more generally; most recently, *In Search for a New Image of Thought: Gilles Deleuze and Philosophical Expressionism* (University of Minnesota Press, 2012).

**Jay Lampert** works on the philosophy of time. His books include *Synthesis and Backward Reference in Husserl's Logical Investigations, Deleuze and Guattari's Philosophy of History*, and *Simultaneity and Delay*. His current book project concerns the futural noema of decisions. He teaches Philosophy at the University of Guelph and Duquesne University.

**Beth Lord** is Senior Lecturer in Philosophy at the University of Aberdeen. She is the author of *Kant and Spinozism: Transcendental Idealism from Jacobi to Deleuze, Spinoza's* Ethics: *An Edinburgh Philosophical Guide* and several articles on Kant and Deleuze.

**Craig Lundy** is a Research Fellow in the Institute for Social Transformation Research at the University of Wollongong, Australia. He is the author of *History and Becoming: Deleuze's Philosophy of Creativity* (Edinburgh University Press, 2012) and various papers on the philosophy of history, socio-political philosophy and European philosophy.

**Arkady Plotnitsky** is a Professor of Theory and Cultural Studies at Purdue University. He has published extensively on Romanticism, continental philosophy and the philosophy of mathematics and science. His most recent books are *Epistemology and Probability: Bohr, Heisenberg, Schrödinger and the Nature of Quantum-Theoretical Thinking* and *Niels Bohr and Complementarity*.

**Anne Sauvagnargues** is a Full Professor at Paris West University. Her publications include: *Deleuze and Arts* (Paris, 2005; Continuum/Bloomsbury, 2013); *Deleuze, L'Empirisme Transcendantal* (Paris, 2010; forthcoming English translation with Edinburgh University Press); and *Ecology of Images: Simondon, Deleuze, Guattari* (Edinburgh University Press, 2014).

**Daniel W. Smith** teaches in the Department of Philosophy at Purdue University. He is the author of *Essays on Deleuze* (Edinburgh University Press, 2012) and the editor, with Henry Somers-Hall, of *The Cambridge Companion to Deleuze* (Cambridge University Press, 2012).

**Henry Somers-Hall** is a senior lecturer in philosophy at Royal Holloway, University of London. He is the author of *Hegel, Deleuze and the Critique of Representation* (SUNY Press, 2012), and *Deleuze's* Difference and Repetition (Edinburgh University Press, 2013), and co-editor of the *Cambridge Companion to Deleuze* (Cambridge University Press, 2012).

**Daniela Voss** lectures in philosophy at the Free University of Berlin and is an Honorary Fellow at Deakin University, Melbourne. She received her PhD at the Free University and is author of *Conditions of Thought: Deleuze and Transcendental Ideas*, published by Edinburgh University Press in 2013.

**Alistair Welchman** is an Associate Professor of Philosophy at the University of Texas at San Antonio. His edited collection *Politics of Religion/Religions of Politics* has just been published, and he has collaborated on translations of Schopenhauer (Cambridge University Press) and Maimon (Continuum, 2010) as well as publishing a large number of articles.

**Nathan Widder** is a Professor of Political Theory at Royal Holloway, University of London. He is author of *Genealogies of Difference* (University of Illinois Press, 2002), *Reflections on Time and Politics* (Penn State University Press, 2008) and *Political Theory after Deleuze* (Bloomsbury Press, 2012).

# Introduction: Deleuze and Post-Kantian Thought – Method, Ideas and Aesthetics

*Daniela Voss and Craig Lundy*

Without doubt, Immanuel Kant's transcendental idealism constituted a major event in philosophy – one that continues to be actualised in multifarious ways today. It has provided the terms of reference and inspiration for several philosophical traditions, most notably German Idealism and Romanticism, but also various currents across the spectrum of contemporary philosophy.[1] In the work of Gilles Deleuze, Kant's presence is pronounced. Despite Deleuze's famous remark that his book on Kant's critical philosophy was intended 'as a book about an enemy',[2] this proclaimed hostility towards Kant rather proves that he regarded Kant as an important 'intercessor'[3] whose concepts could be made to work in a new problematic setting. In fact, Deleuze expresses a kind of involuntary admiration for Kant: 'there functions a sort of thinking machine, a sort of creation of concepts that is absolutely frightening'.[4] And in *Difference and Repetition*, Deleuze compares Kant to 'a great explorer' since he is 'the one who discovers the prodigious domain of the transcendental'.[5] Kant's transcendental philosophy meant turning away from metaphysical projects of grounding philosophy on transcendent principles and values; it replaces the concept of essence with the concept of sense or appearance and the search for the conditions of appearances;

---

[1] Indeed, for those who find value in the so-called 'analytic' and 'continental' divide, it is not uncommon for Kant to be identified as the branching point of these two trajectories (bearing in mind, of course, that this divergence is retrospectively fabricated).

[2] Gilles Deleuze, *Negotiations*, trans. Martin Joughin (New York: Columbia University Press, 1995), p. 6.

[3] Ibid. p. 125.

[4] Gilles Deleuze, 'Synthesis and Time', Lecture Course on Kant held at Vincennes, 14 March 1978, available at <www.webdeleuze.com>

[5] Gilles Deleuze, *Difference and Repetition*, trans. Paul Patton (New York: Columbia University Press, 1994), p. 135.

it introduces time as a structure of empirical consciousness. For Deleuze, the 'greatest initiative of transcendental philosophy' is the introduction of difference in the 'I': the subject is fractured in the transcendental 'I' that thinks, and thereby generates its own empirical passive self in the form of time.[6] In this regard, Deleuze claims that Hölderlin, rather than Fichte or Hegel, is the true descendant to Kant,[7] because he poses the problem of the pure and empty form of time on the level of Greek tragedy, showing its shattering effect in Sophocles' *Oedipus Rex*. On Deleuze's reading, Oedipus is guilty of committing a crime – specifically, the excessive act of separating himself from the gods and doing away with divine judgement – and is therefore compelled to err along the straight line of pure and empty time.[8]

Remarks like these on Kant's descendants (such as Maimon, Fichte, Hölderlin, Schelling and Hegel) occur throughout Deleuze's corpus; and yet, a close assessment of these connections remains missing. Thus, while Deleuze's debt to Kant is clear and well acknowledged, a great deal remains to be said on both the manner of his relations to many post-Kantian thinkers and indeed the post-Kantian tenor of his own thought.

An exception is perhaps Deleuze's relationship to Hegel, which has received much attention of late in Deleuze scholarship. Generally, Deleuze is seen as an anti-Hegelian thinker[9] – an impression solidified by his book on Nietzsche, which is unambiguously written with an anti-Hegelian edge. As is often remarked, Deleuze criticises Hegel's dialectic for its appeal to concepts of negation: ontological difference is misrepresented as contradiction, leading to a 'negation of negation' that precludes any affirmation of difference.[10] Hegel is thus regarded as having betrayed the philosophy of difference – a result that is rectified in Nietzsche. However, a more favourable reading of Hegel can be found in Deleuze's 1954 review of Jean Hyppolite's book *Logic and Existence*. There, Deleuze affirms Hyppolite's interpretation of Hegelian dialectis

---

[6] Ibid. p. 87.

[7] Ibid. pp. 58 and 87.

[8] Deleuze, 'Synthesis and Time'. See also Gregory Flaxman, 'Chronos is Sick: Deleuze, Antonioni and the Kantian Lineage of Modern Cinema', in this volume, pp. 307–29.

[9] Cf. Deleuze's distaste for Hegel is clearly expressed in his 'Letter to a Harsh Critic': What I most detested was Hegelianism and dialectics', in *Negotiations*, p. 6. However, in spite of this frequently cited enmity, recent scholarship also highlights the thematic connections and points of convergence between Deleuze and Hegel. See Nathan Widder, 'State Philosophy and the War Machine', in this volume, pp. 190–211.

[10] Cf. Gilles Deleuze, *Nietzsche and Philosophy*, trans. Hugh Tomlinson (New York: Columbia University Press, 1983), p. 196.

as an ontology of sense, which is to say, an ontology of expression: *'Philosophy must be ontology, it cannot be anything else; but there is no ontology of essence, there is only an ontology of sense.'*[11] The main claim of the book, according to Deleuze, is that philosophy has to rid itself of anthropology. Thus Hegel criticised the Kantian conception of reality, which remains tied to subjective representational experience or self-consciousness. Kantian concepts are extrinsic to the thing-in-itself, Hegel says, and 'no fit terms to *express* the Absolute'.[12] For Hegel, there is nothing outside the concept: it fully expresses the dialectical development of the Absolute, consisting in the stages of unity, difference and unity-in-difference. In Hyppolite's words, it expresses the sense or meaning of the Absolute. While Deleuze endorses Hyppolite's account of Hegel's dialectics as a model of immanent self-differentiation, where the concept is revealed as the expression of the Absolute, he nonetheless asks 'whether an ontology of difference couldn't be created that would not go all the way to contradiction, since contradiction would be less and not more than difference'.[13] This remark already anticipates Deleuze's own elaboration of a philosophy of difference as well as his own logic of sense.

Deleuze's engagement with post-Kantian philosophy owes much to his teachers: besides his lecturer Jean Hyppolite, this is most notably Martial Guéroult. Olivier Revault, a longtime friend of Deleuze during his time as a Sorbonne student, reports that they admired Martial Guéroult for his close readings and structural method: 'I always found Gilles to be a great student of Guéroult.'[14] In fact, explicit traces of Guéroult can be found in the footnotes of many of Deleuze's books. When discussing the work of Maimon or Fichte, Deleuze usually refers to Gueroult's book *La Philosophie transcendantale de Salomon Maïmon* (1929) or the two volumes of *L'Évolution et la structure de la doctrine de la science chez Fichte* (1930). It seems likely that Deleuze knew Maimon and Fichte first and foremost through reading Guéroult. Of course, the most obvious homage to Guéroult is Deleuze's 1969 article 'Gueroult's General Method for Spinoza', which was

---

[11] Gilles Deleuze, 'Jean Hyppolite's *Logic of Existence*', in David Lapoujade (ed.), *Desert Islands and Other Texts (1953–74)*, trans. Michael Taormina (New York: Semiotext(e), 2004), p. 15.

[12] G. W. F. Hegel, *Encyclopedia Logic*, trans. William Wallace (Oxford: Oxford University Press, 1975 [1830]), §44, p. 72.

[13] Deleuze, 'Jean Hyppolite's *Logic of Existence*', p. 18.

[14] Cited in François Dosse, *Gilles Deleuze and Félix Guattari: Intersecting Lives* (New York: Columbia University Press, 2010), p. 97.

published only one year after Guéroult's extensive study of part I of the
*Ethics*.[15]

So far, we have traced the autobiographical encounters by which
certain ideas of German Idealism – of Maimon, Fichte and Hegel –
influenced Deleuze's philosophy. Beyond that, the aim of this volume
is to show the common themes and concepts that Deleuze shares with
post-Kantian thought. Deleuze is certainly not a post-Kantian thinker
in the manner of German Idealism and Romanticism. Nevertheless, as
Christian Kerslake has argued, many of his '*questions* and *problems*
emerge from within the post-Kantian tradition of philosophy'.[16] Indeed,
Kerslake goes so far as to claim that 'Deleuze's own conception of his
philosophical project is fundamentally post-Kantian in its assumptions'
– a strong thesis that he justifies primarily with regard to Deleuze's
1956–7 lecture series *Qu'est-ce que fonder?*[17] This early lecture course
is the most coherent and explicit engagement of Deleuze with the post-
Kantian tradition and, as Kerslake claims, it already sets the course for
Deleuze's attempt 'to transform Kantianism from within, and to produce
a self-grounding post-Kantian system of complete self-differentiation'.[18]
Kerslake interprets Deleuze's philosophy as a continuation of the
Kantian project, as carrying out a 'Copernican revolution which opens
up the possibility of difference having its own concept'.[19] But while
Kerslake's careful and detailed argumentation has a lot to commend it,
it is debatable whether Deleuze's philosophical thinking can be systema-
tised to the extent that Kerslake suggests. The aim of this book is com-
parably modest: as a collection, the contributions seek to identify some
significant common problems and interests that link Deleuze in various
ways to the diverse tradition of post-Kantian thought.[20] As way of introduction, we will discuss a few themes that seem to entail eminent points
of resonance between Deleuze's thought and post-Kantian philosophy:

[15] Martial Guéroult, *Spinoza/1, Dieu (Ethique, I)* (Paris: Aubier-Montaigne, 1968);
Gilles Deleuze, 'Gueroult's General Method for Spinoza', in David Lapoujade (ed.),
*Desert Islands and Other Texts (1953–74)*, trans. Michael Taormina (New York:
Semiotext(e), 2004), pp. 146–55.
[16] Christian Kerslake, *Immanence and the Vertigo of Philosophy: From Kant to Deleuze*
(Edinburgh: Edinburgh University Press, 2009), p. 3.
[17] Ibid.
[18] Ibid. p. 26.
[19] Deleuze, *Difference and Repetition*, pp. 40–1.
[20] Perhaps Joe Hughes' contribution to this collection 'Ground, Transcendence and
Method in Deleuze's Fichte' comes closest to Kerslake's suggestion, as the common
problem that he identifies for both Deleuze and Fichte is 'the completion of the
Kantian enterprise'. See this volume, p. 148.

(1) the notion of a synthetic and constructive method; (2) the Idea or the Absolute; and (3) Aesthetics.

## THE NOTION OF A SYNTHETIC AND CONSTRUCTIVE METHOD

The German Idealists were disappointed by Kant's attempt to ground experience and knowledge in the *a priori* mental structure of the transcendental subject. Kant presupposed *a priori* facts about cognition, i.e. forms and categories that were supposed to secure an objective standard of knowledge, but the German Idealists found his justification wanting. Kant's transcendental deduction of the pure concepts of the understanding is built on formal logic; it takes as its inspiration the Aristotelian table of logical forms of judgement and proceeds by formal logical inference. However, convinced by Jacobi, the German Idealists doubted that general logic is an adequate model for philosophy, since it is entirely formal and completely abstracts from all relation to empirical reality. Maimon was the first to ask: 'how is it conceivable that *a priori* concepts of the understanding like those of cause and effect can provide determinations of something *a posteriori*?'[21] The underlying problem is the fundamental distinction between formal logic and the real. In fact, it was Kant's great achievement to have rejected traditional metaphysics by insisting on the distinction between 'logical' relations and 'real' relations. In the 'Remark to the amphiboly of the concepts of reflection', Kant accuses Leibniz of misrepresenting the real relations of space and time: Leibniz draws these representations into the concept and thus reduces them to merely logical and intelligible relations of things.[22] However, in the wake of this distinction, Kant had to struggle with the hiatus between logical concepts and real relations. A possible solution to this predicament was sketched out by certain post-Kantian philosophers: 'Should not transcendental logic be deduced from its principle *independently* of general logic?'[23] Maimon, Hölderlin, Novalis, Schlegel, Schelling and Hegel, each in his own way, were searching for a more compelling derivation or sufficient reason which would provide a

---

[21] Salomon Maimon, *Essay on Transcendental Philosophy*, trans. Nick Midgley, Henry Somers-Hall, Alistair Welchman and Merten Reglitz (London, New York: Continuum, 2010 [1790]), p. 41.

[22] Immanuel Kant, *Critique of Pure Reason*, trans. and ed. Allen W. Wood (Cambridge: Cambridge University Press, 1998), A275–26/B331–2.

[23] Paul Franks, 'Serpentine Naturalism and Protean Nihilism: Transcendental Philosophy in Anthropological Post-Kantianism, German Idealism, and Neo-Kantianism', in Brian Leiter and Michael Rosen (eds), *Oxford Handbook of Continental Philosophy* (Oxford: Oxford University Press, 2007), p. 258.

basis for the real relations of space and time, no less than for the matter of experience itself. What was needed was a foundation for empirical reality as a whole. Ironically, the German Idealists returned to the pre-Kantian metaphysicians, and in particular to Spinoza, in order to improve on Kantian transcendental philosophy.[24]

As Spinoza has argued, 'the true method of discovery is to form thoughts from some given definitions'.[25] However, a complete or perfect definition must satisfy some requirements: it should not simply *postulate* the existence of the thing with all its properties. On the contrary, it must be possible to *deduce* the innermost essence of the thing including all its properties from the definition. As an example for an incomplete definition of a thing, Spinoza takes the nominal definition of a circle:

> If a circle is defined as a figure, such that all straight lines drawn from the centre to the circumference are equal, every one can see that such a definition does not in the least explain the essence of a circle, but solely one of its properties.[26]

Instead, a definition is required which provides an explanation for the *production* of the figure – that is, a real definition explaining how it arises. In the case of the circle it can be a dynamic rule of construction, such as 'the figure described by any line whereof one end is fixed and the other free'.[27] Salomon Maimon discusses the example of the definition of the circle in his *Essay on Transcendental Philosophy* and similarly comes to the conclusion that a nominal definition is insufficient, because we would only 'know the meaning of the rule or condition of the circle' but not its mode of genesis. As Maimon says: 'Should it be incapable of fulfilment, then the concept here expressed in words would have no objective reality: its synthesis would be found only in words but not in the thing itself.'[28] He therefore demands a 'real definition', which supplies an explanation of the way that things arise, i.e. a method of generation that also provides the basis for the 'material completeness' of the thing. In analogy to the geometrical method by means of which synthetic concepts can be constructed, philosophy needs to find a genetic and synthetic method to explain the genesis of objects.

[24] Ibid. p. 256.
[25] Benedict de Spinoza, *On the Improvement of the Understanding*, in Spinoza, *On the Improvement of the Understanding, The Ethics & Correspondence*, trans. R. H. M. Elwes (New York: Dover, 1955), §94, pp. 34–5.
[26] Ibid. §95, p. 35.
[27] Ibid. §96, p. 35.
[28] Maimon, *Essay on Transcendental Philosophy*, p. 50.

While this is not the place to engage in a full discussion of Maimon's solution to the problem of the genesis of things, we can nevertheless see the way in which geometry and its method of construction of concepts served as an inspiration for philosophy. This sympathy for the geometric method is largely due to Spinoza, which he had rendered reputable through the application of the *more geometrico* in his *Ethics*.

As Martial Guéroult argued, Spinoza's use of definitions, propositions and demonstrations by no means follows a formal logic of inference. Spinoza does not begin with a self-evident principle from which all other beliefs are derived in a chain of deduction. Instead, Spinoza arrives at the definition of a single substance or God within the first eight propositions of the *Ethics*: in the beginning, he defines the attributes as qualified substances, which are distinct in reality but not numerically distinct. Together they constitute one and the same substance. In Guéroult's words: 'God is motley, but unfragmentable, constituted of heterogeneous but inseparable attributes.'[29] According to this interpretation, the attributes are genealogical elements of substance whose definition is derived by means of a genetic and synthetic method. Thus, Spinoza's geometric method is essentially synthetic – and therefore resembles the geometric method in mathematical constructions. In his article on Guéroult, Deleuze emphasises that Spinozism as a 'genetic and constructive philosophy is inseparable from a synthetic method'.[30] In the same article he also praises Guéroult for having demonstrated a 'deep Spinozism of Fichte': Fichte also pursued a synthetic method, 'which is opposed to Kant's analytic method'.[31] In his Lecture course *Qu'est-ce que fonder?*, Deleuze explains that the Kantian transcendental project is based on facts of consciousness, or at least makes use of a hypothesis: if we have objective experience, then the categories must be objectively valid.

> In the Kantian attempt a simple hypothesis subsists. Kant remains tied to simple facticity, Fichte says, while he, Fichte, seeks genesis. . . . Therefore Fichte claims 'Kant has never elevated himself to the transcendental analysis. His analysis is only regressive.'[32]

Fichte took issue with the Kantian presupposition of the transcendental 'I'. It seemed not acceptable that the unconditioned ground of

---

[29] Guéroult, *Spinoza*, pp. 234, 447. Cited in Deleuze, 'Gueroult's General Method for Spinoza', p. 150.

[30] Deleuze, 'Gueroult's General Method for Spinoza', p. 151.

[31] Ibid. p. 147.

[32] Deleuze, *Qu'est-ce que fonder?*, trans. Daniela Voss. The lecture series is available at <www.webdeleuze.com>

experience and of all objects of experience was an unknowable self, and that this unknowable self was at the same time the necessary condition to render free action possible. Fichte demanded access to the unconditioned, self-grounding subject and developed a theory of intellectual intuition resorting to the theory of mathematical construction. 'Just as we prove a proposition in geometry through the construction of a figure in pure intuition, so in philosophy we should demonstrate the forms of the mind by constructing them in a pure intuition.'[33]

Ironically, Kant himself had written on the method of construction in the first chapter of 'The Transcendental Doctrine of Method', but he explicitly relegated this method of cognition to the field of mathematics and argued against any attempt to draw metaphysical conclusions by mathematical constructions.

> Mathematics is thoroughly grounded on definitions, axioms and demonstrations. I will content myself with showing that none of these elements, in the sense in which the mathematician takes them, can be achieved or imitated by philosophy; and that by means of his method the geometrician [Meßkünstler] can build nothing in philosophy except houses of cards . . . [P]hilosophy consists precisely in knowing its bounds.[34]

The main distinction between mathematics and philosophy, Kant argues, lies in two different uses of reason: The philosophical use 'is called the use of reason in accordance with concepts'.[35] It can provide nothing but a rule of synthesis, a pure concept, under which possible empirical intuitions can be subsumed. Thus it only amounts to discursive knowledge achieved by mere concepts. The mathematical use of reason 'is the use of reason through construction of concepts':[36] it allows the construction of synthetic concepts in pure intuition – that is, the pure objects themselves as spatio-temporal magnitudes (*quanta*). According to Kant, there is a great difference 'between the discursive use of reason in accordance with concepts and its intuitive use through the construction of concepts'.[37] However, the German Idealists did not seem to be convinced.

In his essay 'Über die Construktion in der Philosophie', Schelling argues that the Kantian distinction between philosophy and mathemat-

---

[33] Frederick Beiser, *German Idealism: The Struggle Against Subjectivism, 1781–1801* (Cambridge, MA: Harvard University Press, 2002), p. 296. See also Frederick Amrine, '"The magic formula we all seek": Spinoza + Fichte = x', in this volume, pp. 168–89.

[34] Kant, *Critique of Pure Reason*, A726–7/B754–5 (translation modified by Daniela Voss).

[35] Ibid. A723/B751.

[36] Ibid. A724/B752.

[37] Ibid. A719/B747.

ics cannot be upheld.[38] On the contrary, the geometrical method is supposed to be analogous to the method in philosophy. The mathematician, in constructing a geometrical figure, realises the universal within the particular, the ideal within the real, just as the philosopher's task is to abstract from the contingent features of the particular and see it as an instantiation of the Absolute. The only difference lies in the nature of the universal: in geometry, the universal is the pure forms of intuition (space and time), while philosophy is concerned with the universe as a whole, i.e. the Absolute. In order to grasp the Absolute, the philosopher has to resort to 'intellectual intuition', which is a means to construct the identity of all things as archetypes or manifestations of the absolute principle. For Schelling, the mathematical method of construction played a vital role in his late Jena philosophy of intellectual intuition.[39] No doubt, Kant would have insisted that Schelling regresses to pre-Kantian metaphysics, that he has given up reflective thinking and affirmed speculative thought. Indeed, 'as speculative philosophy, German Idealism speaks ontologically once more: it considers "what everything is in itself"'.[40]

We have already referred to Deleuze's approval of the synthetic and constructive method and he explicitly praises it as an achievement of the post-Kantians. In his lecture course *Qu'est-ce que fonder?*, he declares that the common theme of Maimon and Fichte is the substitution of a synthetic and genetic method for the Kantian discursive method of gaining knowledge from mere concepts. Even Hegel understands the dialectic as a synthetic and genetic method – in fact, as an ontological, dialectical movement of the things themselves.[41] In what way does Deleuze take up this synthetic and genetic method in his own philosophy?

In a paper given to the members of the French Society of Philosophy on 28 January 1967, Deleuze explains his conception of 'the method of dramatization'.[42] With this method Deleuze picks up on the Kantian theory of schematisation, which is supposed to settle the difficulties of mediation between concepts and intuition, and sketches a solution in his own way: he 'dramatizes' the schema and renders it dynamical. What he has in mind is something akin to Maimon's 'ideas of the understanding'

---

[38] F. W. J. Schelling, 'Über die Construktion in der Philosophie', in H. M. Baumgartner, W. G. Jacobs, H. Krings and H. Zeltner (eds), *Werke: Historisch-Kritische Ausgabe* (Stuttgart–Bad Cannstatt: Frommann-Holzboog, 1976–), vol. V, pp. 125–34.

[39] Cf. Beiser, *German Idealism*, pp. 585–8.

[40] Franks, 'Serpentine Naturalism and Protean Nihilism', p. 268.

[41] Cf. Deleuze, *Qu'est-ce que fonder?*, available at <www.webdeleuze.com>

[42] Gilles Deleuze, 'The Method of Dramatization', in David Lapoujade (ed.), *Desert Islands and Other Texts (1953–74)*, trans. Michael Taormina (New York: Semiotext(e), 2004), pp. 94–116.

or 'differentials' – i.e. non-representational, intensive elements that generate spatio-temporal intuition through reciprocal determination.

> In a certain way, all the post-Kantians have tried to elucidate the mystery of this hidden art [schematisation], according to which dynamic spatio-temporal determinations genuinely have the power to dramatize a concept, although they have a nature totally different from the concept.[43]

Spatio-temporal dynamisms, according to Deleuze, create particular spaces and times; they generate both the quantitative and qualitative nature of things[44] as well as their generic and specific characteristics (e.g. the way that an animal inhabits its territory, organises space). Spatio-temporal dynamisms also specify concepts, but not in the Kantian sense of synthesising possible sensations under empty logical forms; rather, the concepts themselves are generated. In other words, concepts don't pre-exist, they are not dependent on mental structures, nor are the concepts derived from logical forms of judgement. Rather, concepts are generated in practical encounters, in real experience.[45] More precisely, the genesis of the act of thinking has its sufficient cause in an intensive reality that impinges on the sensible and nervous system of the body. This is what Deleuze calls 'a strange theatre' that affects the body and soul of 'larval subjects' (alluding to Antonin Artaud's theatre of cruelty[46]). What it also shows is that spatio-temporal dynamisms are not completely without a relation to subjectivity. As is generally known, Deleuze – just like Hölderlin, Novalis, Schlegel, Schelling and Hegel – completely abandons the Cartesian conception of self-consciousness, or the autonomous and self-sufficient Kantian–Fichtean subject as the starting point of philosophy. For the German Idealists, the subject still has an important role to play as the highest manifestation of the Absolute, the implicit *telos* of its self-differentiation. For Deleuze, however, the subject is not inherent as a *telos*, it is a real thing, a 'larval subject' that is open to processes of individuation and metamorphoses.

---

[43] Ibid. p. 99.

[44] As an example, Deleuze refers to the 'dynamics of the egg', i.e. the 'cellular migrations, foldings, invaginations, stretchings' that constitute a field of individuation for the embryo. A possible example of spatio-temporal dynamisms concerning inorganic nature could be the foldings and stretchings of barrier reefs or, as Deleuze says, 'the geographical dynamism of the island (island as rupture with the continent, and island as an eruption from the deep)'. Deleuze, 'The Method of Dramatization', pp. 96 and 98.

[45] For instance, the concept of truth gains its material signification through dramatic dynamisms that specify *'who wants the true, when and where, how and how much?'* Cf. Deleuze, 'The Method of Dramatization', p. 98.

[46] Ibid. p. 98. See also Henry Somers-Hall, 'Feuerbach and the Image of Thought', in this volume pp. 253–71.

What Deleuze presents in his paper on 'The Method of Dramatization' is a model of genesis and differentiation that in many ways is constructed along the lines of post-Kantian ideas. He accepts the post-Kantian critique that 'Kant held fast to the point of view of conditioning without attaining that of genesis.'[47] His own model therefore accounts for the genesis of objects and subjects, thought and concepts, and presupposes as sufficient reason or transcendental condition a field of intensive differences, 'an intensive *spatium* that preexists every quality and every extension'.[48] In Deleuze's system, this intensive field is the 'virtual Idea' and the function of spatio-temporal dynamisms is to 'dramatize' or actualise the Idea.

> The answer perhaps lies in a direction that certain post-Kantians have indicated: pure spatio-temporal dynamisms have the power to dramatize concepts, because first they actualize incarnate Ideas.[49]

## THE IDEA OR THE ABSOLUTE

German Idealism, in spite of its variety and diverse tradition, can be regarded as a philosophy of the Absolute or the Idea, which must be interpreted as something unconditioned, infinite and impersonal. The German Idealists thought of it as a sufficient reason or self-grounding principle. They thereby followed their 'mentor' Spinoza who defined substance as 'that which is in itself, and is conceived through itself' and argued that from 'the idea of God . . . an infinite number of things follow in infinite ways'.[50]

Schelling often refers to his philosophy as 'the doctrine of ideas' (*Ideenlehre*), and in his 1804 *System der gesammten Philosophie* describes the Absolute as something which is 'from itself and through itself' (*von sich selbst und durch sich selbst*).[51] Hegel held that all finite things exist in the 'universal divine idea', just as Spinoza argued that 'modes . . . can neither be, nor be conceived without substance; wherefore they can only be in the divine nature, and can only through it be

---

[47] Deleuze, *Difference and Repetition*, p. 170.
[48] Deleuze, 'The Method of Dramatization', p. 97.
[49] Ibid. p. 99.
[50] Benedict de Spinoza, *Ethics*, in Spinoza, *On the Improvement of the Understanding, The Ethics & Correspondence*, trans. R. H. M. Elwes (New York: Dover, 1955), Book I, def. 3, p. 45 and Book II, prop. 4, p. 85.
[51] F. W. J. Schelling, *Sämtliche Werke*, ed. K. F. A. Schelling, 14 vols (Stuttgart: Cotta, 1856–61), vol. VI, p. 148, §7.

conceived'.[52] Of course, in his *Lectures on the History of Philosophy*, Hegel criticised Spinoza's system, arguing that the modes are only affections without reality and that they completely disappear in the substance. Spinozism, according to Hegel, is 'acosmic' insofar as 'all this that we know as the world has been cast into the abyss of the one identity. There is therefore no such thing as finite reality.'[53] Although Hegel never mentions Maimon in this context, it seems that he fully adopted Maimon's view, who had first characterised Spinoza's system as an 'acosmism' in his autobiography. There, Maimon says that Spinoza denies the reality of the world of multiple diverse and finite things: 'In this system *unity* is real, but *multiplicity* is merely *ideal*.'[54] Whatever the correct interpretation of Spinoza (certainly, Deleuze would disagree emphatically), it is important to note that for Maimon and Hegel, as well as for Schelling or the early Romantics (Hölderlin, Novalis, Schlegel), the ideal is real. In other words, idealism and realism are not understood as oppositions.[55] In a similar vein, Deleuze defines the nature of virtual Ideas as real, borrowing a formulation of Proust: Ideas are 'real without being actual, ideal without being abstract'.[56] For Deleuze, the virtual Idea possesses a full intensive reality, consisting of differential elements and relations, singularities and poles. It does not merely have a regulative function like Kantian ideas, but acts as a sufficient reason: it is 'the reason of the sensible, the condition of that which appears'.[57] Virtual Ideas are also the indispensible conditions for the generation of thought: they are problems or problematic structures that need to be actualised in a corresponding field, be it a mathematical theory, a physical or biological system, the social field or an artwork. Deleuze's dialectic of Ideas is not connected with any particular example, but articulates the virtual matrix of any actual system or structure. According to Deleuze, virtual reality is not something transcendent, but rather a transcendental field, a genetic condition which generates the actual but does not resemble it. In his late text 'Immanence: A Life', Deleuze again talks of the transcendental field and defines it as a plane of immanence: 'The transcendental field then

---

[52] Spinoza, *Ethics*, Book I, prop. 15, demonstration.

[53] G. W. F. Hegel, *Lectures on the History of Philosophy: Medieval and Modern Philosophy*, Part III, trans. E. S. Haldane and F. H. Simson (Lincoln: University of Nebraska Press, 1995), p. 281.

[54] Salomon Maimon, *Solomon Maimon: An Autobiography*, trans. J. Clark Murray (London: Gardener, 1888), p. 113.

[55] Cf. Beiser, *German Idealism*, p. 353.

[56] Deleuze, 'The Method of Dramatization', p. 101. See also *Difference and Repetition*, p. 208.

[57] Deleuze, *Difference and Repetition*, p. 222.

becomes a genuine plane of immanence that reintroduces Spinozism into the heart of the philosophical process.'[58] The plane of immanence is 'absolute immanence',[59] which is not *in* something; it is not immanent to anything other than itself, neither to a self-consciousness or transcendental subject, nor to an object. Rather, subjects and objects evolve from the plane of immanence; they are ontologically secondary. As the title of the essay already announces, Deleuze equates the plane of immanence with 'a life', an indeterminate and inorganic life, which is not yet individualised.

> We will say of pure immanence that it is A LIFE, and nothing else. . . . A life is the immanence of immanence, absolute immanence: it is complete power, complete bliss. It is to the degree that he goes beyond the aporias of the subject and the object that Johann Fichte, in his last philosophy, presents the transcendental field as *a life*, no longer dependent on a Being or submitted to an Act – it is an absolute immediate consciousness whose very activity no longer refers to a being but is ceaselessly posed in a life.[60]

Here Deleuze refers to Fichte's late philosophy of his *Second Introduction to the Science of Knowledge* (1797), in which Fichte seems to rethink and redefine the starting point of transcendental philosophy. While in his Jena years he held that the principle of all philosophy lies in an original and reflective act (*Tathandlung*) of self-consciousness – i.e. in a free and self-positing 'I' – he later did not hesitate to evoke an 'Absolute' (Absolute Being or God) or 'a life', thereby abandoning the analysis of the self as a philosophical starting point. His new 'Doctrine of Being, Life and Blessedness'[61] clearly approaches speculative philosophy: 'It is the living and efficient Ex-istence of the Absolute itself which alone has power *to be* and *to exist*, and beside which nothing *is*, nor truly *exists*.'[62] This absolute Being, 'which in itself and in God is pure activity and Life',[63] can only be and exist through itself. Like Spinoza's substance, it is an unconditioned, self-grounding principle or sufficient reason. Fichte, just like the young Romantics and Schelling had done long before him, *vitalised* Spinoza's concept of substance: the Absolute becomes alive and

---

[58] Gilles Deleuze, 'Immanence: A Life', in *Pure Immanence: Essays on A Life*, trans. Anne Boyman (New York: Zone Books, 2001), pp. 27–8.

[59] Ibid. p. 26.

[60] Ibid. p. 27.

[61] Johann Gottlieb Fichte, *The Way towards the Blessed Life; or The Doctrine of Religion*, trans. William Smith (London: Chapman, 1849), p. 190, available online at <https://archive.org/stream/waytowardsbless00fichgoog#page/n6/mode/2up>.

[62] Ibid. p. 54.

[63] Ibid. p. 78.

dynamic.[64] The pressing question then became: How can the Absolute, which is necessarily lasting, without beginning and end, be 'formed and moulded into a particular World, and indeed into an infinitely varied World, flowing onward in a never-ending stream of new and changing forms'?[65] The conception of the organism served as a powerful model for the development of the Absolute. Hölderlin, Novalis, Schlegel, Schelling and (last but not least) Hegel all formulated the idea of dialectical development, which they found characteristic of all organic things: 'it begins from a stage of inchoate unity; it then differentiates itself; and it then reintegrates itself, so that its development consists in the stages of unity, difference, and unity-in-difference'.[66]

Although the ideas of self-differentiation, difference and differentials were of fundamental importance in the post-Kantian tradition, the concept of difference still remained subordinated to identity, organic unity, or totality. Deleuze compares Leibniz and Hegel, stating that they both pursued the thought of difference – the former as infinitely small differences, the latter as contradiction, the opposite extreme limit of difference. They therefore both entertained a model of 'infinite representation'. However, the problem with infinite representation, according to Deleuze, is that

> it does not free itself from the principle of identity as a presupposition of representation. . . . Infinite representation invokes a foundation. While this foundation is not the identical itself, it is nevertheless a way of taking the principle of identity particularly seriously, giving it an infinite value and rendering it coextensive with the whole, and in this manner allowing it to reign over existence itself.[67]

Deleuze, by contrast, ascribes primacy to the concept of difference. Difference must receive its own concept, such that it is no longer negatively defined as a lack of identity. It must free itself from a primary unity. When Deleuze repudiates the concept of foundation, what he aims to prevent is the sublation or reconciliation of difference in a higher identity of 'identity and difference'. It does not mean, however, that he completely abandons the idea of foundation. Rather, in *Difference and Repetition*, he modifies the idea and elaborates an account of 'a universal ungrounding' or 'groundlessness',[68] which tries to elude the

[64] Cf. Beiser, *German Idealism*, p. 367.
[65] Fichte, *The Way towards the Blessed Life*, p. 79.
[66] Beiser, *German Idealism*, p. 367.
[67] Deleuze, *Difference and Repetition*, p. 49.
[68] Ibid. p. 91.

trap of identity, unity or totality, and along with it, the mystical idea of a universal organism or rational plan, a purposiveness or teleology in nature. In this sense, he keeps closer to Spinoza and his banishment of final causes. However, besides difference, the second most fundamental 'transcendental principle', or condition of genesis, for Deleuze, is repetition. Repetition, production and reproduction are the major functions of the faculty of imagination, which for the German Romantics becomes a constitutive faculty of central importance. As Deleuze writes in his early lecture course *Qu'est-ce que fonder?*, after he has talked about the post-Kantian account of genesis and in particular about Novalis' philosophy of the imagination:

> What is unveiled (in the last chapter) is the true structure of the imagination, that is its meaning which can only be understood through the enterprise of grounding, which far from supposing the point of view of the infinite, is nothing other than the principle of the imagination.[69]

The faculty of imagination not only produces images; it also corresponds to a movement of reproduction in nature. It thus acts as a constitutive principle, that is a real movement of things themselves or a pure dynamism in nature. For the German Romantics, therefore, the boundary between philosophy and art, especially poetry, becomes blurred.

## AESTHETICS

In his *Critique of Pure Reason*, Kant ranks the faculty of the imagination among the lower cognitive faculties and ascribes to it a mediating role. Its task is the synthesis of reproduction, which remains subject to the determining, *a priori* concepts of the understanding. It is only in his third *Critique* that Kant allows a certain 'free play' of the imagination. The faculty of the imagination reflects the aesthetic form of the beautiful object and, beyond that, exercises a spontaneous and inventive production of images, entirely unrestrained by determining concepts. In fact, it cannot be taken merely 'as reproductive, as subjected to the laws of association, but as productive and self-active (as the authoress of voluntary forms of possible intuitions)'.[70] By way of example, Kant refers to English landscape gardens or baroque furniture whose extravagant

[69] Cf. Deleuze, *Qu'est-ce que fonder?*, trans. Daniela Voss.
[70] Immanuel Kant, *Critique of the Power of Judgment*, ed. Paul Guyer, trans. Paul Guyer and Eric Matthews (Cambridge: Cambridge University Press, 2000), 5: 240. (The pagination corresponds to the standard German edition of Kant's works, *Kant's Gesammelte Schriften*, edited by the Royal Prussian Academy of Sciences.)

variety of forms 'pushes the freedom of the imagination almost to the point of the grotesque'.[71] Likewise, in natural instances such as 'the changing shapes of a fire in a hearth or of a rippling brook' imagination sustains its free play.[72] In the Kantian theory of the sublime, the faculty of the imagination also plays a crucial role, because its failure to represent the infinite (the mathematically sublime) or its powerlessness in view of violent natural forces (the dynamically sublime) gives us, in the last resort, the feeling of something supernatural: Ideas of reason. This is to say that the imagination makes us aware of the superiority of reason and its regulative Ideas. Although it can never fully represent rational Ideas and therefore remains in stark contrast to reason, it attains a certain harmony with the higher cognitive faculties, because it acts in agreement with the moral interest of reason: it strives to incarnate rational Ideas in sensible nature by creating aesthetic Ideas.

Kant's reflections on beautiful objects in art and nature, as well as on the sublime, certify a certain Kantian 'Romanticism'. As Deleuze says: in his aesthetic of the Beautiful and of the Sublime, Kant gives access to a realm 'in which the sensible is valid in itself and unfolds in a *pathos* beyond all logic'.[73] The German Romantics were looking for just that: a form of knowledge which is nonconceptual and indemonstrable, but which we know to be true through direct experience. They found it in immediate aesthetic intuition, thereby ascribing enormous power to the imagination. What they had done was to transfer the traditional concept of intellectual intuition as an exercise of the infinite intellect into the aesthetic sphere. The Romantics claimed that we could know the absolute through aesthetic experience. Poetry, painting and music became the province of the ineffable, i.e. that which is inexpressible in words from the point of view of logic. The same goes for our ordinary sense perception: our sensuous experience of colours, sounds and tastes also cannot be verbalised adequately or proved by means of formal logical inference. Nature as a whole was considered as a work of art and as the expression of the absolute or infinite. Thus, Schlegel said in his lectures on transcendental philosophy: 'Idealism regards nature as a work of art, as a poem.'[74] The German Romantics no longer separated aesthetics as rigor-

---

[71]  Ibid. 5: 242.

[72]  Ibid. 5: 244.

[73]  Gilles Deleuze, *Kant's Critical Philosophy: The Doctrine of the Faculties*, trans. Hugh Tomlinson and Barbara Habberjam (London: Continuum, 2008), p. xi.

[74]  Friedrich Schlegel, *Vorlesungen über Transcendentalphilosophie*, in Ernst Behler, Jean-Jacques Anstett and Hans Eichner (eds), *Kritische Friedrich Schlegel Ausgabe* (Paderborn: Ferdinand Schöningh, 1958–), vol. XII, p. 105 (trans. by Daniela Voss).

ously as Kant had done into a doctrine of objective sense experience on the one hand, and on the other a theory of the beautiful and the sublime. Kant's critical claims about the limitation of our cognitive powers were put into question by reintroducing a sort of intellectual intuition, a transcendent exercise of the imagination. As Deleuze says, Kant's theory of the free and unregulated play of imagination paved the way for Romanticism and, against his intention, became its 'foundation'.[75]

In *Difference and Repetition*, Deleuze himself develops a theory of the transcendent exercise [*exercice transcendant*] of the faculties, according to which each faculty is unhinged and ceases to collaborate with the other faculties in 'common sense'. That is to say, the faculties no longer converge with the aim of recognising one and the same object, which can be sensed, recalled, imagined or conceived. Rather they are confronted with something that is not communicable within the context of a common sense: the 'imperceptible' or 'the being of the sensible'.[76] This something, according to Deleuze, 'moves the soul, "perplexes" it – in other words, forces it to pose a problem: as though the object of encounter, the sign, were the bearer of a problem'.[77] What impinges on the senses and forces their transcendent exercise, is a transcendental Idea or problem. In this sense, Deleuze agrees with the post-Kantian Idealists who 'insist that their ideas play the same transcendental role as the categories: they too are necessary conditions of possible experience'.[78] Or, more precisely, they are genetic conditions of real experience and of thought.

Deleuze's dialectic of Ideas combines the two halves of the aesthetic treated separately by Kant: differential or intensive Ideas serve at the same time as genetic conditions of experience and of the production of the work of art.[79] As Deleuze explicates in his book on Francis Bacon, the challenge of a work of art is to capture the invisible, intensive forces – that by which the sensible is given, or the condition of sensation.[80] In aesthetic experience, we are encouraged to an activity of thought beyond empirical representation, i.e. an exploration of the transcendental domain of sensibility. In spite of the obvious parallels to German Romanticism, there are considerable differences. The Romantics, for

---

[75] Deleuze, *Kant's Critical Philosophy*, p. xi.
[76] Deleuze, *Difference and Repetition*, p. 140.
[77] Ibid.
[78] Beiser, *German Idealism*, p. 166.
[79] See Daniel Smith, 'Deleuze, Kant and the Transcendental Field', in this volume, pp. 25–43.
[80] Cf. Gilles Deleuze, *Francis Bacon: The Logic of Sensation*, trans. Daniel W. Smith (London: Continuum, 2004), pp. 56–7.

instance, claim that aesthetic contemplation reveals purposiveness, rationality and values that are intrinsic to nature itself; they took the second part of Kant's *Critique of the Power of Judgment* on teleological judgement in a metaphysical sense and introduced a form of teleology into the natural order. Of course, from a postmodern point of view the presupposition of an inherent harmony or beauty, rationality or purposiveness in nature is not tenable. For Deleuze, the transcendental field is rather a violent 'chaosmos' that forces transformations and metamorphoses, which can only be sustained by larval subjects at the border of the liveable: 'it would entail the death of any well-constituted subject endowed with independence and activity'.[81] Thus, Deleuze does not outline a theory of aesthetic contemplation but rather one of violent encounter. Moreover, it is not the Absolute which reveals itself: Deleuze's transcendental empiricism eschews any reassuring transcendence and totality. It is not a speculative idealism of the Absolute, but a philosophy of immanence: the immanence of a multiplicity of transcendental, differential and problematic Ideas.

## OUTLINE OF THE VOLUME

The contributions of this volume are divided into three parts. Part I focuses directly on the engagement between Deleuze and Kant's philosophy, with particular emphasis on Maimon's intermediary role. Part II explores Deleuze's relation to key thinkers and concepts in post-Kantian Romanticism and Idealism, while the final part of this collection pursues various lines of post-Kantian thought and the manner in which they transverse and are augmented by Deleuze.

### Part I: Deleuze, Kant and Maimon

For the volume's opening chapter, 'Deleuze, Kant and the Transcendental Field', Daniel W. Smith explores the way in which Deleuze takes up yet inverts the Kantian critical project by rethinking Kant's definition of the transcendental. Deleuze's major source of inspiration, Smith argues, is Salomon Maimon's account of differentials, which was not pursued as such by post-Kantian philosophy. This Deleuzian-Maimonian redefinition of the transcendental condition has significant effects in each of the five domains that structure the critical project: dialectics, aesthetics, analytics, politics and ethics.

---

[81] Deleuze, *Difference and Repetition*, p. 118.

In Chapter 2, Anne Sauvagnargues investigates the different sources that inspired Deleuze's account of 'transcendental empiricism', focusing on Maimon and his central role in the critique of the Kantian method of conditioning and the invention of a method of genesis. Deleuze appropriates Maimon's theory of differentials or Ideas, while abandoning the transcendental idealism of the divine understanding. But as Sauvagnargues shows, Deleuze alters the definition of Ideas through an engagement with structuralism, as well as the works of Albert Lautman and Gilbert Simondon, giving rise to the definition of Ideas as virtual and differentiated structures that solicit the creation of concepts through processes of differenciation.

In her chapter 'Maimon, Kant, Deleuze: The Concepts of Difference and Intensive Magnitude', Daniela Voss analyses Maimon's account of difference and identity as the transcendental conditions of perception in general. Following a historical-critical and exegetical analysis, Voss discusses the questions of the nature of difference as differential and intensive magnitudes, as well as its precise status as a regulative or constitutive principle. While the post-Kantian philosophers still ascribed primacy to the principle of identity, Deleuze embraces Maimon's challenge and renders the notion of difference the fundamental principle of his own transcendental philosophy.

Rounding off the opening section of the Volume, Beth Lord's contribution, 'Deleuze and Kant's *Critique of Judgment*', critically examines Deleuze's reading of Kant's third *Critique* and his emphasis on the free accord of the faculties as a presupposition of the genesis of thought. What is completely missing in Deleuze's seemingly psychological and romantic account of the faculties, Lord suggests, is the political dimension of the *Critique of Judgment*, which Hannah Arendt has famously pointed out in her 1970 *Lectures on Kant's Political Philosophy*. Lord juxtaposes both readings and thereby elucidates Deleuze's particular interest that guided his interpretation of Kant.

## Part II: Deleuze, Romanticism and Idealism

Heinrich von Kleist experienced Kantian philosophy as a crisis in his life and thought. As a response, Brent Adkins argues, Kleist created a literary 'war machine' against Kant's statist image of thought, which subordinates thought to the interiority of the concept. For Kleist, thought must be opened to an outside – to external forces – only then can it produce something new. In his stories and plays he puts this idea into practice. As Adkins shows in his chapter 'What is a Literature of War?:

Kleist, Kant and Nomadology', both Kleist and Deleuze turn to affects in an attempt to deterritorialise Kant's philosophy.

In Chapter 6 'The Calculable Law of Tragic Representation and the Unthinkable: Rhythm, Caesura and Time, from Hölderlin to Deleuze', Arkady Plotnitsky presents a rich investigation of Friedrich Hölderlin's place within Deleuze's scholarship, moving across the fields of science, art and philosophy. Plotnitsky's aim is to explore Hölderlin's concept of rhythm, as it is developed in his analysis of ancient Greek tragedy, and to outline its major philosophical contribution: the invention of a nonclassical, Romantic ontology. This ontology, Plotnitsky says, is concerned with the unthinkable – that which is beyond the reach of thought and cannot be captured by classical ontological concepts. The unthinkable is the ultimate efficacy of all rhythmic effects and counter-rhythmic movements on the level of actual events. It also bears important links, Plotnitsky elaborates, with Deleuze's concept of chaos as the virtual.

While Deleuze rarely comments directly on Johann Gottlieb Fichte, a connection between both can nevertheless be established when reading Fichte's own texts. In his chapter, 'Ground, Transcendence and Method in Deleuze's Fichte', Joe Hughes shows how, outlining several parallel structures that emerge with regard to their respective methods and conceptions. Specifically, Hughes elicits and examines the resonances between their conceptions of subjectivity, transcendence and real experience, and he further points out the affinities between their methods of genesis and the absolute positing of a self-grounding principle. What he shows is that both engage with a common problem: the completion of the Kantian project.

Continuing the volume's exploration of Deleuze and Fichte, Frederick Amrine's chapter '"The magic formula we all seek": Spinoza + Fichte = x', reintroduces the figure of Spinoza to the equation, elucidating the thematic connections in all three thinkers. Several points of convergence are identified, including the ontology of expression, the priority of imagination, the privileging of intuition over discursive thinking or logic, self-positing concepts and the conception of a pure life. Amrine concludes that those three thinkers 'are deeply connected by a Deleuzian rhizome stretching across four centuries'.[82]

In Chapter 9, 'State Philosophy and the War Machine', Nathan Widder undertakes a fresh analysis of Hegel's political philosophy with respect to Deleuze and Guattari. As he reveals, beyond the common presumption of Deleuze's anti-Hegelianism lies a complex and subtle set

---

[82] Amrine, '"The magic formula we all seek": Spinoza + Fichte = x', in this volume, pp. 168–89.

of connections – including, Widder claims, a shared understanding of political structure as an assemblage of desire. In explicating a series of affinities as well as departures, Widder ultimately argues that the relation between Hegel and Deleuze and Guattari is best described as one of a 'disjunctive synthesis'.

Sean Bowden's chapter, 'Tragedy and Agency in Hegel and Deleuze', sheds light on Deleuze's largely implicit account of action and agency in *The Logic of Sense* and compares it with Hegel's view, as interpreted by thinkers such as Speight, Brandom and Pippin. It argues that both Hegel and Deleuze share an *expressivist* understanding of action and agency, which comes to the fore in their respective interpretations of Sophocles' *Oedipus Rex*. The account of expressivist action and agency is summarised in three structural features: retrospectivity, publicness and heroism.

### Part III: Deleuzian Lines of Post-Kantian Thought

The final part of this collection, which embarks on a number of post-Kantian adventures under the guidance of Deleuze, begins with Alistair Welchman's piece 'Schopenhauer and Deleuze'. It could be noted that Deleuze's engagement with Schopenhauer is rather limited and arguably encapsulated by his criticism of the ascetic and pessimistic tone of Schopenhauerian philosophy. But as Welchman provocatively suggests, Deleuze's rejection is premature; indeed, Schopenhauer's break with Kant, along with his critique of representation, could be said to have much in common with Deleuze's own post-Kantian project. For instance, both of them pose the question of what lies beyond representational experience. Furthermore, Schopenhauer's metaphysical conception of the will, Welchman argues, traverses Deleuze and Guattari's *Anti-Oedipus* and opens the space for the Deleuzo-Guattarian notion of a transcendental, impersonal and productive unconscious.

Taking up the problem of 'beginnings' in philosophy and the nature of philosophical critique, Henry Somers-Hall's chapter 'Feuerbach and the Image of Thought' carries out an appraisal and comparison of Feuerbach's critique of Hegel with Deleuze's criticism of the 'dogmatic image of thought' – the chapter of *Difference and Repetition* nominated by Deleuze as his most important and enduring.[83] What Somers-Hall finds is a striking resemblance between the two. In the closing passages of his chapter, however, Somers-Hall also isolates a key moment of

---

[83] Deleuze, *Difference and Repetition*, p. xvii.

divergence in their conception of the 'encounter' – that which provides the opening onto truly philosophical thought.

In Chapter 13, 'Deleuze's "Power of Decision", Kant's =X and Husserl's Noema', Jay Lampert analyses the nature and time-structure of decisions. Following a consideration of the Kantian object=X, the Fichtean-Hegelian-Husserlian understanding of '=', and Deleuze's account of decision as a divergence-point of incompossible timelines, Lampert arrives at what could be referred to as an ethical account of a 'decision=X'. In doing so, the following challenge is advanced: What is our relation to decisions made in the past, and the multiple paths that appear to stem from them? In what sense have we lived them all, or not?

In the penultimate chapter of the collection, Gregg Lambert explores the family history of contemporary French philosophy, analysing in particular the kinship between Kant and two of his bastard children – Deleuze and Lyotard. As Lambert puts it, these two thinkers are 'pure bastards', insofar as they refuse much of their philosophical inheritance and similarly nurture an ambivalent relation to the vogue of Hegelianism and twentieth-century phenomenology. In order to explain, Lambert zeros in on Deleuze and Lyotard's peculiar breed of Kantianism, and in particular their engagement with Kant's third *Critique*. From this he shows how Deleuze and Lyotard succeed in reworking Kantianism, and further how the culture of modernist art produces the conditions for a new understanding of the Kantian sublime.

Finally, Gregory Flaxman's chapter 'Chronos is Sick: Deleuze, Antonioni and the Kantian Lineage of Modern Cinema', explores the way in which modern European cinema repeats, on its own terms and under its own conditions, the 'revolution' that took place in philosophy through Kant's concept of the pure and empty form of time. By way of Hölderlin's conception of time, which according to Deleuze elaborates Kantian time on the level of Greek tragedy, Flaxman outlines three figures of time and traces them in Antonioni's mature works of the 1960s and 70s. As Flaxman argues, Antonioni realises the three figures in the expression of three types of time-image.

# Part I
# Deleuze, Kant and Maimon

# Chapter 1

# Deleuze, Kant and the Transcendental Field

*Daniel W. Smith*

## INTRODUCTION

The last article Deleuze published before his death in November of 1995, entitled 'Immanence: A Life . . .', opens with the following question: 'What is a transcendental field?'.[1] In a certain sense, this Kantian problem, which Deleuze here takes up at the end of his career, is the question that animated his work from the start. Deleuze's first book, *Empiricism and Subjectivity* (1953), proposed a reading of Hume's empiricism by making use of post-Kantian questions that, in themselves, were foreign to Hume's own philosophy, but already pointed to the possibility of what Deleuze would later call a 'transcendental empiricism' (that is, a transcendental field freed from the constraints of a transcendental subject).[2] Whereas Kant had asked, 'How can the given be given to a subject?', Hume had asked, 'How is the subject (or what he called "human nature") constituted within the given?'. *Nietzsche and Philosophy*, published nine years later (1962), though on the surface an anti-Hegelian tract, is more profoundly a confrontation with Kant that interprets Nietzsche's entire philosophy as 'a resumption of [Kant's] critical project on a new basis and with new concepts'. Its central chapter is entitled, precisely, 'Critique'.[3] The project of

1 Gilles Deleuze, 'Immanence: A Life . . .', in David Lapoujade (ed.), *Two Regimes of Madness*, trans. Ames Hodges and Mike Taormina (New York: Semiotext(e), 2006), pp. 384–9.
2 Gilles Deleuze, *Empiricism and Subjectivity: An Essay on Hume's Theory of Human Nature*, trans. Constantin V. Boundas (New York: Columbia University Press, 1991), p. 87.
3 Gilles Deleuze, *Nietzsche and Philosophy*, trans. Hugh Tomlinson (New York: Columbia University Press, 1983), p. 52: 'We believe that there is, in Nietzsche, not only a Kantian heritage, but a half-avowed, half-hidden rivalry . . . Nietzsche seems to have sought (and to have found in the "eternal return" and the "will to power")

*Anti-Oedipus* (1972), which was, for a time at least, perhaps Deleuze and Guattari's most famous work, is defined in explicitly Kantian and transcendental terms: just as Kant set out to discover criteria immanent to the syntheses of consciousness in order to denounce their illegitimate and transcendent employment in metaphysics, so Deleuze and Guattari set out to discover criteria immanent to the syntheses of the unconscious in order to denounce their illegitimate use in Oedipal psychoanalysis.[4] In Deleuze's magnum opus, *Difference and Repetition* (1968), the presence of Kant is almost ubiquitous, to the point where it can be read as both a completion and an inversion of the *Critique of Pure Reason* (just as *Anti-Oedipus* can be read as a completion and inversion of the *Critique of Practical Reason*).[5] Even Deleuze's 1981 book *Francis Bacon: The Logic of Sensation* can be seen as a reworking of the Transcendental Aesthetic.[6]

Deleuze's philosophy, from this viewpoint, can be rightly interpreted as a transcendental philosophy, but one that defines the transcendental field in a completely different manner than does Kant: it is a problematic, differential and virtual field populated with singularities and events, which constitutes a condition of *real* and not merely *possible* experience. In what follows, rather than trying to describe this transcendental field – which in effect would entail an elucidation of Deleuze's entire philosophy – I would simply like to make some fairly general observations on how this Kantian concern can serve as a guiding thread for interpreting the trajectory of Deleuze early writings. To be sure, this is only one of many approaches one can take on Deleuze's work, which encompasses an

a radical transformation of Kantianism, a re-invention of the critique which Kant betrayed at the same time as he conceived it, a resumption of the critical project on a new basis and with new concepts.'

[4] Gilles Deleuze and Félix Guattari, *Anti-Oedipus*, trans. Robert Hurley, Mark Seem and Helen R. Lane (New York: Viking Press, 1977), p. 75: 'In what he termed the critical revolution, Kant intended to discover criteria immanent to the understanding so as to distinguish the legitimate and the illegitimate uses of the syntheses of consciousness. In the name of *transcendental* philosophy (immanence of criteria), he therefore denounced the transcendent use of syntheses such as appeared in metaphysics. In like fashion, we are compelled to say that psychoanalysis has its metaphysics – its name is Oedipus. And that a revolution – this time materialist – can proceed only by way of a critique of Oedipus, by denouncing the illegitimate use of the syntheses of the unconscious as found in Oedipal psychoanalysis, so as to rediscover a transcendental unconscious defined by the immanence of its criteria, and a corresponding practice we shall call schizoanalysis.'

[5] Gilles Deleuze, *Difference and Repetition*, trans. Paul Patton (New York: Columbia University Press, 1994).

[6] Gilles Deleuze, *Francis Bacon: The Logic of Sensation*, trans. Daniel W. Smith (Minneapolis: University of Minnesota Press, 2005).

immense diversity and scope. But it has the advantage of allowing us to explore the strategies Deleuze used in his early work in the history of philosophy to marshal resources for his reconceptualisation of the transcendental field. Historically, first, it explains why Deleuze wound up appealing to a 'minor' tradition of post-Kantian philosophy (Maimon, Nietzsche, Bergson) as opposed to what has come to be received as its 'major' tradition (Fichte, Schelling, Hegel). Substantively, second, it will permit us to examine the way Deleuze modified Kant's concept of the transcendental field in five crucial domains that defined the critical project: dialectics, aesthetics, analytics, ethics and politics. In each case, we will discover what it means to define the transcendental field with a method of genesis rather than a method of conditioning.

## THE HISTORY OF PHILOSOPHY

Consider first the monographs Deleuze wrote in the history of philosophy. In addition to his short study on Kant, Deleuze wrote books on Hume, Spinoza and Leibniz (pre-Kantians), as well as books on Bergson and Nietzsche (post-Kantians). The question we have to ask is: Why did Deleuze choose to write on these particular thinkers, and not others? The answer is given by Deleuze himself. It is often said that pre-Kantian philosophy found its principle in the notion of God (that is, the analytic identity of an infinite substance), whereas post-Kantianism found its principle in the notion of the Self (that is, the synthetic identity of the finite Self).[7] Deleuze pointed out, however, that these God-Self permutations were of little interest to him, since it changes nothing in philosophy to put Man in the place of God. Indeed, it was in Kant himself, in a 'furtive moment' in the *Critique of Pure Reason*, that Deleuze found the hint of the possibility of a transcendental field that would entail not only the death of God, but also the dissolution of the Self (what Foucault would later call the death of Man) as well as the destruction of the world – the Self, the World and God being the three great terminal points of metaphysics.[8] Indeed, if these are the three endpoints of metaphysics, it is because they are the three great forms of identity: the

---

[7] See Deleuze, *Difference and Repetition*, p. 58.

[8] Ibid.: 'Rather than being concerned with what comes before and after Kant (which amounts to the same thing), we should be concerned with a precise moment within Kantianism, a furtive and explosive moment which is not even continued by Kant, much less by post-Kantianism. For when Kant puts rational theology in question, in the same stroke he introduces a kind of disequilibrium . . . into the pure self of the "I think" . . . [that is] insurmountable in principle.'

identity of the person as a well-founded agent, the identity of the world as its ambient environment, and the identity of God as the ultimate foundation – to which Deleuze might add the identity of bodies as the base of the person, and the identity of language as the capacity to *denote* everything else.[9] One can sense two minor battles in these last two characterisations: against the phenomenological notion of the 'body image' as the final avatar of the theological concept of the soul,[10] and against the analytic preoccupation with the analysis of propositions and the theory of reference, which appears in Kant in the theory of judgement (one of Deleuze's great themes is 'to have done with judgement', which above all means the form of judgement in propositions, and not merely moral judgement).

How then does Deleuze marshal the resources of the history of philosophy to expand on this furtive moment in Kant (i.e., the idea of a transcendental field free from the coordinates of the Self, the World and God – that is, from the form of identity)? One of his chief influences here was the figure of Salomon Maimon, whose *Essay on Transcendental Philosophy* – which was published in 1790, one year before the appearance of Kant's third *Critique* – laid down the basic objections against Kant that would come to preoccupy the post-Kantian philosophies of Fichte, Schelling and Hegel.[11] Maimon's basic objection was this: Kant

---

[9] See Gilles Deleuze, *Logic of Sense*, trans. Mark Lester, with Charles Stivale, ed. Constantin V. Boundas (New York: Columbia University Press, 1990), pp. 293, 294: 'The order of God includes the following elements: the identity of God as the ultimate foundation; the identity of the world as the ambient environment; the identity of the person as a well-founded agent; the identity of bodies as the base [as Deleuze says elsewhere, the phenomenological concept of the "body image" is one of the final avatars of the old concept of the "soul"]; and finally the identity of language as the power of *denoting* everything else . . . The order of the Antichrist is opposed point by point to the divine order. It is characterised by the death of God, the destruction of the world, the dissolution of the person, the disintegration of bodies, and the shifting function of language, which now only expresses only intensities.' Cf. p. 176: 'The divergence of affirmed series form a "chaosmos" and no longer a world; the aleatory point which traverses them forms a counter-self, and no longer a self; disjunction posed as a synthesis exchanges its theological principle for a diabolical principle . . . The Grand Canyon of the world, the "crack" of the self, and the dismembering of God.'

[10] See Deleuze and Guattari, *Anti-Oedipus*, p. 23: 'The "body image" – the final avatar of the soul, a vague conjoining of the requirements of spiritualism and positivism.'

[11] Maimon's now neglected work lies at the root of much post-Kantian philosophy; as Frederick Beiser notes, to study Fichte, Schelling, or Hegel without having read Maimon is like studying Kant without having read Hume; see Frederick Beiser, *The Fate of Reason: German Philosophy From Kant to Fichte* (Cambridge, MA: Harvard University Press, 1987), p. 286. See also Jules Vuillemin, *L'héritage kantien et la révolution copernicienne* (Paris: PUF, 1954), p. 55: In the criticism of scepticism, 'what corresponds to the Kant-Hume relationship is now the Fichte-Maimon relationship'.

had ignored the demands of a *genetic* method. This criticism means two things.

First, Kant relied on what he himself called 'facts', for which he then searches for conditions. In the *Critique of Pure Reason*, Kant does more than simply claim that reason implies *a priori* knowledge; he adds that the so-called 'universal' knowledges of pure sciences such as mathematics are the knowledges in which reason necessarily manifests itself. They are the *a priori* 'facts' of reason. In the *Critique of Practical Reason*, Kant similarly takes as his point of departure the 'fact' of the judgement of value and moral action. Kant assumed these original facts of reason – the 'fact' of knowledge and the 'fact' of morality – and then sought their conditions of possibility in the transcendental. But this was a vicious circle that made the condition (the possible) refer to the conditioned (the real) while reproducing its image. In other words, Kant's conception of the transcendental entailed a *conformism* – the value of knowledge and morality are never placed in question. Maimon, by contrast, argued that Kant's claim to ground his critique on reason alone would be valid only if these *a priori* knowledges had been *deduced* or engendered from reason as the necessary modes of its manifestation. In other words, the immanent ambitions of Kant's critical project could be realised only if, rather than simply assuming these 'facts' as given, it provided a *genetic* account of knowledge and morality. Second, Maimon argued that this genetic demand could be fulfilled only through an account that described the transcendental conditions of *real* experience, and not merely those of possible experience. Even if the categories of the understanding are applicable to objects in general, the category itself can never specify which object it belongs to in *real* experience. By confining himself to possible experience, Kant was unable to provide the faculty of judgement a rule for determining *when* a given category was applicable to real experience. The concept of causality may indeed be applicable to certain irreversible causal sequences, as Kant argues in the Second Analogy (fire causes smoke, because fire always precedes

Kant himself, in his letter to Marcus Herz of 26 May 1789, wrote of the *Essay on Transcendental Philosophy*: 'But one glance at the work made me realize its excellence and that not only had none of my critics understood me and the main questions as well as Mr. Maimon does but also very few men possess so much acumen for such deep investigations as he.' Immanuel Kant, *Philosophical Correspondence*, ed. and trans. Arnulf Zweig (Chicago: University of Chicago Press, 1967), p. 151. In a letter to Reinhold, Fichte wrote: 'My respect for Maimon's talent is limitless; I firmly believe, and am willing to prove, that the critical philosophy has been overturned by him.' Fichte, *Briefwechsel*, III/2, p. 282, as quoted in Beiser, *The Fate of Reason*, p. 370, note 2.

smoke in the order of time). But the concept itself gives us no means of distinguishing, within experience, between *necessary and universal connections* and *contingent and constant conjunctions*. Hume's scepticism, in other words, remains unanswered, and Kant's duality between concept and intuition remains unbridgeable. Maimon, by contrast, was the first to argue that this duality could only be overcome through the formulation of a principle of difference. Whereas identity is the condition of possibility of thought in general, *it is difference that constitutes the genetic condition of the real.*

These two Maimonian themes – the demand for a *genetic method* and the positing of a *principle of difference* – reappear as leitmotifs in almost every one of Deleuze's books through 1969, even if Maimon's name is not always explicitly mentioned. The reason for this is not difficult to ascertain. The post-Kantian philosophers all took up Maimon's challenge, but in some fashion each of them still subordinated the principle of difference to the principle of identity. Deleuze, I would argue, returns to Maimon in order to take up the one option that was not pursued as such by post-Kantian philosophy (though Schelling no doubt remains closest to Deleuze). For Deleuze, 'difference-in-itself' (the title of the first chapter of *Difference and Repetition*) becomes the genetic element of real experience, from which all other relations are derived (identity, analogy, resemblance, opposition, contradiction, negation, and so forth). Indeed, these two Maimonian themes will become two requirements of Deleuze's 'transcendental empiricism', that is, a transcendental field without a transcendental subject or a thing-in-itself, both of which introduce elements of transcendence into the transcendental field. (It is important to recall that, for Kant, 'transcendence' and 'transcendental' are diametrically opposed terms: his *transcendental* philosophy was a method of immanence whose aim was to critique the *transcendent* illusions of reason.) In Deleuze, there are no subjects, although there are processes of subjectivation; there are no objects, but there are processes of objectivation; there is no 'pure reason', but there are historically variable processes of rationalisation, and so on. This is why Deleuze can say that the transcendental field is a principle of critique *as well as* a principle of creation.

*The Pre-Kantian Tradition: Hume, Leibniz, Spinoza*

It is not coincidental that Maimon described his own reformulation of transcendental philosophy as a 'coalition system' [*Koalitionssystem*] that incorporated various elements from the systems of Hume, Leibniz,

Spinoza. Nor is it coincidental that Deleuze devoted a separate mono-graph to each of these thinkers. In this sense, Maimon functions as one of the primary philosophical precursors to Deleuze. At one level, Deleuze's books on Hume, Leibniz and Spinoza, are simply brilliant monographs in the history of philosophy; but when Deleuze *uses* these pre-Kantian thinkers in his constructive works such as *Difference and Repetition* – when he treats them as contemporaries, as it were – he always asks the post-Kantian question: How would their systems function if they were freed from the metaphysical illusions of the Self, the World and God that were criticised by Kant in the *Critique of Pure Reason*? What would happen if one removed the theological exigency of a pre-established harmony from Leibniz's philosophy? Or if one removed the identity of a single substance from Spinoza's philosophy?[12] This is how Deleuze transforms pre-Kantian thinkers into post-Kantian resources for his own thought, as way of reconfigur-ing the transcendental field. (We have already seen how Deleuze saw in Hume's philosophy an inversion of the Kantian question: 'How is the subject constituted in the given?' rather than 'How is the given given to a subject?')

Consider Leibniz's philosophy, for instance, from this post-Kantian viewpoint. First, *God* would no longer be a Being who compares pos-sible worlds and allows the 'best' of all possible worlds to pass into existence; rather, he would become a pure process that affirms incom-possibilities and passes through them. Second, the *World* would no longer be a world of continuity defined by its pre-established harmony; instead, divergences, bifurcations and incompossibles would now be seen to belong to *one and the same universe*, a chaotic universe in which divergent series trace endlessly bifurcating paths, and give rise to violent discords and dissonances that are never resolved into a harmonic tonal-ity: a 'chaosmos', as Deleuze puts it (borrowing a portmanteau word

---

[12] On these points, see the letter to Martin Joughin, cited in the 'Translator's Preface' to *Expressionism in Philosophy: Spinoza*, trans. Martin Joughin (New York: Zone Books, 1990), p. 11: 'What interested me most in Spinoza wasn't his Substance, but the composition of finite modes. I consider this one of the most original aspects of my book. That is: the hope of making substance turn on finite modes, or at least of seeing in substance a *plane of immanence* in which finite modes operate, already appears in this book. What I needed was both (1) the expressive character of particular individu-als, and (2) an immanence of Being. Leibniz, in a way, goes still further than Spinoza on the first point. But on the second, Spinoza stands alone. One finds it only in him. This is why I consider myself a Spinozist, rather than a Leibnizian, though I owe a lot to Leibniz.'

from Joyce's *Finnegans Wake*), and no longer a world.[13] Leibniz could only save the 'harmony' of *this* world by relegating discordances and disharmonies to *other* possible worlds. Third, individuals (the *Self*), rather than being closed upon the compossible and convergent world they express from within, would now be torn open, and kept open through the divergent series and incompossible ensembles that continually pull them outside themselves. The 'monadic' subject, as Deleuze puts it, becomes the 'nomadic' subject.[14] The Leibnizian notion of *closure* is here replaced by the Deleuzian notion of *capture*.

One could say that Deleuze effects a similar type of conversion in his reading of Spinoza. For Deleuze, there can be neither a single substance nor essences (even singular essences), and thus, strictly speaking, no third kind of knowledge, since there is nothing to know at this level.[15] It is the first and second kinds of knowledge – affections/affects and concepts – that give us the most adequate access to Being. Although Deleuze likes to consider himself as Spinozist, that does not mean he accepts everything in Spinoza; far from it. The same holds for Bergson: even though Deleuze can rightly be considered a Bergsonian (as much as a Kantian, or a Leibnizian, or a Spinozist), Bergson's first book, *Time and Free Will*, contains a sustained critique of the concept of intensity, which Deleuze explicitly rejects.[16]

---

[13] The term 'chaosmos' can be found in James Joyce, *Finnegans Wake* (London: Penguin, 1999 [1939]), p. 118: 'every person, place and thing in the chaosmos of Alle anyway connected with the gobblydumped turkery was moving and changing every part of the time'.

[14] See Deleuze, *Logic of Sense*, p. 17: 'Instead of a certain number of predicates being excluded from a thing in virtue of the identity of its concept, each "thing" is open to the infinity of predicates through which it passes, and at the same time it loses its center, that is to say, its identity as a concept and as a self' (translation modified).

[15] See Deleuze's critique of Spinoza's notion of substance in *Difference and Repetition*, pp. 40–1: 'Nevertheless, [in Spinoza] there still remains a difference between substance and the modes: Spinoza's substance appears independent of the modes, while the modes are dependent on substance, but as though on something other than themselves. Substance must itself be said *of* the modes and only *of* the modes. Such a condition can be satisfied only at the price of a more general categorical reversal according to which being is said of becoming, identity of that which is different, the one of the multiple, etc. That identity not be first, that it exist as a principle but as a second principle, as a principle *become*; that it revolve around the Different: such would be the nature of a Copernican revolution which opens up the possibility of difference having its own concept, rather than being maintained under the domination of a concept in general already understood as identical.'

[16] See Deleuze, *Difference and Repetition*, p. 239: 'This is why the Bergsonian critique of intensity seems unconvincing. It assumes qualities ready-made and extensities already constituted.'

*The Post-Kantian Tradition: Maimon, Nietzsche, Bergson*

Deleuze's strategy with regard to the post-Kantian tradition of Fichte, Schelling and Hegel – which constitutes the history of the synthetic identity of the finite Self – is slightly different. Deleuze occasionally appeals to aspects of their thought that escapes this synthetic identity, such as Schelling's theory of power.[17] More importantly, though, Deleuze creates his own 'minor' tradition of post-Kantian philosophy which finds its shining points in Maimon, Bergson and Nietzsche, who made no appeal to the synthetic self.

In his book *Bergsonism*, Deleuze examines Bergson's famous critique of the notion of the possible, which has certain parallels with Maimon's critique. Bergson considers a number of metaphysical questions – 'Why is there order rather than disorder?' 'Why is there something rather than nothing?' 'Why is there this rather than that?' – and argues that these are false questions derived from a misplaced use of negation. Why? (1) What is given in experience is *order*, but we negate that order, and then speak of *disorder*, when we encounter an order we did not expect or do not understand (order + negation = disorder). (2) What is given in experience is *being*, but we negate that being, and then speak of non-being or 'nothingness', when a being does not correspond to our expectation and we experience it as a lack, or as the absence of what interests us (being + negation = non-being). (3) Finally, what is given in experience is the *real*, but we negate that real, and then speak of the possible, when we consider or desire that the real could have been otherwise (the real + negation = the possible). In each of these cases, we fall into the same error: we mistake the more for the less, or an after for a before. We behave as though non-being existed *before* being, disorder *before* order, and the possible *before* existence – as though being came to fill in a void, order to organise a preceding disorder, the real to realise a pre-existing possibility. As Deleuze writes: 'Being, order, and the existent are truth itself; but in the false problem there is a fundamental illusion, a "retrograde movement of the true", in which being, order, and the existent project themselves back into a possibility, a disorder, a nonbeing that are supposed to be primordial.'[18]

One can see the parallels with Maimon's critique of Kant: for

[17] See, e.g., Deleuze, *Difference and Repetition*, pp. 190–1.
[18] Gilles Deleuze, *Bergsonism* (New York: Zone Books, 1988), p. 18, quoting from Bergson, *The Creative Mind: An Introduction to Metaphysics*, trans. Mabelle L. Andison (Totowa, NJ: Littlefield, Adams & Co, 1975), p. 118.

Bergson, the possible is a false notion, a source of false problems. When we think of the possible as somehow 'preexisting' the real, we think of the real as something more than possible, that is, as the possible with existence added to it. We then say that the possible has been 'realised' in the real. This process of realisation, Deleuze suggests, is subject to two rules: resemblance and limitation. The real is supposed to *resemble* or to be 'in the image of' the possible that it realises: the concept of the thing is already given as possible, and simply has existence or reality added to it when it is realised. On the other hand, since not every possible is realised, the process of realisation involves a *limitation* by which some possibles are supposed to be repulsed or thwarted, while others pass into the real. But this is where the slight of hand becomes obvious: if the real is supposed to resemble the possible, is it not because we have retrospectively or retroactively 'projected' a fictitious image of the real back into the possible? In fact, it is not the real that resembles the possible, it is the possible that resembles the real. As Deleuze would later write in *Logic of Sense*, 'the error of all determinations of the transcendental as consciousness is to conceive of the transcendental in the image and resemblance of what it is supposed to found'.[19] One can see why Deleuze, following Bergson, would reject the notion of 'conditions of possibility', and will replace the possible-real opposition with the virtual-actual couplet: every phenomenon is an actualisation of virtual elements, relations and singularities that are themselves real.[20]

*Nietzsche and Philosophy*, in turn, is animated by similar Kantian concerns, though we will not explore them in detail here. In general, Deleuze argues that it is Nietzsche who finally fulfilled Kant's transcendental project by bringing the critique to bear, not on false claims to knowledge and morality, as in Kant, but on knowledge and morality themselves, on true knowledge and true morality – and indeed on the very notion of truth itself. Deleuze interprets the will to power and eternal return as genetic principles that give a genealogical account of the meaning and value of knowledge, morality and truth.[21]

In these early works, Deleuze explicitly sets out a certain number of criteria for thinking about the status of the transcendental field. First, the condition must be a condition of real experience, and not merely of possible experience: 'it forms an intrinsic genesis, not an extrinsic

---

[19] Deleuze, *Logic of Sense*, p. 105.
[20] Deleuze, *Bergsonism*, pp. 94–103; Deleuze, *Difference and Repetition*, pp. 208–14.
[21] Deleuze, *Nietzsche and Philosophy*, pp. 51–2, 93–4.

conditioning'.[22] Second, this means that the condition cannot be in the image of the conditioned, that is, the structures of the transcendental field cannot simply be traced off the empirical. Third, to be a condition of real experience, the condition can be no broader than what it conditions; the condition must therefore be determined *along with* what it conditions, and must *change* as the conditioned changes (conditions are not universal but singular). Fourth, to remain faithful to these exigencies, 'we must have something *unconditioned*' that would be capable of 'determining *both* the condition and the conditioned'.[23] This is the crux of Deleuze's debate with Hegel: Is this unconditioned the 'totality' (Hegel) or the 'differential' (Deleuze)? Is it external difference (the 'not-X' of Hegel) or internal difference (the $dx$ of Deleuze)? Fifth, the nature of the 'genesis' in the genetic method must therefore be understood, not as a dynamic genesis – that is, as a historical or developmental genesis – but rather as a static genesis (i.e., a genesis that moves from the virtual to its actualisation).

Deleuze's work in the history of philosophy, it seems to me, was organised, in a rather conscious manner, around this aim of rethinking the nature of the transcendental field. When Deleuze claims that the limitations of the Kantian theory can only be overcome through a theory of singularities, it is because singularities (or events) escape the system of the Self, the World and God. As Deleuze constantly says, they are 'impersonal' [escaping the form of the Self], pre-individual' [escaping the form of God] and 'a-cosmic' [escaping the form of the World]'.[24] It would not be difficult, I think, to show that Deleuze's use of prior figures in the history of philosophy – such as Plato, Aristotle, the Stoics, Lucretius, Duns Scotus – are also put in the service of this transcendental project, and it is this overriding concern that bestows that particularly 'Deleuzian' tone to his monographs.

## KANT AND DELEUZE'S CONSTRUCTIVE PHILOSOPHY

This Kantian theme becomes even more revealing when one turns from Deleuze's work in the history of philosophy to his elaboration of his own philosophical system. I use the term 'system' advisedly. 'I feel that I am a very classical philosopher', Deleuze once wrote. 'I believe in philosophy as a system . . . [But] for me, the system must not only be in

---

[22] Deleuze, *Difference and Repetition*, p. 154.
[23] Deleuze, *Logic of Sense*, pp. 122–3.
[24] Ibid. p. 177.

perpetual heterogeneity, it must be a heterogenesis, something which, it seems to me, has never before been attempted.'[25] *Heterogenesis*: this means, following Maimon, that the system must be a genetic system that accounts for the genesis of the heterogeneous, the creation of difference, the production of the new. Our second question then becomes: What would Deleuze's 'system' look like if one attempted to describe it in Kantian terms? I would like to briefly take a stab at this here, using five Kantian rubrics that roughly parallel the architectonic of Kant's own system: Dialectics, Aesthetics, Analytics, Ethics and Politics.

a. *Dialectics* (Theory of Ideas). Consider first Deleuze's conception of Dialectics, that is, his theory of Ideas (what can only be *thought*). Deleuze's philosophy is far too quickly identified as an 'anti-dialectical' mode of thought. It is true that Deleuze is anti-Hegelian: what he criticises in the Hegelian dialectic is its reliance on the mechanisms of contradiction and 'the labour of the negative', which Deleuze replaces with movements of difference and the joy of affirmation. It is also true that he is anti-Platonic, at least insofar as Plato defined Ideas in terms of their self-identity and their transcendence; for Deleuze, Ideas are immanent and differential.

But Deleuze develops his own theory of Ideas primarily by reconsidering Kant's Dialectics. If Kant critiqued the concept of the world, it was because the true object of that Idea is the category of causality, and the causal nexus that extends infinitely in all directions, and can never be unified. When we believe we can unify this causal nexus and assign an object to it – we can call it the World, or the Universe, or the totality of what is –, we are then in a transcendent illusion. The true object of that idea, its immanent object, is the category of causality itself, the extension of which we experience as a *problem*. This is the aspect of Kant that Deleuze takes up: Ideas are *objectively problematic structures*. Deleuze's claim that he is a pure metaphysician amounts to saying that Being – ultimate reality – is a *problem*: it always presents itself to us under a problematic form (we experience the world, and everything in the world, initially in the form of a problem – something we do *not* recognise, but rather something that forces us to think).

In a way, Deleuze here takes up and develops a theme first proposed

---

[25] Gilles Deleuze, 'Lettre-préface de Gilles Deleuze', in Jean-Clet Martin, *Variations: La Philosophie de Gilles Deleuze* (Paris: Payot, 1993), p. 7. See also Gilles Deleuze and Félix Guattari, *What is Philosophy?*, trans. Hugh Tomlinson (New York: Columbia University Press, 1994), p. 9: 'Today it is said that systems are bankrupt, but it is only the concept of the system that has changed.'

in Heidegger's book, *Kant and the Problem of Metaphysics*.[26] For Heidegger, the great problem in Kant was the relation between thought and being – that is, the relation between concepts and intuitions. Kant himself effected a mediation between the two via the operations of *synthesis* and *schematisation*, which are operations of the productive imagination. But in the third *Critique* (written after Maimon's *Essay*), Kant showed (against Heidegger) that the secret of the Kantian project does not lie in the imagination, but in the theory of Ideas: when synthesis breaks down it produces the experience of the *sublime*, and when schematising breaks down, it produces the operation of *symbolising*. Now both the sublime and the symbol (along with genius and teleology) are means through which Ideas appear in Nature itself, in the sensible. This is what it means to say that Deleuze's theory of Ideas is purely immanent: Ideas are problematic ontological structures that are immanent to experience as such. They do not simply exist in our heads, but are encountered here and there in the constitution of the actual world. The history of humanity, as well as the history of nature (or rather, its 'becoming'), can be conceived of as a history of *problematisations* – a notion Foucault would later adopt from Deleuze.[27]

However, when it comes to fleshing out the exact nature of these problematic structures (or Ideas), Deleuze turns not to Kant, but to Leibniz. Many of the concepts he uses to characterise the nature of problems can be found in Leibniz: problematic structures are multiplicities, constituted by singularities (or events), which are themselves defined in terms of the differential relation between indeterminate and purely virtual elements, and so forth. As Deleuze once commented in a seminar: 'All the elements to create a genesis as demanded by the post-Kantians are virtually present in Leibniz.'[28]

One can already sense here the revolution Deleuze is in the process of introducing into the history of philosophy. If Deleuze can consider himself a metaphysician, and rejects the Heideggerian theme of the end of metaphysics, it is because be believes – naively, as he puts it – that it is possible to construct a new metaphysics that replaces the old one (where the Self, the World and God were the highest forms of identity): the concept of multiplicity replaces that of substance, singularities or

---

[26] Martin Heidegger, *Kant and the Problem of Metaphysics*, trans. Richard Taft (Bloomington: Indiana University Press, 1997).

[27] See, for instance, Michel Foucault, 'Polemics, Politics and Problematizations', *Essential Works of Foucault*, ed. Paul Rabinow, vol. 1, *Ethics* (New York: The New Press, 1998).

[28] Deleuze, seminar of 20 May 1980, available online at <www2.univ-paris8.fr/deleuze>.

events replace the notion of essence, and so forth. If the theory of Ideas is a response to the Socratic question 'What is. . .?', one could say that, for Deleuze, anything that *is* is a multiplicity (and not a substance), constituted by a convergence of singularities (and not by an essence), which are virtualities (and not possibilities), and so on. The aim of Deleuze's theory of Ideas, in other words, is to provide us with a means of thinking the nature of being, even if he would later call into question the concept of ontology by suggesting that the term '*est*' (is) should be replaced with the word '*et*' (and).

b. *Aesthetics* (Theory of Sensation: Space and Time). We turn now, second, to the question of aesthetics. If the question of sensibility plays an important role in Deleuze's work, it is because in themselves such problematic structures are primarily *sensed* rather than apprehended: they affect us, and provoke us to think. This is why Deleuze calls them problematic multiplicities, as opposed to theorematic structures that begin with well-defined axioms. Kant himself had separated the theory of sensation (aesthetics) into two isolated parts. In the 'Transcendental Aesthetic' of the *Critique of Pure Reason*, aesthetics designated the theory of sensibility as the form of *possible* experience: this was the *objective* element of sensation as conditioned by the *a priori* forms of space and time. In the 'Critique of Aesthetic Judgment' in the *Critique of Judgment*, which includes the Analytics of the Beautiful and the Sublime, aesthetics designated the theory of art as a reflection upon *real* experience: this was the *subjective* element of sensation as incarnated in the feeling of pleasure and pain.

For Deleuze, by contrast, space, time and sensation are themselves differential Ideas. He locates the conditions of sensibility in an *intensive* conception of space and a *non-chronological* conception of time, which are actualised in a plurality of extended spaces, and a complex rhythm of actual times, which is the object of Deleuze's analyses in the 'Repetition' chapter of *Difference and Repetition*. Moreover, since for Deleuze the aim of art is to produce a sensation, these genetic principles of sensation are also the principles of composition of the work of art, and conversely, it is the structure of the work of art that reveals these conditions. Deleuze's theory of sensation in this way reunites the two halves of aesthetics dissociated by Kant: the theory of forms of experience (as the 'being of the sensible') and the work of art (as a 'pure being of sensation').

One of Deleuze's most important works in this regard is his two-volume study of the cinema. Whatever their importance for film studies, *The Movement-Image* and *The Time-Image* are essentially an elaboration of Deleuze's Transcendental Aesthetic. One of the characteristics of film is that it presented a new type of image: an image that moves, and that moves in time. The philosophical question Deleuze poses in these works is: 'What exactly does the cinema show us about space and time that the other arts do not show?'[29] He presents the work as a classification of the multiplicity spaces and times actualised in modern cinema. In his book on Proust, he likewise examines the various structures of time revealed in *In Search of Lost Time*. If one of the characteristics of modern art was to have renounced the domain of representation and instead to have taken the *conditions* of representation as its object, Deleuze's numerous writings on the arts are in effect explorations of this transcendental domain of sensibility: the subtitle of his study of the painter Francis Bacon is 'the logic of sensation'.

c. *Analytics* (Theory of the Concept). Consider now the third division of Kant's first *Critique*, the Analytic of Concepts. Deleuze agrees with Kant that philosophy can be defined as 'knowledge through pure concepts', but he takes the further step, against Kant, that concepts can never be given ready-made or *a priori*. Rather, concepts must always be created, invented, or fabricated (which is why Deleuze considered himself to be an empiricist), and they are always created in response to a specific problem.[30] One can note the deduction of these domains in Deleuze: (1) being (reality) presents itself under the form of a problem (*Dialectics*); (2) these problematics (differential multiplicities) are not known by us, they are primarily sensed, and these sensed intensities provoke us to think (*Aesthetics*); (3) one of the outcomes of this thought process (though by no means the only one) is the creation of concepts (*Analytics*).

In *Difference and Repetition*, however, Deleuze is highly critical of concepts, but primarily *insofar* as they are subordinate to the model of judgement, which consists of subsuming the particular under the general – whether these are the genus and species of Aristotle, or the Kantian categories. 'Every philosophy of categories', writes Deleuze, 'takes judgment as its model'.[31] Judgement has two functions: common sense and good sense. *Common sense* is a faculty of identification that can be

---

[29] Gilles Deleuze, *Negotiations: 1972–1990*, trans. Martin Joughin (New York: Columbia University Press, 1995), p. 58.

[30] See Deleuze and Guattari, *What is Philosophy?*, p. 7: 'The following definition of philosophy can be taken as being decisive: knowledge through pure concepts.' This phrase is qualified by the more famous line: 'philosophy is the art of forming, inventing, and fabricating concepts' (p. 2).

[31] Deleuze, *Difference and Repetition*, p. 33.

defined in terms of both the subjective identity of the self and its faculties, and the objective identity of the things to which these faculties refer. Since we no more find ourselves before a universal indeterminate object than we are a universal self, however, judgement requires a second faculty of *good sense* (the French *sens* here meaning 'direction'), which subsumes diversity under the common form of the Same, reducing the more differentiated to the less differentiated, the singular to the regular, ultimately equalising difference by relating it to the form of an object or the identity of a subject. This is the orientation that one finds in Kant's Table of Categories, which are derived from the various forms of judgement: the categories provide an *a priori* direction that everyone must follow, and they are distributed in an *a priori* manner that everyone must share. The type of distribution offered in the Table of Categories, as Kant himself noted, is inseparable from the agrarian problem: it implies the establishment of enclosures, the delimitation of territories, the assignation of 'property' and the instituting of 'classes'.

It was not until *What is Philosophy?*, published in 1991, that Deleuze put forward his own analytic of concepts, for which his motto, one might say, was 'to have done with judgement' (even reflective judgement). The sedentary distribution of categories found in Kant (and Aristotle) is imposed upon a prior nomadic and problematic distribution of elements, relations and singularities (multiplicities) that Deleuze has analysed in his Dialectics. (Like Kant, Deleuze distinguishes Ideas from concepts, albeit in an original manner.) This is the import of Deleuze's doctrine of univocity, derived, in modified form, from Duns Scotus: Being speaks in one voice, but what it speaks is difference-in-itself (or problematics). Categories, whether Kantian or Aristotelian, can only have an analogical relation to Being, never a univocal relation – which is why a philosophy such as Deleuze's can never have categories (unless, like Peirce, for example, one creates a new concept of a 'category'). The basis for Deleuze's Analytics thus lies in his Dialectics: a concept, Deleuze tells us, is a *heterogenesis*:[32] it actualises a certain number of singularities and renders them consistent within itself. In this sense, concepts do not have a referent, since their object is created at the same time the concept is created. Deleuze thus distinguishes concepts from the 'functions' of science and logic, which – although they are equally creative – are necessarily referential, and are developed in discursive systems.

The earliest, and perhaps still the most concrete, example of Deleuze's approach to concepts can already be found in his 1967 study of

[32] Deleuze and Guattari, *What is Philosophy?*, p. 20.

*Masochism.*[33] It criticises the Hegelian presumptions (of complementarity and opposition) implied in the notion of 'sado-masochism', and instead presents a differential analysis of the component elements of the concepts 'sadism' and 'masochism', showing that each of these concepts define incommensurate objects, separate universes between which there is no communication.

d. *Ethics* (Theory of Affectivity). Fourth, what is Deleuze's relation to the second *Critique*, the *Critique of Practical Reason*. Deleuze often uses the term 'morality' to define, in very general terms, any set of 'constraining' rules (e.g. a moral code) that consists in judging actions and intentions by relating them to *transcendent* values (this is good, that is evil. . .). It is this Kantian model of judgement and the appeal to universals that Deleuze rejects. What he calls 'ethics' is, on the contrary, a set of 'facultative' rules that evaluate what we do, say, or think according to the *immanent* mode of existence that it implies. One says or does this, thinks or feels that: what mode of existence does it imply? As both Spinoza and Nietzsche showed, modes of existence are defined *intensively* as a degree of power, a capacity for affecting or being affected that is necessarily actualised at every moment. Each in their own way showed that there are certain things one cannot do *or even think* except on the condition of being weak, base, or enslaved, unless one harbours a vengeance or *ressentiment* against life (Nietzsche), unless one remains the slave of passive affections (Spinoza); and there are other things one cannot do or say or feel except on the condition of being strong, noble, or free, unless one affirms life or attains active affections.

Moreover, one would have to argue that the concept of desire that lies at the basis of Deleuze's ethico-political philosophy – notably in *Anti-Oedipus* – is an explicit attempt to rework the fundamental theses of Kant's *Critique of Practical Reason*. Kant presents the second *Critique* as a theory of desire, and he defines desire, somewhat surprisingly, in *causal* terms: desire is 'a faculty which by means of its representations is the *cause* of the actuality of the objects of those representations'. In its lower form, the products of desire are fantasies and superstitions; but in its higher form (the will), the products of desire are acts of *freedom* under the moral law – actions which are, however, irreducible to mechanistic causality. Deleuze takes up and modifies Kant in two fundamental ways. First, if desire is productive or causal, then its product is itself *real* (and not illusory or noumenal): the entire socio-political field,

---

[33] Gilles Deleuze, *Masochism: Coldness and Cruelty*, trans. Jean McNeil (New York: Zone Books, 1989).

Deleuze argues, must be seen as the historically determined product of desire. Second, to maintain this claim, Deleuze appeals to the theory of Ideas outlined above. In Kant, the postulates of practical reason are found in the transcendent Ideas of God, World, and the Soul, which are themselves derived from the types of judgement of relation (categorical, hypothetical, disjunctive). For Deleuze, by contrast, desire is determined by a set of constituting passive syntheses (connective, disjunctive, conjunctive), which in turn appeals to Deleuze's genetic and differential theory of Ideas. In this sense, what one finds in Deleuze is at once an inversion as well as a completion of Kant's critical philosophy.

e. *Politics* (Social Theory). Consider, finally – and very briefly – the question of politics, which is developed primarily in the works Deleuze co-authored with Félix Guattari. The link between ethics and politics is, for Deleuze, redefined as the link between desire and power: *desire* (the difference between active and reactive forces in a given mode of existence) never exists in a spontaneous or natural state, but is always 'assembled' [*agencé*] in variable but determinable manners in concrete social formations, and what assembles desire are relations of *power*. Deleuze remains 'Marxist' in that his social theory is necessarily tied to an analysis of capitalism, which he defines by the conjunction or differential relation between the virtual quantities of labour and capital. What he calls 'schizophrenia' is an absolute limit that would cause these quantities to travel in a free and unbound state on a desocialised body: this is the 'Idea' of society, a limit that is never reached as such, but constitutes the ideal 'problematic' to which every social formation constitutes a concrete solution. For Deleuze, the central political question concerns the means by which the singularities and states of difference of the transcendental field are assembled in a given socius. *Capitalism and Schizophrenia* consequently outlines a typology of four abstract social formations – 'primitive' or segmentary societies, States, nomadic 'war machines' and capitalism itself – that aims to provide the conceptual tools for analysing the diverse dimensions of concrete social structures: How are its mechanisms of power organised? What are the 'lines of flight' that escape its integration? What new modes of existence does it make possible? These types of social formations are not to be understood as stages in a progressive evolution or development; rather, they sketch out a topological field in which each type functions as a variable of coexistence that enters into complex relations with the other types.

CONCLUSION

These, to be sure, are only very general schematic characterisations of the structure of Deleuze's project. The conclusions I would like to draw from them are modest: first, that in both his historical and constructive work, Deleuze was pursuing the elaboration of a philosophical system (one that is open, differential, problematic, and so on); and second, that this system is a transcendental system, one that both completes and inverts Kant's critical project. Historically, in working out this transcendental project, Deleuze primarily made use of three pre-Kantian thinkers (Hume, Spinoza and Leibniz) and three post-Kantian thinkers (Maimon, Nietzsche and Bergson) – all of whom provide Deleuze with the resources to think through a metaphysics stripped of the presuppositions of both God and Man, infinite substance and finite subject. Constructively, I have tried to sketch out the implications of Deleuze's project in five Kantian domains – dialectics, aesthetics, analytics, ethics and politics – showing how, in each case, Deleuze introduces into his analyses a consideration of the role of heterogenesis. Finally, I might note that Deleuze himself summarises his distance from Kant in terms of two fundamental inversions: the repudiation of universals in favour of the *singular*, and the repudiation of the eternal in favour of the *new*, that is, the genetic conditions under which something new is produced (heterogenesis).[34] These are perhaps the two essential themes that mark Deleuze's reconceptualisation of the transcendental field towards a 'transcendental empiricism'.

---

[34] Deleuze frequently makes both these points; see, for instance, the conclusion of 'What is a *dispositif?*' in *Michel Foucault: Philosopher*, trans. Timothy J. Armstrong (New York: Routledge, 1992), pp. 159–68.

Chapter 2

# The Problematic Idea, Neo-Kantianism and Maimon's Role in Deleuze's Thought

*Anne Sauvagnargues*[1]

Maimon is a decisive factor in the deflagration of the Kantian critique, to which Deleuze reverts systematically in the first part of his œuvre. Drawing from Kant the definition of philosophy as critique, along with his transcendental inspiration, but all the while reconfiguring the status of experience and that of the transcendental, Deleuze carries out a renewal of the Kantian project in the tradition of Neo-Kantianism. This shows the role of Maimon for Deleuze, who was hailed from 1960 up to *The Fold*[2] as the one who permits a true genesis of experience and of thought, since he substitutes for the orthodox divide between categories and sensibility in Kant his account of the differential or the Idea, which 'is fully differentiated in itself, before *differenciating* itself in the actual'.[3] Deleuze elaborates this turn towards a new transcendental method by integrating and displacing the Maimonian critique of the Kantian schematism, in order to release it from its oscillation between transcendental idealism and sceptical 'empiricism'. In 1967, the method of dramatisation constituted a first step of this transformation of the Kantian transcendental method that passes from conditioning to genesis, taking up the definition of the Idea according to Maimon and transforming it considerably through the Spinozist resumption of structuralism, the work of Lautman, and Simondon's definition of the intensive field of individuation.[4]

[1] Chapter translated by Daniela Voss.
[2] Gilles Deleuze, 'Lecture Course on Chapter Three of Bergson's *Creative Evolution*'. Presentation at the Ecole Supérieure de Saint-Cloud, 14 March 1960, trans. Bryn Loban, *SubStance*, issue 114, 36:3, (2007), pp. 72–90. Gilles Deleuze, *The Fold: Leibniz and the Baroque*, trans. Tom Conley (Minneapolis: University of Minnesota Press, 1993), p. 89.
[3] Gilles Deleuze, 'The Method of Dramatization' ('La Méthode de dramatisation', 1967), in David Lapoujade (ed.), *Desert Islands and Other Texts (1953–1974)*, trans. Michael Taormina (New York: Semiotext(e), 2004), p. 94 (translation modified by DanielaVoss).
[4] Ibid. pp. 94–116.

In what follows, I will trace the passage from a conditioning empiricism to a superior empiricism, which gives up the fixed structures of representation closed off within a transcendental subject, and propose a new conception of a dehumanised, real experience. It is Maimon who first initiated this turn towards real experience, which is not simply given but must be produced genetically. Thus the second part of the chapter sketches the way in which Maimon resolves the problem of Kantian schematism by claiming a continuity between the passive affection of sensibility and the activity of the understanding. For Maimon, the matter of intuition results from a differential production of the understanding, which remains largely unconscious. As will be shown, Deleuze departs from Maimon in many ways: the Idea is released from the viewpoint of differential calculus and becomes a virtual ideality, which is to say an Idea-problem that actualises or differenciates itself through spatio-temporal dynamisms interior to the Idea. As virtual structures, Ideas-problems no longer refer to an unconscious activity of the understanding and cease to be defined as the infinitely small. In closing this chapter, I will examine Deleuze's critique of the Cartesian criteria of clear and distinct evidence. The act of thinking in thought arises through the encounter with the virtual Idea, which is distinct and necessarily obscure because it does not pre-exist in consciousness before its actualisation. Thus, as we will see, Deleuze replaces the Cartesian model of recognition through clear evidence with what he refers to as an apprenticeship by distinct and obscure Ideas.

## FROM CONDITIONING TO GENESIS

In his transfigured resumption of the transcendental, Deleuze takes up the neo-Kantian objection according to which Kant holds on to the point of view of conditioning without reaching that of genesis. Here Maimon appears as a precursor. It is Maimon who raises the objection that the Kantian transcendental critique remains empirical because it is limited to stating the difference *de facto* between the determining concept and the determinable intuition without succeeding in producing it genetically. 'Maimon's genius lies in showing how inadequate the point of view of conditioning is for a transcendental philosophy.'[5]

Deleuze's turn to Maimon sheds light on his use of the notion of empiricism and the subtle ambiguity that allows him to call for a

---

[5] Gilles Deleuze, *Difference and Repetition*, trans. Paul Patton (New York: Columbia University Press, 1994), p. 173.

'transcendental empiricism', while blaming Kant, as Maimon does, for retaining an 'empirical' version of the transcendental. These two opposing uses of empiricism correspond to a reconfiguration of the experience: 'empiricism' in the first case designates pejoratively the moulding [*la mise en forme*] of a conditioned experience through representational reduplication. Experience is thus placed in resemblance to the image of thought, whereas in the second case transcendental empiricism leaves us grappling with a real, and not only possible, experience – like an encounter or violence to thought: this is the 'superior' or genetic empiricism.

Passing from this conditioning empiricism to a superior empiricism defines the philosophy of difference as a critique of representational reason that Deleuze conducts in *Difference and Repetition* on both fronts – the Dialectic and the Analytic: thwarting the pathologies of thought (stupidity) through a clinic of thought allows for the attainment of a 'transcendental empiricism' that transforms at the same time the status of the transcendental and that of empiricism. This clinic of thought extends the Kantian transcendental dialectic by a critique of representational reason, which Deleuze calls 'the image of thought' (Chapter 3). If this clinic is carried out, the philosophy of difference breaks with Kantianism, with the Aesthetic and the Transcendental Logic – the asymmetrical synthesis of the sensible and the ideal synthesis of difference of Chapters 4 and 5 – which grant access to 'real' experience, and not to its merely possible image.

Maimon proposes a new distribution of the empirical and the transcendental by establishing a differential continuity through a return to Leibniz at this point, where Kant separated intuition and the categories within the finite intellect and radically split the human understanding from the infinite divine understanding. According to Deleuze, it is Maimon 'who proposes a fundamental reformulation of the *Critique* and an overcoming of the Kantian duality between concept and intuition'.[6] The difference between sensibility and understanding, as well as their articulation, due to the schematism of the imagination, can only be recorded (*quid facti*), not legitimised *quid juris*. The Kantian conditioning of a possible experience, closed off within a given subject, remains exterior to what it conditions, too large, merely possible. It is this conditioning that Deleuze criticises in terms of the image of thought. Maimon encourages Deleuze on this road, still implicitly in *Nietzsche and Philosophy* (1962) and developed in a perfectly explicit way along Chapter 3 of *Difference and Repetition*, 'The Image of Thought', which

---

[6] Ibid.

carries out the Transcendental Dialectic of representational thought subjected under common sense.

This allows us to reassemble the critique that Deleuze, following Maimon, proposes of the Kantian philosophy. Kant holds to a simple conditioning (*quid facti*) in order to take account of the merely exterior harmony of the faculties due to the *deus ex machina* of the schema, and thus justify the postulates of the image as agreed upon by thought.[7] Because Kant traces the philosophical image of thought from the natural image of a thought, subjected to 'empirically' given values (*doxa*), he substituted for transcendental empiricism a tracing of the transcendental from the empirical, i.e. experience as it is moulded by representation.[8]

What does this turn of experience then consist in? All of the first part of his œuvre is dedicated to this problem. Deleuze characterises the different authors to whom he devotes a work (Hume, Nietzsche, Proust and Bergson) by crediting them with the different stages of his deflagration of Kantianism in the manner of a free indirect discourse. Since *Empiricism and Subjectivity* (1953), Deleuze assumes the Kantian project by defining the philosophy of Hume as 'a plan of analysis in order to undertake and conduct the examination of the structures of consciousness (critique), and to justify the totality of experience'.[9] But the totality of experience is not given in advance, conditioned by the structure of a given subject. In 1962, by reference to Nietzsche, he points out that the fact that 'Kant had not carried out a true critique' is first and foremost 'one of the principal motifs of Nietzsche's work', because Kant 'was not able to pose the problem of critique in terms of values'.[10] The image of thought, presupposed by Kantian philosophy, merely restores the well-recognised values of thought (truth, morality, transcendental psychology and theology). Kant, the 'great explorer', 'who discovers the prodigious domain of the transcendental', thus traces the so-called transcendental structures from empirical acts of an ordinary psychological consciousness.[11] From this follows, in the first edition of the *Critique of Pure Reason*, the primacy of the synthesis of recognition which conditions an unspecified object as correlate of the 'I think' to which all the

---

[7] Ibid. p. 167.

[8] Ibid. p. 143.

[9] Gilles Deleuze, *Empiricism and Subjectivity: An Essay on Hume's Theory of Human Nature*, trans. Constantin V. Boundas (New York: Columbia University Press, 1991), p. 87.

[10] Gilles Deleuze, *Nietzsche and Philosophy*, trans. Hugh Tomlinson (London: Athlone Press, 1983), p. 1.

[11] Deleuze, *Difference and Repetition*, p. 135.

faculties are related. The genius of Kant – having conceived a total and immanent critique – 'turns into the politics of compromise',[12] which safeguards and justifies each ideal: the subject, God, the world. This is why 'there is still too much empiricism in the *Critique*',[13] meaning here too much compromise with common sense, too much submission to established fact. 'Critique has everything – a tribunal of justices of the peace, a registration room, a register – except the power of a new politics which would overturn the image of thought'.[14]

When Deleuze writes, 'But Nietzsche does not rely on anyone but himself to conceive and accomplish the true critique. This project is of great importance for the history of philosophy',[15] there is no doubt that Deleuze defines thus his own project. In his 1960 *Lecture Course* on Bergson, Deleuze defines Bergson as 'the anti-Kant'[16] and following in the wake of Maimon as the philosopher who approaches the neo-Kantian problem of genesis. Bergsonian intuition counts as a transcendental method of analysis because it goes beyond given experience (*doxa*) towards the transcendental conditions, which are no longer, in the manner of Kant, 'the conditions of every possible experience', but rather conditions of real (and not given) experience.[17] That is to say, intuition rises from individuated perception to its transcendental conditions in order to capture real experience 'at its source, or rather above that decisive *turn* where, taking a bias in the direction of our utility, it becomes properly *human* experience'.[18] With Bergson, as with Nietzsche, Deleuze releases experience from its moulding [*mise en forme*] through an originary subject: experience is no longer, in the manner of phenomenology, a seizure of originary conditions of the given for consciousness. On the contrary, Bergson confronts us with a decentred, de-psychologised experience, released from its predicates that are traced from a transcendental Ego postulated by a psychological subject.

The transcendental assumes here a rigorous genetic sense: the conditions of experience do not concern the abstract conditions of a mental and already conditioned experience, but the reciprocal genesis of thought in an encounter with experience, such that the positions of objects and

---

[12] Deleuze, *Nietzsche and Philosophy*, p. 89.

[13] Deleuze, *Difference and Repetition*, p. 170.

[14] Ibid. p. 137.

[15] Deleuze, *Nietzsche and Philosophy*, p. 88.

[16] Deleuze, 'Lecture Course on Chapter Three of Bergson's *Creative Evolution*', p. 78.

[17] Gilles Deleuze, *Bergsonism*, trans. Hugh Tomlinson and Barbara Habberjam (New York: Zone Books, 1988), p. 23.

[18] Henri Bergson, *Matter and Memory*, trans. Nancy Margaret Paul and W. Scott Palmer (New York: Zone Books, 1991), p. 184.

subjects appear as derivations. Passing from conditioned experience to a true conditioning implies this turn towards a de-humanised (real) experience, which ceases to be moulded anthropologically, shaped by the doxical uses of perception and action of an already given subject. Owing to this 'turn of experience', Deleuze finds in Bergson a transcendental Aesthetic which is not reduced to the Kantian psychological version. The transcendental illusion consists in projecting onto experience an abstract tracing of the given, posed retrospectively as logically possible, starting from a constituted subject which predetermines the field of experience. Deleuze thus resumes the Bergsonian critique of the possible, an abstract and retrospective tracing from the given: the transcendental no longer concerns the conditions of possible experience, constructed retroactively in resemblance to the real that it is supposed to constitute, but its real, genetic conditions that are 'no larger than the conditioned'. Substituting for the simply logically possible a real that is neither given nor actualised but virtual, Deleuze opens experience onto a dynamics of unpredictable differenciation, an actual shock [*choc*] to thought, an encounter at the point where the realisation of the possible implies nothing but an abstract resemblance with the mental concept of the thing. There still remains the problem of specifying this genesis as an encounter with an experience, not at all determined in advance, though real, which implies a double determination of difference: as differenciation (with a c), or actualisation, as individuation of thought in a pre-individual, intensive field, through the encounter with an Idea, which is itself virtually differentiated (with a t), determined through the variation of differential relations and the distribution of singularities. The transcendental is no longer closed off, as in Kant, through realisation of a logically possible (resemblance) but makes itself virtual differenc/tiation through divergence.

The transcendental critique of the image of thought implies this struggle against representation, the insubordination towards values established by common sense and recognition, which condition *a priori* the field of experience. The critique proceeds by untying thought from the configuration of a consciousness, and as regards Kant, this is how he fails to carry out the critique. Proust shows how to reverse this image of thought, pointing us to a pathic [*pathique*] genesis of thought that breaks forth [*sursauter*] under the violence of the sign, and substituting an Aesthetic of violent encounter with the Idea to the representational *doxa* of recognition. The image of thought derives from representation and rests on the identity in the concept, the opposition in determination, the analogy in judgement and the resemblance in the object, according to the table of categories of the representational understanding. It cedes its position to a philosophy of difference, which leaves experience exposed to a real, dangerous and unpredictable encounter, and not as a possible tracing from already fixed structures of an objectality [*objectalité*] closed off within a personal and conscious transcendental subject. The transcendental field, constituted by impersonal singularities, proves (real) experience to be like an encounter operating case by case, and not given once and for all.

Thought is no longer an innate given of the mind but the result of a violent encounter and constraint, it becomes engendered, genital, as Artaud said. Via this determination of thought as powerlessness, the passivity of which explains creation, Deleuze is able to transpose Nietzsche's genealogy and Bergson's intuition in a theory of Ideas, while effectively linking in an unexpected manner Maimon, Nietzsche and Bergson, and equally presupposing a theory of problems that invokes Lautman and Simondon, Plato and Kant, and rests on the dissolution of any transcendental Ego. One can understand then how Deleuze proceeds with Maimon while displacing him.

## MAIMON, IDEAS-PROBLEMS AND THE METHOD OF DRAMATISATION

In his *Essay on Transcendental Philosophy*,[19] Maimon proposes to resolve the problem of Kantian schematism, conceiving the gap between sensibility and the categories as a passage to the limit of the infinitesimally small, that is, the mathematical differential. Such is the Leibnizian solution by means of which he intends to save the Kantian schematism, which Kant, according to him, determines only *quid facti*, in an empirical manner, and not *quid juris*, by right. In order to guarantee the schematism, it has to be produced genetically such that the passive affection of sensibility and the activity of the understanding can appear as one passing into the other. With recourse to the Leibnizian principle of con-

---

[19] Salomon Maimon, *Essay on Transcendental Philosophy*, trans. Nick Midgley, Henry Somers-Hall, Alistair Welchman und Merten Reglitz (New York and London: Continuum, 2010). Deleuze's reading of Maimon is based on the fine studies of Martial Guéroult, *La philosophie transcendentale de Salomon Maïmon* (Paris: Alcan, 1929) and of Jules Vuillemin, *L'héritage kantien et la révolution copernicienne* (Paris: PUF, 1954), even if he draws diametrically opposite conclusions (Deleuze, *Difference and Repetition*, pp. 174, 324 n. 6), he cites them in the extremely revealing bibliography which closes *Difference and Repetition*. See also the excellent book of Juliette Simont, *Essai sur la quantité, la qualité, la relation chez Kant, Hegel, Deleuze: Les 'fleurs noires' de la logique philosophique* (Paris: L'Harmattan, 1997).

tinuity, Maimon thus posits the matter of intuition as the differential of the activity of the understanding, as its extreme limit, which is equal to passivity, a *pathos*.

As passive affection is produced as a passage to the limit of the spontaneity of the understanding, the sensible given becomes the differential of an activity of the understanding, produced unconsciously by transcendental imagination. This discussion clarifies the transcendent use of the faculties and the methodological role of differential calculus in *Difference and Repetition*, in keeping with the *Anticipations of perception* and the theory of intensive magnitudes in Kant. Deleuze pursues with precision the discussion between Kant and Maimon, which has to be reproduced in order to elucidate the status of the Idea, which is neither real, nor fictive, but virtual and differential.[20]

In the *Anticipations of perception*, Kant demonstrates that all intuition has an intensive magnitude or degree: as regards the nature of the matter that fills [the forms of] intuition, we can anticipate that it must necessarily have an intensive magnitude, such that it cannot be divided into units, but which consists of a summation of infinitesimals. Any sensation has an intensive magnitude: for instance, the colour red spreads between the degree zero of consciousness and the perfectly actualised sensation of colour. In an intensive manner, through infinitesimal variation, consciousness runs through all the intermediaries of the absence of consciousness to full consciousness, from degree zero of sensation to its perfect actualisation, so that it runs through all the degrees of luminosity between degree zero of consciousness and degree one of sensation.

For Maimon, these differentials, provided by the understanding and produced through an unconscious activity of the self [*moi*], are themselves obscure, in view of their status as infinitely small and as the liminal degree [*degré limite*] of consciousness. For them to appear for consciousness, [the faculty of] imagination has to do a summation in order to produce an object of a finite, determined magnitude. This way, the infinitely small, the summation of which constitutes the degree $n$ of empirical consciousness, is in fact the differential of an unconscious production of transcendental imagination. The passivity of reception, to which Kant devoted himself in terms of the passive encounter of sensible affection, becomes, for Maimon, the differential of an unconscious activity of the self. These differentials of objects, or Ideas of reason, are the *noumena*, while the objects that arise from them, are the *phenomena*.[21]

---

[20] Deleuze, *Difference and Repetition*, pp. 178, 173–4.
[21] Maimon, *Essay on Transcendental Philosophy*, p. 32.

Thus Maimon resolves [the problem of] transcendental schematism by positing a common source of intuition and the categories: the divine understanding, of which our finite understanding is nothing but a mode. Since the matter of intuition actually consists in the production of differentials provided by the understanding, though at its limit, and thus identical to passive elements, the merely apparent distinction between understanding and sensibility is due to the finitude of our understanding. But human understanding is not of a different nature from the divine understanding, which is active through its syntheses, and intuitive as much as it posits the content itself. The finitude consists only in a limitation that renders the understanding unconscious of that part of its activity which is the production of differentials. This allows Maimon, by means of a generalised idealism, to eliminate the thing-in-itself from the *dispositif*: the *noumenon* becomes the differential of objects, which affect us as phenomena.

Deleuze carries out this whole discussion on the ground of transcendental empiricism, while liquidating the transcendental idealism of divine understanding. The method of dramatisation explicitly takes up the problem of Kantian schematism and shows at the same time how Deleuze partly resumes Maimon's solution and transforms it. Whenever the spatio-temporal dynamisms dramatise the concepts of the understanding, they actualise Ideas, endowed with their own consistency, such as Maimon's Ideas of reason. Yet, Deleuze does not at all intend to resolve the Ideas into the activity of the thinker, neither into the infinite understanding of God: they persist [*insister*], without being constituted by a mental activity, on account of virtual multiplicities, that is as differentiated structures. Therefore, the Idea is not the concept, a mental representation, but a differentiated complex that solicits the creation of concepts. It is necessary to reserve the name of Ideas 'not for pure *cogitanda* but rather for those instances which go from sensibility to thought and from thought to sensibility',[22] in the manner of differentials as in Maimon. Resuming Maimon's Ideas of reason, capable to produce their object, Deleuze situates his own distinction between Idea and concept in the distinction, as established by Maimon, between Ideas of reason (*noumena*) that produce sensible affection, and the Ideas of the understanding. Conceiving the differential limit of the sensible and of thought as an intensive differenciation, not as the unconscious production of an activity of the thinker which is based on the divine understanding, Deleuze also demonstrates how he departs from Maimon.

---

[22] Deleuze, *Difference and Repetition*, p. 146.

As a renewed transcendental method, the method of dramatisation unravels and transforms the Kantian schematism, while substituting for the peaceful neutrality of the *logos* the pathetic depth [*épaisseur pathétique*] of a *drama* which infuses the noetic relations with a spatio-temporal cinematic and injects into the neutral intelligibility of the concept the pathic power [*puissance pathique*] of an encounter that carries thought to the limit of its powerlessness. The Kantian schema converted logical possibility into transcendental reality and ensured the compatibility of the categorical structure with the spatio-temporal dynamisms of intuition. Deleuze substituted the virtual reality of the Idea for the merely logically possible of analytic thought and conceived the dynamism no longer as exterior of the concept, like in Kant, but as interior of the Idea, as really dramatising the emergence of the concept, the genesis of thought. 'The answer perhaps lies in a direction that certain post-Kantians have indicated: pure spatio-temporal dynamisms have the power to dramatize concepts, because first they actualize, incarnate Ideas.'[23]

So how can we specify the determinacy of the virtual Idea without dissolving it into God (transcendental idealism), nor resolving it into a mental act? Deleuze here turns to Lautman in order to analyse the virtual differentiation of the Idea, and to Simondon in order to explain its differenciation or actualisation. In his analysis of the differential calculus, Lautman introduces the concept of singularities to mathematics. The geometrical interpretation of differential equations brings to the fore two distinct mathematical realities: the field of directions with its topological accidents concerning the existence of singular points to which no direction is attached, and the integral curves which take a determined form in the neighbourhood of singularities of the field of directions. These two challenges [*attaques*] are of course complementary, because the nature of singularities is defined by the form of curves in their neighbourhood, but their mathematical reality is distinct.[24] Indicating this difference of kind between the existence and distribution of singular points, which refer to the Idea-problem, the problem-instance, and their specification in the solution-instance, Lautman shows that the problem conditions are irreducible to their treatment in thought.

Integrating this Lautmanian distinction between problem and solution,

---

[23] Deleuze, 'The Method of Dramatization', p. 99.
[24] Albert Lautman, 'Essay on the Notions of Structure and Existence in Mathematics', in *Mathematics, Ideas and the Physical Real*, trans. Simon Duffy (London, New York: Continuum, 2010), Book II, p. 181 and Albert Lautman, 'Symmetry and Dissymmetry in Mathematics and Physics', in *Mathematics, Ideas and the Physical Real*, Book IV, p. 259.

Deleuze releases the differential Idea from the infinitesimal calculus and takes up again the virtual ideality of the problem according to the research he had just carried out on structuralism [*pensées structurales*].[25] In linguistics, anthropology and psychoanalysis (Saussure, Lévi-Strauss, Lacan), structuralist thought provisionally serves as a relay for Deleuze, because it sets a new domain of idealities, between intellectual essence and the empiricism of the state of things. The explication [of the virtual ideality], which is irreducible to empirical reality, but not transcendent to it, develops differentially from the list of empirical determinations, but is not reduced to them. In 'How Do We Recognize Structuralism?', a text which is written in the same year as 'The Method of Dramatization', Deleuze maintains for the time being the concepts of the symbolic and of structure which he will criticise with Guattari from *Anti-Oedipus* onwards and expounds the virtual differentiation of the structure that allows him to specify the status of the Idea as a positional, serial, constraining but not principal multiplicity, a determining but not antecedent condition. This virtual plane is endowed with a power of internal organisation that is capable of conferring a relational value to the elements that are systematically distributed.

It is in this context that 'the birth of structuralism at this point coincides with the death of any genetic or dynamic ambitions of the calculus'.[26] The differentials no longer refer to the infinitely small, but to a new conception of limit which loses its phoronomic character and is from then on rated as a cut, a variation of the remarkable and the regular. As a cut, the ideal cause of continuity, the Maimonian limit no longer indicates a passage between intuition and categories, but the production of differential singularities. The virtual ideality of the Idea has reconfigured the relation between empiricism and intelligibility. Following Lautman, Deleuze distinguishes the ideal order of problems and the empirical series of solutions, and defines the problem as a transcendental instance that does not exist exterior to the solutions that it determines.

Lautman also allows Deleuze to distance himself from structuralism: if the problem is neither real nor fictive, it is also not symbolic in a structuralist sense either, depending on the reciprocal assignation of signifying and signified series.[27] The virtual takes precedence over the

---

[25] For a detailed analysis, see my work *Deleuze: L'Empirisme transcendantal* (Paris: PUF, 2010), chap. VII 'Spinoza et le structuralisme' and chap. VIII 'Série, effet de surface, différenciant'.

[26] Deleuze, *Difference and Repetition*, p. 176.

[27] Ibid. p. 178.

determination of this third order, which is irreducible to the real and to the imaginary, and the problematic, as we have now defined it, displaces the symbolic and substitutes it. Like the structure, the problem is immanent to the empirically real for which it traces the noetic diagram, but contrary to it, it is also genetic, a real source of individuation, and the singularities of which it is composed are not signifying but differential. The objectivity of the problem is thus irreducible to an anthropological structure, be it linguistic, social or unconscious, and Deleuze connects the problematic in Simondon and in Lautman: 'problems are Ideas themselves'.[28] As a pre-individual field of singularities, the problem corresponds now to the dramatisation of the Idea, to its distinct-obscure actualisation, produced by a violent encounter in the life of the thinker. Deleuze connects the Simondonian disparation with the Bergsonian tradition of an epistemology of the problem. This treatment assures the transfer of Simondon's energetics to a physics of thought: a displaced structuralism renews and prolongs the intensive philosophy of Simondon, and allows one to consider the virtual under the point of view of ideal differentiation, not any more under the point of view of individuation.

THE DISTINCT/OBSCURE APPRENTICESHIP OF THE IDEA
AGAINST THE RECOGNITION OF CLEAR AND DISTINCT
EVIDENCE

In place of the 'clear and distinct' parameters of the Cartesian model of recognition, Deleuze substitutes the 'distinct-obscure' of discordant thought. The clarity of the Kantian possible gives way to the distinct-obscure differenc/tiation of the Idea. According to Maimon, the Idea presents itself to consciousness as its liminal, infinitesimal degree, thus as obscure affection. For Deleuze, the Ideas have to be conceived as virtual multiplicities, made up of differential relations and singular points, which thought apprehends in the differential mode of dizziness, fainting or obscure imperceptibility, of the problematic encounter.

Recapturing the Leibnizian valorisation of the obscure within the framework of the distinction of the virtual and the actual, Deleuze firmly distinguishes the obscure apprenticeship of the Idea from the clear recognition of knowledge (*doxa*). As it is not yet actualised in a concept,

---

[28] Ibid. pp. 146, 162 and Gilles Deleuze, 'Ninth Series of the Problematic', in *The Logic of Sense*, ed. Constantin V. Boundas, trans. Mark Lester with Charles Stivale (New York: Columbia University Press, 1990), pp. 52–7.

the virtually distinct Idea is necessarily obscure, because it does not pre-exist in consciousness before its actualisation. On the other hand, evidence, enjoying the suspect clarity of recognition, remains of the order of the confused, the well-known, stupidity, of the order of those propositions that are not produced creatively by the actualisation of an Idea. Such is the confused knowledge of school textbooks, of *doxa*, of the order of common sense. This critique of clear evidence, which is constant in Deleuze from 'The Method of Dramatization' to *The Fold*, merges with the struggle against stupidity as recognition. Thus the Idea (with a capital I) does not amount to an intellectual representation, a mental given. It is not constituted by an inner psychic projection in the thinker, but consists in a virtual complex of ideal connections. We have seen by reference to Lautman, that Deleuze refuses to make a human, psychological, noetic given of the Idea, but contrary to Plato, the Idea does not plunge into the separated atmosphere of an eternal intelligible. Deleuze conceives it as a real multiplicity, subjected to a virtual cinematics, animated by spatio-temporal dynamisms, rhythms and differential speeds, which case by case form a rule of specification for the concepts.

While determining these differential movements and tendencies of actualisation, this dramatisation of the Idea takes place in a necessarily obscure, though distinct mode: the minute perceptions composing the Idea of the sea are obscure, because they are not yet differenciated in consciousness, although they are for themselves perfectly distinct, composed of differential relations and defined singularities, even if they are not clearly made out. As such, if Cartesian clarity remains confused and doxical, this is because it is not an object of an effective dramatisation. It remains a given knowledge in the mode of recognition, whose apparent clarity is the price to pay for the absence of originality and creativity. Vice versa, all that is distinct is necessarily obscure, because it concerns an Idea which is not yet differenciated for consciousness. The obscurity of the Idea which gives rise to the creation of thought thus distinguishes itself from the natural light of *doxa* and straight opinion.

By means of this discussion with Maimon, we now understand the role that Deleuze accords to differentials, to the distinct-obscure, and to the concept and the Idea respectively. The actualisation of the concept must not be understood in terms of a logic of the possible and the pre-existence of truth, whereupon the concept realises itself in thought according to an analysis in terms of the part and the whole; it must rather be understood according to this new logic of the virtual, for which the actualisation of the concept results from a differenciation of the Idea. Deleuze can thus conclude: 'The nature of the Idea is to be distinct and obscure. In other words, the Idea is precisely *real without being actual, differentiated without being differenciated, and complete without being entire.*'[29] In other words, it consists in a virtual, perfectly singularised and distinguished complex, a virtual multiplicity which solicits a response from thought, its actualisation.

Thus the Idea is not given in thinking as something innate. In distinguishing the Idea and the concept, Deleuze separates ideality and thought, and posits the concept as a response, a reaction to sensible intrusion, to the affection by the Idea. Ideas are the differentials of thought which they produce through encounter with the sensible. Deleuze thus credits Maimon with injecting receptivity into the spontaneity of the understanding, and conversely, spontaneity into affection. This is what he wants to express when he declares to capture, under the notion of *drama*, the pathic (*pathiques*) dynamisms that determine the Idea to actualise itself, the passive genesis of the Idea. These *dramas* are not exclusively dependent on the typology of thinkers (Nietzsche), neither on an intuitive access to an experience which cannot be socialised (Bergson), but on the 'logical drama'[30] which, according to Lautman, is played out on the plane of problems. Therefore, the problem is not at all anterior to its realisation within a theory (solution), even if it is not confused with it: as problematics, Ideas differ in kind from concepts which do not resemble them. This transcendence of the Idea with regard to the solutions that actualise it empirically, but also its immanence in the solutions that cover it, define the new transcendental plane. The Idea-problem remains immanent to the solutions, which actualise it, with which, however, it does not identify itself; and this relative transcendence does not imply any supremacy, neither anteriority. This relation between problem and solution is tied back to the relations between substance and its modes in Spinoza: the solution actualises the problem, which subsists and insists in its actualisation. But if the problem does not identify itself with the solution, it also does not pre-exist in a heaven of Ideas, and has no existence outside the solution. For Deleuze, there is no ready-made problem. 'A problem is determined only by the singular points which express its conditions',[31] it determines itself nowhere else but in the solution, it has no prior conceptual or principal signification with regard to its solutions. If it is not mixed up with the solution, it

[29] Deleuze, *Difference and Repetition*, p. 214.
[30] Lautman, 'Essay on the Notions of Structure and Existence in Mathematics', p. 189.
[31] Deleuze, *The Logic of Sense*, p. 54; *Difference and Repetition*, p. 278.

depends, however, on the empirical effectuation of the solution, without which it cannot be constructed. But it is determined as a problem to which the solution responds without being confused with it. Thus the problem concerns the ideal, virtual event, while the solution, which effectuates the problem on a spatio-temporal plane, appears as its actual differenciation. 'All concepts are connected to problems without which they would have no meaning and which can themselves only be isolated or understood as their solution emerges.'[32]

This accounts for Deleuze's interest in the Proustian approach. The apprenticeship which *In Search of Lost Time* describes shows that the sign gives access neither to a given objectivity, nor to a subjective discovery, but to – what Deleuze, in 1964, with difficulty calls – the apprenticeship of 'essence', an apprenticeship which is nevertheless empirical, factual, contingent and affective. We only learn by surrendering to the sensible, to the extent that thought is stirred up through singular signs: not only is each faculty raised to its transcendent (involuntary, says Proust) exercise through the violence of a multiplicity which affects it, but learning also becomes the living passage between ignorance (*non-savoir*) and knowledge, which accounts for the production of new thought under the force of problematic signs. Learning means raising a faculty to its transcendent exercise, within a disjointed relation that indicates the encounter with the Idea. 'To learn is to enter into the universal of the relations which constitute the Idea, and into their corresponding singularities.'[33]

The signs make up problems, Deleuze writes, and they release the structure of the Idea which may seem to be posed like a Platonic Idea, because it designates the objectivity of the problem. In fact, as we have just confirmed the analysis of the Idea as a differential multiplicity, and as we could equally show by means of an analysis of the sign as individuation, learning means confronting oneself with the differentiation of the Idea, whereas knowing means being satisfied with the doxical possession of a rule of solutions. Signs are thus an object of apprenticeship, of an exploration of the Idea, which consists in forming a problematic field with the Idea. This is why exploring the Idea or carrying a faculty to its points of transcendent exercise comes down to the same thing. Learning, making the experience of a sublime disproportion between thought and Idea – this means making the experience of a dramatisation where the

[32] Gilles Deleuze and Félix Guattari, *What is Philosophy?*, trans. Hugh Tomlinson and Graham Burchell (New York: Columbia University Press, 1994), p. 16.
[33] Deleuze, *Difference and Repetition*, p. 165.

remarkable points of our body, for example while swimming, enter in relation to the singular points of the Idea of the river, in such a way that thought, pushed to its limits of power, springs up under the involuntary intrusion of the sign.

Chapter 3

# Maimon, Kant, Deleuze:
# The Concepts of Difference and
# Intensive Magnitude

*Daniela Voss*

## INTRODUCTION

Maimon's *Essay on Transcendental Philosophy* from 1790 is written as a commentary to Kant's *Critique of Pure Reason*. In this loose collection of commentaries, supplementary notes and appendices, Maimon develops ideas that give rise to new movements in philosophical thought. Chief amongst these is the way Maimon thinks of the relation between identity and difference. According to Martial Guéroult, Maimon oscillates between two solutions:[1]

1. The first solution presupposes the primacy of identity. Identity is considered as the supreme principle, and difference fulfils only a subordinate function as limitation or opposition. As Maimon says: 'Difference is not actually a special form in its own right, but signifies simply lack of identity.'[2] In his book on Fichte, Guéroult shows how Fichte will follow this train of thought and develop it further to a philosophy of identity. Contrary to Maimon, however, Fichte will not think identity as a formal identity but as an infinite reality. Difference will function as a rule of limitation of the infinite ego.
2. The second solution, however, leads in a different direction. Maimon regards identity and difference first and foremost as relational concepts, which means that one concept cannot be thought without the other. For our finite understanding, they function as forms of

---

[1] Martial Guéroult, *L'Evolution et la Structure de la Doctrine de la Science chez Fichte*, vol. 1 (Paris: Les Belles Lettres, 1930), p. 126.

[2] Salomon Maimon, *Essay on Transcendental Philosophy*, trans. Nick Midgley, Henry Somers-Hall, Alistair Welchman and Merten Reglitz (London, New York: Continuum, 2010 [1790]), p. 112. The page numbers refer to the original German edition and are marked in the English translation at the top of each page.

thought. As Maimon holds against Kant, they are the most fundamental forms of thought insofar as they are transcendental conditions of perception in general. However, Maimon does not stop here.
In order to answer the question of the real, he turns difference into
a positive and productive principle. Maimon develops the idea of
pure differentials that operate as rules by which everything given to
consciousness arises.

In this chapter, I would like to pursue this second solution – a solution
that will become an important reference point for Deleuze's philosophy
of difference. In leaving behind the primacy of identity and turning difference into a principle of its own – that is, into a genetic principle for
the production of the real – Deleuze could be said to follow and renew
Maimon's post-Kantian project.

## IDENTITY AND DIFFERENCE AS TRANSCENDENTAL CONCEPTS

Maimon defines identity and difference as relational concepts
(*Verhältnisbegriffe*) and as 'universal forms of thought by means of
which the understanding brings unity to the manifold'.[3] Relational
concepts always come along in reciprocally defining pairs, such that
one of the terms cannot be thought without the other. As further examples, Maimon lists the concepts of cause-and-effect and substance-and-
accident. These concepts can also be found in Kant's table of categories
under the title of pure concepts of relation, whilst the concepts of difference and identity are conspicuously left out. Maimon's aim is to prove
against Kant that the concepts of difference and identity have a transcendental status. In fact, he holds them to be the most fundamental of all
categories, because they are the necessary precondition for thinking any
synthesis of a manifold at all.[4]

Kant also deals with the concepts of difference and identity in his
chapter on 'The Amphiboly of the Concepts of Reflection' in the
*Critique of Pure Reason*, where they appear as one of the four pairs of
reflective concepts (the others being agreement and opposition, inner
and outer, matter and form). Concepts of reflections are used for comparing representations with one another. According to Kant, two kinds
of uses must be distinguished: whether they are employed with regard
to logical objects (concepts), or to empirical objects (spatio-temporal

[3] Ibid.
[4] Ibid. pp. 130–1.

representations). In this chapter, Kant takes the opportunity to criticise Leibniz for his 'misuse' of reflective concepts, especially his misuse of the concept of difference. For Leibniz, any difference is a conceptual difference: if we find that two empirical objects differ in some way, this difference must have a sufficient reason in the individual concepts of the objects. Ultimately, this leads Leibniz to claim that no two objects have exactly the same properties. Even two drops of water must be distinguished with respect to their intrinsic conceptual properties. According to Kant, Leibniz's error was to universalise the so-called principle of the 'identity of indiscernibles', while he maintains that it can only be applied in the case of concepts and not in the case of empirical reality. Kant argues that empirical objects can be completely identical with regard to their intrinsic properties but differ with regard to their external relations in space or time.

The crucial thought experiment that Kant puts forward against Leibniz is that of incongruent counterparts.[5] Suppose that there are two objects that are completely identical with regard to their intrinsic properties. Kant chooses as an example someone's right and left hand (or the mirror image of the right hand – this latter example of the right hand and its mirror image allows him to eliminate all tiny quantitative and qualitative differences that might pertain between right and left hand). Now given that there are no intrinsic differences that the understanding can grasp, these two objects are nonetheless distinct. This fact can easily be proven, since the right hand will never be congruent with the left hand (or its mirror image, which is also a left hand). Kant's argument is supposed to show that there are differences, namely spatio-temporal differences, which are only apparent to the senses and which cannot be intellectualised by the understanding. Thus, for Kant, space and time are *a priori* forms of sensible intuition, which are irreducible to conceptual differences.

The solution that Maimon puts forward is an attempt to reconcile Leibnizian and Kantian views. Maimon agrees with Kant's claim that space and time are *a priori* forms of consciousness, but they are so only for our consciousness of representation. Space and time are schemata[6] or fictions[7] produced by the faculty of imagination; their objective ground, however, has to be traced back to the *a priori* concepts of dif-

---

[5] Immanuel Kant, 'Prolegomena zu einer jeden künftigen Metaphysik, die als Wissenschaft wird auftreten können', in *Kants Werke*, Akademie Textausgabe, vol. IV (Berlin: Walter de Gruyter, 1968 [1783]), §13, pp. 285–6.

[6] Maimon, *Essay on Transcendental Philosophy*, pp. 179, 346.

[7] Ibid. p. 19.

ference and identity. Maimon departs from the Kantian use of the term 'schema' in a remarkable way. Although Kant also defines a schema as 'a product of the imagination',[8] he reserves it for a very specific use. For Kant, the schema signifies a rule in accordance with which the imagination can apply concepts to appearances. A schema is called 'transcendental' if it makes the application of pure concepts of the understanding to appearances in general possible. The use of schemata is thus restricted to the realm of experience. As Samuel Atlas emphasises:

> Kant's very definition of the function of the *schema* implies a limitation, namely, a limitation restricting its application to the realm of experience. [...] The function of the categories is confined and restricted through the *schemata* to the objects of sensibility; their application beyond the realm of sensibility is not warranted.[9]

Maimon, on the contrary, uses the concept 'schema' as an image for something which is beyond our experience, namely for differences that only the understanding can think.[10] He thus takes sides with Leibniz's rationalistic claim that space and time can in principle be reduced to pure intelligible relations between things.[11] Consequently, he claims that the concept of difference is more fundamental than the relation of 'being outside one another':

> Being outside one another in time and space has its ground in the difference between things, i.e. the imagination, which is the ape of the understanding, represents things *a* and *b* as external to one another in time and space because the understanding thinks them as different.[12]

In other words, space and time function as schemata, by means of which the faculty of imagination is able to represent something which is beyond our capacity of representation: purely conceptual differences or intelligible relations of difference. Again, Maimon first of all argues in unison with Kant and then departs from the Kantian line of thought.

---

[8] Immanuel Kant, *Critique of Pure Reason*, trans. and ed. Allen W. Wood (Cambridge: Cambridge University Press, 1998), A140/B179.

[9] Samuel Atlas, *From Critical to Speculative Idealism: The Philosophy of Solomon Maimon* (The Hague: Martinus Nijhoff, 1964), p. 104.

[10] Referring to the German mathematician and philosopher Ben David, Maimon says that '[p]erhaps *Ben David* understands the term "differential magnitudes" to mean something that cannot be presented in intuition; but if these cannot be represented in themselves, they can nevertheless be represented through a schema [...]' (Maimon, *Essay on Transcendental Philosophy*, p. 276).

[11] 'I speak here as a Leibnizian, who treats time and space as universal undetermined concepts of reflection that must have an objective ground [...]' (Ibid. p. 133).

[12] Ibid. pp. 133–4.

Like Kant, he maintains that consciousness only arises with synthesis and that synthesis is a function of the imagination, 'without which we would have no cognition at all, but of which we are seldom even conscious'.[13] However, Maimon emphasises the fact that synthesis always implies a unity of difference. In other words, we always have to presuppose difference, that is, the diversity of a given manifold, such that a synthesis in one intuition can be effectuated. In Maimon's words, 'something must be given that is thought by the understanding as a manifold (through unity of difference)'.[14] Consequently, the concepts of identity and difference are the necessary precondition for thinking any synthesis at all. Contrary to Kant, Maimon not only considers spatio-temporal representations as products of synthesis, but literally anything given to consciousness. This includes sensations, for example the sensation of colour. As Peter Thielke explains:

> In order for us to be conscious of a sensation, the sensation itself must be thought of as composed of a unified manifold, even though the manifold must be unified *pre-* or *sub*-consciously. For sensation to be present in consciousness, we cannot posit it as merely given, but must think of it as a unified composite.[15]

In this way, Maimon attempts to reduce anything given in consciousness to a pre- or subconscious differential manifold, which is supposed to be the objective ground (*ens reale*) for any synthesis produced by the imagination.

For Maimon, the concepts of identity and difference are the most fundamental forms of thought, because they are not only effective with regard to intuition, that is, spatio-temporal representations, but already with regard to sensation. In other words, they are not only formal conditions for synthesising quantitative magnitudes but also qualitative magnitudes. Thus, Maimon concludes that both identity and difference are *formal conditions of perception in general.*[16] He thereby goes much further than Kant who only acknowledges formal conditions of experience, that is, the categories. As Maimon says:

> The concepts of reflection, identity and difference, are the highest (most universal) forms of thought because the use of the categories properly

---

[13] Kant, *Critique of Pure Reason*, A78/B103.
[14] Maimon, *Essay on Transcendental Philosophy*, pp. 130–1.
[15] Peter Thielke, 'Intuition and Diversity: Kant and Maimon on Space and Time', in Gideon Freudenthal (ed.), *Salomon Maimon: Rational Dogmatist, Empirical Skeptic* (Dordrecht: Kluwer, 2003), p. 116.
[16] Maimon, *Essay on Transcendental Philosophy*, pp. 131, 214–15.

called extends only to objects of experience (to the objective reality of subjective perception), while the use of these concepts of reflection extends not only to objects of experience but also to objects of perception itself.[17]

Having shown that identity and difference are transcendental concepts that must be presupposed for any conscious perception, Maimon needs to specify now the nature of the differences that constitute the objective ground, that is, the pre- or subconscious manifold that makes up the matter of perception.

## DIFFERENCE AS A GENETIC PRINCIPLE FOR THE PRODUCTION OF CONSCIOUS PERCEPTION

Maimon's ambition to reduce anything given in consciousness to intelligible relations or differentials has to do with the problem *quid juris*, that is, the question in what way *a priori* concepts can justifiably be related to given intuition. Maimon criticises the solution that Kant develops in his chapter on Schematism, involving the intermediate *a priori* intuition of time and space. He argues that the Kantian transcendental schema of pure intuition is an impossible representation. Even if we were able to imagine such a thing as pure intuition, i.e., a spatial or temporal whole which is emptied of all content, it would be nothing but an illusion, incapable of fulfilling its synthetic function.[18] In order to bridge the gap between *a priori* concepts and given intuition, we have to think of the given itself as a product of synthesis, the elements of which are a pure rational manifold of differentials, or as Maimon also says, ideas of the understanding. In fact, Maimon solves the problem *quid juris* by dissolv-

---

[17] Ibid. pp. 129–30. In this quote, Maimon may also be alluding to the distinction between 'judgements of experience' and 'judgements of perception', which Kant makes in section 18 and section 29 of the *Prolegomena*. According to Kant, judgements of perception present a mere constant conjunction among perceptions in experience and are therefore only subjectively valid, while judgements of experience claim a necessary relation in the object and are therefore objectively valid. Thus, Kant distinguishes between the judgement 'when the sun shines on a stone it grows warm', which is a mere subjective perception, and the judgement 'the sun warms the stone', which involves the *a priori* concept of cause-and-effect. In the *Critique of Pure Reason*, Kant no longer makes this distinction; instead he claims that without the categories we would have no experience at all. Contrary to Kant, Maimon adopts the skeptical position that it is impossible to prove necessary connections among perceptions in experience and that we have to acknowledge a subjective level of experience, namely 'perception in general' (cf. Maimon, *Essay on Transcendental Philosophy*, pp. 186–7).

[18] I reconstruct the full argument that Maimon advances against Kant in my article 'Maimon and Deleuze: The Viewpoint of Internal Genesis and the Concept of Differentials', *Parrhesia*, 11, (2011), pp. 62–74.

ing the whole problem: he no longer conceives concepts and intuitions as heterogeneous, stemming from two different sources of human cognition, sensibility and understanding, but instead considers them both as products of the understanding that converge to one another at infinity.[19]

Maimon borrows the concept of differentials from Leibniz, who introduced the term to solve the mathematical problem of tangents, i.e., the determination of gradients of curves. The tangent to a curve at a particular point is the visible expression of the law that determines the gradient of the curve at that point. According to Leibniz, the law consists of the quotient between two infinitely small values, the differentials dy and dx. The symbol dx represents an infinitely small difference in relation to x, which corresponds to an infinitely small difference dy in relation to y. By means of the ratio dy/dx, one can determine the course of the curve in the immediate neighbourhood of the given point, that is, its manner of rising or falling.

During the days of Leibniz and Newton and the foundation of differential calculus, there was a controversial debate as to the correct interpretation of differentials: differentials were characterised as 'ultimate differences', 'quantities smaller than any given quantity', 'qualitative or relative zeros', 'ghosts of departed quantities', 'evanescent quantities', and 'momentary increments or decrements of a flowing quantity'.[20] However, it is important to note that, generally, differentials were not conceived as extended quantities, however small, but rather as intensive qualities. Being smaller than anything given to consciousness, differentials could not be assigned any determinate value. Yet, their ratio could generate a finite quantity, expressing the value of the gradient of the tangent to the curve at a given point. The ratio of differentials was thus defined as a generative law determining the qualitative behaviour of the curve.

Maimon's ingenuity consists in the application of the mathematical

[19] 'Suppose it is true that we possess experiential propositions (in Kant's sense) and that we apply the pure concepts of the understanding to appearances for their sake; then the possibility of all this or the *quid juris?* is easily explained according to my theory because the elements of appearances [i.e. ideas of the understanding or differentials], what the pure concepts of the understanding are subsequently applied to, are not themselves appearances. If someone asks me: but how does the understanding recognize that these elements pertain to these relations? I answer: because the understanding itself makes them into real objects by means of these relations and because the appearances themselves approach these relations more and more closely (to infinity)' (Maimon, *Essay on Transcendental Philosophy*, pp. 192–3).

[20] Carl B. Boyer, *The History of the Calculus and its Conceptual Development* (New York: Dover Publications, 1959 [1949]), pp. 12–13, 212, 216, 219.

term of differentials to the specific philosophical problem of the nature of sensation. However, one can say that the definition of sensation in terms of differentials was already prefigured in Kant, insofar as he pointed to the *intensive* nature of sensation. Since the identity of intensive magnitudes and the infinitely small was a commonplace in those days, as Hermann Cohen suggests, it was only a small step to conceive sensation in terms of differentials.[21] Yet, Kant did not make this move. For Kant, sensation is the matter of perception, which somehow 'fills' the forms of intuition, space and time. He explains sensation as 'a merely subjective representation, by which one can only be conscious that the subject is affected, and which one relates to an object in general'.[22] Thus, sensation is the effect of a modification of our faculty of sensibility, and this modification can be characterised in terms of *degree*. For instance, we distinguish temperature in degrees of heat, or colours according to degrees of hue, lightness and saturation. Kant discusses this matter in the 'Anticipations of Perceptions' in the *Critique of Pure Reason*. There he states that in contrast to intuition, that is, extensive magnitudes, which are apprehended by a successive synthesis, sensation is neither extended nor divisible, and the apprehension of sensation does not happen successively but in an instant. He concludes that sensations have to be conceived as *intensive magnitudes*. One of the main characteristics of intensive magnitudes is that they cannot be described as the summation of distinct units or parts, but rather as the limitation of a continuous inner multiplicity. A given intensive magnitude comprises 'a continuous nexus of many possible intermediate sensations, whose difference from one another is always smaller than the difference between the given one and zero, or complete negation'.[23] Hence the possibility of inner variation moves between the degree zero, in which the sensation would entirely disappear for our empirical consciousness, and its given degree of reality.

---

[21] Hermann Cohen, *Das Prinzip der Infinitesimal-Methode und seine Geschichte* (Frankfurt/M: Suhrkamp, 1968), pp. 57–8. It must be noted, however, that Cohen notoriously neglects Maimon's contribution to the interpretation of sensation as the infinitely small or intensive magnitude. He is not even mentioned in Cohen's book on the principle of the infinitesimal method – a lack of attention that already Friedrich Kuntze criticises in his magnum opus on Maimon from 1912. Only in his book *Kant's Theory of Experience*, Cohen briefly acknowledges that 'Salomon cogently argued for the connection between consciousness and differential in his investigations of transcendental philosophy'. See Hermann Cohen, *Kants Theorie der Erfahrung*, 4th edn (Berlin: Bruno Cassirer, 1925), p. 389 (my translation).

[22] Kant, *Critique of Pure Reason*, A165/B207.

[23] Ibid. A168/B210.

The idea of an intensive magnitude, which is generated in relation to zero and that gradually changes in accordance with the principle of continuity, corresponds to Leibniz's mathematical concept of differentials or infinitely small differences, which continuously become smaller as they approach the particular numerical values for any of the curve's points. Maimon capitalises on this link between sensation, intensive magnitude and differential.

> The extensive magnitude is, so to speak, the schema of the intensive magnitude because intensive magnitude, along with its relations, cannot be perceived directly and in itself but only by means of extensive magnitude. For example, the different degrees of heat and cold are perceived by means of the rising and falling of a thermometer: it is given as a unity and thought as a plurality through comparison. With quanta, intensive magnitude is the differential of the extensive, and the extensive is, in turn, the integral of the intensive.[24]

Maimon distinguishes here between the thought (or concept) of intensive magnitudes and the perception of intensive magnitudes. Thus, we can only conceive of an intensive magnitude if we make use of extensive magnitudes as a schema or image of their inner plurality. For instance, with the help of a thermometer, we can express the degree of temperature by referring to the number that the column of mercury indicates at the temperature scale. We can only *conceive* but never perceive the inner plurality of intensive magnitudes directly. This is so, because intensive magnitudes are *given* to our consciousness only as an already synthesised representation. Prior to any synthesis, intensive magnitudes are equal to zero in intuition. Only as parts of a synthesis can we become conscious of them, that is, when they are arranged in reciprocally determining relations to produce the representation of a quality or thing. Hence, for Maimon, it is the differential relation of intensive magnitudes, which provides the law of production of our conscious perception.

As we have seen, Maimon describes the relation between extensive and intensive magnitudes in terms of the relation between the integral and its differential, and in this way he goes beyond Kant. They both define sensation as intensive magnitudes, but while for Maimon intensive magnitudes can be explained by means of differentials or laws of production, for Kant, intensive magnitudes are only described from the point of view of their effect, that is, as subjective modifications of the mind. Kant adheres to a psychological definition of intensive magni-

---

[24] Maimon, *Essay on Transcendental Philosophy*, pp. 122–3.

tude, insofar as he reduces the real to an influence on the senses, which is simply given but not further explicable. Perhaps Kant was aware of the awkward psychological character of his definition of intensive magnitudes, and this is why he may have changed the formulation of the alleged *a priori* principle of 'Anticipations of Perception' from the first to the second edition of the *Critique of Pure Reason*. In the 1781 edition, the general principle is formulated as follows: 'In all appearances the sensation, and the *real*, which corresponds to it in the object (*realitas phaenomenon*), has an *intensive magnitude*, i.e., a degree' (A166). Having rephrased the principle in the 1787 edition, it then reads as '*In all appearances the real, which is an object of the sensation, has intensive magnitude*, i.e., a degree' (B207). Perhaps he may have wanted to bestow a more objective character upon intensive magnitude by defining it as 'the real' and the 'object of sensation', but in the paragraph that follows, sensible reality is still explained as an influence on the senses, that is, as sensation. Thus, Kant did not dispense with psychology but held fast to empirical-psychological considerations, although there certainly is a problem with how something subjective such as sensation could be anticipated by an *a priori* principle. Kant's concerns about this problem are clearly expressed in the following quotation:

> Nevertheless there must always be something striking about this anticipation of perception for a researcher who has become accustomed to transcendental consideration and thereby become cautious, and some reservation is aroused about the fact that the understanding can anticipate a synthetic proposition of the sort which that concerning the degree of everything real in appearance is, and thus about the possibility of the inner variation of the sensation itself if one abstracts from its empirical quality, and it is therefore a question not unworthy of solution, how the understanding can assert something synthetic *a priori* about appearances, and indeed anticipate them in that which is really merely empirical, namely what pertains to sensation.[25]

Maimon, on the contrary, attempts to 'objectify' intensive magnitudes and explain their *a priori* nature by identifying them with differentials. Differentials make up a completely rational manifold, which remains subconscious from the viewpoint of our consciousness of representation. Their reciprocal determination is a continuous process, which proceeds 'until the degree necessary for consciousness is reached'.[26] In this way, qualities as well as quantities are produced. All appearances are thus

---

[25] Kant, *Critique of Pure Reason*, A175/B217.
[26] Maimon, *Essay on Transcendental Philosophy*, p. 31.

continuous magnitudes, which the understanding can only think as 'flowing':[27]

> it [the understanding] can only think an object by specifying the way it arises or the rule by which it arises: this is the only way that the manifold of an object be brought under the unity of the rule, and consequently the understanding cannot think an object as having already arisen [*entstanden*] but only as arising [*entstehend*], i.e. as flowing [*fliessend*].[28]

The 'flowing' object of the understanding has its objective ground in the manifold of differentials, which are real or, as Maimon says, an *ens reale*. Differentials provide a way of explaining how both qualities and quantities are generated according to the principle of continuity. For Maimon, this is also the only way to solve the problem *quid juris* satisfactorily: the pure concepts of the understanding do not apply to some heterogeneous matter given in intuition, but only to differentials. This means that the task of the understanding consists not merely in providing the universal forms by means of which objects can be thought, but in actively producing objects from the differential relations of their elements. As Maimon says, the understanding 'not only has a capacity [*Vermögen*] to *think* universal relations between determined objects of intuition, but also to *determine* objects by means of relations'.[29] In other words, the understanding produces objects and their relations 'from the real relations of their differentials'.[30]

> As a result, the understanding does not subject something given *a posteriori* to its *a priori* rules; rather it lets it arise [*läßt entstehen*] in accordance with these rules (which I believe is the only way to answer the question *quid juris?* in a wholly satisfactory way).[31]

---

[27] In the *Critique of Pure Reason*, Kant makes use of the term 'flowing' when he characterises space and time as '*quanta continua*' or continuous magnitudes. However, what is designated by the expression 'flowing' is simply the continuous process of the productive synthesis of imagination, and thus it only says that time elapses, while this psychological process takes place (Kant, *Critique of Pure Reason*, A170/B211). By contrast, for Maimon, the flowing character is linked to the 'real' differential rules, which produce objects in accordance with the principle of continuity. In other words, the differential or intensive magnitude is itself a positive, productive magnitude, from which every extensive magnitude arises and in which it has its ground.

[28] Maimon, *Essay on Transcendental Philosophy*, p. 33.

[29] Ibid. p. 356.

[30] Ibid. pp. 355–6.

[31] Ibid. p. 82.

## THE IDEA OF AN INFINITE UNDERSTANDING

In the *Critique of Pure Reason*, Kant tackles the problem of analysing the human faculties of cognition, in particular the faculty of the understanding, which harbours the seeds to pure concepts, 'where they lie ready, until with the opportunity of experience they are finally developed and exhibited in their clarity by the very same understanding'.[32] Kant's epistemic theory relies on the idea of affection and being affected from the outside: something is given to the human mind within the pure forms of sensible intuition and then further processed according to the pure concepts of the understanding. Kant contents himself with the fact of the given and the harmonic accord of our faculties without asking how all this comes about. Thus, his transcendental philosophy remains within the bounds of epistemic immanence, which becomes clear in his response to Maimon's critical *Essay on Transcendental Philosophy*:

> But how such a sensible intuition (as time and space), a form of our sensibility is possible, or such functions of the understanding as those which logic develops out of it are possible, or how it happens that one form is in harmony with another in a possible cognition, [all] this is absolutely impossible for us to explain any further, because to do so we would need another kind of intuition than the one we have and another understanding so that we could compare our understanding to it and moreover, an understanding that could present things determined in themselves to each of us. But we can judge all understanding only by means of our understanding and likewise all intuition only by means of our intuition. And in any case it is not necessary to answer this question.[33]

For Maimon, the Kantian position is clearly insufficient. He wants to know how it is possible that two heterogeneous faculties such as sensibility and understanding agree with one another, and how it is that the given conforms to the rules of the understanding. He asks for the genesis of the given and tries to determine a sufficient reason or real ground from which the given arises. These questions imply that we have to leave epistemology behind and turn to metaphysical or ontological problems. To Maimon, it seems obvious that the faculty of thought is not bound to the touchstone of experience and naturally strives to reach a *'maximum*

---

[32] Kant, *Critique of Pure Reason*, A66/B91.

[33] See Kant's Letter to Herz, 26 May 1789, in Immanuel Kant, *Gesammelte Schriften*, vol. XI (Letters 1789–1794), ed. Königlich-Preussische Akademie der Wissenschaften (Berlin 1902), pp. 48–55 (Letter No. 362 [340]). An English translation of this letter can be found in Maimon, *Essay on Transcendental Philosophy*, Appendix II, p. 233.

in thinking'.[34] The mathematical science serves Maimon as an example of just how far thought protrudes into realms that can no longer be represented in intuition, such as the realm of the infinitely small. The fact that our knowledge always remains incomplete to some degree should not discourage us but rather act as an incentive to push forward in thought. Maimon maintains that

> reason commands us to *progress to* infinity, so that what is thought ever increases and on the other hand what is given becomes infinitely small. The question here is not how far we can go in this, but simply: what point of view we must consider the object from, in order to be able to judge correctly about it. But this [point of view] is nothing other than the idea of the most-complete-of-all [*allervollkommensten*] faculty of thought, to which we must approach ever closer to infinity.[35]

Contrary to Kant, Maimon indeed introduces a viewpoint beyond our finite human understanding, namely the idea of an infinite understanding, in which everything is thought and nothing given, that is, for which the object and the concept of the object are one and the same.[36] However, it is important to note that Maimon does not start with a metaphysical doctrine of an infinite understanding and then derives the world and its phenomena. Bergman argues that Maimon introduces the infinite understanding

> as a methodological notion to clarify the relation between representation and object and the objectivity within it. In this respect Maimon is a disciple of Leibniz who also employs the distinction between the finite and the infinite understanding as a methodological aid to understand the structure of consciousness.[37]

According to this reading, the infinite understanding is to be understood as a limit concept or idea, towards which we keep approaching but which we never reach, and not as a metaphysical, all-embracing reality.

In Samuel Atlas' view, Maimon's idea of an infinite understanding has a direct 'metaphysical' and 'constitutive' function,[38] and in this

---

[34] Maimon, *Essay on Transcendental Philosophy*, p. 2.

[35] Salomon Maimon, 'Herr Maimon's reply to the previous article', *Berlinisches Journal für Aufklärung*, IX/I (1790), pp. 52–80. The English translation can be found in Maimon, *Essay on Transcendental Philosophy*, Appendix III, p. 244.

[36] 'For an infinite understanding, the thing and its representation are one and the same' (Maimon, *Essay on Transcendental Philosophy*, p. 365). See also ibid. p. 210.

[37] Samuel Hugo Bergman, *The Philosophy of Solomon Maimon*, trans. from the Hebrew by Noah J. Jacobs (Jerusalem: The Magnes Press, The Hebrew University, 1967), p. 16.

[38] Atlas, *From Critical to Speculative Idealism*, pp. 74, 96.

way Maimon clearly deviates from Kant's definition of regulative ideas. Maimon himself describes his difference from Kant as follows:

> So I differ from *Kant* merely in this: instead of the three ideas that he assumes, I assume a single idea (of an infinite understanding), and I ascribe objective reality to this idea (not, it is true, viewed in itself – for this is contrary to the nature of an idea – but only in so far as it acquires objective reality for us in so many ways by means of objects of intuition).[39]

Atlas argues that Maimon provides a sort of 'transcendental deduction' for the idea of an infinite understanding, inasmuch as it is a necessary and indispensable concept for demonstrating how the given is generated and cognition of things is possible. If we hold our experiential knowledge to be true, then we have to grant objective validity (or according to Maimon, even objective reality) to the idea of an infinite understanding. This 'deduction' resembles Kant's transcendental argument for the objective validity of the categories in the *Prolegomena*. Thus, Atlas claims: 'The idea of an infinite mind approximates the status of an idea deduced by the transcendental method.'[40]

Whenever Maimon invokes the infinite understanding, he usually takes caution to call it an idea. When he refers to the finite human understanding, he calls it a *schema*: 'our understanding is the schema for the idea of an infinite understanding. In this case, the schema indicates the idea, and the idea indicates the thing itself or its existence, without which this idea and its schema would themselves be impossible.'[41] Maimon's statement does not really make it evident how he understands the relation between the finite and the infinite understanding. According to Atlas, the finite understanding serves as a schema, that is, an *image* for the infinite understanding, a metaphysical reality, of which we can only have an idea.[42] In the last part of the quote, Maimon does speak of the infinite understanding as a metaphysical reality, a 'thing itself' that really exists and provides a sufficient reason or real ground for both the idea and the schema. He certainly plays with the conception of an immanent ontology, that is, the thought that our understanding would be part of an infinite understanding, which acts as an immanent productive principle:

> We assume an infinite understanding (at least as idea), for which the forms are at the same time objects of thought, or that produces out of itself all possible kinds of connections and relations of things (the ideas). Our

---

[39] Maimon, *Essays on Transcendental Philosophy*, p. 366.
[40] Atlas, *From Critical to Speculative Idealism*, pp. 96–7.
[41] Maimon, *Essay on Transcendental Philosophy*, p. 365.
[42] Atlas, *From Critical to Speculative Idealism*, p. 104.

understanding is just the same, only in a limited way. This idea is sublime and will, I believe (if it is carried through), overcome the greatest difficulties of this kind.[43]

If we take Maimon's suggestion seriously and 'carry through' the idea of an infinite understanding, we will have to think of the knowing subject and the cognised object as both *within* an infinite and productive understanding. This is the philosophy of Spinoza, according to which minds and bodies are only *modes* of God. Maimon does not explicitly make use of Spinoza, but he undoubtedly felt much sympathy towards his system and defended it against the criticism of his friend and benefactor Moses Mendelssohn.[44] As Beth Lord suggests, Maimon did not openly refer to Spinoza in his writings out of respect for his amicable relations with Mendelssohn and for political reasons, given the rather hostile, anti-Spinozistic intellectual climate in those days.[45] Lord argues that, deep down, Maimon is a Spinozist, and his purpose in the *Essay on Transcendental Philosophy* is 'to show that transcendental idealism cannot work unless it posits the reality of a *Spinozistic* supersensible substrate underlying appearances'.[46] According to this reading, Maimon goes beyond Kant's doctrine of epistemic immanence and outlines a theory of ontological immanence, in which the infinite understanding reveals an immanent productivity.

Maimon's affinity with Spinoza is indeed indubitable and can be explained by means of their common background in Jewish religion and philosophy. Maimon had a great admiration for the medieval philosopher Moses Maimonides, whose name he adopted.[47] He wrote a commentary on Maimonides' *Guide of the Perplexed* and also devoted a part of his *Autobiography* for the exposition of Maimonides' philosophy.[48] Maimonides advanced the doctrine that the *intellectus,* the *ens*

---

[43] Maimon, *Essay on Transcendental Philosophy*, pp. 64–5.

[44] Salomon Maimon, *Salomon Maimons Lebensgeschichte: Von ihm selbst geschrieben,* ed. Octavia Winkler (Berlin: Union Verlag, 1988), chap. 21, p. 145: 'I read *Spinoza*; I very much liked the deep thought of this philosopher and his love of truth, and since I was led to his system already in Poland by Kabbalistic writings, I began to think about it once more, and I became so convinced of its truth that all efforts by Mendelssohn to dissuade me from it were fruitless.' (my translation)

[45] 'Through the influence of Mendelssohn, and perhaps to avoid embarrassing him, Maimon came to accept that it was impolitic to proclaim oneself a Spinozist. His published texts consequently play down his Spinozism, proclaiming instead a reliance on Leibniz' (Beth Lord, *Kant and Spinozism: Transcendental Idealism and Immanence from Jacobi to Deleuze* (New York: Palgrave Macmillan, 2011), p. 110).

[46] Ibid. p. 105.

[47] Maimon's birth name is Shlomo or Salomon ben Joshua.

[48] Cf. Maimon, *Salomon Maimons Lebensgeschichte*, chap. 22, pp. 151–2.

*intelligens* and the *ens intelligibile* are one and the same.[49] This doctrine is again inspired by Aristotle's view that for God, the cognised object is nothing but himself; in other words, the knowing subject and the object of cognition are identical. Following this Aristotelian and Maimonidean tradition, 'Maimon identifies the world with the *ens intelligibile*, God with the active *ens intelligens*, and the human soul with the potential *intellectus*.'[50] However, Maimon reconstructs Maimonides' doctrine in Kantian and Leibnizian terms:

> According to Leibniz, understanding and perception are not two separate things that are objectively different in a real sense but two things that differ only in a formal sense; every material conception can be dissolved into an intellectual conception since the former is only a confused [*verworren*] form of the latter; hence, the *intellectus, ens intelligens* and the *ens intelligibile* are one not only from the standpoint of intellectual form posited by cognition (as in Kant's system) but also from the standpoint of the relationship of the intellectual form to the object of the understanding or of the sensibility; and thus the difference between the infinite Understanding, praised be he, and our understanding, as I have explained, will only be formal, that is, the infinite Understanding, praised be he, produces with the help of the forms of the understanding the objects themselves which are the *intelligibilia*. This possibility becomes evident in arithmetic where numbers are both intellectual forms and their objects as well.[51]

In this quote Maimon expresses a monistic interpretation of Leibniz, claiming that the finite and the infinite understanding are of the same metaphysical essence and that the distinction between sensible and intellectual knowledge, being just a difference of degree, not a difference of kind, is due to the limitations of our human understanding. As Maimon himself admits, his transcendental philosophy embodies a 'coalition system' of Spinoza, Hume, Leibniz and Kant, and, as we have just seen, of medieval Aristotelian Jewish doctrines.[52] As a consequence

---

[49] Moses Maimonides, *The Guide for the Perplexed*, trans. from the original Arabic text by M. Friedlander, 2nd edn (New York: Dover Publications, 1956), part I, chap. 68.

[50] Bergman, *The Philosophy of Solomon Maimon*, p. 212.

[51] This is a quotation from Maimon's Hebrew commentary *Giva'at ha-Moreh*, p. 107; quoted and translated by Bergman 1967, pp. 36–7.

[52] For Maimon's description of his philosophy as a 'coalition system' of Spinozistic, Humean, Leibnizian and Kantian views, see *Salomon Maimons Lebensgeschichte*, chap. 26, p. 188. Abraham P. Socher, among others, argues for the crucial impact of Maimonides on Maimon's philosophy: 'I suggest that the leading member of Maimon's coalition system was, in fact, Maimonides' (Abraham P. Socher, *The Radical Enlightenment of Solomon Maimon: Judaism, Heresy, and Philosophy* (Stanford: Stanford University Press, 2006), p. 92, see also pp. 85–6).

of this mixture of heterogeneous sources it is sometimes difficult to assess Maimon's position. Perhaps Maimon did not even have a definite and settled view of the matter, and this may explain the rather diverging readings of Maimon in secondary literature emphasising either the Leibnizian or the Spinozist elements. Lord argues that

> Maimon aligns himself with Spinozism in the sense that he takes the infinite understanding to be the infinite idea of all reality, of which our own minds (and all our objects of intuition) are modes. Furthermore, he suggests that our idea of the infinite understanding cannot be the idea of a merely *possible being*; we necessarily think it as *actualizing* itself as our own minds and the objects of our sensible intuition. That is, we necessarily think of the infinite intellect as actual because our understanding is a mode of the infinite intellect, and our thinking is a limited instance of its thinking. The idea of the infinite intellect is *in us* because we are *in it*.

The thought that the human finite understanding is only a mode of the infinite understanding would deny an independent existence to the human intellect. This thought would be in contradiction with Leibniz's claim that there are substances that are created by God but exist outside him. It further contradicts Maimon's earlier claim that the human understanding is a *schema* of the infinite understanding, as this suggests rather an analogical relation in the sense that '[t]he finite reason is seen in the light of, or brought into relation with, the infinite reason, but not in the sense that the infinite mind is considered as operating through the finite mind'.[53] The conception of an infinite mind actualising itself through the human finite mind will be of paramount importance for the speculative, metaphysical systems of Fichte, Schelling and Hegel. Atlas, however, vehemently denies that such a thought can already be found in Maimon. He argues that 'the conception of the human mind as a *schema* is a whole world away from the metaphysical conception of the human mind as a medium of the absolute spirit'.[54] For Atlas, the importance of Maimon's thought lies in its contribution to a revival of critical idealism, that is, not of the whole body of Kantian doctrines, but of the critical method.[55]

Bergman underscores the Spinozistic elements in Maimon, in particular with respect to Maimon's solution to the question *quid juris?*. However, he also points to the fact that for Maimon, the identity of the infinite intellect, the world and the human finite understanding remains a goal or an idea to be approached, but which we can never reach. There

---

[53] Atlas, *From Critical to Speculative Idealism*, p. 100.
[54] Ibid.
[55] Ibid. p. 19.

remains room for '"the full force" of Humean scepticism'.[56] This seems to come closest to Maimon's position. Maimon himself says in his *Essay* that the triple identity of God, the world and the human soul 'is a *focus imaginarius* –! How far I am in agreement with Kant here [and with Spinoza and Leibniz, one may add], I leave to the judgement of Kant himself, as well as to the judgement of every thinking reader'.[57]

## DELEUZE'S PHILOSOPHY OF DIFFERENCE

In the Maimon scholarship, his philosophy is almost unanimously interpreted as paving the way for German Idealism, that is, a philosophy of identity. But recently, Maimon's transcendental philosophy has been rediscovered in contemporary European philosophy, due to Deleuze's reference to Maimon in several of his works, including his major text *Difference and Repetition*.[58]

It would perhaps be an exaggeration to say that Maimon was a precursor of a postmodern philosophy of difference – Maimon's philosophical thinking is deeply enrooted in medieval Jewish philosophy and the modern European philosophy of his time – but it is certainly right that there exist certain thematic and conceptual connections with a contemporary philosophy that emphasises the thought of difference and abandons the modern ideals of identity, subjectivity and representation. Deleuze's special interest in Maimon is tied to his concept of difference as intrinsic difference and as a genetic principle of the production of the real.

---

[56] Bergman, *The Philosophy of Solomon Maimon*, p. 218.

[57] Maimon, *Essay on Transcendental Philosophy*, p. 208. Kant himself acknowledged the 'excellence' of Maimon's *Essay*, but nevertheless judged it as 'for the most part directed *against me*'. He did not hesitate to regard Maimon as a Spinozist: 'Mr Maimon's way of presenting things [*Vorstellungsart*] is in fact one and the same as Spinoza's; and if this is conceded [*ex concessis*] it could serve very well to refute the Leibnizian.' Kant's letter to Herz, 26 May 1789, see Maimon, *Essay on Transcendental Philosophy*, Appendix II, pp. 231 and 236.

[58] See for instance, Gilles Deleuze, *Nietzsche and Philosophy*, trans. Hugh Tomlinson (London: Athlone Press, 1983 [1962]), p. 52 footnote; *Difference and Repetition*, trans. Paul Patton (New York: Columbia University Press, 1994 [1968]), pp. 170, 173–4, 192–3, 310, 324, 326; *The Fold: Leibniz and the Baroque*, trans. Tom Conley (Minneapolis: University of Minnesota Press, 1993 [1988]), p. 89; 'The Idea of Genesis in Kant's Aesthetic', in *Desert Islands and Other Texts (1953–74)*, ed. David Lapoujade, trans. Michael Taormina (New York: Semiotext(e), 2004), p. 61; seminar on Kant of 14 March 1978 (available at <www.webdeleuze.com>). The longest and most detailed exposition of Maimon's philosophy can be found in Deleuze's 1956–1957 lecture course 'Qu'est-ce que fonder?', given at the Lycée Louis le Grand (available in French at <www.webdeleuze.com>).

The concept of difference takes centre stage in Deleuze's book *Difference and Repetition*, as is clear from his title. 'Identity', the second term of the traditional conceptual couple, is conspicuously absent, substituted by the term 'repetition'. Contrary to Maimon, Deleuze does not refer to 'difference and identity' as relational concepts or forms of thought, but instead to 'difference and repetition' as material principles or processes.

In fact, Deleuze distinguishes two different forms of difference and repetition.[59] In the first case, difference and repetition are related to series of representations that can be brought under a common concept, but differ in time and space and the materials they are made of. This means that the differences between them are only external and do not affect the conceptual identity under which they are subsumed. Deleuze probably has in mind here Kant's discussion of difference in 'The Amphiboly of the Concepts of Reflection' and his argument of incongruent counterparts:

> However far you go in the concept, Kant says, you can always repeat – that is, make several objects correspond to it, or at least two: one for the left and one for the right, one for the more and one for the less, one for the positive and one for the negative.[60]

The difference implicated in these repetitions will always be external, that is, only an external difference between the ordinary instances of a concept. 'Repetition thus appears as a difference, but a difference absolutely without concept; in this sense, an indifferent difference.'[61] Deleuze refers to this type of repetition as 'bare, mechanical and stereotypical repetitions'[62] that appear to our consciousness of representation.

However, Deleuze claims that the essence of 'repetition cannot be explained by the form of identity in concepts of representation, [. . .] it demands a superior "positive" principle'.[63] He thus distinguishes from the first type a second type of repetition, which he calls 'secret, disguised and hidden repetitions'.[64] In this second sense, repetition essentially repeats difference, and through relating difference to difference it produces the real of experience. Difference and repetition are conceived as material and dynamic principles that operate in a sub-representational,

---

[59] Deleuze, *Difference and Repetition*, pp. 23–4.
[60] Ibid. p. 14.
[61] Ibid. p. 15.
[62] Ibid. p. xix.
[63] Ibid. p. 19.
[64] Ibid. p. xix.

transcendental realm. The representation of objects of experience is only a secondary or derived phenomenon, which cannot exhaust the diversity of perception. As Deleuze states in the Preface: 'All identities are only simulated, produced as an optical "effect" by the more profound game of difference and repetition.' As original and positive principles, difference and repetition constitute what Deleuze calls a 'transcendental' or 'superior empiricism'.[65] This empiricism is supposed to be superior because it no longer contents itself with the order of representation, that is, with what is evident to our consciousness of representation, but protrudes into a sub-representational and dynamic order of internal differences or Ideas. 'For in the dynamic order there is no representative concept, nor any figure represented in a pre-existing space. There is an Idea, and a pure dynamism which creates a corresponding space.'[66]

For Deleuze, an Idea is constituted by internal or intrinsic differences. Just like Kantian external differences, internal differences are differences without a concept. That is to say, they have to be distinguished from conceptual differences, i.e. those differences that refer to the identity of a concept, dividing it and at the same time preserving its identity. A perfect example of a conceptual difference is Aristotle's specific difference, which constitutes a new species and at the same time preserves the identity of the genus. For instance, given the genus 'animal', the specific differences 'terrestrial' and 'aquatic' divide the common genus animal by constituting two different species, terrestrial animals and aquatic animals. However, the specific differences differ only *within* the identity of the genus 'animal', that is, *within* the identity of the concept. Thus, Deleuze designates them as conceptual differences. Internal differences, on the contrary, are not internal to a concept, but 'internal to an Idea' and 'external to the concept which represents an object'.[67]

Deleuze derives the term of internal differences from Leibniz's mathematical concept of infinitely small differences or differentials.[68] He is intrigued by the fact that these 'evanescent differences' still pertain when the terms of the relation disappear, that is, when the given in intuition vanishes for our consciousness of representation. The relation between the infinitely small differences is nevertheless *real* and operates as a rule according to which finite quantities are generated.[69] Regarding Deleuze's

[65] Ibid. pp. 56, 144.
[66] Ibid. p. 20.
[67] Ibid. p. 26.
[68] Ibid.
[69] Cf. also Deleuze's remarks on differential calculus in his lecture on Leibniz, held in Vincennes on 22 April 1980 (available at <www.webdeleuze.com>).

interest for Leibniz's differential calculus, the parallel to Maimon cannot be missed, and Deleuze explicitly acknowledges Maimon's philosophical 'reinterpretation of the calculus'.[70] Deleuze also takes the differential dx as a symbol for the Idea, but contrary to Maimon, he conceives the Idea not as an idea of the understanding. The Idea, for Deleuze, is a very complex thing: 'a system of *differential relations* and the result of a distribution of remarkable or singular points (ideal events)'.[71] An Idea always connects at least two heterogeneous series of differences, which are put into reciprocal resonance with one another by a differenciator, i.e. the 'dark precursor'. What becomes evident in Deleuze's definition of Ideas is the influence of structuralism: Ideas are open systems or structures of differential relations.[72] They are not located within an infinite understanding, but in a 'virtual' realm, which Deleuze describes as an 'unextended or formless depth',[73] an 'intensive *spatium*'.[74] By means of spatio-temporal dynamisms in a particular field of individuation, Ideas become *actualised* or incarnated in empirical terms.[75]

Deleuze develops his 'dialectic of Ideas' in rather abstract terms, meaning them to serve as 'categories of every system in general'.[76] He suggests all different kinds of Ideas: sensible Ideas, physical or biological Ideas, psychological Ideas, socio-economic Ideas, philosophical Ideas and so on. Sensible Ideas, which Deleuze describes as systems of differences in the form of intensity and as 'the reason of the sensible',[77] come closest to the function that Maimon ascribes to his differentials or ideas of the understanding, namely as the sufficient reason or genetic principle for real experience. Moreover, just as Maimon defines differentials as 'limits of objects of experience'[78] and as elements 'that we never reach in intuition',[79] Deleuze locates sensible Ideas at the extreme limit of sensibility, which cannot be reached from the point of view of the empirical exercise of our faculties. As Deleuze says,

> [i]t is difference in intensity [. . .], which constitutes the being 'of' the sensible. [. . .] It is intensity or difference in intensity which constitutes

---

[70] Deleuze, *Difference and Repetition*, p. 170.
[71] Gilles Deleuze, 'The Method of Dramatization', in *Desert Islands*, p. 94.
[72] For Deleuze's engagement with structuralism, see his essay 'How do we Recognize Structuralism?', in *Desert Islands*, pp. 170–92.
[73] Deleuze, 'The Method of Dramatization', p. 98.
[74] Ibid. p. 97.
[75] Cf. Deleuze, *Difference and Repetition*, p. 245.
[76] Deleuze, 'The Method of Dramatization', p. 98.
[77] Deleuze, *Difference and Repetition*, p. 222.
[78] Maimon, *Essay on Transcendental Philosophy*, p. 186.
[79] Ibid. p. 351.

the peculiar limit of sensibility. As such, it has the paradoxical character of that limit: it is the imperceptible, that which cannot be sensed because it is always covered by a quality which alienates or contradicts it, always distributed within an extensity which inverts and cancels it.[80]

According to Deleuze, the differences in intensity, which give rise to both sensible qualities and extensive quantities, that is, which create diversity, tend to be covered up or eliminated in extensity and quality. This means that empirical enquiry will not discover pure differences or intensities but only 'an impure mixture'.[81] Therefore, like Maimon, Deleuze calls for a 'transcendental enquiry'[82] to retrace these differences in intensity or sensible Ideas under the surface of intuitable qualities and extensities. He further argues that time and space as well result from an intensive depth. With regard to Kant he remarks that 'while he [Kant] refuses a logical extension to space and time, Kant's mistake is to maintain a geometrical extension for it, and to reserve intensive quantity for the matter which fills a given extensity to some degree or other'.[83] Deleuze envisages a dynamic construction of space from internal differences or differentials. Whilst he could have been referring to Maimon, Deleuze mentions the Neo-Kantian Hermann Cohen, who pursued and developed the Maimonian project of a transcendental, genetic and differential philosophy.[84] Deleuze comes to the conclusion that internal differences or differentials have to be considered as a transcendental principle, that is, as genetic conditions for the production of real experience:

> Finally, while the conditions of possible experience may be related to extension, there are also subjacent conditions of real experience which are indistinguishable from intensity as such.[85]

However, despite the apparent parallels to Maimon and Cohen, Deleuze's model of a 'transcendental' or 'superior empiricism' differs considerably from their versions of philosophical idealism. Deleuze goes along with Maimon's and Cohen's definition of intensive magnitudes as the real (*ens reale*) and their refutation of Kant's psychologism, but he does not ground them in differential laws of the understanding. He conceives intensities or differentials as an extralogical, sensible principle, or as sensible Ideas located within a virtual realm that is immanent to the

---

[80] Deleuze, *Difference and Repetition*, pp. 236–7.
[81] Ibid. p. 223.
[82] Ibid. p. 240.
[83] Ibid. p. 231.
[84] Ibid. pp. 231–2.
[85] Ibid.

empirical world. Thus every object has to faces: a virtual or ideal half and an empirical half.[86] Each is immersed in an intensive, abyssal depth. '[T]he entire world may be read [. . .] in the moving depth of individuating differences or differences in intensity.'[87] There is an inner world of intensities, which cancels itself out in extension. Deleuze thus takes sides with Nietzsche, capitalising on his conception of the 'will to power' as an internal differential structure of forces. As Nietzsche notes in 1885:

> The victorious concept 'force', by means of which our physicists have created God and the world, still needs to be completed: an inner world must be ascribe to it, which I designate as 'will to power', i.e., as an insatiable desire to manifest power; or as the employment and exercise of power, as a creative drive, etc.[88]

Nietzsche was interested in scientific energy studies, in particular the work of Roger Joseph Boscovich (1711–87), a mathematician and physicist born in Ragusa, Dalmatia (present-day Dubrovnik in Croatia). Boscovich is the author of *Philosophiae naturalis theoria* (*Theory of Natural Philosophy*, 1785), in which he develops a dynamic interpretation of the world according to which phenomena are explained in terms of force, instead of mass. Nietzsche cites him as the one who won the greatest triumph over the senses by renouncing 'the belief in the last part of the earth that "stood fast" – the belief in "substance", in "matter", in the earth-residuum, and particle-atom'.[89] By following Boscovich, Nietzsche does not want to claim that our material world is a mere delusion or appearance. Instead, he intends to find the genetic principle of it all, a more rudimentary world of forces and affects, which allows organic forms and functions to develop and differentiate.

Deleuze himself refers to energy studies, that is, to the scientific

---

[86]  Ibid. p. 209.
[87]  Ibid. p. 247.
[88]  Friedrich Nietzsche, *The Will to Power*, trans. Walter Kaufmann and R. J. Hollingdale (New York: Vintage Books, 1968), sect. 619 (1885), pp. 332–3 (translation modified). The line 'an inner world must be ascribed to it' is based on Nietzsche's original handwritings. In the printed version, edited by Nietzsche's sister Elisabeth Förster-Nietzsche and Peter Gast, this line was rendered as 'an inner will must be ascribed to it'. Note that the Kaufmann/Hollingdale translation still reproduces this original 'error'. For more on the textual criticism of *The Will to Power*, see Wolfgang Müller-Lauter, '"Der Wille zur Macht" als Buch der "Krisis" philosophischer Nietzsche-Interpretation', in Behler et al. (eds), *Nietzsche Studien: Internationales Jahrbuch für die Nietzsche-Forschung*, vol. 24 (Berlin: Walter de Gruyter, 1995), pp. 223–60.
[89]  Friedrich Nietzsche, *Beyond Good and Evil*, in Walter Kaufmann (ed.), *Basic Writings of Nietzsche* (New York: The Modern Library, 1968 [1886]), Book I, sect. 12, p. 210.

research of Carnot and Curie,[90] but at the same time he says that he seeks to define 'energy in general':

> However, energy in general or intensive quantity is the *spatium*, the theatre of all metamorphosis or difference in itself which envelops all its degrees in the production of each. In this sense, energy or intensive quantity is a transcendental principle, not a scientific concept.[91]

Like Nietzsche, Deleuze extracts from the empirical concept of energy a transcendental or metaphysical principle of internal differences or intensities: 'The will to power is the flashing world of metamorphoses, of communicating intensities, difference of differences.'[92] This 'fluid world of Dionysus'[93] affects our sensibility in a way that undermines the common exercise of our faculties. Each faculty is confronted with its own limit: the imperceptible, the immemorial, the unthinkable.[94] While Maimon hopes to progress to the limits of experience by continuously pushing forward in infinite thought, Deleuze invokes a transcendent exercise not only of thought but of all the faculties. Moreover, this transcendent exercise is not understood as orthodox rational thought proceeding by method, but rather as a violent encounter with something 'paradoxical' which obtrudes itself upon our senses and *forces* us to think.[95] The highest object of sensibility, that is, 'the sublime',[96] which arouses our faculties to a dissociated activity and carries them to their utmost limit, is intensity or difference in itself.

As we have seen, Deleuze's model of transcendental empiricism and the concomitant theory of the transcendent exercise of the faculties contain elements of Leibniz, Maimon, Kant and Nietzsche. The conceptions of difference and intensive magnitude are at the heart of his philosophical thought, which dispenses with the logic of representation and the primacy of identity. In this regard, Deleuze's debt to Maimon's philosophy is indubitable. At the same time, Deleuze is important for the revival of Maimon. Due to his intervention, contemporary readers are guided back to the point, at which Maimon's thought bifurcates: while one movement leads to Fichte and absolute idealism, the other is taken up by Deleuze's transcendental philosophy of productive and

---

[90] Deleuze, *Difference and Repetition*, pp. 222–3.
[91] Ibid. pp. 240–1.
[92] Ibid. p. 243.
[93] Ibid. p. 258.
[94] Ibid. p. 227.
[95] Ibid. pp. 141, 227.
[96] Ibid. p. 146.

genetic difference. Maimon's ambivalent philosophy of difference can be regarded as the 'differenciator' that puts the divergent series of (transcendental and absolute) idealisms and contemporary European philosophy in resonance with one another.

Chapter 4

# Deleuze and Kant's *Critique of Judgment*

*Beth Lord*

## INTRODUCTION

Twentieth-century continental philosophers have typically read Kant's *Critique of Judgment* against the grain of the first *Critique*, finding within it Kant's thinking of the non-rational and the unrepresentable.[1] Those thinkers find in the third *Critique* evidence of Kant's own post-Kantianism and even postmodernism. His consideration of non-cognitive modes of thought in reflective judgement seems to point beyond the limits of transcendental idealism, while new possibilities for nature, art and politics seem to be hinted at throughout the text. This extension of the Kantian project has been as potent for recent philosophers as it was for the early Romantics.

Gilles Deleuze is an exception to this trend. For Deleuze, the *Critique of Judgment* contains several 'new discoveries', but is largely consistent with the *Critique of Pure Reason* as he interprets it. The key theme of Deleuze's many writings on Kant is that in thinking its own being, the Kantian 'I' generates its own difference from itself.[2] This self-generated,

[1] See, for example: Jean-Francois Lyotard, *Lessons on the Analytic of the Sublime: Kant's Critique of Judgment*, trans. Elizabeth Rottenberg (Stanford: Stanford University Press, 1994), pp. 23–9; Philippe Lacoue-Labarthe and Jean-Luc Nancy, *The Literary Absolute: The Theory of Literature in German Romanticism*, trans. Philip Barnard and Cheryl Lester (Albany: SUNY Press, 1988); and essays by Lyotard, Lacoue-Labarthe, Nancy and Elaine Escoubas in Jeffrey Librett (ed. and trans.), *Of the Sublime: Presence in Question* (Albany: SUNY Press, 1993).

[2] See especially Gilles Deleuze, *Difference and Repetition*, trans. Paul Patton (London: Athlone, 1994), pp. 58 and 85–6; and Gilles Deleuze, 'On Four Poetic Formulas that Might Summarise the Kantian Philosophy', published in 1984 as the Preface to Gilles Deleuze, *Kant's Critical Philosophy: the Doctrine of the Faculties*, trans. Hugh Tomlinson and Barbara Habberjam (Minneapolis: University of Minnesota Press, 1984). For further discussion of this topic see Beth Lord, 'Deleuze and Kant', in Daniel Smith and Henry Somers-Hall (eds), *The*

self-differentiating difference founds transcendental idealism but is also covered over by it, becoming nearly undetectable in Kant's system of conceptual judgements applied externally by a unified subject. In the *Critique of Pure Reason*, judgement is strictly determinative: it brings *a priori* concepts to the intuited manifold and thereby makes it determinate and objective. Deleuze criticises Kant's focus on judgement for making determination too 'external',[3] while indicating the points where Kant reveals a deeper, more internal, and non-conceptual kind of determination in the I. In the *Critique of Judgment* Kant introduces reflective judgement, which brings an intuited manifold to subjective feeling, leaving it conceptually indeterminate. In aesthetic judgement, the beautiful object diverts the cognitive faculties away from cognition and into free play, generating pleasure instead of knowledge. It is not reflective judgement itself that is interesting for Deleuze: an indeterminate form of judgement is still applied 'externally' to objects and does not accomplish the internal ontological determination that he demands. What is interesting about aesthetic judgement, for Deleuze, is its revelation of difference within the subject.

That Deleuze's reading of the *Critique of Judgment* is on the same plane as his reading of the *Critique of Pure Reason* is not immediately apparent. His interpretation of the third *Critique*, presented in *Kant's Critical Philosophy* and his essay 'The Idea of Genesis in Kant's Aesthetics', appears overly psychological and idealist. In his view, it seems the purpose of the *Critique of Judgment* is to unfold the inner drama of the faculties and the genetic story of their accord: the inner turmoil of the faculties generates their eventual harmony, such that the judgement of taste is the outcome of a process encased within the mind. Deleuze focuses almost exclusively on the Critique of Aesthetic Judgment, paying little attention to the second, teleological half of the text, which indicates that the purpose of the *Critique of Judgment* is to establish that nature is a suitable arena for free human action. Kant states that the significance of reflective judgement is that it 'makes possible the transition from the domain of the concept of nature to that of the concept of freedom'.[4] On this basis, thinkers including Hannah Arendt have unfolded the text's political dimension.

For Arendt, the key relation developed in the *Critique of Judgment* is

*Cambridge Companion to Deleuze* (Cambridge: Cambridge University Press, 2012), pp. 82–102.

[3] Deleuze, *Difference and Repetition*, p. 170.

[4] Immanuel Kant, *Critique of Judgment*, trans. Werner S. Pluhar (Indianapolis: Hackett, 1987), p. 196 (Akademie pagination).

that between the subject and the community, drawn out through Kant's discussion of the *sensus communis* and the universal communicability of judgements of taste. For Deleuze, Kant's text reveals a different kind of relation between the subject and the non-subjective. The non-subjective, and indeed any sense of political relation, is located within the Kantian subject itself. This results in a reading of the *Critique of Judgment* that looks fairly limited in that it is centred on the subject and its mental powers. Yet Deleuze's reading of the third *Critique* is consistent with his general strategy for reading Kant as a philosopher who internalises difference and the non-subjective. Indeed, these 1963 texts on the third *Critique* are precursors to the more advanced thinking about Kant featured in 1968's *Difference and Repetition*. In this chapter, I follow some aspects of Deleuze's interpretation of the *Critique of Judgment* to show both its limitations as a reading of Kant, and its anticipation of the motif of the self-differing subject that characterises Deleuze's later work on Kant.

1.

Deleuze's 'The Idea of Genesis in Kant's Aesthetics', published in 1963, starts from an interpretation of the Kantian cognitive faculties that Deleuze had developed in his book of the same year, *Kant's Critical Philosophy*. While Kant's differentiation of the faculties of sensibility, understanding, and reason is much criticised for reflecting an outmoded 'faculty psychology', Deleuze sees this differentiation as the basis of productive relations internal to the subject. These relations generate outcomes including cognition and free action depending on which faculty legislates, and in which of our rational interests. The different faculties enter harmonious accords under legislation, but what makes these accords possible is the faculties' *a priori* capacity for a free, unlegislated, and indeterminate accord. The latter, Deleuze argues, is itself grounded in a more fundamental discord that reflects the faculties' difference in kind. The faculties' free and unlegislated accord is the subject matter of the *Critique of Judgment*; their original discord is revealed in the Analytic of the Sublime. Thus Deleuze takes the *Critique of Judgment* to have a special status in Kant's philosophy, establishing what grounds and generates the harmonic relations of the faculties – and all that follows from them – in the first two *Critiques*.[5]

---

[5] See Deleuze, *Kant's Critical Philosophy*; and Gilles Deleuze, 'The Idea of Genesis in Kant's Aesthetics', trans. Daniel W. Smith, *Angelaki* 5:3, (2000), pp. 57–70; and Daniel W. Smith's introduction to the latter on pp. 57–8.

Deleuze discusses the faculties in terms that are alternately political and organic, drawing out two different senses in which faculties are *powers*. Kant's term *Vermögen*, generally translated as 'faculty' due to Kant's occasional addition of the Latin *facultas*, means ability, capacity, or power. Sensibility and understanding are sometimes referred to as capacities of intuition and cognition in the first *Critique*, and Kant sometimes uses *Vermögen* interchangeably with *Kraft*, a term indicating natural force, strength, or efficacy. Seen in this context, the faculties appear less as discrete divisions of the mind and more as conative powers through which the mind strives to enact and perfect its determined functions. The purpose of the mind is, on Deleuze's interpretation, to determine the nature of its own rational interests, to subject its interests to critique, and to realise those that pass the test: the mind strives to realise its legitimate interests through the harmonic relations of its powers, resulting in cognition of the world and consciousness of the mind's own freedom. Understood in this way, knowledge and moral action are by-products of reason's broader project to perfect itself through its own power. Unlike early modern thinkers of *conatus*, however, the 'power' of Kantian reason is differentiated, relational, and capable of metacritique.[6]

Deleuze distinguishes two senses of 'faculty' (or 'power') in Kant's texts. First, a faculty is a type of relation between the subject, a representation, and its object. The faculty of knowledge is a relation of agreement between the subject's representation and an object; the faculty of desire is a causal relation through which the subject's representation causes an object to come about; and the faculty of pleasure and pain is a relation in which a representation of an object strengthens or weakens the subject's vital force. These 'higher' faculties are powers in the sense that they govern appearances in accordance with reason's speculative or practical interest. In the second sense, faculties are sources of representations, as in the faculties of sensibility, understanding, and reason. These lower-order faculties are powers in the sense that they *produce* their objects, that is, the various kinds of representations in the mind (intuitions, concepts, ideas), in order to realise rational interests. The distinction is between governing powers that determine the purposes of rationality, and productive powers that realise those purposes through their working.[7]

The two kinds of power are construed politically, on Deleuze's

[6] Deleuze, *Kant's Critical Philosophy*, pp. 2–3.
[7] Ibid. pp. 3–9.

reading: in striving both to determine and to realise its own interests, reason internalises a political division between the power to legislate and the power to produce. Kant presents an externalised version of just this division in his essay 'The Conflict of the Faculties'. This essay concerns the discrepancies between philosophy and theology faculties in the university. Kant does not intend an association between academic faculties (*Fakultäten*) and mental faculties (*Vermögen*), but Deleuze's claim that Kant's critical philosophy is a 'Doctrine of the Faculties' suggests an analogy. 'The Conflict of the Faculties' shows how university politics determines freedom of thought: Kant evokes earlier struggles to free philosophy from theology and to establish the freedom to think and speak without interference from religious authority. The power structures between the faculties of the university unquestionably determine what the faculties of the mind have the power to do. Kant distinguishes the 'higher' faculties of theology, law, and medicine from the 'lower' faculty of philosophy, which encompasses all the arts and sciences. The 'higher' faculties are sanctioned by government because they concern the well-being of the populace which needs to be carefully managed. By contrast, the 'lower' faculty of philosophy is free of such control, because it concerns learning and truth based on rational thought. The higher faculties legislate for the use of knowledge in the interests of a still higher power, whereas the lower faculty of philosophy produces new knowledge and evaluates it according to its own judgement.[8]

By analogy, the 'higher' faculties of the university correspond to the 'higher' (governmental) faculties of the mind: theology is aligned with the faculty of knowledge and the *Critique of Pure Reason*; law with the faculty of desire and the *Critique of Practical Reason*; and medicine with the faculty of the feeling of pleasure and pain and the *Critique of Judgment*. The 'lower' faculty of philosophy, the 'departments' of which produce knowledge in natural science, history, and so on, corresponds to the 'lower' (productive) faculties of the mind that produce their objects of knowledge: sensibility produces intuitions, understanding produces concepts, and reason produces ideas. The lower faculties must interact and harmonise to produce anything. Unlike the philosophical faculties of the university, which are free from control, the mental faculties of the first two *Critiques* are harmonised by a dominant lower faculty, in line with a presiding higher faculty and the interest it pursues. Understanding in the *Critique of Pure Reason* produces objects and

8 Immanuel Kant, *The Conflict of the Faculties*, trans. Mary J. Gregor (New York: Abaris, 1979).

reports to the higher faculty of knowledge in reason's speculative interest; practical reason in the *Critique of Practical Reason* produces moral legislation and reports to the higher faculty of desire in reason's practical interest. In the *Critique of Judgment*, however, the lower faculties operate without a dominant lower faculty, and are free of higher facultative governance and rational interest. The interaction of imagination and understanding that results in our 'liking' is 'free' of cognitive and moral determination and 'devoid of all interest'.[9] Only in the *Critique of Judgment*, then, do we see something analogous to the faculty of philosophy that thinks freely and legislates for itself.

In the *Critique of Judgment* there can be a conflict of faculties because none of the lower faculties is dominant. The faculties, here, produce feelings of pleasure and pain based on their relations as prompted by an object. If the object purposively prompts the faculties to harmonise they produce pleasure; if the object prompts them to conflict, they produce pain. When the faculties of imagination and understanding harmonise as if they were going to produce knowledge, but, being free of cognitive and conceptual determination, they do not produce knowledge, they enter what Kant calls a state of 'free play'. In free play, imagination and understanding harmonise as if they were going to combine the manifold and unify it in a concept, without either of them taking the lead to cause that to happen.[10] Instead of conceptual determination, this harmonic free play leads to a feeling of pleasure in the object. In the first and second *Critiques*, the lower faculties are free to pursue truth but one of them dominates the others, to direct truth in a certain direction (i.e. scientific knowledge or moral action). In the third *Critique*, these faculties are free to pursue truth without such direction: what interests us is not the truth but the free process by which the faculties pursue it. What results instead is the judgement of taste: to feel the harmonisation of the faculties in their free play is not only to feel pleasure, but also 'to prove that I have taste'.[11]

Deleuze sees the origins of Romanticism in the free, unregulated relationships of the Kantian faculties as 'elective affinities' that combine, separate, and harmonise without conceptual jurisdiction. Kant's Romanticism consists in 'an aesthetic of the Beautiful and of the Sublime, in which the sensible is valid in itself and unfolds in a *pathos* beyond all

---

[9] Kant, *Critique of Judgment*, pp. 203–4; Deleuze, *Kant's Critical Philosophy*, p. 47.
[10] Kant, *Critique of Judgment*, p. 217.
[11] Ibid. p. 205.

logic'.[12] Yet Deleuze's interpretation also suggests the political romanticism of an unregulated community which has no leader or laws, and which gestures towards harmony even as it encounters conflict. For Kant, the ideal might be a free philosophy faculty that microcosmically works towards the kingdom of ends. Deleuze, again revealing his early modern sensibilities, draws on the language of the state of nature ending in the social compact ('accord', 'concord', and 'discord'). Just as the ungoverned state of nature generates a 'free accord' as a necessary precursor to determinate forms of government, the ungoverned play of the faculties in the third *Critique* must generate a 'free and indeterminate accord' as a necessary precursor to the determinate relations of dominance between the faculties in the first two *Critiques*. How could the faculties enter into relations of governance in those texts unless they had first passed through the state of nature and entered *freely* into the social compact? Or, as Deleuze puts it:

> How can a faculty, legislative in a given interest, induce the other faculties to indispensable complementary tasks, if all the faculties together were not first of all capable of a free spontaneous accord, without legislation, with neither interest nor predominance?[13]

Deleuze's interpretation makes the *Critique of Judgment* a story of political harmony achieved through free elective affinity: combination and conflict that are purposive without purpose.

This is a major theme of Kant's essays on politics and history. In Kant's own variant of the narrative of the state of nature, human beings start from a Rousseauist pastoral situation and are compelled to move forward through seemingly random formations and dissolutions of communities towards the political harmony of the whole human species. The human species, taken in the large and over all of history, has no governing body, yet it moves inexorably towards political harmony. Just as the faculties produce a purposive harmony through undirected free play, human individuals progress purposively through their apparently contingent free activity. In Kant's 'Idea for a universal history with a cosmopolitan aim', he uses the language of free play that he will later use in the *Critique of Judgment*:

> History . . . allows us to hope . . . that if it considers the play of the freedom of the human will *in the large,* it can discover within it a regular course; and that in this way what meets the eye in individual subjects as confused and

---

[12] Deleuze, *Kant's Critical Philosophy*, p. xii.
[13] Deleuze, 'Idea of Genesis', p. 60.

irregular yet in the whole species can be recognised as a steadily progressing though slow development of its original predispositions.[14]

When individual people play freely, without direction or determination, they are nevertheless bound to harmonise and to fulfil humanity's rational predispositions. This harmony is achieved through antagonism or 'unsocial sociability': our 'propensity to enter into society, which is combined with a thoroughgoing resistance that constantly threatens to break up this society'.[15] Humans are pulled between sociability and isolation because of our free will, which leads us to want to be with other free wills, but also to resist them. This resistance drives us to act and to 'obtain a rank among [our] fellows, who [we] cannot *stand*, but also cannot *leave alone*'.[16] This, Kant suggests, is how humanity got out of the state of nature:

> Thus happen the first true steps from crudity toward culture, which really consists in the social worth of the human being; thus all talents come bit by bit to be developed, taste is formed, and even, through progress in enlightenment, a beginning is made toward the foundation of a mode of thought which can with time transform the rude natural predisposition to make moral distinctions into determinate practical principles and hence transform a *pathologically* compelled agreement to form a society finally into a *moral* whole.[17]

Socio-political harmony is based on prior antagonism and discord, without which human beings would have lived an eternally 'pastoral life of perfect concord' with no moral worth or rational development. 'The human being wills concord; but nature knows better what is good for his species: it wills discord.'[18] Through this dialectic of sociality and antagonism we enter into free accords – 'pathologically compelled agreements' – which, through unsocial sociability, can develop into more sophisticated forms of government. There can be no sovereignty, governance, culture, or taste without discord. As Hannah Arendt puts it, 'discord, indeed, is so important a factor in nature's design that without it no progress can be imagined'.[19]

---

[14] Immanuel Kant, 'Idea for a universal history with a cosmopolitan aim', trans. Allen W. Wood, in *Anthropology, History, and Education*, ed. Günter Zöller and Robert B. Louden (Cambridge: Cambridge University Press, 2007), p. 8:17 (Akademie pagination).

[15] Ibid. p. 8:20.

[16] Ibid. p. 8:21.

[17] Ibid.

[18] Ibid.

[19] Hannah Arendt, *Lectures on Kant's Political Philosophy*, ed. Ronald Beiner (Brighton: Harvester Press, 1982), p. 52.

In the passage above, it is no coincidence that judgements of taste become possible only after the free harmonisation of human individuals has occurred. For the harmony of the faculties in the judgement of taste is thoroughly bound up with the drive towards both the political harmony of free thinkers, and a 'universal' harmony between humanity and nature. Even in their free play, when they are not governed by the interests of reason, the faculties nevertheless fulfil reason's interests: judgements of the beautiful are not determined by any interest, but beautiful objects turn out to be 'interesting' to reason. They are interesting because they indicate that nature is suitable for human knowledge and freedom, thereby supporting reason's project to fulfil its purposes in nature.[20] The faculties in the *Critique of Judgment* appear free and undetermined not because legislation is absent (as Deleuze suggests), but because legislation comes from a sovereign force that is too big to be seen: the pull of the universe itself, as it were. The free accord of the faculties, like the free accord of human beings, emerges from discord because nature wants reason to perfect itself in fulfilling its purposes.

2.

No one has better analysed the political dimension of the *Critique of Judgment* than Hannah Arendt who, in her 1970 *Lectures on Kant's Political Philosophy*, argues that Kant's text poses two questions of humankind's purpose. First, in line with 'Idea for a universal history with a cosmopolitan aim', what is the purpose and direction of the human species taken in the large? Second, in line with Kant's texts on anthropology, what is the purpose and direction of human beings, as 'actual inhabitants of the earth'? The first question concerns how humanity relates to nature, and is addressed by the Critique of Teleological Judgment; the second question concerns how human beings relate to each other, and is addressed by the Critique of Aesthetic Judgment. (A third question, *what is man as rational being*, or how a human being relates to itself, is addressed by the first two *Critiques*.)[21] Arendt's contention is that Kant thinks the 'end' of human beings is sociability, which enables the human species to progress towards its 'end' of cosmopolitan harmony. If there is a mental activity that shows that sociability is our end, and that shows *only* this, it is the judgement of taste: a judgement that is detached from knowledge and morality,

[20] Kant, *Critique of Judgment*, p. 300.
[21] Arendt, *Lectures*, pp. 26–7.

whose purpose is to generate a mental state that can be communicated socially. On Arendt's account, the free accord of the faculties in the judgement of taste is directly linked to the free accord of human beings in sociability. The purpose of the 'discordant accord' of the faculties is to further our 'unsocial sociability'.

This parallel is strengthened by Kant's doctrine of the *sensus communis* or 'common sense', a term which seems intentionally ambiguous. It refers to the feeling of the faculties working together, but it also refers to the communicability of that feeling in society. Kant introduces the *sensus communis* as an effect of the faculties' free play:

> [By] common sense . . . we do not mean an outer sense, but mean the effect arising from the free play of our cognitive powers – only under the presupposition of such a common sense, I maintain, can judgments of taste be made.[22]

Kant adds that this common sense, shared by all judging human beings, is a necessary condition of communicability, and suggests that taste is itself just such a shared sense.[23] Common sense is both the effect of a commonality in the mind, and the condition of possibility of commonality with others. It is both a sense *of* inner commonality and a sense *for* outer commonality, such that it bridges the private and the social. If taste *is* this common sense, then taste once again joins the free play of the faculties with the free play of sociability. Taste is our socially-harmonising ability to judge the communicability of our feelings of facultative harmony. Accordingly, Arendt indicates that *sensus communis* is the 'community sense', and that our possession of a faculty of judgement presupposes that we exist in a community. 'One judges always as a member of a community, guided by one's community sense, one's *sensus communis*. But in the last analysis, one is a member of a world community by the sheer fact of being human; this is one's "cosmopolitan existence".'[24]

For Deleuze, aesthetic common sense is parallel to the free, indeterminate relation of the faculties. Just as the indeterminate relation of the faculties in the judgement of taste grounds the determinate relations of those faculties in judgements of cognition and morality, aesthetic common sense grounds the empirical and moral common senses of the first two *Critiques*. And Deleuze demands genetic explanations for both the free accord of the faculties and for the *sensus communis aestheti-*

---

[22] Kant, *Critique of Judgment*, p. 238.
[23] Ibid. pp. 238–9, 293, 295.
[24] Arendt, *Lectures*, p. 75.

*cus.* Kant simply says that common sense must be *presupposed* because without it, there could be neither taste nor communication.[25] Indeed, it seems that common sense is bestowed by nature, not unlike our capacity to be affected by the given in sensibility. But Deleuze insists that we cannot escape the question of where this common sense comes from; or, put otherwise, why humans have this drive to commonality. Arendt shows that this question is answered by the Critique of Teleological Judgment: our faculties are driven towards commonality because human beings are driven towards community and the human species is driven towards communion with the cosmos. Even without Arendt's analysis, however, it is evident that Kant can only answer the question, *where does common sense come from?* (just like the question, *where does our intuitive capacity come from?*) through a teleological account of humanity's purpose.

Rather than finding the reason for these features of aesthetic experience in teleology, Deleuze wants to explain the origin of facultative harmony and common sense genetically, in the mind:

> How can we explain that our faculties, differing in nature, enter spontaneously into a harmonious relationship? We cannot be content to presume such an accord. We must engender it in the soul. This is the only issue: to establish the genesis of aesthetic common sense, to show how the free accord of the faculties is necessarily engendered.[26]

Deleuze draws explicitly on Kant's idealist critic Solomon Maimon here. Like Maimon, Deleuze is dissatisfied whenever Kant invokes necessary presuppositions, requiring that the thing in question be accounted for in terms of genesis. Also like Maimon, and in contrast to Kant's readers on the side of *Naturphilosophie*, Deleuze locates genesis in the mind and makes its products ideal. Maimon insisted that certain problems in Kant's philosophy could be solved only by making transcendental idealism at once more empirical and more ideal, and accounting for the genesis of the matter of sensation through a limited, human version of the intuitive intellect.[27] On this interpretation, taste, facultative harmony, common sense, and our sense of human community are not caused in us by a nature that wants rational ends to be realised. Instead, they must be products of a quasi-intuitive intellect that generates its objects from ideas. The political dimension of Kant's thought about free

---

[25] Kant, *Critique of Judgment*, p. 239.
[26] Deleuze, 'Idea of Genesis', p. 62.
[27] See Salomon Maimon, *Essay on Transcendental Philosophy*, trans. Nick Midgley et al. (London: Continuum, 2010). For brief discussion, see Lord, 'Deleuze and Kant'.

play, accord, and discord is, for Deleuze, wholly internal to the mind and its inner conflicts.

This is exemplified in Deleuze's treatment of the Analytic of the Sublime. Whereas the judgement of the beautiful involves a relation of imagination and understanding, the judgement of the sublime involves a relation of imagination and reason. The faculties are not so much in play as in 'seriousness', and our liking for the sublime is an indirect or negative pleasure, a pleasure that arises from the conflict of imagination and reason.[28] Reason demands the comprehension of something infinitely large in one whole; imagination is inadequate to this task, but in attempting it, proves its vocation to harmonise with rational laws in general. The imagination inflicts a violence on inner sense which, while painful, is 'purposive *for the whole vocation* of the mind'.[29] Thus the feeling of the sublime is a displeasure that results in pleasure; a discord of the faculties that reveals their suitability for accord. Deleuze goes further, stating that

> [t]he accord of the imagination and reason is effectively engendered in this discord. Pleasure is engendered within pain. Furthermore, everything happens as if the two faculties were fecundating each other reciprocally and found the principle of their genesis, one in the proximity of its limit, the other beyond the sensible, and both in a 'point of concentration' which defines the most profound point of the soul as the suprasensible unity of all the faculties.[30]

Deleuze sees the feeling of the sublime as a 'discordant accord' that is generated from a 'point of concentration' that is 'the most profound point of the soul'. These phrases invoke Maimon, who had argued that objects are generated from 'differentials', concentrated relations of differences that the mind thinks. The 'discordant accord' also recalls the state of nature, but the sublime is a state of nature that is all in the mind. The sublime is an inner drama, an 'emotion' in which a person feels his rational being and its moral superiority to his merely *natural, human* being.[31] For Deleuze, it is the model by which we are to understand how the free accord of the judgement of the beautiful is generated.

Deleuze posits that the free accord of understanding and imagination is engendered through reason's 'intellectual interest in the beautiful'.

---

[28] Kant, *Critique of Judgment*, pp. 245–6, 258. Deleuze's analysis focuses on the mathematical sublime.

[29] Ibid. p. 259.

[30] Deleuze, 'Idea of Genesis', p. 63.

[31] Kant, *Critique of Judgment*, p. 264.

As we have seen, reason is interested in the external harmony of nature with our capacity to judge, as revealed by the beautiful object. Reason's interest in the beautiful is connected to the matter of the object: its colours and sounds, which can be connected to reason's ideas through symbolisation. Reason's activity here is free of cognitive constraints: intuitions of colours are freely associated with concepts of moral qualities (white with innocence, orange with courage).[32] Deleuze suggests that in its own free activity, determined by its interest, reason causes the understanding's concepts to expand and frees the imagination of cognitive constraints. It is reason, therefore, that is responsible for the genesis of the free accord of understanding and imagination:

> The analytic of the beautiful as exposition only allows us to say: in the aesthetic judgment, the imagination becomes free at the same time that the understanding becomes undetermined. But how did it free itself? How did the understanding become indeterminate? It was through reason, which thereby secures the genesis of the free indeterminate accord of the two faculties in the judgment.[33]

Reason's interest in the harmony between humanity and nature – the harmony that validates the purposes of history and politics – turns out to generate the inner harmony of the faculties. But this is not because facultative harmony has a social purpose, as it does for Arendt. For Deleuze, facultative harmony is in reason's gift; and reason can accomplish this 'transcendental genesis' because it has passed through 'the genetic model of the sublime'.[34] Reason passes through its own internal state of nature – the sublime – frees itself, and then frees the other faculties to join indeterminate accords. The purpose of reason's genesis of these free accords is to constitute 'the soul, that is, the suprasensible unity of all our faculties, the "point of concentration", the vivifying principle from which each faculty is "animated", engendered in its free exercise, and in its free accord with the others'.[35]

The *Critique of Judgment*, on this reading, is entirely inward looking, concerned with the mind and its powers. For Deleuze, the *Critique of Judgment* grounds the other two *Critiques*, and the free accord of the faculties grounds the more determinate relations the faculties have in those texts. The political and cosmopolitan purpose of the free accord of the faculties – to push human beings towards sociality and the human

---

[32] Ibid. p. 302.
[33] Deleuze, 'Idea of Genesis', p. 65.
[34] Ibid. p. 66.
[35] Ibid. p. 68.

species into harmony with nature – is lost to a psychological and romantic purpose, to supply an explanatory ground for the structure of the
mind. Kant tells us that the structure of the mind is incapable of explanation and therefore can *only* be presupposed, whereas Deleuze insists
that it must be genetically explained. In his interpretation of the *Critique
of Judgment*, the result is the reduction of aesthetic judgement and its
purposes to a faculty of reason that seeks transcendental genesis – much
like Maimon's intuitive intellect. Looked at in this way, Deleuze appears
to be the crudest kind of respondent to Kant's critical system, demanding grounding explanations where there can be none, and inventing
them where Kant does not supply them. It is not surprising that Deleuze,
like Kant's idealist critics, fails to notice that the vitalist soul and the
concept of genesis are heavily criticised in the second half of the *Critique
of Judgment*.

3.

Deleuze's interpretation can, however, be seen in a better light if it
is taken as part of his general strategy for reading Kant. Deleuze's
project is to show that 'what can only be presupposed' is not itself a
presupposition, but something that *gives itself* to presupposition, and
therefore something that the relevant faculty can, and must, transcendentally investigate. Retrospectively, it is clear why Deleuze demands a
genetic explanation for aesthetic common sense, for the question 'Why
should we assume a common sense at all?' is prominent in *Difference
and Repetition*. Common sense, he argues there, is part of the 'image
of thought': the image thought gives itself of what it means to think.
Philosophers concern themselves with the appearance of thinking – a set
of clichés about what thinking is, including recognition, representation,
and common sense – none of which amounts to thinking. Kant, though
frequently guilty of this himself, is also a philosopher who thematises
the image of thought: he shows in the transcendental deduction of the
B-edition of the *Critique of Pure Reason* that thinking *cannot think
itself*, that it can *only* access itself as appearance.[36] Kant understands
that there is a problem with thinking about thinking, but he nevertheless
falls back on models of representation and common sense. For Deleuze,
if we are to understand what thinking is, it cannot be through *thinking*
about it, which only leads us to more images of thought.

[36] Immanuel Kant, *Critique of Pure Reason*, trans. Norman Kemp Smith (London:
Macmillan, 1929), p. B157–9 (Akademie pagination).

For Deleuze, philosophy is not thinking about thinking; it is being *forced* to think, violently, against our will. The force comes from a contingent encounter through the senses, an encounter with 'something that can only be sensed' – an imperceptible intensity accessible only to sense and not to the other faculties. It is not something that can be represented, recalled, or shared in a 'common sense'.[37] This encounter does not move sensibility and thought into a 'joint labour', but instead 'perplexes' the soul and forces it to pose a problem, the real stuff of thinking. Here, thought is forced to grasp that which can only be thought, but which also cannot be accessed *through* thought and which is therefore, in a way, unthinkable. Deleuze develops a 'doctrine of the faculties' in *Difference and Repetition* based on discord and divergence:

> Rather than all the faculties converging and contributing to a common project of recognizing the object, we see divergent projects in which, with regard to what concerns it essentially, each faculty is in the presence of that which is its 'own'. Discord of the faculties, chain of force and fuse along which each confronts its limit, receiving from (or communicating to) the other only a violence which brings it face to face with its own element, as though with its disappearance or its perfection.[38]

The discord of the faculties, the communication of violence between them, and the confrontation of the limits of the imagination – threatening either its disappearance or its perfection – are all features of Kant's sublime and of Deleuze's explication of it. Deleuze replaces the faculties' free play with a mutual violence which unhinges common sense and leads each faculty to pursue what is proper to it alone.

There is nevertheless a commonality of the faculties which allows for a kind of communication and even a harmony. It is the harmony of elements that explode in sequence because they are drawn together by a lit fuse; a 'discordant harmony' that is not resolved in a common sense:

> We saw how the discord between the faculties, which followed from the exclusive character of the transcendent object apprehended by each, nevertheless implied a harmony such that each transmits its violence to the other by powder fuse, but precisely a 'discordant harmony' which excludes the forms of identity, convergence and collaboration which define a common sense. This harmonious Discord seemed to us to correspond to that Difference which by itself articulates or draws together. There is thus a point at which thinking, speaking, imagining, feeling, etc. are one and the same thing, but that thing affirms only the divergence of the faculties

---

[37] Deleuze, *Difference and Repetition*, pp. 139–40.
[38] Ibid. p. 141.

in their transcendent exercise. It is a question, therefore, not of a common sense but, on the contrary, of a para-sense.[39]

Para-sense indicates a commonality through divergence, a difference that draws together. The conflict of the faculties, here, is not to be reconciled, because it is the very structure of the mind. The mind is indeed sublime, for Deleuze, because it is a harmonious discord, but the harmony is not the kind that Kant recognised. It does not unify differences, but allows differences to be constitutive of it. The sublimity of the mind is open-ended, and is not resolved in self-reflexive admiration of the subject's moral vocation. Instead, the *genesis* of commonality from difference is highlighted and is allowed to persist. This is why Deleuze is so interested in those moments – the sublime, the B-edition transcendental deduction – where Kant approaches this kind of genesis.

As we have seen, Deleuze thinks that Kant's Critique of Aesthetic Judgment shows how the genesis of commonality is directed by reason, by way of its discordant accord with imagination in the sublime. We have also seen that Deleuze emphasises what happens after reason's experience of its own sublimity: reason finds itself interested in the beautiful and frees itself to associate concepts and intuitions playfully or symbolically. This is described in the Deduction of Pure Aesthetic Judgments, the section of the *Critique* where Kant justifies the fact that judgements of taste, while apparently personal, are made with universal validity. Kant's deductions make genesis thematic; the transcendental deduction of the *Critique of Pure Reason* concerns the genesis of the 'object' and the objective reality of concepts. The deduction of the *Critique of Judgment* concerns the genesis of a common sense: it asserts 'that we are justified in presupposing universally in all people the same subjective conditions of the power of judgement that we find in our-selves'.[40] In the *Critique of Pure Reason* deduction, what seemed to be *subjective* – that is, our own representations – turned out to be *objective*, due to our generating their objectivity in judging them determinatively. In the *Critique of Judgment* deduction, what seems to be personal – that is, our own feeling of pleasure – turns out to be universal, due to our generating its universality in making reflective judgements of taste. Where Kant focuses on the genesis of the objective, the common, and universal, Deleuze delves into the discord and difference that make these geneses possible. For Deleuze, the discord of the sublime and the genesis that ensues can only be internal to reason.

---

[39] Ibid. pp. 193–4.
[40] Kant, *Critique of Judgment*, p. 290.

What Deleuze finds most interesting in the deduction of the first *Critique* is the 'fractured I': the self breaks apart and differs from itself when it has to appear to itself in order to think itself.[41] All the commonalities of objectivity, selfhood, and conceptual thought delineated in the *Critique of Pure Reason* rest on that original difference, on Deleuze's account. In the deduction of the *Critique of Judgment*, Deleuze is similarly interested in an original difference that grounds commonality. The subject, in order to think its own purpose, must have an experience that causes a feeling of sublimity and an explosion of difference in the faculties. His language here anticipates the language of *Difference and Repetition*:

> [The] harmony of the sublime is highly paradoxical. Reason and the imagination accord with each other only within a tension, a contradiction, a painful laceration. There is an accord, but a discordant accord, a harmony in pain. And it is only this pain that makes the pleasure possible. Kant insists on this point: the imagination submits to a violence, it even seems to lose its freedom.[42]

In fact, Kant states that the sublime is 'a subjective movement of the imagination by which it does violence to the inner sense'; in other words, the imagination does not submit to but *enacts* violence.[43] In its attempt to obey reason's demand, the imagination forces inner sense into a paradox of time, requiring it to comprehend an infinite amount of apprehended material in one instant. It is not the difference between reason and imagination that matters here, but the difference of imagination from itself, as it demands of itself a temporal synthesis that it cannot accomplish. In the sublime, imagination is forced, by its own nature, to the point of its limit. Here we have the conflict of the faculties, in the differing of one faculty from itself which makes possible the commonality and universality that the deduction establishes.

For Deleuze, Kantian deductions concern the interior difference that underlies the more familiar Kantian commonalities and unities. The key commonalities of the Critique of Aesthetic Judgment – taste, community, reason's vocation in nature – are based on this original difference of imagination. On Arendt's reading, the Deduction of the third *Critique* aims to reconcile private experience with our sociality: 'Kant was very early aware that there was something nonsubjective in what

[41] See the references in notes 2 and 36, above.
[42] Deleuze, 'Idea of Genesis', p. 63.
[43] Kant, *Critique of Judgment*, p. 259.

seems to be the most private and subjective sense.'[44] For Arendt, the nonsubjective is intersubjectivity; commonality and community are built into our private sense. Arendt thus gives us a reading of Kant that builds outwards towards Hegelian idealism and a dialectical reconciliation of the private with the public. For Deleuze, building on the inwardness of Maimonian idealism, there is similarly something nonsubjective within the subjective, but it is metaphysically nonsubjective, i.e. the *difference* of subjectivity. Deleuze presents a reading of Kant that builds inwards, that reconstitutes the mind from the outside in, that relates the subjective to the nonsubjective *within* the mind. This is an idealist reading of Kant, but it is one that highlights that most puzzling feature of Kantian judgement: the relation of the subject to what is nonsubjective within it.

[44] Arendt, *Lectures*, p. 67.

Part II

# Deleuze, Romanticism and Idealism

# Part II.
## Deleuze, Romanticism and Idealism

# Chapter 5

# What is a Literature of War?: Kleist, Kant and Nomadology

*Brent Adkins*

## INTRODUCTION

Deleuze's first public discussion of Kleist was at a conference in Milan in May 1974.[1] Soon after this, in a book on Kafka co-authored with Guattari, Kleist is mentioned again. It is a brief reference, but it appears that by this time their interpretation of Kleist had progressed to the point where his work could be organised around the question, What is a literature of war? In the context of the Kafka book this question serves two purposes. First, it supports the affinity that Kafka felt for Kleist. Second, it serves to contrast Kleist and Kafka, insofar as their works revolve around distinct questions.[2] It is not until *A Thousand Plateaus* in 1980, though, that Deleuze and Guattari's Kleist interpretation is fully explored in the context of the war machine plateau.

In addition to the war machine, Kleist illustrates some of Deleuze and Guattari's other key concepts, such as affect, becoming, and line of flight. All of these intersect in Kleist's work to form a literature of war. Before I pursue this further, though, a couple of clarifications are necessary. First, a literature of war does not have war as its object in precisely the same way that the war machine does not have war as its object. Kleist is not interested in the representation of war. A literature of war does not seek to mirror war. Second, a literature of war does not

---

[1] Gilles Deleuze and Félix Guattari, *Two Regimes of Madness: Texts and Interviews, 1975–1995*, ed. David Lapoujade, trans. Ames Hodges and Mike Taormina (Cambridge, MA: MIT Press, 2006), pp. 11–12, 401. See also Ronald Bogue's 'Deleuze, Guattari, and the Kafka-Kleist Connection: Toward a Literature of War', in Petr Kouba and Tomas Pivoda (eds), *Franz Kafka: Minority Report* (Prague: Litteraria Pragensa Books, 2011), pp. 62–86.

[2] Gilles Deleuze and Félix Guattari, *Kafka: Toward a Minor Literature*, trans. Dana Polan (Minneapolis: University of Minnesota Press, 1986), p. 55.

seek to represent the war machine. A literature of war does not represent anything. It produces. It creates. What is a literature of war? A literature that creates a war machine. I will argue that the war machine that Kleist writes aims to deterritorialise Kant's thought, and this is precisely why Deleuze and Guattari find him so compelling.

## THE TROUBLE WITH KANT

Both Deleuze and Kleist have a complicated history with Kant. One of Deleuze's earliest monographs is an analysis of Kant's work, while all of Kleist's major works follow upon what has come to be known as his 'Kant Crisis'. Deleuze's engagement with Kant cannot be character-ised as a crisis, but Kant remains a touchstone throughout much of his career. Furthermore, I argue below that both Deleuze and Kleist settle on the notion of affect (*Gemüt*) as a deterritorialising response to Kant, though they arrive at this notion by very different means.[3]

### Kant the Enemy

In a letter to Michel Cressole, Deleuze writes, 'My book on Kant is different, I like it very much, I wrote it as a book on an enemy. . .'.[4] Despite this admission, and other claims by Deleuze to have given Kant a 'monstrous child', Deleuze is not explicit about the precise way in which Kant is an enemy or in what the monstrousness of his reading consists. I would go so far as to say that Deleuze himself wasn't entirely clear about the degree to which he would diverge from Kant in his later works. I do, however, think that in this early work on Kant there are nascent themes that become more fully fleshed out in later works, even when the reference to Kant is no longer explicit. The theme I would like to focus on here is the theme of ontological continuity, or what I take to be the same thing, univocity. Univocity is, of course, a crucial theme in Deleuze's work, beginning with *Expressionism in Philosophy: Spinoza* and *Difference and Repetition* through *The Logic of Sense*. In his later work with Guattari, univocity is recast in terms of consistency and immanence. What is at stake in all of these accounts of ontologi-

---

[3] Matthieu Carrière, *Für eine Literatur des Krieges, Kleist* (Basel: Stroemfeld, 1981), pp. 23–5; 65ff. Carrière's work on Kleist is referred to as an 'unpublished study' in *A Thousand Plateaus*.

[4] Quoted in 'Translator's Introduction' to Gilles Deleuze, *Kant's Critical Philosophy*, trans. Hugh Tomlinson and Barbara Habberjam (Minneapolis: University of Minnesota Press, 1984), p. xvi.

cal continuity is a way of doing metaphysics that does not depend on a transcendent, formal ordering of matter, which generates two orders of being (form and content) that can only be related analogically. It is precisely on this score that Deleuze takes Kant to be an enemy. The issue is not formality, as such, but the idea that form is ontologically discontinuous with the content that it forms. Deleuze's project, the project of univocity, is the attempt to think form as ontologically continuous with its content.[5]

We see Deleuze edging towards this position in the Kant book in the way that he takes up the issue of reflective judgement in the third *Critique*. For Kant, the distinction between reflective judgement and determining judgement is that while determining judgements are made by subsuming the judgement under a concept, reflective judgements have no such subsuming concept. For Kant, this discovery of a new kind of judgement is treated as important, but not in such a way that it modifies the results of the first two *Critiques*. In fact, in a letter to Reinhold, Kant describes the entire critical project in this way:

> My inner conviction grows, as I discover in working on different topics that not only does my system remain self-consistent but I find also, when sometimes I cannot see the right way to investigate a certain subject, that I need only look back at the general picture of the elements of knowledge, and of the mental powers pertaining to them, in order to make discoveries I had not expected.[6]

Kant goes on to say in the letter that he has discovered a 'new sort of *a priori* principle' related to the faculty of feeling pleasure and displeasure. Insofar as a faculty has *a priori* principles it can be subject to a critique, just as the faculties of cognition and desire were subject to critique. The picture that Kant paints here is of three distinct faculties, each with its own critique. Furthermore, it is clear from the first *Critique* that Kant's intention is to subject cognition to critique precisely so that he can make room for the practical or moral deployment of reason. The primacy of the moral use of reason is carried through the third *Critique* as Kant finds in both aesthetic and teleological judgement an analogue to morality and a ground for morality in the postulate of an ordered universe, respectively.

[5] I pursue these themes at length in Brent Adkins and Paul Hinlicky, *Rethinking Philosophy and Theology with Deleuze: A New Cartography* (London: Bloomsbury, 2013) and Brent Adkins, *Deleuze and Guattari's* A Thousand Plateaus: *A Reader's Guide and Critical Introduction* (Edinburgh: Edinburgh University Press, 2015).

[6] Quoted in 'Editor's Introduction' to Immanuel Kant, *Critique of the Power of Judgment*, ed. and trans. Paul Guyer (Cambridge: Cambridge University Press, 2000), pp. xiii–xiv.

Deleuze, of course, acknowledges Kant's explicit intentions with regard to the critical project as a whole, but turns Kant's own question against him. Deleuze asks: What is the condition for the possibility of determining judgement? Deleuze shows, with gleeful perversity, that the condition for the possibility of determining judgement is in fact reflective judgement. He argues that it might be tempting to think that reflective judgement remains adjunct to determining judgement since reflective judgement does not legislate, but a 'faculty would never take on a legislative and determining role were not all the faculties together in the first place capable of this free subjective harmony'.[7] Thus, the ground for cognition or desire legislating in accord with concepts is dependent on what Kant calls the 'free play of the faculties' that arises when there is no determining concept to legislate.

Deleuze argues the same point with respect to teleological judgement, as well. First, he shows that teleological judgement is also a kind of reflective judgement. Second, he shows that the kind of reflective judgement found in a concept of natural ends also grounds determining judgement. The conclusion that Deleuze reaches, and the monstrous child he forces Kant to acknowledge, is this: 'Thus the first two *Critiques* set out a relationship between the faculties which is determined by one of them; the last *Critique* uncovers a deeper free and indeterminate accord of the faculties as the condition of the possibility of every determinate relationship.'[8]

For our purposes, here two observations need to be made. First, Deleuze forces Kant to ground both cognition and desire (in Kant's sense) in affect. Second – and this is related – this move allows Deleuze to convert Kant's metaphysics from discontinuity to continuity. The grounding of both cognition and morality in affect recalls not only one of the dominant themes of *Nietzsche and Philosophy*, published in the year prior to the Kant book, but also points forward to his later discussions of Spinoza and his work with Guattari. It is within this larger context of affect that we find Deleuze and Guattari's discussions of Kleist. Showing that Kant presupposes a univocal metaphysics in direct opposition to his stated intentions, beginning with the Inaugural Dissertation and running through the critical period, foreshadows Deleuze's concern with the theme of univocity that runs through *Logic of Sense* and *Difference and Repetition*, as well as the theme of immanence that runs through the work with Guattari and informs their reading of Kleist.

[7] Deleuze, *Kant's Critical Philosophy*, p. 50.
[8] Ibid. p. 68.

*Kleist's Kant Crisis*

In contrast to Deleuze's ability to hold Kant at arm's length, Kleist seems overwhelmed by his encounter with Kantian philosophy. In 1801, it left him 'deeply and painfully shaken', and in a letter to Wilhelmine von Zenge he writes that, in Kant's wake, 'We cannot decide whether what we call truth is truly truth or whether it only seems so to us.' All of Kleist's earlier beliefs about the importance of a life plan, and not being subject to fate, are shattered: 'My highest and only goal has sunk and now I have none.'[9] The vertigo induced by Kant sent Kleist into a frenzied production over the next ten years, a period in which he produced all his major works. Kant's restriction of the understanding to appearance, rather than things-in-themselves, seems to have created an ontological problem for Kleist. His response to this problem was to create art in which expectations are overturned, in which people lose control of their lives, in which affect dominates reason.

The difficulty, at least as far as Kleist scholarship is concerned, is that it's not entirely clear what Kleist is reacting to. In the letter to von Zenge, for example, he refers to the 'new, the so-called, Kantian philosophy'. Does this mean he read Kant? Does it mean he read one of Kant's followers? Reinhold or Fichte, perhaps? Or, is 'Kantian philosophy' a synecdoche for 'German Enlightenment'? Kleist himself gives no clear indication here.[10] Initially, Kleist scholarship took it that 'Kantian philosophy' was 'Kant', and so debates revolved around which Kantian text prompted Kleist's crisis. Ludwig Muth argues in *Kleist und Kant* that the third *Critique* plays the decisive role in Kleist's transformation. Cassirer, in contrast, argues that it was not so much Kant but Kantians that precipitated the crisis – namely Fichte's *The Vocation of Man*. More recent scholarship has abandoned the idea that Kleist's shift after 1801 can be tied to any one text, whether by Kant or another contemporary. Instead, contemporary Kleist scholars, such as Mehigan and Fischer, focus on his intellectual milieu, in particular the strain of scepticism they see evident in the German Enlightenment. Thus, the more recent Kleist scholarship no longer has to go searching through specific texts in order to find parallels. It can also dispense with arguments about whether or not Kleist

---

[9] Heinrich von Kleist, *Selected Writings*, ed. and trans. David Constantine (Indianapolis: Hackett Publishing, 2004), pp. 421–2.

[10] There's a reference to the *Metaphysics of Morals* in 'On the gradual production of thoughts while speaking', an essay discussed below. There's also a reference to 'South Sea Islanders' in the letters, that might be construed as an oblique reference to the *Groundwork*.

was a good interpreter of Kant or Kantianism. At the same time though, recent Kleist scholarship also has the disadvantage of painting Kleist's milieu in very broad strokes. Furthermore, arguing that Kleist was reacting to something 'in the air' is certainly true, but trivially true. The result is an unsatisfying explanation of Kleist's Kant crisis.[11] It's precisely at this point that Deleuze and Guattari's use of Kleist becomes instructive. On their reading, Kleist's Kant crisis is precipitated by Kant's statist image of thought, and his response is the mobilisation of affect to deterritorialise this image of thought.

## THE WAR MACHINE

For Deleuze and Guattari, one of the primary ways of talking about the mobilisation of affect is in terms of the war machine. It is tempting to read the Treatise on Nomadology as an argument for nomads and war machines at the expense of states. Read in this way the Nomadology becomes a moral treatise, arguing that we ought to be more nomadic. I do not think, though, that the Nomadology, or any of *A Thousand Plateaus*, is moral in that sense. Rather, I think that *A Thousand Plateaus* is ethical for precisely the same reason that Spinoza's major work is entitled the *Ethics*. Both begin with ontology and show what follows from this ontology. While Spinoza's ontology is one of substance and modes, Deleuze and Guattari's ontology is one of assemblages. Each of the plateaus in *A Thousand Plateaus* concerns a particular type of assemblage. An assemblage is a heterogeneous but consistent arrangement of parts that is more or less stable over time. Thus, the contents of my desk are an assemblage. I'm an assemblage. The Himalayas are an assemblage. At the same time, however, an assemblage also has two opposed tendencies: one towards stasis and one towards change. These two tendencies form abstract poles on an ontologically univocal continuum. The Himalayas assemblage is much closer to the stasis pole, while the contents of my desk are closer to the change pole. Importantly, though, the abstract poles that orient any assemblage are not different in kind; they are only different in degree.

In the Nomadology, Deleuze and Guattari are interested in political assemblages. The two abstract poles of any political assemblage are

---

[11]  Mehigan gives a nice summary of the history of Kleist scholarship with regard to the Kant crisis in his '"Betwixt a false reason and none at all": Kleist, Hume, Kant, and the "Thing in Itself"', in Bernd Fischer (ed.), *A Companion to the Works of Heinrich von Kleist* (Rochester, NY: Camden House, 2003), pp. 165–88.

the state and the war machine. Deleuze and Guattari illustrate the difference between these two poles by discussing the difference between two games: chess and Go.[12] 'Chess is a game of State.' Go is a game of the war machine. Why? 'Chess pieces are coded.' They are coded not only according to their allowable moves, but their shape. Pawns look like other pawns, but not like knights. Pawns always move in the same way, which is manifestly not like a knight. Despite the astronomical number of combinations these pieces can enter into, chess is fundamentally static. In contrast to this, Go is played with flat stones that are indistinguishable from one another. The function of any given piece is completely determined by its external relation to the other pieces on the board, whereas internal relations determine the function of chess pieces. Go thus expresses the abstract pole of change. Any political assemblage, then, will be some combination of these tendencies towards both the state pole and the war machine pole. Deleuze and Guattari's task in the Nomadology is to show the importance of the war machine pole in understanding the political assemblage. Their claim is that the political traditionally has been understood solely from the perspective of the state pole. This has resulted in the privileging of particular molar formations at the expense of molecular becomings. This accounting of the war machine, though, is not an invitation to replace all state forms with nomadic war machines. The state pole is irreducible and ineradicable. It cannot be eliminated, and political assemblages cannot be understood without it.

### The War Machine as Affective

As we saw above, both Deleuze and Kleist respond to Kant by turning to affect. This point of overlap is crucial because it's the way in which both thinkers replace Kant's commitment to discontinuity with continuity. Since the beginning of Kant's critical turn, signalled by the 1770 Inaugural Dissertation, Kant distinguishes his philosophical method through his commitment to the *a priori* distinction between the sensible and the intelligible. All of the major distinctions in Kant's critical philosophy can be traced to this fundamental diremption between transcendental form and empirical content. The difference that Kant proposes here is a difference in kind. What distinguishes both Kleist and

---

12  Gilles Deleuze and Félix Guattari, *A Thousand Plateaus: Capitalism and Schizophrenia*, vol. 2, trans. Brian Massumi (Minneapolis: University of Minnesota Press, 1987), p. 352.

Deleuze from Kant is their reframing of metaphysics in terms of affect in a way that does not depend on the positing of a transcendental form that makes incomprehensible matter coherent. Kant's philosophy is hylomorphic, while Deleuze and Kleist are proposing a hylozoism, the idea that matter is self-forming.

In the case of the war machine the turn to affect manifests itself in an account of the political that is not dependent on the state-form as an image of thought for all human organisation. Rather, both the state and the war machine are tendencies within all political assemblages, which are themselves ways of organising affects. In order to understand how political assemblages are ways of organising affects, we'll turn again to Spinoza. For Spinoza, the identity of any entity is the ratio of motion and rest among its parts. This ratio places limits on the ways in which any entity can affect and be affected. For example, the relation of my parts to one another is such that I cannot fly unaided or breathe underwater without special equipment. For Spinoza, as well as Deleuze, we can ask similar questions about political entities. What is a particular group of people capable of? Is the power of the group increased or decreased by having mountain borders? Access to the sea? The ability to work metals? Obviously, none of these questions can be answered absolutely, or binarily. Whatever increases the power of a group in some respects may decrease it in other respects. What was once, on balance, an increase in a group's power, may now be a decrease.

The tendency of political entities to maintain their power through reducing the number of ways of affecting and being affected, Deleuze calls the state. It is also in these terms that we can think coding and territorialisation. A political assemblage fixes the relations among its various parts by coding them. In short, the political assemblage becomes chess-like. Furthermore, in such an assemblage the parts are organised such that every part refers to some organising principle, whether it be a king or government. This organisation is what Deleuze and Guattari refer to as territorialisation. Territorialisation refers not only to the way that a state organises its geographic territory, but the way that it organises a whole host of territories, such as people, animals, and plants. A college student is territorialised not merely by the fact that she is on a college campus. She remains a college student whether on or off campus. At the same time being a college student organises when and where she goes. The campus itself is spatially territorialised, but for the student her time is also organised as she fits herself into the rhythms of the day and semester. Mondays, Wednesdays, and Fridays may have a different rhythm from Tuesdays and Thursdays, which in turn may differ from the weekends. Territorialisation is the belonging generated by fitting oneself to a rhythm.

## The War Machine as Assemblage

As we've already seen, the difference between the state and the war machine is one of opposing tendencies between stasis and change. Deleuze and Guattari state this explicitly: 'It is in terms not of independence, but of coexistence and completion *in a perpetual field of interaction*, that we conceive of exteriority and interiority, war machines of metamorphosis and State apparatuses of identity ... The same field circumscribes its interiority in States, but describes its exteriority in what escapes States or stands against States.'[13] Notice, however, that in addition to 'metamorphosis' and 'identity' as descriptors of the war machine and the state, Deleuze and Guattari also speak of the difference between the exterior and the interior. The exteriority of the war machine is the first axiom of the Nomadology and it is opposed to the interiority of the state. In this context exterior and interior do not refer to a simple geographical boundary that runs through a homogeneous space. Rather, exterior and interior are two opposed ways of describing space itself. As we saw briefly above in the discussion of Go and chess, the distinction here is between the smooth space of the exterior and the striated space of the interior.

Deleuze and Guattari signal their interest in exteriority in the opening plateau 'Rhizome'. One of the characteristics of a rhizome is that it is always open to the outside, always making heterogeneous connections. It is also precisely at this point that Kleist is mentioned for the first time. A war machine is thus an assemblage that is composed of lines of flight, open to heterogeneous connections. It is precisely for this reason that the war machine is always trying to ward off the state. State formations block lines of flight and reproduce only homogeneous connections. The state converts the war machine's exteriority to a selfsame interiority. By the same token the state is always trying to co-opt the war machine. The state's identity is dependent on foreclosing exteriority but realising that lines of flight are endemic to any assemblage. As a result, the state seeks through law (overcoding) to channel these lines of flight to serve its own ends. What this means in political terms is that the war machine gets converted into a military that serves the state and is highly regulated. The war machine, however, is not limited to the military. *Any* assemblage

---

[13] Deleuze and Guattari, *A Thousand Plateaus*, pp. 360–1.

that exceeds the state form and opens it to heterogeneous connections is a war machine. Thus, for Deleuze and Guattari a political lobby is a war machine. Love is a war machine. Religion is a war machine. And, most important for our purposes here, Kleist writes the war machine.

### The War Machine as Anti-Kantian

In order to see more clearly how Kleist writes the war machine, let's return to Kant and his relation to war. It would not be an exaggeration to say that Kant's critical project is a project wholly concerned with boundaries: boundaries between appearances and things-in-themselves, boundaries between freedom and nature, boundaries between reason and the understanding, boundaries between morality and inclination, boundaries between enlightenment and enthusiasm. The problem as Kant sees it is that philosophy has failed to properly set the boundaries between these realms, and as a result philosophy has devolved into a series of border disputes.[14] 'The battlefield of these endless controversies is called metaphysics.'[15] Kant laments that there was a time when metaphysics was called 'queen of the sciences'. Her rule was despotic and carried by dogmatic administrators. These administrators eventually fell to fighting amongst themselves. Their efforts were further hampered by 'nomads [sceptics] who abhor all permanent cultivation of the soil, [and] shattered civil unity from time to time'.[16] The dogmatists always managed to rebuild but not in an orderly way, since they still disagreed with one another. Kant, of course, posits the critical philosophy as a solution to the internecine battles among the dogmatists and a bulwark against the disruptive incursions of the nomads. Kant thus fights a war on two fronts. One of the fronts is internal. It concerns delimiting the pretensions of dogmatists. Kant attempts here to limit the domain of metaphysics. Metaphysics may only colonise objects of possible experience. It must limit itself to appearances to which it gains access through synthetic *a priori* judgements.

The real problem here, though, is the sceptics, these nomadic anarchists that do not respect the rule of metaphysics. They have no interest in permanence, no wish to maintain 'civil unity'. They seek only to destroy what others have built. They arrive without warning from the

---

[14] See my chapter on Kant in Adkins and Hinlicky, *Rethinking Philosophy and Theology with Deleuze*.

[15] Immanuel Kant, *Critique of Pure Reason*, ed. and trans. Paul Guyer (Cambridge: Cambridge University Press, 1998), Aviii.

[16] Ibid. Aix.

outside. The only fortunate thing that Kant can see about the nomads is that there are so few of them. They attack and then melt back into the hinterlands. It's always possible to rebuild. Kant's strategy in the face of this anti-state, anti-metaphysical threat is the strategy of all states with regard to nomads – appropriate them. Turn them into the military wing of the state. Kant neutralises the threat of scepticism by absorbing it into the critical project. Kant deploys scepticism in his battle against dogmatism to restore peace in the land of metaphysics. Kant delimits the pretensions of dogmatism by showing that dogmatism exceeds the boundaries of the understanding by making theoretical judgements about things in themselves. Kant brilliantly shows in the dialectic of the first *Critique* that all of the problems of philosophy arise from making theoretical claims about the ideas of reason (world, soul, and God). Kant's strategy here is not the dogmatic strategy of arguing for the 'true' conception of world, soul, and God, but the sceptical strategy of arguing that since these are not objects of possible experience we can have no theoretical knowledge of them. Kant thus deflates dogmatism and appropriates scepticism for his own ends in one fell swoop.

For Deleuze and Guattari, Kant is the exemplary state philosopher. 'It was all over the moment the State-form inspired an image of thought.'[17] As we have seen, Kant is explicit about this as he likens the state of metaphysics to a badly run political state. The queen's rule is in question. Stateless nomads have breached the city walls. The ministers of state quibble endlessly among themselves instead of looking after the affairs of state. The solution is to both solidify and delimit the queen's rule by replacing the dogmatic ministers of state with nomads. The price the nomads pay is their absorption into the interior of the state. They are no longer exterior to the state but part of it. The war machine is necessarily opposed to the state, and as such it is necessarily opposed to the Kantian philosophy. The war machine would be a thought that does not take the state-form as its image, a thought that does not seek to reproduce the architectonic of the state with its interiority and homogeneity. The war machine is a thought that remains exterior and opens the interior of the state onto the heterogeneous.

*Writing the War Machine*

Deleuze and Guattari return to Kleist at precisely the point that they're differentiating the statist thought of Kant from the war machine. Given

---

[17] Deleuze and Guattari, *A Thousand Plateaus*, p. 376.

what we've seen of Deleuze's earliest interpretations of Kant, it's no surprise that they focus on the notion of *Gemüt* in Kleist, particularly his short essay 'On the Gradual Production of Thoughts whilst Speaking'.[18] *Gemüt* is a difficult word to translate, and would normally be translated as 'mind', 'soul', 'heart', or 'disposition'. The problem with translating the word in this way is the unavoidable connotations of interiority that Deleuze and Guattari are trying to avoid. In this context it's clear that the better translation is 'affect', insofar as it suggests a connection between the speaker and an exteriority that produces something new. What Kleist argues in the essay is that speech is not controlled by the interiority of the concept, but rather that when speech is under pressure from external forces, only then can it produce new thoughts. He proposes the following method for producing new ideas: 'I put in a few unarticulated sounds, dwell lengthily on the conjunctions, perhaps make use of apposition where it is not necessary, and have recourse to other tricks which will spin out of my speech, all to gain time for the fabrication of my idea in the workshop of the mind [*Vernunft*].'[19] The reference to *Vernunft* (reason) here is crucial, since it plainly reverses the Kantian project. For Kant, reason is a tribunal that dispenses determining judgements that keep concepts within their appointed boundaries. For Kleist, reason is a workshop that creates ideas under the pressure of having to speak. Here we are not too far from Deleuze's contention in *Kant's Critical Philosophy* that the determining judgements of reason presuppose a free play of the faculties.

Even in this essay about the relation between speaking and new ideas, Kleist uses metaphors of war. The kind of war Kleist refers to, though, is fundamentally different from Kant's use of military images. While Kant uses images of war in support of the state and its unity, Kleist uses images of war that suggest the externality of the war machine.

> And in this process nothing helps me more than if my sister makes a move suggesting she wishes to interrupt; for such an attempt from outside to wrest speech from its grasp still further excites my already hard-worked mind and, *like a general* when circumstances press, its powers are raised a further *degree*.[20]

Notice that the general's task here is not to restore order but to increase intensity on the basis of external circumstances. This shift to the register of intensity is reinforced later in the essay and also in martial terms when

---

[18] Kleist, *Selected Writings*, pp. 405–9.
[19] Ibid. p. 406.
[20] Ibid. (emphasis mine).

he writes: 'And in general if two men have the same clarity of thought the *faster* speaker will always have an advantage since he brings, so to speak, more *forces* to the battle than his opponent.'[21] For Kleist, the clarity of thought is not a sufficient guarantee of success. Thought must be opened to an outside. Opening to an outside does not result in the determination of the outside by thought. Rather, external intensities draw transversal lines between the well-ordered points of thought, which fashions new thoughts and 'with a convulsive movement, take fire, seize a chance to speak and bring something incomprehensible into the world'.[22]

This production of new thoughts by engaging with the external through speech returns us to *Gemüt* or affect. Affects are impersonal, non-subjective, and non-signifying. They are not the possession of a subjective interiority or thought. Affects are external to every interiority and in fact are the conditions for the possibility of interiority. What Kleist provides in this essay is a method for mobilising *Gemüt* in order to open thought to its outside. He makes this explicit when he writes: 'For it is not *we* who know things but pre-eminently a certain *condition* of ours which knows.'[23] Knowledge is not a property for Kleist as it is for Kant. Knowledge is also not guaranteed by a transcendental unity of apperception. Knowledge is external to the subject and located in affect. Learning something new is not a matter of securing one's boundaries and subjecting every entrant to the tribunal of reason. Bringing something incomprehensible into the world must risk opening thought to the outside. 'A thought grappling with exterior forces instead of being gathered up in an interior form, operating by relays instead of forming an image; an event-thought, a haecceity, instead of a subject-thought, a problem-thought instead of an essence-thought or theorem; a thought that appeals to a people instead of taking itself for a government ministry'.[24]

*Michael Kohlhaas*

While his essay on the production of new thoughts describes a method, it is in his stories and plays that Kleist puts this method into practice. Reading Kleist there is a sense of breathlessness. This is created in part by the fact that his stories have no breaks, no sections or chapters. They simply flow continuously. In *Michael Kohlhaas*, Kleist tells the story

---

[21] Ibid. p. 408 (emphasis mine).
[22] Ibid.
[23] Ibid. (emphasis in original).
[24] Deleuze and Guattari, *A Thousand Plateaus*, p. 378.

of a sixteenth-century, German horse dealer who is cheated out of two horses by a petty baron, the Junker von Tronka. Kohlhaas does his best to work within the legal system to get redress. At one point the baron agrees to give the horses back, but they have been worked very hard and are no longer a sufficient repayment for Kohlhaas' losses. At this point Kohlhaas sees that he can no longer work within the strictures of the state and becomes an outlaw. He gathers a small band of men around him and lays siege to the baron's castle, destroying it. The baron narrowly escapes, and Kohlhaas pursues, while his band of outlaws continues to grow. Fear begins to spread across the countryside as various forces try to bring Kohlhaas to heel, but invariably fail as he outwits them at every turn. It is clear by this point in the story that Kohlhaas' war is no longer against a local baron but against the state itself, which refuses him justice. Kohlhaas is now a war machine that disturbs civil unity at every turn.

Kohlhaas' disturbance of the peace is so great that even the leader of the Protestant reformation, Martin Luther, weighs in. Luther writes a letter to Kohlhaas, which so disturbs him that he travels to Wittenberg in disguise to meet with him. Upon meeting him Luther exclaims, 'Your breath is a pestilence, your presence perdition ... Damnable, terrible man! ... Who gave you the right – other than you yourself – to fall upon the Junker von Tronka and then, not finding him in his castle, to visit with fire and sword the whole community that is protecting him?'[25] Kohlhaas' reply turns on the notion of community. 'The war I am waging on the community of humankind is an evil deed if I was not ... expelled from it.'[26] Luther is baffled by Kohlhaas' thinking here. It is inconceivable that one be outside the state. 'Expelled! ... What madness seized your thinking? Who could have expelled you from the community of the state in which you lived? Indeed, has it ever been the case, since states existed, that any man, whoever he might be, has been expelled from one?'[27] For Luther, one necessarily belongs to the state. There is nothing outside the state. In Kleist's story theology has also taken the state-form as the image of thought. The parallels with Kant are clear. The nomads disrupting the civil unity of state philosophy must be incorporated into the state. They cannot remain external.

Kohlhaas cannot remain external either. In the end he agrees to submit to the justice of the sovereign in this matter, so long as he sees justice

[25] Kleist, *Selected Writings*, p. 236.
[26] Ibid.
[27] Ibid. pp. 236–7.

done to the Junker von Tronka in the matter of the horses. Ultimately, Kohlhaas receives his horses back in fine form, just before he is led to his execution. For Deleuze and Guattari this seems to be the fate of every war machine. 'As for Kohlhaas, his war machine can no longer be anything more than banditry. Is it the destiny of the war machine, when the State triumphs to be caught in this alternative: either to be nothing more than the disciplined, military organ of the State apparatus, *or to turn against itself*, to become a double suicide machine for a solitary man and a solitary woman?'[28] Even if Kleist's war machines fail, he still succeeds in giving us another image of thought. An image of thought predicated on speeds and slowness. Kohlhaas is always too quick for the authorities. He always shows up where he's not expected. It is also an image of thought that is generated by affect rather than determining judgements. Kohlhaas is driven by anger and sadness, but it's not an anger or sadness that belongs to him. It belongs to the band of outlaws. It spreads and grows along with Kohlhaas' fame. 'Affects transpierce the body like arrows, they are weapons of war.'[29] These affects are a madness that seizes not only Kohlhaas' reason, but also infect the entire country.

## 'Penthesilea'

Kleist's plays work in much the same way as his stories. They do not have acts, and, in fact, when Goethe staged one of Kleist's plays and recast it into acts, Kleist was incensed.[30] Kleist's plays are rather a series of continuous scenes. The play that best exemplifies the war machine is 'Penthesilea'. 'Penthesilea' stages the tragic confrontation between Achilles and Penthesilea, leader of the Amazon army, during the Trojan War. Both sides hear of the Amazons' approach and rush to meet them. The Trojans arrive first and are promptly attacked. The Greeks assume that the Amazons are on their side and seek to make a treaty with them. When the Greeks approach to make a pact they are rebuffed, and the Amazons turn on them. Two states are at war. Each is trying to assert its sovereignty over the other. They wrongly assume that the Amazons are also interested in statecraft. The Amazons are not a state, though; they are a war machine. Odysseus relays his incomprehension to Antilochus:

[28] Deleuze and Guattari, *A Thousand Plateaus*, pp. 355–6. The reference to the 'double suicide machine' is to the way that Kleist ended his own life in a suicide pact with another woman.

[29] Ibid. p. 356.

[30] On Kleist and Goethe see Joachim Maass, *Kleist: A Biography*, trans. Ralph Manheim (New York: Farrar, Strauss and Giroux, 1983), pp. 151ff.

Plump in the middle of our quarrel – she
Must seek her friends on this side or on that;
And we may well believe her friend to us
Since to the Trojans she is patent foe.[31]

Odysseus' incomprehension, much like Martin Luther's in *Michael Kohlhaas*, arises from the fact that he can't imagine any choice except between two molar state-forms, either the Trojans or the Greeks. The Amazons, though, occupy the smooth space between states. They are the middle that Odysseus' logic demands be excluded. For Odysseus there are only states, molar formations of striated space. The idea that one could belong to a pack that is not a state simply never occurs to Odysseus. Achilles, however, recognises that the Amazons do not belong to a state, and thus asks Penthesilea directly about her motivations:

What urges thee, in steel caparisoned,
Full of insensate rage, most like a Fury,
To fall thus headlong on the tribes of Argos?[32]

Penthesilea's answer is that they attack to capture men in order to mate and thus produce more Amazons. The war machine propagates by alliance not filiation by a series of heterogeneous connections. The relation between the Amazons and the Greeks is not the relation between two states but the relation between the wasp and orchid, infectious and rhizomatic.

The war machine of the Amazons runs transversally across the striations of both the Greek and Trojan states. The deterritorialising edge of the war machine is Penthesilea herself. She leads the charge that so bewilders Greeks and Trojans alike. Importantly, though, it is not through Penthesilea as subject that this deterritorialisation occurs. Rather, Penthesilea is the locus of affects that infect both Trojans and Greeks. In particular, Kleist's drama focuses on the infection of Achilles. The change wrought by this infection is reciprocal. Both Achilles and Penthesilea undergo a transformation as a result. Achilles enters into a becoming-woman, and Penthesilea enters into a becoming-dog. Penthesilea's becoming-dog does not turn her into a pet or a species. She is not the member of a family, nor the representative of a genus. Her becoming-dog is not achieved through imitation, but through channelling affect. Kleist writes of Penthesilea:

---

[31] Heinrich von Kleist, 'Penthesilea', in *Plays*, ed. Walter Hinderer (New York: Continuum, 1982), scene i.
[32] Ibid. scene xv.

She's in a frenzy now among her dogs,
Her lips all flecked with foam, calling them sisters.[33]

Even though she still carries a bow and leads the pack, the other Amazons recognise that Penthesilea has become something other than human:

HIGH PRIESTESS: Take her and throw her to the ground! Bind her!
AN AMAZON: Bind whom, Your Grace? The Queen?
HIGH PRIESTESS: I mean that dog (*Hündin*)!
– There's no restraining her with human hands.[34]

It's crucial to note at this point that even though Penthesilea is recognised as a dog, that recognition does not arise through resemblance. Becoming-animal does not occur through imitation. Penthesilea does not become-dog by barking. It's that calling the dogs 'sisters' circulates the same affect as barking. Penthesilea becomes-dog by effectuating the same diagram as the pack, occupying the same problematic as the pack.

Examples could be multiplied from Kleist's other works. Kleist's work is full of fainting spells, catatonias, misunderstandings, flights of passion, and mob rule. All of the best laid plans come to ruin in Kleist's *œuvre*. More importantly for our purposes here, all of the best laid plans come to ruin in Kleist because they are overwhelmed by affect. In *Saint Cecilia*, for example, four Protestant brothers set out to disrupt a Catholic religious service only to be overwhelmed by the power of the music. They spend the rest of their lives in an asylum silent except to sing the *gloria in excelsis*. In *Betrothal in Santa Domingo*, the main character betrays her household for love, is misunderstood by her fiancé, and subsequently killed. Both Deleuze and Kleist turn to affect in their attempts to come to terms with Kant, even though they reach this result by very different means.

## CONCLUSION

Deleuze and Kleist are both post-Kantian in the sense that they rehabilitate the role of affect in their work. Sensation is no longer subordinated to the understanding, nor is inclination subordinated to reason. As Deleuze argues and as Kleist illustrates, understanding and reason are both effects of affect. Furthermore, these affects are non-subjective and non-signifying. Affects do not have their source in a transcendental

---

[33] Ibid. scene xxii.
[34] Ibid.

unity of apperception. Any unity that might be called a subject is the result of flows and coagulations of affect. Furthermore, affects do not resemble or reproduce analogically the categories of the understanding or reason's search for the unconditioned. Affects are becomings. They occupy a plane of consistency with relations of speeds and slowness. They are Penthesilea's frozen rigidity upon first seeing Achilles, as well as the speed and ferocity with which she attacks. They are Kohlhaas' anger that slowly spreads throughout the countryside and infects some with anger and others with fear. These same affects clash with one another and transform one another. Kleist experienced Kant as a blockage. He didn't know where to go after reading Kant. His work after the Kant crisis shows him circumventing the blockage by writing the war machine. A war machine aimed not only at the strictures of the Kantian philosophy, but a war machine aimed at a thought predicated on the state-form. Although, Deleuze never had a Kant crisis, he too aimed his war machine at any thought predicated on the state-form. This certainly included Kant, but encompassed the major tradition of Western thought itself.

# Chapter 6

# The Calculable Law of Tragic Representation and the Unthinkable: Rhythm, Caesura and Time, from Hölderlin to Deleuze

*Arkady Plotnitsky*

## INTRODUCTION: THE PROBLEM OF RHYTHM AND THE PROBLEM OF FRIENDSHIP

Although sparse in Gilles Deleuze's oeuvre or in his collaborations with Félix Guattari, invocations of Friedrich Hölderlin occur at important, even crucial junctures of their work, as in his 1968 *Difference and Repetition*[1] or in their 1991 *What is Philosophy?*[2] – two books that frame the period of Deleuze's most influential work. On the first of these occasions, with which I shall be primarily concerned in this essay, Deleuze draws on Hölderlin for his examination of 'the problem of rhythm', referring in particular to Hölderlin's concept of rhythm [*Rhythmus*], as it is developed in his analysis of ancient Greek tragedy. This concept includes the concepts of 'counter-rhythm' and 'caesura' as defining components of its architecture, and it is also fundamentally connected to and indeed coextensive with Hölderlin's concept of time, developed in the same analysis and equally defined by its fractured, 'caesured', character.

I use the terms 'problem' and 'concept' in Deleuze and Guattari's sense in *What is Philosophy?*, which defines them as correlative to each other, building on Deleuze's earlier argument concerning 'problems' and 'ideas' in *Difference and Repetition*.[3] For the sake of economy, I shall henceforth mostly speak of concepts (a broader *concept* that subsumes ideas), even though my argument will primarily concern *Difference*

---

[1] Gilles Deleuze, *Difference and Repetition*, trans. Paul Patton (New York: Columbia University Press, 1994), pp. 85–91.
[2] Gilles Deleuze and Félix Guattari, *What is Philosophy?*, trans. Hugh Tomlinson and Graham Burchell (New York: Columbia University Press, 1994), pp. 101–2.
[3] Deleuze and Guattari, *What is Philosophy?*, p. 16; Deleuze, *Difference and Repetition*, pp. 153–64.

*and Repetition*. A concept in this sense is not merely a generalisation from particulars (which commonly defines concepts) or any general or abstract idea.[4] Instead, a concept is always a multi-component entity, composed of other concepts and connections between them: 'there are no simple concepts'.[5] A concept has a structure and even rhythm or (they are related but not the same) at least refrain: 'it is a refrain, an opus with its number (*chiffre*)', which also makes a concept 'composed', like a poetry line, or a poem.[6] Indeed, if 'there are no simple concepts', any concept, even if it is a component of a larger concept, is irreducibly non-simple, and opens itself to new delineations, which enables a concept to remain 'always new' and make philosophy a creation of 'concepts that are always new'.[7] A concept is always singular, unique: 'the concept as a specifically philosophical creation is always a singularity', a trajectory of thought (*heicceity*), and a concept always carries a signature underneath it.[8] Each concept is, furthermore, defined as a problem – a multifaceted problem in turn. A problem in this sense, while it can and must be solved, does not disappear in its solutions, but 'exists and *persists* in [them]': it is 'determined at the same time as it is solved' and is 'at once both transcendent and immanent in relation to its solution'.[9] This persistence helps to make a problem and the concept associated to it always new.

Hölderlin's concepts of rhythm, caesura and time are such concepts-problems, and as the creator of these and other concepts, Hölderlin is a philosopher, both in his literary and philosophical works. These three concepts are, again, connected and may be seen as forming a single concept. While the confluence of rhythm, caesura and time is manifested more immediately in the case of poetry – in which, indeed in the structure of the poetic line, these concepts in part originate – it is also found elsewhere: in mathematics, physics, philosophy, history, ethics, and politics. '*Everything is rhythm*', Hölderlin is reported (by Bettina von Arnim) to have said: '*the entire destiny is a single celestial rhythm, just as the work of art has a unique rhythm*'.[10] Whether Hölderlin said exactly this or not, one could hardly doubt that he thought that rhythm or, it follows, caesura, are found everywhere. In this reach, it is analogous to Deleuze's and Deleuze and Guattari's concept of refrain, which, while congruent

---

4  Deleuze and Guattari, *What is Philosophy?*, p. 24
5  Ibid. p. 19.
6  Ibid. p. 21.
7  Ibid. p. 5.
8  Ibid. p. 7.
9  Deleuze, *Difference and Repetition*, p. 163 (emphasis added).
10  Bettina von Arnim, *Die Günderode* (Leipzig: Insel Verlag, 1983), p. 294.

with Hölderlin's concept of rhythm, signed by Hölderlin, is *Deleuze and Guattari's* concept and is 'signed' by them.[11]

Hölderlin's concepts of rhythm, caesura and time enable him to make another major philosophical contribution: a new concept of ontology. By 'ontology', I understand a description or conception of what is possible to say or, in the first place, to think concerning the ultimate constitution of things in a given domain. Accordingly, ontology is not only a claim concerning the *existence* of something (say, material bodies in physics or thoughts in philosophy or psychology), but also and indeed primarily a claim concerning the *character* of this existence.[12] Although associated by Hölderlin himself with the ancient Greek thinking, which is to say, his *interpretation* of this thinking, this ontology does not appear to have been developed before Hölderlin or his fellow Romantics, such as Heinrich von Kleist in Germany, or Percy Bysshe Shelley and John Keats in England. One might further argue that it was in part a response to Hume's and then Kant's philosophy, by taking it to the limit that Hume and Kant had not envisioned or had been reluctant to accept. I shall, accordingly, call this ontology 'Romantic ontology', although it may also be called 'nonclassical ontology', which is a more conceptual designation – helpful because this ontology, juxtaposed to 'classical ontology' (defined below), is found beyond the Romantics. Romantic ontology is a more historical designation.

This ontology is defined by the scepticism concerning the possibility of capturing the ultimate workings of matter or thought *by thought*, and, at the limit, by assuming that this possibility is in principle excluded. By contrast, classical ontological thinking *always* leaves room for such a possibility, at least in principle, and it can be defined accordingly. Nonclassical ontology makes the ultimate working of matter or thought inconceivable, *un*thinkable, ultimately unthinkable even as unthinkable. The word 'the unthinkable' (*das Undenkbare*) is used by Hölderlin in speaking of human understanding as 'wandering beneath the unthinkable'.[13] Hölderlin also speaks of *das Unförmliche*.[14]

---

[11] Deleuze, *Difference and Repetition*, p. 123; Gilles Deleuze and Félix Guattari, *A Thousand Plateaus*, trans. Brian Massumi (Minneapolis: University of Minnesota Press, 1987), pp. 310–50.

[12] My discussion of ontology may be linked to Heidegger's work, indebted to Hölderlin, and, for a helpful contrast with Heidegger, or Deleuze, that of Alain Badiou, whose thinking is indebted to Hölderlin as well. These connections are, however, beyond my scope here.

[13] Friedrich Hölderlin, *Essays and Letters* (New York: Penguin, 2009), p. 327 (translation modified).

[14] See, for example, ibid. p. 263.

Deleuze invokes *das Unförmliche* in considering the third synthesis of time, which, however, ultimately relates to the unthinkable, in *Difference and Repetition*.[15] While the definition of ontology given above in effect defines classical ontology, there is no contradiction in speaking of nonclassical ontology as 'ontology'. This is because, under these conditions, properly ontological architectures (it follows, classical in character) emerge at intermediate levels. It is only impossible to speak of ontology at the ultimate level considered. Nonclassical ontology is 'ontology without the ultimate ontology'.

### THREE CONCEPTIONS OF CHAOS AND NONCLASSICAL ONTOLOGY, FROM THE PRE-SOCRATICS TO HÖLDERLIN

I would like to begin by positioning nonclassical thinking in relation to Deleuze and Guattari's argument concerning thinking as the confrontation between the brain and chaos in *What is Philosophy?*.[16] What they call *thought* is a creative form of this confrontation, manifested in art, science, and philosophy, as against *opinion*, which merely 'protects us from chaos', like 'a sort of umbrella'. 'But art, science, and philosophy require more: they cast planes over the chaos', and thus open new spaces of creative thought. Accordingly, Deleuze and Guattari see chaos not so as much an enemy but as a friend, even the greatest friend of thought, and its best ally in its struggle against opinion: 'the struggle with chaos ... the instrument in a more profound struggle', that 'against opinion, for the misfortune of people comes from opinion. ... And what would *thinking* be, if it did not constantly confront chaos?'.[17]

Deleuze and Guattari approach chaos itself by means of a particular and, in philosophy, rarely (if ever) used concept. This concept owes more to some of the key developments of modern physics, in particular the so-called quantum field theory, than to philosophy.[18] According to Deleuze and Guattari:

Chaos is defined not so much by its disorder as by the infinite speed with which every form taking shape in it vanishes. It is a void that is not a nothingness but a *virtual*, containing all possible particles and drawing out all

---

[15] Deleuze, *Difference and Repetition*, p. 92.
[16] Deleuze and Guattari, *What is Philosophy?*, pp. 201–18.
[17] Ibid. pp. 202, 206 and 208.
[18] Arkady Plotnitsky, 'Chaosmologies: Quantum Field Theory, Chaos, and Thought in Deleuze and Guattari's *What is Philosophy?*', *Paragraph* 29:2 (2006).

possible forms, which spring up only to disappear immediately, without consistency or reference, without consequence. Chaos is an infinite speed of birth and disappearance.[19]

This conception of chaos may be termed *chaos as the virtual*, and it is indeed essential for our understanding of thought. I would contend, however, that thought also confronts two other forms of chaos, which (especially the first one) are manifestly important for Hölderlin and which in effect enter Deleuze and Guattari's discussion of thought in *What is Philosophy?* as well. The first, correlative to nonclassical ontology and corresponding to Hölderlin's *Undenkbarem*, is *chaos as the unthinkable*. This concept can be traced to, and was likely derived by, Hölderlin from the ancient Greek idea of chaos as *areton* or *alogon* – that which is beyond all comprehension, and hence beyond ontology. The link between this concept of chaos and chaos as the virtual arises because of the possibility that the processes responsible for the creation or annihilation of forms, for their birth and disappearance, may not be conceivable by any means available to us. The second conception is that of *chaos as randomness and chance*, or more accurately, as the efficacity of randomness and chance. This concept is not entirely put aside by Deleuze and Guattari's definition of chaos as the virtual. For, saying that 'chaos is defined *not so much* by its disorder' suggests that it is still defined by disorder due to the randomness or chance found in the emergence and disappearance of forms in the virtual, which brings probability into our encounter (in the actual) with chaos as the virtual, or as the unthinkable. *As* unthinkable, the unthinkable cannot, however, be thought of as random, and not all effects of the unthinkable are random either. Henceforth, I shall understand chaos in all three senses – the virtual, the unthinkable, and the random – joined together.

One can, then, describe Romantic or nonclassical ontology as follows. The ultimate constitutive entities of the domain under investigation do exist. There are, however, uncircumventable *epistemological* limits upon how far our thought concerning this character can reach, even in principle. This precludes assigning of any ontology and thus applying any terms, including those used at the moment (entities, constitutive, ultimate, workings, being, becoming, time, and so forth) beyond this limit, and hence to the ultimate nature of this existence, which is literally unthinkable, ultimately unthinkable even as unthinkable. The application of these terms is possible only at the level of *effects*, where our

---

[19] Deleuze and Guattari, *What is Philosophy?*, p. 118.

thinking and hence ontology remain classical, while the (acausal) *efficacity* of which is beyond the reach of thought. It follows that 'efficacity', too, is a provisional name and is ultimately inapplicable. In Deleuze's terms, these effects appear at the level of *the actual* and this efficacity corresponds to *the virtual*.

Nonclassical ontology reaches beyond Kant's ontology of noumena or things-in-themselves, at least as it is expressly delineated by Kant. While unknowable, Kant's things-in-themselves are still in principle thinkable, even thinkable as causal, which makes Kant's ontology classical in the present definition.[20] It is true that this thinking cannot be guaranteed to be right, and it may, Kant says, only need to be justified practically rather than theoretically.[21] However, this thinking could in principle be right, and what Kant calls reason [*Vernunft*] has at least (Kant in fact claims more) a chance to be right. Accordingly, the ultimate nature of existence is not placed beyond thought altogether, in the way it is under the conditions of nonclassical ontology, in which one cannot apply the terms things-in-themselves, or noumena, or again, any other term or concept at the ultimate level. This also makes the suspension of causality at the ultimate level automatic, because causality is a thinkable attribute (although causality is possible at intermediate levels considered). As noted above, the unthinkable could not be thought of as random either. But then, we may not be able to conceive of the absolutely random, which makes randomness different from causality in this regard. One should not, however, identify the unthinkable with the absolutely random, in part because certain collective effects of the unthinkable are ordered, and hence cannot arise from that which is absolutely random. The recourse to probability becomes unavoidable under the conditions of nonclassical ontology, and for fundamental reasons, rather than merely practical ones, as would be the case in a classical causal ontology that might require the use of probability, and, as Wittgenstein thought, conceivably all classical ontologies are causal.[22] I shall adopt the Bayesian definition of probability, as a *degree of belief*, which is especially suitable in nonclassical ontology, because it also applies to single, unrepeatable events, rather than only to repeatable ones, such as a coin toss.[23]

[20] Immanuel Kant, *Critique of Pure Reason*, trans. Paul Guyer and Allen W. Wood (Cambridge: Cambridge University Press, 1997), p. 115.

[21] Ibid. p. 115.

[22] Ludwig Wittgenstein, *Tractatus Logico-Philosophicus*, trans. Charles Kay Ogden (London: Routledge, 1985), p. 175.

[23] On the Bayesian philosophy of probability, see Edwin Thompson Jaynes, *Probability*

A famous and spectacular example of classical ontology is Sophocles' *Oedipus the King*, where the apparently random or chance events are ultimately predetermined by the inescapable necessity of fate, no matter how one tries to circumvent it. Or, such is the case if one so reads the ultimate ontology of the events and temporality in the play – a reading that Hölderlin's reading appears to question, allowing, however, that this ontology is presumed by Oedipus or other characters in the play. In Hölderlin's reading, the tragic fate is determined otherwise. It is a form of necessity without causality, manifested (at the level of the actual) in the structure of tragic representation, as the interplay of rhythm and caesura. The characters' ontological decisions or bets, 'calculations', such as Oedipus' decision to pursue, against Tiresias' advice, his investigation of the murder of Laios, are measured against this fate and in relation to this structure, especially caesuras, which reflect the fact that the tragic fate will defeat these bets and plunge the characters into chaos, without return. This is how the structure of tragedy is defined or 'calculated' by Sophocles, in Hölderlin's reading – that is, according to a precise 'calculable law', which nevertheless relates the calculable to that which is unthinkable and, hence, incalculable.[24]

## THE STRUCTURE OF TRAGEDY AND THE ARCHITECTURE OF TEMPORALITY IN HÖLDERLIN: RHYTHM, CAESURA, AND THE UNTHINKABLE

The nonclassical scheme itself outlined above is very general and leaves space for differences in the architecture of the effects a given version of this scheme would contain – effects that are thinkable or knowable, even if their efficacity is beyond the reach of thought. Indeed, while always unthinkable, this efficacity is not the same even in the case of a given field, let alone as governing all possible fields. While each time unthinkable, it is each time different, different even in the case of each new effect or new set of effects. What is, then, the specific ontological architecture of Hölderlin's vision that lead him to, or emerged from, his reading of tragedy?

The most immediately manifested effects are those of the rhythmic

*Theory: The Logic of Science* (Cambridge: Cambridge University Press, 2003), pp. xix–xxviii. Deleuze sees probability as a degree of belief and thus on Bayesian lines in connection with Hume and empiricism, although Hume's ontology is ultimately classical. See Gilles Deleuze, *Pure Immanence: A Life* (New York: Zone Books, 2005), p. 44.

24 Hölderlin, *Essays and Letters*, p. 317.

successions of events or, importantly, 'representations [*Vorstellungen*]', such as are developed through the tragic hero, successions altered by caesura, which also represent the tragic *agon*, and as Lacoue-Labarthe rightly argues, becomes the governing principle of the structure of tragedy.[25] However, in the present reading of Hölderlin's scheme, there is a further discreteness or, as it were, 'caesuration', underlying this structure, which is as follows. At the ultimate *ontologically available* limit, all individual events (which could also be events of thought), including those composing each rhythmic succession, are always *discrete* or *singular* with respect to each other, while the ultimate efficacity of all events is *not available* to thought, is *das Undenkbare*, and hence is beyond ontology.[26] These ultimate underlying events are not only isolated from their background, which defines events in general, but are also, when they comprise a multiplicity, disconnected, 'caesured', from each other, without any causal or otherwise lawful relationships between any *two events* (I shall explain this emphasis presently). This is the case even when these events occur in a temporal sequence, to the degree and within the limits that the concept of sequence can apply, because their temporal succession may only be apparent even ontologically. The concept of sequence or even temporality cannot apply to the ultimate *efficacity* of these events, which is unavailable to thought. In other words, at this ultimate available level of the constitution of events, all events are always separated from each other, and any *two of them* are unrelated to each other. This underlying manifold of events can be random overall, although it may appear ordered or rhythmic at a lower resolution. However – and this is a crucial aspect of the nonclassical ontological architecture – in certain, but not all, circumstances, some collectivities of such underlying events can have an order or rhythm to them. The overall structure of such collectivities is not random, even though *any two events* still cannot be connected by any law (hence my emphasis here and above). In the case of tragedy, this order or rhythm reflects the nature of fate as a form of necessity without causality. I shall return to this apparently (but as will be seen, only apparently) paradoxical ontological architecture below.

For the moment, if considered more coarsely, a given event-field may

---

[25] Ibid. pp. 317, 325 (translation modified); Philippe Lacoue-Labarthe, *Heidegger, Art, and Politics*, trans. Chris Turner (Cambridge: Blackwell, 1990), p. 41.

[26] An event in the sense discussed here is connected to but is different from an event or singularity in Deleuze's sense of *heicceity*, defined by a trajectory, a line of flight, which, in the present view, would still be underlined by a discrete manifold (Deleuze and Guattari, *What is Philosophy?*, pp. 156–7).

include intervals or trajectories of continuity and continuous temporality or intervals that have discrete rhythmic structures, even if the underlying, more coarsely grained, manifold of events does not. The possibility of such continuous intervals and discontinuous rhythmic sequences (in this case one could speak of sequentiality), along with the counter-rhythm and caesuras that interrupt them, are central for Hölderlin's concepts of rhythm and caesura. However, at the ultimate available level of resolution any such interval would always resolve into a multiplicity, either random or itself rhythmic, of discrete events that might, but need not, have occurred in close temporal proximity to each other. It is this proximity, whether temporally defined or not, that prevents one from perceiving their discreteness. On the other hand, it is this discreteness that gives rise to any caesura and its counter-rhythmic effects, which interrupt a given rhythmic sequence, continuous or discontinuous. An interruption may occur, and generally does (especially, in the structure of tragedy), due to an intersection between two rhythmic sequences, but even then each of these sequences is still ultimately discrete. It is, I argue, the corresponding broken and nonsequential – 'caesured' – temporality that is at stake in Hölderlin, who formally represents it by the structure of tragedy. Placed beyond the reach of thought, as *das Undenkbare*, the efficacity of all events and sequences (rhythmic or broken by a caesura) considered cannot be assumed to be either continuous or discontinuous, or forming a mixture of both. Nor can it be seen as temporal, unless one defines this efficacity as time, which one would be reluctant to do because one would then *name*, as 'time', this efficacity. It is true that 'efficacity' is also a name. However, it is assumed here to be a provisional and ultimately inapplicable name. It also has strategic neutrality, which is difficult to have in the case of time. Hölderlin, too, uses *das Undenkbare* or *das Unförmliche*, and not *Zeit*, in (un)naming this efficacity.

The architecture just outlined, again, defines and is partly extracted from, or constructed by, Hölderlin on the basis of his reading of *Antigone* and *Oedipus the King*, but also on the basis of his reading of, among other things, Kant's philosophy. In both plays, counter-rhythmic caesuras, marked by the intervention of Tiresias in the end (ancient tragedy) of the first and the beginning (modern tragedy) of the second play, introduce a disjunction between two sets of events.[27] As noted above, a caesura breaks a possible rhythmic or causal connection (causality is replaced by fate, as a form of necessity without causality)

---

[27] Hölderlin, *Essays and Letters*, p. 324.

between two rhythmic tragic representations, and relates them not in terms of succession but in terms of a kind of equilibrium, as the structure of representation as such. According to Hölderlin:

> In the rhythmic succession of representations [*Vorstellungen*] wherein the *transport* [in French in the original] represents itself demands a counter-rhythmic interruption, a pure word, *that which in metric is called a caesura*, in order to counteract the turbulent [successive] alternation of ideas at its climax, so that that it is not the alternation of representations that now appears but a representation as such.[28]

However, 'the tragic *transport* [itself] is essentially empty, and is the most unbounded of all', devoid of all connections.[29] This emptiness and unboundedness of the tragic transport is in accord with the argument given here concerning the ultimately discrete character of all events, including those of thought, so that every one of them could, in principle, lead to a caesura. The rhythm of any life can radically alter at any point, revealing this underlying 'caesured' discontinuity, rarely completely random, even if not always manifesting a tragic fate, and hence making this caesura belong to the structure of tragic or tragic-like representation. Such is the case unless instead of an unthinkable efficacity one assumes an ultimate underlying continuity that classically (and causally) connects everything. I shall return to this possibility below. According to Lacoue-Labarthe:

> In tragedy, but also in history, of which tragedy is more than emblematic (in reality it is its structural matrix or, alternatively, the tragic Law is historicity itself), the law finitude takes the form of the 'categorical turning away (*kategorische Umkehr*)' of the God, which renders *imperative* for man a turning back toward the earth. . . . For Hölderlin (as for Hegel, but at a quite other level), Sophoclean tragedy was the 'testament' of the Greek experience of the divine, that is to say, the document attesting to the necessary withdrawal of the divine. By the same token, as for Hegel, too (at least the Hegel who is not yet Hegelian), it held the secret of historicity, of the destiny of history as nothing other than erratic accomplishment of the Law of finitude (and there, as everyone knows, Hölderlin probably has nothing to do with Hegel). In these conditions – it little matters whether this lies outside Hölderlinian 'theology' or not – it is not perhaps impossible to raise the caesura to the rank of a concept, if not *the concept*, of historicity. A caesura would be that, within history, which interrupts history and opens up another possibility of history.[30]

---

[28]  Ibid. p. 317 (translation modified).
[29]  Ibid. p. 317.
[30]  Lacoue-Labarthe, *Heidegger, Art, and Politics*, pp. 43, 45.

It might be more accurate to say that a caesura opens a possibility of another, different – 'erratic' or rather (it is not entirely erratic) 'caesured' – history, and in the first place, reveals a different, rhythmic temporality, which is the *condition* of all history. I would also prefer to speak, as in fact Hölderlin does, of *the condition* of history in the sense of Deleuze's transcendental empiricism in *Difference and Repetition*, rather than *the condition of the possibility* of history of Kant's transcendental idealism. However, Lacoue-Labarthe is right to see caesura as a concept.

The conceptual architecture just outlined defines, I argue, both Hölderlin's thought and the Hölderlin-Deleuze juncture. Admittedly, one could read either Hölderlin or Deleuze differently. It is, for example, not clear whether Lacoue-Labarthe's reading sees Hölderlin's thinking in strictly nonclassical terms, although he comes close when questioning the assumption of an underlying continuum beneath the fractured temporality defined by caesura, which, as will be seen, some of Hölderlin's statements might invite. Deleuze's virtual, which is here read in terms of the nonclassical, unthinkable efficacity of the actual, is more often seen as ontologically conceivable, thinkable, and even describable, again, in continuous or causal terms.[31] Even if such is ultimately the case, however, Deleuze's analyses, especially that of the synthesis of time, advanced in *Difference and Repetition*, in conjunction with Hölderlin, suggests a nonclassical architecture of the relationships between the actual, defined in terms of effects, and the virtual, understood as the inconceivable efficacy of these effects. It is true that the virtual is, according to Deleuze, *real*, but that does not mean that it needs to be assumed to be describable by any form of ontological architecture or accessible to thought at all – quite the contrary. Hence, this efficacity cannot be assigned temporality, although it is responsible for all temporality.

It follows that the unthinkable cannot be divine either. It is true that at the moment of caesura, in a tragic representation, the God is, according to Hölderlin, time, is 'nothing but time,' and it is for that reason the God forgets himself at this moment, which may suggest that the God, 'the Father of Time', is the efficacity of time.[32] But, then, this efficacity would not be unthinkable, at least when it comes to actual historicity, even if not in tragedy. The divine, the God, is still thinkable, thinkable as God, even

---

[31] A prominent example is DeLanda, who sees the virtual as continuous and causal, on the model of the so-called 'phase space' of classical physics. See Manuel DeLanda, *Intensive Science and Virtual Philosophy* (Minneapolis: University of Minnesota Press, 2013). For a reading of the virtual on the model of quantum physics, defined by nonclassical ontology, see Plotnitsky, 'Chaosmologies'.

[32] Hölderlin, *Essays and Letters*, p. 323.

if, as in negative or mystical theology, none of God's actual attributes is thinkable. In this respect the situation is parallel to that of causality, and more than parallel, because God is also causality. It is Nietzsche's radical critique of causality in philosophy that leads him to nonclassical ontology and to his concept of the death of God. It is the unthinkable (and hence, again, acausal and un-divine) efficacity that ultimately creates 'the conditions of [pure or empty forms] of time and space', forms exposed, unlike the unthinkable itself (which cannot be exposed), at the moment of a caesura.[33] This move towards the unthinkable appears to be characteristic of Sophocles, who, unlike other Greek tragic writers, knows how to portray human understanding [*Verstand*] 'wandering beneath the Unthinkable' [*unter Undenkbarem wandelnd*], the abyss or (since this word is no longer applicable either) the un-abyss, the beyond-abyss of the unthinkable 'above' the divine.[34] If this is the God's withdrawal, one could (I am not saying Sophocles or even Hölderlin have done so) read it as a tragic representation of the unthinkable and, hence, un-divine efficacity of the divine, and thus, with Nietzsche, as announcing the death of God, or at least a figure of the death of God.

As noted earlier, under these conditions any actual individual event, at least, again, in the ultimate available graining, is irreducibly singular and cannot be comprehended by law, and hence cannot be positioned in a calculable relation to any other event that precedes or follows it.

However, in certain circumstances, collectivities of events exhibit ordered, rhythmic patterns, (which may be interrupted or counter-rhythmically hinged by caesuras), patterns sometimes manifesting, in tragedy or in life, a tragic fate as necessity without causality. In other words, the events involved may be collectively organised, but no two events are lawfully connected to each other: the law or rhythm of this organisation does not allow us to put any single event in a determined or determinable relation to any other single event or group of events, preceding or following it. This situation may appear paradoxical, and it is paradoxical, if considered classically: there is no conceivable logic that could explain how this is possible. The paradox is resolved if one adopts nonclassical ontology: this organisation is possible, indeed actually, historically occurs, but how it comes about is in principle inaccessible to thought. This would be the nonclassical or Romantic meaning of 'chaos-

---

[33] Ibid.

[34] Ibid. p. 326 (translation modified). The phrase 'the abyss above' occurs (in a different set of contexts) in the title of Silke Weineck's book, *The Abyss Above: Philosophy and Poetic Madness in Plato, Hölderlin, and Nietzsche* (Albany: SUNY Press, 2002), which offers an important analysis of Hölderlin.

mic', although Joyce's famous coinage can of course be understood otherwise. Hölderlin's concept of rhythm is a chaosmic conjunction of three key elements – the inaccessible efficacity of all events, the incalculable emergence of individual events, and of rhythmic effects and counterrhythmic movement, giving rise to caesuras, which break or, as in the structure of tragedy, join rhythmic sequences. I would argue (although this argument cannot be fully pursued here) that an analogous, even if not identical, chaosmic architecture defines the concept of refrain in Deleuze and Guattari, or, again, the structure of concepts, which always has a refrain to it.[35]

Now, the structure of tragedy or its law is 'calculable', which is one of Hölderlin's opening points in his theory of tragedy or history, and which Lacoue-Labarthe is right to stress.[36] However, in the present reading, the (nonclassical) calculus of this structure is entirely different from the classical one, for example in Kant, which presupposes the underlying causal order – a difference on which Lacoue-Labarthe does not appear to reflect in his linking of Hölderlin and Kant, thus missing the nonclassical potential of Hölderlin's thought.[37] This calculus is formally rigorous, precise, and it even finds a parallel in the mathematical structure of quantum theory.[38] The law of historicity or of temporality need not depend on, and perhaps cannot be expressed in, mathematical terms, unless we deal with temporality in modern physics, and even there our mathematical representation is limited. Luckily, we have Hölderlin's calculus defined by rhythm and caesura to help us. But if we want to use this calculus in real life, it only allows us to estimate probabilities of possible events, in the absence of an underlying (causal) architecture that could, in principle, guarantee such estimates.

It remains crucial, however, that the effects of the unthinkable, the effects that compel us to infer the unthinkable, are not only random, and arguably cannot be, because then the unthinkable could be just thought of as random, assuming, again, that we can think absolute randomness. Instead, these effects form a complex, chaosmic, interplay of randomness and order, or of all three forms of chaos (the unthinkable,

---

[35] Deleuze and Guattari, *A Thousand Plateaus*, pp. 312–14; Deleuze and Guattari, *What is Philosophy?*, p. 21.

[36] Hölderlin, *Essays and Letters*, p. 217; Lacoue-Labarthe, *Heidegger, Art, and Politics*, p. 41.

[37] See, however, S. Weber, '"Giebt es auf Erden ein Maas?" – "Is There a Measure on Earth?"' (forthcoming), for a more nonclassically oriented reading.

[38] Arkady Plotnitsky, *Epistemology and Probability: Bohr, Heisenberg, Schrödinger, and the Nature of Quantum Thinking* (Berlin and New York: Springer, 2009).

the random, and the virtual) and rhythmic and counter-rhythmic order, an interplay of the particular type, as here described. In dealing with this chaosmos, we are still 'plunged' into chaos, not necessarily in the way, say, Oedipus is, but in the way we are by philosophy, science, and art, by 'casting planes over chaos' and finding chaosmic ways of relating to the world and counteracting opinion.[39]

### THREE SYNTHESES OF TIME, FROM KANT TO HÖLDERLIN TO DELEUZE

Hölderlin's conception of rhythm and caesura originates in poetry, and is transferred, by a way of a structural isomorphism, first to tragedy and then to history. A caesura breaks the rhythm of a line of poetry so as to make the two parts involved not linked sequentially but placed in an equilibrium of a single structure. The concept of caesura has, thus, an essential relation to time. This relation is manifested more immediately in a rhythm of poetry or in a musical composition, but found elsewhere, specifically and paradigmatically in the structure of tragedy, or history. The tragic moment is 'a counter-rhythmic interruption' in the course or succession of events.[40] But, according to Hölderlin, the possibility of caesura also reflects a different form or a different synthesis of time by separating it from movement, linked to the continuous (linear or circular) time of movements of bodies or clocks, a key point for Deleuze. Indeed, the law of rhythm, as a result, extends to and arguably originates in temporality. In both Hölderlin and Deleuze, this extension proceeds via Kant, who separates time from its dependence on movement, and thus in effect gives time an interdependent rhythm, although not counter-rhythm and caesura, as he should have done in Hölderlin's view. The conception of temporality that Hölderlin envisions is defined by the interplay of continuous (or discrete but rhythmic) structures and discontinuous or counter-rhythmic intrusions – by cosmos and chaos (chaosmos), causality (or necessity) and randomness or chance – without, by virtue of its nonclassical character, ever making it possible for us to conceive of the ultimate efficacity of this organisation. This nonclassical rhythmic law of temporality implies the irreducible, rhizomatic multiplicity of temporal effects. Thus, it converts a line into a rhizome, possibly even in the case of the (effect of the) line in mathematics. Thus, this law also links the irreducibly unthinkable and the

---

[39] Deleuze and Guattari, *What is Philosophy?*, p. 202.
[40] Hölderlin, *Essays and Letters*, pp. 318, 325.

irreducibly multiple. The irreducibly unthinkable is arguably the more Hölderlinian and the irreducibly multiple the more Deleuzean aspect of this situation, found in the concept of refrain, which relates to 'the intra-assemblage', the 'organisation' of which is 'very rich and complex'.[41] According to Deleuze:

> The Kantian initiative can be taken up, and the form of time can support both the death of God and the fractured I, but in the course of a quite different understanding of the passive self. In this sense, it is correct to claim that it is neither Fichte nor Hegel who is a descendent of Kant – rather, it is Hölderlin, who discovers the emptiness of pure time and, in this emptiness, simultaneously the continuous diversion of the divine, the prolonged structure of the I, and the constitutive passion of the self. Hölderlin saw in this form of time both the essence of tragedy and the adventure of Oedipus, as though these were complementary figures of the same death drive. Is it possible that Kantian philosophy should thus be the heir of Oedipus?[42]

This heritage is not surprising, for one thing, because 'the Kantian initiative' is a culmination of a longer history beginning with the pre-Socratics and the Greek tragic dramatists, which, as discussed earlier, would also support the idea of the death of God. On the other hand, this type of philosophical and proto-psychoanalytical enrichment of the concept of time, also linking time to thought, 'pure time' to 'pure thought', may appear peculiar. Hölderlin, however, gives this enrichment logic because it occurs at a tragic moment, defined by a caesura. At this point, 'nothing exists besides the conditions of time and space':

> At a moment like this man forgets both himself and God and, in a sacred manner, of course, turns himself round like a traitor. For at the most extreme edge of suffering, nothing exists besides the conditions of time and space. Man forgets himself there because he is wholly in the moment; and God, because he is nothing else than time. And both are unfaithful: time, because at such a moment it reverses categorically – beginning and end simply cannot be connected; and man, because at this moment he must follow the categorical reversal, and therefore simply cannot be in what is to follow after this reversal what he was at the beginning.[43]

In the present reading, both space and time are effects of the unthinkable, which is not temporal. Nor is it divine, as the withdrawal of the God or its becoming time becomes an allegory of the unthinkable giving rise to time, and hence an allegory of or supporting the death of God.

[41] Deleuze and Guattari, *A Thousand Plateaus*, p. 323.
[42] Deleuze, *Difference and Repetition*, p. 87.
[43] Hölderlin, *Essays and Letters*, pp. 323–4.

Deleuze further argues that, prior to Kant, the synthesis of time, as in 'the second synthesis of time', while moving in the direction by grounding time 'in the pure past of the Ideas', does not, nevertheless, sufficiently separate time from movement. Even with Leibniz and Hegel, time remains linked too closely to the time of *physis*, either periodic (circular) or infinite (an infinite continuum). These two forms of time are connected, because the periodic, circular time of hours, days, years, and so forth, essentially periodises the continuum of time, by means of clocks and their continuous movement. Deleuze notes this as well: 'The joint, *cardo*, is what ensures the subordination of time to those properly cardinal points through which pass the periodic movements which it measures (time, number of the movement, for the soul as much as for the world).'[44] This cardinality is that of the continuum, such as that of real numbers, assumed to be in one-to-one correspondence with the points on the straight line and, as numbers, arranged and thus ordered accordingly. This 'natural' idea proved to be problematic by Cantor's set theory, which introduced the concept of cardinal numbers. For the moment, this is also the standard way of measuring or even defining time, physically or (with qualifications) phenomenally. Hence, time is still in effect subordinated to the movement of bodies and clocks (or their images), which was the view of Leibniz, who is mentioned by Deleuze, alongside Hegel.[45]

Although relatively brief, Deleuze's analysis of the pre-Kantian synthesis of time is subtle, and it would be difficult to consider it here. Deleuze's main point suffices to understand his move to the third synthesis of time in Kant and Hölderlin. This point is that the synthesis of time before Kant, and specifically the second synthesis of time, 'creates a circle' by 'introduc[ing] *movement into the soul* rather than *time into thought*', which is a decisive difference on both counts: a shift from movement to time, and a shift from the soul to thought.[46] The question becomes what is the empty form of time, entirely divorced from movement, as the third synthesis of time. The answer is helped by Hölderlin's theory of tragedy, as embodying his law of rhythm and caesura, which defines the concept of time as 'time . . . out of joint'. *Hamlet* is, thus, added to the mix, making the time-out-of-joint tragedy of the Northern prince *joined* to the Northern philosopher's (Kant's) synthesis of pure time, with Hölderlin providing a deeper thinking concerning both

[44] Deleuze, *Difference and Repetition*, p. 88.
[45] Ibid.
[46] Ibid.

concepts and thus bringing Hamlet and Oedipus together yet again. According to Deleuze, who has already linked Kant and Oedipus via Hölderlin:

> What does it mean: the empty form of time or third synthesis? The Northern Prince says 'time is out of joint'. Can it be that the Northern philosopher says the same thing: that he should be Hamletian because he is Oedipal? The joint, *cardo*, is what ensures the subordination of time to those properly cardinal points through which pass the periodic movements which it measures (time, number of the movement, for the soul as much as for the world). By contrast, time out of joint means demented time or time outside the curve which gave it a god, liberated from the overly simple circular figure, freed from the events which made up its content, its relation to movement overturned; in short, time presenting itself as an empty and pure form. Time itself unfolds (that is, apparently ceases to be a circle) instead of things unfolding within it (following the overly simple circular figure). It ceases to be cardinal and becomes ordinal, a pure *order* of time. Hölderlin said it [time] no longer 'rhymed', because it was distributed unequally on both sides of a 'caesura', as a result of which beginning and end no longer coincided. We may define the order of time [time out of joint] as this purely formal distribution of the unequal in the function of a caesura. We can then distinguish a more or less extensive past and a future in inverse proportion, but the future and the past here are not empirical and dynamic determinations of time: they are formal and fixed characteristics which follow *a priori* from the order of time, as though they comprised a static synthesis of time. The synthesis is necessarily static, because time is no longer subordinated to movement; time is the most radical form of change, but the form of change does not change. The caesura, along with the before and after that it ordains one and for all, constitutes the fracture in the I (the caesura is exactly the point at which the fracture appears).[47]

It is clear that, under these conditions, defined by the eruptive counter-rhythmic effect of caesura, the dependence of time on the movement of bodies or the soul and, along with them, the continuity and causality of time are suspended, as against the preceding history of philosophy or science. To make this suspension rigorous, I argue here, one might need to reach beyond Kant, even if against his own grain, as Hölderlin does. This may be why Deleuze is compelled to appeal to Hölderlin at this juncture, and this is, in my view, why, although rarely invoked, Hölderlin is so important for Deleuze. While separating time from movement, Kant, following Newton, still assigns to time, just as he does to space, unity and continuity, which reinstates the continuity of time

---

[47] Ibid. pp. 88–9.

(no caesuras in time itself) and, thus, implicitly movement, insofar as time is ultimately a continuous flow.[48] Kant also maintains the principle of causality throughout. In his view, 'time out of joint' is still an effect of time that is never out of joint, the time of the continuum or the continuum of time, in its ordinality and *implicit* cardinality, implicit because it requires us to move from Kant to Cantor. Ordinality could be continuous as well, as Cantor, who introduced this language and is Deleuze's source here, showed. Deleuze detects in Kant a certain groundness that stands in the way of developing an adequate synthesis of pure time (the third synthesis of time) in the second synthesis of time, and not only in Kant but also in Leibniz and Hegel. But, as Deleuze also says:

> Just as the ground is in a sense 'bent' and must lead us towards a beyond, so the second synthesis of time points beyond itself in the direction of a third which denounces *the illusion of the in-itself* as still a correlate of representation. The in-itself of the past and the repetition in reminiscence constitute a kind of 'effect', like an optical effect, or rather the erotic effect of memory itself.[49]

The language of effects is notable here. But the character of the efficacity of these effects is still a question: indeed, as I argue here, it is *the* question. As I explained, the ultimately continuous ground-ness of this efficacity re-emerges in Kant, and moreover, Kant's 'in-itself', Kant's 'illusion of the in-itself', while no longer correlative to an actual representation, or a representation in the actual, is, as virtual, still thinkable, as against the irreducibly unthinkable efficacity one finds in Hölderlin. In Hölderlin, in the present reading, this efficacity is seen as neither continuous nor discontinuous, nor again as anything else, including anything temporal, however rhythmic or counter rhythmic. Any actual rhythm or counter-rhythm, caesura, and time, continuous or out of joint, and hence 'pure time', are effects of this unthinkable virtual efficacity. Deleuze agrees, at least in closing his discussion of Hölderlin here: 'the extreme formality [of pure time] is there only for an *excessive* formlessness (Hölderlin's *Unförmliche*)'. This point is perhaps missed by Lacoue-Labarthe in discussing space and time as 'pure forms' in Hölderlin.[50] This excessive formlessness may be called 'pure time' only insofar as it is no longer 'time' at all in any sense we can give to such a concept, in this respect

[48] Kant, *Critique of Pure Reason*, pp. 162–70, 178–84.
[49] Deleuze, *Difference and Repetition*, p. 88 (emphasis added).
[50] Ibid. p. 92 (emphasis added); Lacoue-Labarthe, *Heidegger, Art, and Politics*, pp. 43–4. Both Deleuze and Lacoue-Labarthe, however, follow Jean Beaufret, *Hölderlin et Sophocle* (Paris: Gérard Monfort, 1983).

making the term 'pure' more important than 'time', because, under these conditions, nothing we could in principle think could ultimately be pure. The special significance of caesura-like effects is, again, that these effects manifest the fact that, given a sufficient resolution, any apparent continuum, temporal or comprised by events, is ultimately underlined by a discrete manifold. The efficacity of this discrete manifold cannot, in the present view, be assumed to be discontinuous any more than continuous, or, correlatively, be causal. It is this architecture that rigorously prevents us from speaking of subordinating time or event-manifolds to movement.

CONTINUITY AND DISCONTINUITY BEYOND CALCULUS, THE ETERNAL RETURN, AND THE *UNFÖRMLICHE*

Hölderlin's and Deleuze's analyses of rhythm and temporality have important connections to the history of mathematics and specifically to calculus – connections, it is true, that are only implicit in Hölderlin, but expressly developed by Deleuze in *Difference and Repetition*. This is hardly surprising. Both Hölderlin and Deleuze are concerned with the relationships between continuity and discontinuity, and the difficulty of rigorously defining the constitution of a *continuous* manifoldness – say, a straight line – as comprised by *discrete* individual points, corresponding to real numbers, as noted above. This difficulty may indeed be insurmountable in mathematics, as revealed by Cantor's analysis invoked by Deleuze. In the case of Hölderlin's concept of rhythm, this difficulty is reflected in and, in a way, resolved by suspending continuity altogether at the level of the ultimate available *graining* of events, and suspending both continuity and discontinuity at the level of the ultimate efficacity of events.[51] One of the main developments of eighteenth- and then nineteenth-century mathematics was a radical rethinking of the nature of continuity, in conjunction with establishing, around the time of Hölderlin's work, the mathematical foundations of calculus, which until that time, while extraordinarily effective practically, lacked rigorous mathematical definitions of its key concepts.[52] This rethinking

---

[51] As I noted, this type of architecture of effects re-emerged later on in quantum mechanics. I have considered these connections in Arkady Plotnitsky, '"In Principle Observable": Werner Heisenberg's Discovery of Quantum Mechanics and Romantic Imagination', *Parallax* 10:3, (2004), pp. 20–35.

[52] A proper understanding of the difference between continuity and differentiability was part of this history. Although Bernhard Riemann provided some earlier insights, Karl Weierstrass was the first to construct an example of a function that, while continuous

allowed one to more properly address, even if not ultimately resolve, the difficulties and paradoxes plaguing the subject in mathematics, physics, and philosophy from the pre-Socratics on. It is in part because of this history and the way in which it shaped the relationships between mathematics and philosophy that calculus plays a major role in *Difference and Repetition*, also in connection with the synthesis of time, which leads Deleuze to Kant and Hölderlin. Cantor's theory of ordinal and cardinal numbers, to which Deleuze refers in the passage on the third synthesis of time, cited above, is part of this history. Cantor's theory was developed well after the time of Hölderlin and was unlikely to have any connections to Hölderlin's ideas. The theory, however, confronted the problems essentially analogous to those to which Hölderlin's and, after Cantor, Deleuze's thinking responded as well, admittedly, as philosophical, rather than mathematical, problems. But then, these problems were also philosophical, as well as mathematical, for Cantor and other mathematicians who addressed them.

The textual evidence for the connections between Hölderlin's thinking and calculus is indirect, but is manifested in Hölderlin's appeal in his discussion of rhythm and time to 'calculus' and its avatars (*calcul, Rechnung, Berechnung*), as in considering the *calculability* of the law of tragedy by virtue of its rhythmic and counter-rhythmic order that defines it. As the preceding analysis suggests, Hölderlin appears to have questioned the model of continuity analogous to that defining and defined by calculus (and the theory of continuous functions), at least as applicable to temporality, ultimately defined by continuity in Kant, in part following Newton and calculus. In approaching temporality, Hölderlin appears to envision a very different relation between continuity and discontinuity, and a different form of calculus of the temporal, as considered here. As noted earlier, at stake in his analysis of the structure of tragedy and, by the same token, historicity is 'the calculable law'. One must, however, establish 'how the content is different from this law, and by what means; how the particular content relates to the general calculation within a *continuum*, which, though endless, is nevertheless determined throughout; and how the developments and the intended statement, the living sense of which cannot be calculated, may be related to the calculable law'.[53]

at every point, does not allow for a derivative and hence is not differentiable at any point. This roughly means that, if one thinks of it as a curve, one cannot define a tangent to this curve at any point.

[53] Hölderlin, *Essays and Letters*, p. 317 (emphasis added).

It is possible to read this elaboration, and hence Hölderlin's ontology, on the model of calculus, for example, as used by Dedekind to define real numbers, some of which, specifically irrational or transcendental, are incalculable, through the discrete, and thus 'calculable', sequences of rational numbers (speaking very roughly). This definition was introduced in the 1870s, long after Hölderlin's death, but the role of series in differential calculus, which is similar and which in fact was Dedekind's model, might well have been familiar to him (it also plays an important role in Deleuze).[54] In this reading, the calculable law, technically applied to the discrete, could be related to the infinite of a continuum, which would be thus determined without being strictly computed, and then the calculable law of the tragic representation would be related to the incalculable 'living sense' of this representation. This reading is possible, but it would be difficult, if not impossible, to relate it to *das Undenkbare* as opposed to the present reading, which also has a much greater formal generality. The calculable formal law of tragedy or (this is the same *formal* law) of history only relates to the temporal effects of the unthinkable, which is beyond all calculations, including the type of approximation found in calculus, of the continuous by the discrete. This is because the ultimately reachable or establishable architecture of effects is always *discrete*, if sometimes organised, rhythmic, with any continuity appearing only at a coarse, low-resolution, as a second-level effect.[55] It is this underlying manifold that gives rise to any given caesura that interrupts continuity or discontinuous rhythms. Crucially, however, it is not simply a reversal of the ontological order of the continuous and the discontinuous, although this reversal takes place (the discontinuous always underlies the continuous) and is important, but of seeing both as effects of the unthinkable, which is neither continuous nor discontinuous.

The conceptions of temporality available at Hölderlin's time could

---

[54] On the connection between this definition and Deleuze's concept of temporality, see Daniela Voss, *Conditions of Thought: Deleuze and Transcendental Ideas* (Edinburgh: Edinburgh University Press, 2013), pp. 236–41.

[55] This conception is again, different from Kant, or Leibniz or Hegel. Leibniz's case is especially interesting in the present context because he pondered the constitution of the continuous (out of points) even before his work on calculus, where his thinking appears to correspond to what is now known as fractals. See Samuel Levey, 'The interval of motion in Leibniz's *pacidius philalethi*', *Nous* 37:3, (2003), pp. 371–416. And in connection with Deleuze, see Simon Duffy, 'The Question of Deleuze's Neo-Leibnizianism', in Rosi Braidotti and Patricia Pisters (eds), *Revisiting Normativity with Deleuze* (London: Bloomsbury, 2012), pp. 51–642, which follows Levey's analysis. However, this ontology is different and less complex than that of Hölderlin, as considered here, because, while not differentiable, fractal manifolds are *continuous*.

not accommodate this view because they all had assumed an underlying efficacious architecture of such effects as either continuous or discontinuous, as in atomism, which was beginning to enjoy new prominence at the time. Models and calculus analogous to that of Hölderlin are, however, conceivable in modern physics, specifically in quantum theory, and in post-Cantorian mathematical logic. These mathematical models conceptualise the line as irreducibly inaccessible, beyond the reach of thought, which prevents us from assuming that the ultimate constitution of the line is in any way linear, is a line in any sense that we can give to this term. As I said, however, temporality and rhythm need not require rigorous mathematical models, unless they deal with physics. On the other hand, philosophical conceptions of both, possibly supplied by literature, can suggest mathematical models, which can be made rigorous.

Whether Deleuze subscribes to this type of concept of temporality or rhythm may, as I said, depend on a given interpretation and a given juncture of his thought or writing. Even if he does not, however, the conjunction between his thought and that of Hölderlin poses the question of the possibility of such concepts, as his analysis of Hölderlin and the third synthesis of time in *Difference and Repetition* makes apparent. This analysis, I would contend, comes close to this conception of temporality, as his conclusion suggests by bringing together Hölderlin and Nietzsche, via eternal return. The connections between Nietzsche's eternal return and the third synthesis of time in Deleuze would require a separate discussion. I shall limit myself to citing the conclusion of a long paragraph, which closes this analysis on an 'excessive formlessness' of Hölderlin's *Unförmliche*, although *das Undenkbare* is at stake here as well:

> [T]he order of time, time as pure and empty form [discovered by Hölderlin], has precisely undone that circle [the overly simple circle that has as its content the passing present and as its shape the past of reminiscence]. It is undone in favor of a less simple and much more secret, much more tortuous, much more nebulous circle, an externally eccentric circle, the decentered circle of difference which is re-formed uniquely in the third time of the series. The order of time has broken the circle of the Same and arranged time in a series only in order to re-form a circle of the Other at the end of the series. The form of time is there only for the revelation of the formless in the eternal return. The extreme formality is there only for an excessive formlessness (Hölderlin's *Unförmliche*). In this manner, the ground has been superseded by a groundlessness, a universal ungrounding which turns upon itself and causes only the yet-to-come return.[56]

---

[56] Deleuze, *Difference and Repetition*, p. 91.

In the present reading, this irreducibly excessive formlessness of Hölderlin's *Unförmliche* and, finally, *Undenkbare* is the ultimate efficacy of all rhythmic and counter-rhythmic effects or their interplay, pure temporal or other. All rhythmic effects, however, wherever they occur, do involve temporality, which is why one is compelled to speak of *rhythm* and *time* (no capitals), also in juxtaposition, to *Being* and *Time*, especially when capitalised, as they were by Heidegger.[57] As explained earlier, under these conditions, recourse to probability in assessing possible future events becomes unavoidable in principle, which are also the conditions of the death of God, and both concepts, the death of God and the eternal return, were introduced, as correlative to each other, in *Thus Spoke Zarathustra*.[58] This is because there is no hidden underlying causal architecture that would make this recourse merely a practical matter. It follows that the return of the-yet-to-come could never be certain. It does not follow, however, that Romantic or nonclassical ontology, the ontology of *rhythm and time*, is limited to randomness and chance, which would indeed mean that it is limited to counter-rhythm and caesura. For these random events may under certain circumstances, enigmatically or mysteriously (but without mysticism), 'conspire' to form chaosmic rhythmic orders, as the orders of the multiple, which is also why we must assume their efficacity to be unthinkable. Deleuze provides literary examples of such chaosmic orders – Joyce himself, Borges, Gombrowicz, and Proust, who initiates this excursion into literature.[59] The return of the-yet-to-come, of a future or a possible later future, which, in accordance with Deleuze's concept of repetition, is never quite identical to the yet-to-come of which it is a 'return', could never be guaranteed. But, as Hölderlin taught us, such a return may not be entirely random. This is because it is a product of the interplay of rhythm and caesura, an interplay, to which we can apply calculable laws, established already by the Greek tragedy, and thus assess how likely this return may be, but which arise from the unthinkable, *das Undenkbare*, which is beyond law and hence deprives these assessments of certainty.

[57] Martin Heidegger, *Being and Time*, trans. Joan Stambaugh (Albany: SUNY Press, 2010).

[58] Friedrich Nietzsche, *Thus Spoke Zarathustra*, trans. Adrian Del Caro (Cambridge: Cambridge University Press, 2013).

[59] Deleuze, *Difference and Repetition*, p. 123.

Chapter 7

# Ground, Transcendence and Method in Deleuze's Fichte

*Joe Hughes*

> Philosophy must constitute itself as the theory of what we are doing, not as a theory of what there is. What we do has its principles; and being can only be grasped as the object of a synthetic relation with the very principles of what we do.
>
> Gilles Deleuze, *Empiricism and Subjectivity*[1]

> The real, understood as the object, aim and limit of affirmation; affirmation understood as acquiescence in or adhesion to the real: this is the meaning of braying.
>
> Gilles Deleuze, *Nietzsche and Philosophy*[2]

## INTRODUCTION

There are not many standards by which Johann Fichte could be said to be one of Gilles Deleuze's central interlocutors, at least not at first sight. Deleuze rarely cites Fichte. When he does, it is in admittedly important places and contexts, but these citations are almost always unexpected and fleeting. Think, for example, of the suggestion in 'Immanence: A Life. . .' that Fichte is one of the very few thinkers to have grasped absolute immanence as a life;[3] or the footnote of *Expressionism in Philosophy* which cites, of all texts, Fichte's letter to Schelling on Maimon's concept of quantitability – a concept which would become the first moment of sufficient reason in *Difference and Repetition*.[4] These moments of direct

---

[1] Gilles Deleuze, *Empiricism and Subjectivity: An Essay on Hume's theory of Human Nature*, trans. Constantin Boundas (New York: Columbia University Press, 1991), p. 133.

[2] Gilles Deleuze, *Nietzsche and Philosophy*, trans. Hugh Tomlinson (New York: Columbia University Press, 2006), p. 183.

[3] Gilles Deleuze, *Pure Immanence: Essays on A Life*, trans. Anne Boyman (New York: Zone Books, 2001), p. 27.

[4] Gilles Deleuze, *Spinoza et le problème de l'expression* (Paris: Minuit, 1968), p. 180 n. 15.

citation are, however, rare. But perhaps this is not the best way to gauge Fichte's importance for Deleuze. As Deleuze himself points out, the checklists of philosophers' libraries never actually reveal the apologetic and polemical directions of their work.[5]

In fact, if we turn to Fichte's own texts, a whole world of resonances begins to emerge. Take, for example, Fichte's insistence that thinking begins in a pre-representational and impersonal field. Even though his thought was, and still is, characterised as an absolute egoism, Fichte frequently complained that this view 'accepted by friends and enemies equally', is 'simply impossible'. Pure knowing is neither objective nor subjective.[6] His is 'a system whose beginning and end and whole nature is concerned with forgetting individuality in theory and rejecting it in practice'.[7] This conception of an impersonal and pre-individual knowing is a crucial proposition for Deleuze studies, which is still hesitant to follow Deleuze himself in grasping the virtual and its Ideas as unavoidably linked to a pre-individual and impersonal faculty of thought.[8]

Or consider Fichte's use of language. It develops two procedures central to Deleuze's own practice. First, Fichte resists a stable terminology: 'I have sought so far as possible to avoid a fixed terminology – the easiest way for literalists to deprive a system of life, and make dry bones of it.'[9] Each concept is translated and transformed and becomes designated by a different name. But, second, despite this process of transformation, Fichte insists that behind its instability lies another form of coherence: 'in the nature of our science, *the same thing* is constantly repeated in the most various terms and for the most diverse purposes'.[10] In this way, Fichte creates the conditions for a fulgurating thought, one

---

[5] Deleuze, *Nietzsche and Philosophy*, p. 162.

[6] Johann Gottlieb Fichte, *The Science of Knowledge*, trans. Peter Heath and John Lachs (Cambridge: Cambridge University Press, 1991), pp. 25–6; For Fichte's break with representation, see Johann Gottlieb Fichte, *Foundations of Transcendental Philosophy: (Wissenschaftslehre) Nova Methodo (1796/99)*, trans. Daniel Breazeale (Ithaca: Cornell University Press, 1992), pp. 86–97.

[7] Fichte, *The Science of Knowledge*, p. 84; cf. pp. 34–5.

[8] Gilles Deleuze, *Difference and Repetition*, trans. Paul Patton (New York: Columbia University Press, 1994), pp. 199–200. See also Gilles Deleuze, *The Logic of Sense*, trans. Mark Lester and Charles Stivale, ed. Constantin Boundas (New York: Columbia University Press, 1990), pp. 217–23. See also Gilles Deleuze and Félix Guattari, *What is Philosophy?*, trans. Hugh Tomlinson and Graham Burchell (New York: Columbia University Press, 1994), p. 211.

[9] Fichte, *The Science of Knowledge*, p. 90.

[10] Johann Gottlieb Fichte, *The Science of Knowing: J. G. Fichte's 1804 Lectures on the Wissenschaftslehre*, trans. Walter E. Wright (Albany: SUNY Press, 2005), p. 48 (original emphasis).

that will 'spring up by itself, like a *lightning flash*'.[11] In much the same way and for similar reasons (the resistance to dry bones, cliché[12] or dead representation[13]), Deleuze continually transforms the names of his concepts while, at the same time, creating the conditions under which a monotonous conceptual structure is able to flash forth.[14]

Or consider Fichte's insistence on the futility of conversation,[15] his attempt to discover the unity of the theoretical and the practical within a transcendental theory of the drive (a project Deleuze took up and deepened with the resources of psychoanalysis), his sustained methodological reflection on the meta-philosophical problematic of standpoint, or his unique synthesis of Kantianism and Spinozism.[16] Or consider Fichte's reading of the first *Critique* as ushering in a world of immanence and of the third *Critique* as discovering the genetic principle at the heart of the critical project – which is to say two of the central and distinctive features of Deleuze's own reading of Kant.[17] And, of course, there is Fichte's well-known assertion of the primacy of the practical, which Deleuze will transform through Bergson, Nietzsche and Spinoza, but which will nevertheless remain a central position of his thought, already articulated on the final page of *Empiricism and Subjectivity* in a claim that hovers over the rest of Deleuze project like a mist giving it its sense: 'Philosophy must constitute itself as the theory of what we are doing, not as a theory of what there is.'[18]

What all of these resonances suggest is that if there is a case to be made for pursuing the question of Deleuze's relation to Fichte, it cannot be made at the level of citations. Rather, it has to be made at the level of a common problem, and that problem is quite clearly the task that both Deleuze and Fichte set themselves: the completion of the Kantian enterprise.

---

[11] Ibid. p. 48 (original emphasis).

[12] Gilles Deleuze, *Francis Bacon: The Logic of Sensation*, trans. Daniel W. Smith (London: Continuum, 2003), pp. 93–4. See also Gilles Deleuze, *Cinema 2: The Time-Image*, trans. Hugh Tomlinson and Robert Caleta (Minneapolis: University of Minnesota Press, 1989), pp. 20–2.

[13] Deleuze, *The Logic of Sense*, p. 146.

[14] Manuel DeLanda, *Intensive Science and Virtual Philosophy* (London: Continuum, 2002), p. 202. See also Alain Badiou, *Deleuze: The Clamor of Being*, trans. Louise Burchill (Minnesota: University of Minnesota Press, 2006), p. 15.

[15] Fichte, *The Science of Knowledge*, p. 79.

[16] See Martial Guéroult, *L'évolution et la structure de la doctrine de la science chez Fichte*, 2 vols (Paris: Belles Lettres, 1930), pp. 164–5.

[17] Fichte, *The Science of Knowing*, pp. 31–2.

[18] Deleuze, *Empiricism and Subjectivity*, p. 133.

## THE KANTIAN ENTERPRISE

Throughout his early work Deleuze often positions his philosophical project as a reworking of Kantianism. Sometimes this is only implicit, as in his deeply Kantian reading of Hume in *Empiricism and Subjectivity* or in his reactivation of a genetic account of the faculties in *Proust and Signs*. Most of the time, though, it is explicit. *Nietzsche and Philosophy*, for example, sets Kant up as one of Nietzsche's two hidden interlocutors, and many of Nietzsche's central concepts are read in relation to fundamental Kantian problems: the status of synthesis, of the moral law, of universal history and the ends of humanity, the problem of genesis (grounded now in the will to power), the unity of theoretical, practical, and aesthetic judgement (which we find in the triple affirmation of chance, becoming and multiplicity), and so on. Perhaps the most direct statement of this project comes early in *Difference and Repetition*. 'The Kantian initiative (*l'initiative kantienne*) can be taken up', Deleuze writes there, but only 'in the course of a quite different understanding of the passive self.'[19] Deleuze's language here recalls that of his 1956 course *Qu'est-ce que fonder?* (hereafter *What is Grounding?*). Heidegger's *Kant and the Problem of Metaphysics*, Deleuze says, 'invites us to a repetition of the Kantian enterprise (*l'entreprise kantienne*)'.[20]

I'll return to the central importance of Heidegger below, but it is worth saying that this concern to take up and repeat the Kantian enterprise is not merely an announced programme or problematic. It is reflected in the distribution of Deleuze's central concepts. Take, for example, *Difference and Repetition*. Its central concepts – intensity, virtuality, representation, grounding, repetition, difference – are all organised around a linked series of syntheses divided into two basic movements of the imagination. The first movement, developed in the second chapter, 'Repetition for Itself', is a succession of passive syntheses. The imagination operates a first passive synthesis that binds the intensities of sensibility. A second synthesis gathers together these bindings. A third passive synthesis tries to bring the first two under a rule. Sometimes it

---

[19] Deleuze, *Difference and Repetition*, p. 87. See also Deleuze, *Francis Bacon*, p. 118.
[20] Gilles Deleuze, *Qu'est-ce que fonder?*, lecture course delivered in 1956, found at <http://www.webdeleuze.com/php/sommaire.html> (last accessed 28 September 2014). I'll return to the importance of Heidegger below. But for an extended discussion of the way in which *Difference and Repetition* builds its account of synthesis around Heidegger's *Kant and the Problem of Metaphysics*, see Joe Hughes, *Deleuze's Difference and Repetition: A Readers Guide* (London and New York: Bloomsbury, 2009), p. 97ff.

succeeds; sometimes it doesn't. When the third synthesis fails, the entire system of the passive self dissolves, and thought raises itself to a new power: that of ideal synthesis whose end is the production of Ideas. With Ideas the second movement of the imagination begins, that of dramatisation, actualisation and individuation. The imagination, Deleuze says, carries the newly produced Ideas back into the dissolved passive self, and it thereby gives the formerly passive syntheses a rule which makes them active.[21] The actualisation of Ideas thus unfolds across two active syntheses, that of good sense and that of common sense, which together ensure the cancellation of difference in the extensities and qualities of the world of representation. Because these linked series unfold along a genetic line that rises from intensity to representation we can represent it schematically like this:

8. Representation
> 7. Active synthesis 2 (Common Sense)
> 6. Active synthesis 1 (Good Sense)

5. Ideal Synthesis
> 4. Passive Synthesis 3 (Thought)
> 3. Passive Synthesis 2 (Memory)
> 2. Passive Synthesis 1 (Imagination)

1. Intensity

In *Difference and Repetition*, these two directions are explicitly modelled on the two movements of the imagination in Kant's first *Critique*: (1) the synthetic process which moves from sensibility to understanding by virtue of three syntheses (apprehension, reproduction, and recognition); and (2) the schematism, which moves from the understanding back to sensibility. Deleuze recasts the first movement as a series of passive syntheses ('a quite different understanding of the passive self') and recasts the second as an act of dramatisation in which the imagination gives the passive synthesis the role fashioned for it by the Idea.[22]

Taken as a whole, this structure – a structure that is constantly repeated across Deleuze's work from *The Logic of Sense* to *Cinema I* and *Cinema II* to *What is Philosophy?* 'in the most various terms and for the most diverse purposes' – raises a number of questions. Perhaps

---

[21] Deleuze *Difference and Repetition*, p. 220: 'While it is thought which must explore the virtual down to the ground of its repetitions, it is imagination which must grasp the process of actualisation from the point of view of these echoes or reprises. It is imagination which crosses domains, orders and levels [. . .] guiding our bodies and inspiring our souls, grasping the unity of mind and nature; a larval consciousness which moves endlessly from science to dream and back again.'

[22] Ibid. p. 218.

the first and most basic is the nature of this movement of thought. What is the nature of the becoming of the Deleuzian subject? By which I mean: What is the nature not of the material becoming which Deleuze calls 'intensity', nor the nature of the immaterial and incorporeal becoming he calls 'virtuality' or 'sense', but the nature of that developmental process which transforms itself across various structures as it moves from intensity to virtuality to representation by means of a linked series of syntheses or repetitions? What is it that grounds this post-Kantian conception of subjectivity?

## TRANSCENDENCE AND GROUNDING

Perhaps the most direct response to these questions comes not from Deleuze's major publications, but from two of his lecture courses. Take, for example, his 1980 course on Leibniz. In the final lecture of the course, Deleuze raises the question of grounding, and in the context of this question draws a sharp distinction between the classical conception of the subject and the modern or Kantian subject. For Kant, Deleuze says, the thinking subject is not a thinking thing or a created thing. It is, rather, 'the form of grounding'. To conceive of the subject in this way is to treat the 'finite ego (*moi*) as first principle'.[23]

> Kant's history depends greatly on the reform. The finite ego is the true founding. Thus the first principle becomes finitude. For the Classics, finitude is a consequence, the limitation of something infinite. The created world is finite, the Classics tell us, because it is limited. The finite ego founds the world and knowledge of the world because the finite ego is itself the constitutive founding of what appears. In other words, it is finitude that is the founding of the world. The relations of the infinite to the finite shift completely. The finite will no longer be a limitation of the infinite; rather, the infinite will be an overcoming (*dépassement*) of the finite. Moreover, it is a property of the finite to surpass and go beyond itself. The notion of self-overcoming (*auto-dépassement*) begins to be developed in philosophy. It will traverse all of Hegel and will reach into Nietzsche. The infinite is no longer separable from an act of overcoming finitude because only finitude can overcome itself. Everything called dialectic and the operation of the infinite to be transformed therein, the infinite becoming, become the act through which finitude overcomes itself by constituting or by founding the world. In that way, the infinite is subordinated to the act of the finite.[24]

---

[23] Gilles Deleuze, *Leibniz*, lecture delivered on 20 May 1980, found at <http://www.webdeleuze.com/php/sommaire.html> (last accessed 28 September 2014).
[24] Ibid.

This passage turns on a double transformation: the modern subject is no longer an effect, but a cause. It is conceived not as constituted finitude, but as constitutive finitude, an act of self-transcendence through which it constitutes not only itself but, at the same time, founds the world. Finitude becomes, Deleuze says, a 'first principle'. But, second, this entails a new distribution of the relations of finite and infinite. The subject is no longer a created thing set against the infinite; it is itself infinite in its self-overcoming. The infinite becomes immanent to the act of transcendence. Put differently, and in terms to which I'll return at the end of this essay, the real is no longer the aim and limit of self-transcendence. The act of transcendence just is the real.

Deleuze's language here, in its emphasis on founding, finitude, and transcendence, recalls the language of his 1956 course *What is Grounding?* As Christian Kerslake has persuasively shown, this course, delivered during the period Deleuze described as a hole in his life, represents a pivotal moment in Deleuze's formulation of his philosophical project, determining precisely what it would mean to accept Heidegger's invitation to 'a repetition of the Kantian enterprise'.[25] The central methodological problem of the course turns around the titular question of grounding: What does it mean to ground a claim, either by appeal to the principle of reason or through a deduction in response to the question *quid juris*, or by some other method? Ultimately the explicitly Heideggerian answer Deleuze will give to this question turns around an implicated problem which, Deleuze says, is precisely the problem Kant left for philosophy. 'Kant poses and leaves a problem for philosophy: finitude as such, insofar as it is finitude, is constitutive.'[26]

To think finitude as constitutive requires not only a new conception of the nature of subjectivity but a new conception of the transcendental. Early in the course Deleuze asks what Kant means by this 'mysterious concept: the transcendental'. To answer the question, he says, one must return to Hume and to a historical shift in the conception of the very nature of subjectivity.

> Hume introduced something new [to the problem of the transcendental]: the analysis of the structure of subjectivity. The word 'subject', as it happens, is very rarely used by Hume. This is perhaps not by chance. Hegel too analyses subjectivity without using the word 'subject'. Heidegger goes further and says that the word 'subject' must not be used. One must, rather,

[25] See Christian Kerslake, *Immanence and the Vertigo of Philosophy: From Kant to Deleuze* (Edinburgh: Edinburgh University Press, 2009), pp. 1–46.
[26] Deleuze, *Qu'est-ce que fonder?*

designate it by the essential structure one discovers. Once we have defined the subject, there is no more reason to speak of it. Both Heidegger and Hegel tell us that the subject is that which develops itself. Hegel analyses it dialectically. To develop oneself is to transform oneself, etc. Its essence is mediation. Heidegger says the essence of subjectivity is transcendence, but with a new sense: whereas this term used to refer to the state of something transcendent, with Heidegger, it becomes the movement of self-transcendence. It is the mode of being of the movement that transcends (*le mouvement à ce qui se transcende*).[27]

This passage is striking for a number of reasons. It seems to explain, for example, what happened to the central theme of Deleuze's first book post-1953: it's not that subjectivity lost its status as a problem for Deleuze, but that he focused on designating its essential structure. It is striking, too, in the way it links Heidegger and Hegel together in the elaboration of a philosophical project – and, indeed, throughout the course, Heidegger and Hegel play enormously important roles (and Hegel is very much read with sympathy and insight (and is even defended)). But ultimately, what I want to emphasise here is that this passage performs, in different terms, the shift elaborated in his 1980 course on Leibniz: we must reconceive the transcendental as immanent to a subjectivity conceived as an act of self-transcendence.

Deleuze's development of this conception of subjectivity unfolds through a sustained engagement with two texts: Heidegger's *Kant and the Problem of Metaphysics* and Heidegger's 1929 treatise, 'On the Essence of Ground'. Indeed this latter piece structures the passage above. Heidegger writes, 'If one chooses the title of "subject" for that being that we ourselves in each case are and that we understand as "Dasein", then we may say that transcendence designates the essence of the subject, that it is the fundamental structure of subjectivity.'[28]

There are two ways of misrecognising the nature of transcendence, Heidegger argues. We can think it in spatial terms, as a 'surpassing' which moves from one thing to another, or we can describe it in epistemological terms, as a subject over and against an object. But to conceive transcendence in these terms is precisely to miss the point. The subject, grasped as a structure of transcending,

> surpasses neither a 'boundary' placed before the subject, forcing it in advance to remain inside (immanence), nor a 'gap' separating it from the

[27] Ibid.

[28] Martin Heidegger, 'On the Essence of Ground', in *Pathmarks*, ed. William McNeill (Cambridge: Cambridge University Press, 1998), p. 108.

object. Yet nor are objects – the beings that are objectified – that *toward which* a surpassing occurs. *What* is surpassed is precisely and solely *beings themselves*, indeed every being that can be or become unconcealed for Dasein, thus *including precisely* that being as which 'it itself' exists.[29]

Condensed in this passage are the basic characteristics of transcendence Deleuze himself emphasises in both *What is Grounding?* and his 1980 course on Leibniz: transcendence is neither an object nor the aim and limit of the subject. It is the immanent process of self-overcoming. And ultimately Heidegger will redefine the mysterious concept of the transcendental in just these terms: '[t]his term names all that belongs essentially to transcendence'.[30] In *What is Grounding?* Deleuze alters Heidegger's terms in a way that makes him into a transcendental empiricist who manages to affirm immanence: with Heidegger, Deleuze says, 'the transcendental becomes a structure of empirical subjectivity', it 'is reduced to transcendence, to overcoming', and as a result, 'the word transcendent no longer refers to a being outside or superior to the world, but to an act'.[31]

Is this act of pure transcendence not an unexpected Fichtean moment in Heidegger's thought? In the final section of the treatise, Heidegger writes that the act of surpassing in question is one that takes place 'only in a "will"'.[32] And what's more, this will is a *free* will. It does not surpass as 'an occasional and additional accomplishment'. The act of transcendence, you could say, is not heteronomous. It is autonomous. The transcending will projects its own possibilities as function of its own essence. Whatever casts itself projectively 'in accordance with its essence', Heidegger writes, 'is that which we call freedom'.[33] Indeed, Heidegger's answer to the question – what is grounding? – is that the 'essence of ground', the '*origin of ground in general*' is 'freedom as transcendence'.[34] Whether this is Deleuze's response as well is a question I will return to below. But what I want to signal here is that in presenting this thesis, Heidegger approaches Fichte's position that freedom is 'the ultimate ground and first condition of all being and consciousness'.[35]

[29] Ibid. (original emphasis).
[30] Ibid. p. 109.
[31] Deleuze, *Qu'est-ce que fonder?*.
[32] Heidegger, 'On the Essence of Ground', p. 126.
[33] Ibid. (original emphasis).
[34] Ibid. p. 127 (original emphasis).
[35] Fichte, *Foundations of Transcendental Philosophy*, p. 68. Cf. Fichte, *The Science of Knowledge*, pp. 40–1. For a sustained discussion of the concept of freedom and its systematic function in Fichte, see Günter Zöller, *Fichte's Transcendental Philosophy* (Cambridge: Cambridge University Press, 1998).

There are, of course, important differences between the Fichtean and Heideggerian theses, their respective conceptions of freedom, will, and what Fichte, too, calls 'the possibilities of action'.[36] But if I am drawing attention to these resonances it is because, in his course on Leibniz, Deleuze himself makes this association, explicitly linking the modern conception of subjectivity and transcendence not with Heidegger but with Fichte.

Immediately after characterising the modern subject as an act of transcendence which grounds the world at the same time that it subordinated the infinite to the act of the finite, Deleuze continues:

> What results from this? Fichte has an exemplary page for the Kantian polemic with Leibniz. Here is what Fichte tells us: I can say A is A, but this is only a hypothetical proposition. Why? Because it presupposes 'if there is A'. If A is, A is A, but if there is nothing, A is not A. This is very interesting because he is in the act of overthrowing the principle of identity. He says that the principle of identity is a hypothetical rule. Hence he launches his great theme: to overcome hypothetical judgment to go toward what he calls 'thetic' judgment. To go beyond hypothesis toward thesis. Why is it that A is A if A does exist, because finally the proposition A is A is not at all a final principle or a first principle? It refers to something deeper, specifically that one must say that A is A because it is thought. Specifically, what founds the identity of things that are thought is the identity of the thinking subject. Moreover, the identity of the thinking subject is the identity of the finite ego. Thus the first principle is not that A is A, but that ego equals ego.[37]

Here it is Fichte's conception of the synthetic relation of self to self that now characterises the modern conception of the subject. The principle of identity finds its ground in the finite ego as first principle and this entails an entire redistribution of the relations between the finite and the infinite. As Deleuze puts it later, with Fichte, 'the synthetic identity of the finite ego replaces the infinite analytic identity of God'.[38]

But to what extent does any of this relate to Deleuze's major texts? We might note in this short passage three of the central themes of *Difference and Repetition*: (1) the affirmation that the finite ego in its Fichtean guise is already beyond representation; (2) the problem of the ground; and (3) the basic position of Deleuze's ontology that substance

---

[36] Fichte, *Foundations of Transcendental Philosophy*, p. 69; cf. pp. 167–86. For a lucid discussion of some these issues, see Jürgen Stolzenberg, 'Martin Heidegger Reads Fichte', in *Fichte and The Phenomenological Tradition*, ed. Violetta L. Waibel, Daniel Breazeale, and Tom Rockmore (Berlin: Walter de Gruyter, 2010).

[37] Deleuze, *Leibniz* lecture (translation modified).

[38] Ibid.

must turn around the modes, or as he puts it here, that the 'infinite is subordinated to the act of the finite'.[39] But to understand how the thematics of constitutive finitude and transcendence work their way into a text like *Difference and Repetition*, it is not enough to make these associations which only circle around the question. It is necessary to show that these concepts are represented by the central concepts of Deleuze's works, and to this, it is necessary to make a brief detour through Jean Wahl's 1944 text *Existence humaine et transcendance*.

## TRANSCENDENCE AND REPETITION

Deleuze never cited Wahl's text. He famously cites another text in the early twentieth-century debate about the nature of transcendence to which Wahl's text indirectly responds – Sartre's *The Transcendence of the Ego* – but Deleuze does not seem to have mentioned Wahl. It is clear, though, from even a glance that the text played an enormous role in Deleuze's development as a thinker. It opens, for example, with an argument for a 'transcendental empiricism' which, Wahl says, would have to be characterised by the search for the conditions of real experience and not possible experience.[40] More importantly for my line of inquiry is that Wahl develops an argument Deleuze would take up in *Empiricism and Subjectivity*: the claim that, as Deleuze puts it, the only content we can give the idea of subjectivity is that of transcendence.[41] Wahl develops this idea by surveying the different forms and conceptions of transcendence in Nietzsche, Kierkegaard, Jaspers and Heidegger – which is to say, a significant portion of the set of thinkers Deleuze is concerned with in *Grounding* and in the opening chapters of *Difference and Repetition*.

Of these thinkers and their various conceptions of transcendence, it is Kierkegaard, Wahl says, who 'returns [transcendence], in a way, to immanence', through his concept of repetition. In what way is repetition a mode of immanent transcendence? Wahl explains:

> Repetition is the fact that the past is taken back, as it were, out of the past and returned to a new present, reaffirmed. One could compare it to the way in which Aristotle defines substance: *to ti ên einai*. The individual must be what it was. It is a question of 'remaining what one was' and of reaffirming oneself as such.[42]

---

[39] Deleuze *Difference and Repetition*, p. 304.
[40] Jean Wahl, *Existence humaine et transcendance* (Neuchâtel: Éditions de la Baconnière, 1944), p. 18.
[41] Deleuze, *Empiricism and Subjectivity*, p. 85.
[42] Wahl, *Existence humaine et transcendance*, p. 48.

Repetition is a form of transcendence by virtue of the movement through which the past is affirmed in a new present. Wahl implies that this movement is substantial, but rather than emphasising the reality of transcendence, or perhaps in order to, he goes on to emphasise its temporality. When we repeat, Wahl explains, in either a Kierkegaardian or a Nietzschean mode, 'we make a unity of the present, the past and the future. We attain a moment in which there is an absolute union of what Heidegger called "the three extases of time".'[43]

Deleuze no doubt would have heard the resonance between this account of repetition in Kierkegaard and his account of habit – a different type of repetition – in Hume, if Wahl's account of transcendence and repetition were not already a formative idea behind *Empiricism and Subjectivity*. Habit, Deleuze writes there, is 'the constitutive root of the subject, and the subject, at root, is the synthesis of the present and the past in light of the future'.[44] I will return to this image of time below, as it was developed in *Nietzsche and Philosophy*, but the argument I wanted to make with this detour is just that Wahl shows us the way in which the problem of constitutive finitude is formulated in *Difference and Repetition*. Kierkegaard's conception of repetition, of course, is the very concept Deleuze adopted and modified as a replacement for the Hegelian dialectic (another form of transcendence).[45] But, as Wahl tells us, repetition just is transcendence. It is the category under which we think the subject as constitutive finitude.

## METHOD

Deleuze's most frequent discussion of Fichte, though, turns not on questions of transcendence, but on questions of method. Ultimately these two questions imply one another. But in the final pages of *What is Grounding?*, and in several of his major texts, Deleuze develops Fichte's reflections on method, and he does so, we might say, in a negative and positive direction. Negatively, Fichte is behind two closely related but distinct criticisms of Kant. Throughout his work, Deleuze will say that: (1) Kant held fast to the point of view of conditioning without attaining that of genesis;[46] and that (2) it is not the conditions of all possible experience that must be reached, but the conditions of real experience.[47] Most

---

[43] Ibid.
[44] Deleuze, *Empiricism and Subjectivity*, pp. 92–3.
[45] Deleuze, *Difference and Repetition*, pp. 10 and 308.
[46] Ibid. p. 170.
[47] Gilles Deleuze, *Desert Islands and Other Texts 1953–1974*, trans. Mike Taormina

of the time Deleuze's readers attribute these criticisms to the influence of Maimon on the basis of a passage in *Difference and Repetition*.[48] But if we consider Deleuze's various formulations more widely, it becomes clear they are a complex assemblage of very diverse positions held by many of the post-Kantians. When Deleuze first speaks of a principle that is no wider than the given, he cites Schelling, no doubt following Wahl.[49] When Deleuze writes in *Difference and Repetition* that the conditions of possibility are too wide for real experience, that 'the net is so loose that the largest fish pass through', he is almost certainly thinking of Novalis' famous claim that hypotheses are nets. In most texts, though, it becomes clear that in elaborating this dual critique of Kant, Deleuze is in fact closely following Guéroult's exposition of Fichte's method – an exposition which treats Maimon as a central source for Fichte, but one Fichte goes beyond.[50]

Indeed, both of these claims are central to Fichte's project of coherently completing the Kantian enterprise. He grounds the legitimacy of his system in its ability to account for real experience:

> If the hypothesis of idealism is correct and the reasoning in the deduction is valid, the system of all necessary presentation or the entirety of experience [. . .] must emerge as the final result, as the totality of the conditions of the original premise.[51]

And, what's more, in this passage and in others, he insists that real experience must be grasped genetically. 'So long as the thing is not made to arise as a whole in front of the thinker's eyes', Fichte writes, 'dogmatism is not hounded to its last refuge,'[52]

Deleuze's thought clearly develops itself according to both of these imperatives. As I outlined above, *Difference and Repetition* (to take only one example), is nothing but a genetic line that ends in the genesis of real experience. After the subject has transformed itself across the three passive syntheses, determined itself through an ideal synthesis, and actualised its Ideas through active syntheses, Deleuze's genetic line ends precisely in the

---

(New York: Semiotext(e), 2004), p. 36.

48  Deleuze, *Difference and Repetition*, p. 173.

49  Deleuze, *Desert Islands*, p. 71; Wahl, *Existence humaine et transcendance*, p. 18.

50  See, in particular, the discussion on method in Deleuze, *Qu'est-ce que fonder?* and Deleuze, *Desert Islands*, p. 61.

51  Fichte, *The Science of Knowledge*, pp. 25–6.

52  Ibid. p. 24. Cf. Fichte, *The Science of Knowing*, p. 39. 'Unlike the actual sciences which ground themselves on principles that are only "factually manifest", the science of knowing intends to introduce entirely genetic manifestness and then to deduce the factical from it.'

represented object determined in both its quantity and quality. The thing, you could say, is made to arise whole in front of the thinker's eyes. But there is an important break with Fichte here, too, one which testifies to the importance of Maimon. 'Real experience', for Deleuze, is not only that which appears at the end of the genetic line as for Fichte. It is also there at the beginning in a different, pre-representational form: the corporeal, intensive flux lived by the passive self. At this level too we find a certain distribution of quality and quantity. But quality and quantity have not yet taken on their perceptual form, which will come about only through the actualisation of an Idea's relations and singularities. As Deleuze elaborates in the opening chapters of *Nietzsche and Philosophy*, at this pre-representational level of force, quantity expresses the synthesis of forces; quality expresses the transformation of force brought about by synthesis. In *Difference and Repetition* this form of quantity will be called intensive quantity, and Deleuze will say that 'while the conditions of possible experience may be related to extension, there are also subjacent conditions of real experience which are indistinguishable from intensity as such'.[53]

But Deleuze will also say that these assemblages of intensity function as a 'transcendental principle'.[54] And it is in this positing of a principle in the depths of the passive self that we encounter the positive dimension of Deleuze's relation to the Fichtean method, but with an admittedly significant departure from Fichte. If this principle is to be found at the foundation of the passive self, submerged in a flux of intensity, it would then be significantly different from Fichte's absolute self, a pure abstract point from which experience emerges. It would be an activity characterised not by freedom (as for Heidegger) but by thoroughgoing determination. One of Deleuze's more developed accounts of this problem is in *Nietzsche and Philosophy*, where the will to power comes to function as this first principle of constitutive finitude, but it is a principle which only becomes free under determinate conditions.

FIRST PRINCIPLES

The first time Deleuze characterises the will to power as a principle he describes it as the principle of the eternal return. This means, of course, that the eternal return, as a form of synthesis, is not itself a principle. Rather, it has a principle or expresses a principle. As Deleuze puts it: 'we can only understand the eternal return as the expression of a principle

---

[53] Deleuze *Difference and Repetition*, pp. 231–2.
[54] Ibid. p. 38.

which is the reason of the manifold and its reproduction, of difference and its repetition (*nous ne pouvons comprendre l'éternel retour lui-même que comme l'expression d'un principe qui est la raison du divers et de sa reproduction, de la différence et de sa répétition)*.[55] Deleuze's language in this passage is characteristically both precise and allusive. The allusion is to Kant. The eternal return, as synthesis, has for its principle a principle that is the reason or ground for both the manifold, or difference, and its reproduction, or its repetition. But the eternal return itself is neither the manifold, nor its reproduction. It is, as I'll develop below, a third moment that ties these first two together in a synthetic process which is clearly meant to reconfigure Kant's deduction. In Kant we get:

1. The synthesis of apprehension
2. The synthesis of reproduction
3. The synthesis of recognition

In Deleuze's Nietzsche, we get:

1. Diversity or difference
2. Reproduction or repetition
3. Eternal return

I obviously do not mean that Deleuze is simply replaying Kant here. Kant's synthetic model is very different from Deleuze's Nietzsche on two important points. First, for Deleuze, the manifold is no longer given in the empty form of time. What is apprehended and gathered together in synthesis is force.[56] Apprehension is not the apprehension of formal diversity, but of concrete, material diversity. Second, there are no pre-given categories that can serve as rules for synthesis effectively guaranteeing the act of recognition. Rather, as Deleuze puts it later in the text, 'We require a genesis of reason itself, and also a genesis of the understanding and its categories: what are the forces of reason and of the understanding?'[57] Synthesis then, approaches the empirical at the same time that it becomes genetic.

Deleuze makes several important claims for the will, which is to say, for the principle grounding this genetic process. Let me emphasise two. First, it is a plastic principle. 'How should the term "principle" be understood?', Deleuze asks.

---

[55] Deleuze, *Nietzsche and Philosophy*, p. 49 (translation modified). See Gilles Deleuze, *Nietzsche et la philosophie* (Paris: PUF, 2007), p. 55.
[56] Deleuze, *Nietzsche and Philosophy*, p. 50.
[57] Ibid. p. 91.

Nietzsche always attacks principles for being too general in relation to what they condition, for always having too broad a mesh in relation to what they claim to capture or regulate. [. . .] If [. . .] the will to power is a good principle, if it reconciles empiricism with principles, if it constitutes a superior empiricism, this is because it is an essentially *plastic (plastique)* principle that is no wider than what it conditions, that changes itself with the conditioned and determines itself in each case along with what it determines.[58]

The plasticity of the principle, we could say, has two dimensions. The first is an external relation of the principle to 'what it conditions'. In the context of the will to power, this is the relation of the principle to force. Plasticity, in this sense, means that as a principle of the synthesis of force, the will to power simultaneously modifies and is modified by the nature of the forces brought into relation in the act of synthesis. The eye that binds light is itself bound light. The second dimension of plasticity is an internal relation. The principle is determined not only by the set of forces outside of it, but is self-determining as well. Thus there is a structural plasticity and a genetic plasticity; the determination of the principle by what it gathers together and the determination of the principle by itself. There is plasticity as determination and plasticity as constitution.

Emphasising the plasticity of a first principle radically alters the very status of principles in ways it is impossible to develop here. But notice that this conception at least retains a variation on one of the traditional requirements of first principles: a principle must contain within it the necessity of its own existence. The will to power, in its plasticity, does not necessarily exist, but it is by definition *inseparable* from existence insofar as it modulates in relation to that which it modulates. But Deleuze never claims that this first principle necessarily exists. In fact, there is a very real sense in which it can be said not to exist: it its initial positing, it is indistinguishable from becoming, the pure evanescence of form or the permanent abortion of the instant.[59] It is only in its second dimension, that of self-determination, that the principle becomes capable of existence. Thus a second, more traditional aspect of Deleuze's notion of first principles: as a principle the will to power is productive, and it accounts synthetically for that which follows from it. What follows from the will to power is the thought of the eternal return. If the will to power is genetic or productive, what it produces is the eternal return. Put

---

[58] Ibid. p. 50; cf. p. 85.
[59] Deleuze and Guattari, *What is Philosophy?*, p. 118; Deleuze, *Difference and Repetition*, p. 70.

differently, becoming, which is not, gives rise to Being. Substance turns around the modes; the infinite is subordinated to the act of the finite.

The eternal return, Being, comes second. It is 'formed' by the will to power, 'constituted' by the will to power, 'produced' by the will to power, and so on.[60] It must emerge on the basis of a principle:

> It is the will to power, as differential element, that produces and develops difference in affirmation, that reflects difference in the affirmation of affirmation, and makes it return in the affirmation which is itself affirmed. Dionysus developed, reflected, and raised to the highest power: these are the aspects of Dionysian willing which serve as principles for the eternal return.[61]

The will to power is productive; the eternal return is produced. This passage is structured by a succession of triads which elaborate the way in which the eternal return is constituted:

1. Difference             affirmation               development
2. Reflection of difference  affirmation of affirmation  reflection
3. Return of difference    affirmation affirmed       raising

Each of these triads clearly repeats the reformulation of the Kantian triad outlined above. As we move from difference to its reflection to its return we move across the genetic process grounded in the will to power and its synthesis of forces. What is produced through this genetic process is not, after all, the understanding or reason. As Deleuze argued earlier in *Nietzsche and Philosophy*, our image of the faculty of thought must be reinvented, and this reinvention leads to an image of thought that is independent of reason.[62] What is produced in this process, then, is not reason, but the eternal return, a thought liberated from all reason, a 'thought that would go to the limit of what life could do', becoming the 'affirmative power of life'.[63]

But these triads do not simply repeat that early triad of difference, reproduction, and return. To this previous triad, we now have the triad of the development, reflection and raising of the will coupled with the triad of affirmation. These two latter triads relate to the first according to the distinction I made earlier between the two dimensions of the will's plasticity. What is at stake in the first triad (difference, repetition, return) is the will's external relation to the forces it gathers and its plasticity

[60] Deleuze, *Nietzsche and Philosophy*, pp. 187–8.
[61] Ibid. p. 189 (translation modified), see Deleuze, *Nietzsche et la philosophie*, p. 217.
[62] Ibid. pp. 100–1. This argument was already made in precisely these terms in *Qu'est-ce que fonder?* It appears again in the conclusion to *What is Philosophy?*
[63] Ibid. p. 101.

with respect to what it determines and what determines it. In the final two triads what is at stake is the will's process of self-determination. In the act of synthesising force, the will itself undergoes a process of constitution in which it determines itself and raises itself to its highest power (the thought of the eternal return, the being which is said of becoming).

It is in this dimension that the problem of being becomes resolvable. In developing, reflecting and raising itself to a new power, the principle of synthesis no longer determines itself in relation to the forces of chaos which affect it from the outside. Rather it determines itself in another region, one created by the principle itself.[64] By virtue of this genetic dimension, the will is able to convert determination into constitution, and pull itself out of becoming into an invented being. In this respect we are very much within the conceptual world of *Difference and Repetition* and the doctrine of passive synthesis. There, too, eternal return is the highest form of synthesis, the act by which thought raises itself to the absolute. But thought must necessarily pass through the entire regime of passivity before it is able to raise itself to the higher power of ideal synthesis which, through its becoming, creates the virtual.

## HYPOTHETICAL AND ABSOLUTE POSITING

Deleuze's first principle thus appears as the precise inversion of Fichte's. What is at stake is not the pure activity of the self, but its pure passivity. And whereas Fichte posits a principle which is unconditioned in both its form and matter, the will to power, in its first positing, is determined with respect to both form and content: what it synthesises and the way it synthesises is determined by the nature of the force gathered together. Thus, whereas Heidegger will begin with an immediately free will, Deleuze will begin with a passive will which must become active through a developmental process. And yet, despite these fundamental differences, Deleuze arrives at his principle in a way which he consistently and explicitly modelled after Fichte's own method. Indeed, across his career in both his major texts and in his lectures Deleuze returns to the Fichtean distinction of hypothetical and absolute positing, and repurposes it to meet new ends.[65]

---

[64] Gilles Deleuze and Félix Guattari, *A Thousand Plateaus: Capitalism and Schizophrenia*, trans. Brian Massumi (Minneapolis: University of Minnesota Press, 1987), p. 311.

[65] To cite only the most important discussion of the process, see: Deleuze, *Nietzsche*

This is particularly clear in the final pages of *Nietzsche and Philosophy*. The eternal return and the thinker of the eternal return, the overman, Deleuze says, 'relate to Zarathustra as to the conditioning principle which "posits" them in a merely hypothetical manner' (*ils renvoient à Zarathoustra comme au principe conditionnant qui les 'pose' de manière seulement hypothétique*). By contrast, they relate to Dionysus as to 'the unconditioned principle that is the ground of their apodictic and absolute character' (*à Dionysos comme au principe inconditionné qui fonde leur caractère apodictique et absolu*).[66]

At a minimum, there are three questions this passage raises. First: what is the status of Zarathustra, Dionysus, and, implicitly, Ariadne here? Deleuze speaks as though they were the principles themselves. But we know that Zarathustra, for example, is not the principle. The principle of the eternal return is the will to power. Zarathustra is the one who posits the will in a merely hypothetical manner. Should we say then that Zarathustra or Dionysus represents the meta-philosophical position of the philosopher, the gaze under which the self constructs itself? Perhaps; but it's not entirely clear that a rigorous philosophy of immanence can admit this meta-philosophical positioning of the philosopher above or behind what she thinks.[67] Let us say then that they are, instead, figures of the will to power and of our mode of approach to it.

Second: how does one move from a hypothetical positing to an absolute positing of the will? When Deleuze raises the methodological problem of hypothetical and anhypothetical principles he almost always cites page 174 of Guéroult's *L'évolution et la structure de la doctrine de la science*, and most of the time quotes a particular passage on that page in which Guéroult claims that the analytic method, the movement from a hypothetical principle to an anhypothetical principle, has no other end than its own suppression. But this passage appears within the context of a philosophical *tour de force* in which Guéroult surveys the entire evolution of Fichte's conception of method in just under 30 pages, and this broader account of method often structures Deleuze's own arguments (most notably in Chapter 8 of *Expressionism in Philosophy*).[68]

*and Philosophy*, p. 193; Gilles Deleuze, *Expressionism in Philosophy: Spinoza*, trans. Martin Joughin (New York: Zone Books, 1992), p. 134; Deleuze, *Difference and Repetition*, pp. 197 and 282; Deleuze and Guattari, *What is Philosophy?*, p. 207.

[66] Deleuze, *Nietzsche and Philosophy*, p. 193 (translation modified), see Deleuze, *Nietzsche et la philosophie*, p. 221.

[67] See François Laruelle, *Philosophy and Non-Philosophy*, trans. Taylor Adkins (Minneapolis: Univocal, 2013), p. 29.

[68] See, in particular, Deleuze, *Expressionism in Philosophy*, pp. 134–9.

Guéroult's argument is thus impossible to summarise here, but the basic question animating it is this: Fichte begins with a fact (A=A) and an arbitrary application of the principle of reason to that fact (the principle of identity itself must have a ground); how does one erase these two contingencies, the contingency of fact and the contingency of the application of the principle of reason?

In *Expressionism in Philosophy*, Deleuze puts the problem this way: 'We reach the positing of a principle on the basis of a hypothesis; *but the principle must be of such a nature as to free itself entirely from the hypothesis*, to ground itself, and ground the movement by which we reach it; it must *as soon as possible* render obsolete the presupposition from which we started in order to discover it.'[69] In Fichte, this is accomplished by positing the absolute self and grounding both the hypothetical and the absolute moments in the freedom of the 'I' as it necessarily circulates through the circle sketched above. In Deleuze's reading of Spinoza this is accomplished through a coordination of the *a priori* and *a posteriori* proofs for God's existence: the *a posteriori* proof carries us as quickly as possible to an anhypothetical principle (viz., God); the *a priori* proof establishes this principle on a new ground (power)[70] which allows a progressive and genetic deduction of the real from the idea of God.[71]

*Nietzsche and Philosophy* is initially consistent with this broader procedure. Deleuze posits the will as the principle of the eternal return, but this positing is arbitrary in two ways: it assumes the fact of the eternal return and it assumes an ungrounded application of the principle of reason. As Deleuze puts it, Zarathustra, the hypothetical positing of the will, both assumes the 'constituted eternal return'[72] and grasps the will only through its *ratio cognoscendi*, or our reason for knowing the will. In the absolute positing of the will, however, both the fact and the principle change. The eternal return is no longer assumed, but constituted, and the principle of reason is no longer merely the reason for knowing, but becomes a *ratio essendi*, the reason of essence.[73] How do we move from one to the next?

Deleuze characterises the transition from the *ratio cognoscendi* to the *ratio essendi* as an act of transmutation. This is one of the most obscure moments of the text, but we can see already that Deleuze is

---

[69] Ibid. p. 136 (original emphasis).
[70] Ibid. p. 89.
[71] Ibid. pp. 137–9.
[72] Deleuze, *Nietzsche and Philosophy*, p. 187.
[73] Ibid. p. 188.

Spinozist here. The movement between the two manners of positing the will cannot be accomplished at the level of theoretical judgement or by a transition from theoretical to practical judgement. It has to assume the mutual implication for the theoretical and the practical at the start. This mode of knowing is thus inseparably tied to an ethics, and the transition between hypothetical and absolute positing requires an ethical transformation, a lived mutation in or in relation to thought. This process won't be fully developed until *Difference and Repetition* and *The Logic of Sense*, where Deleuze elaborates in great detail the genetic process by which the passive self dissolves and raises itself to a higher power, and the way in which that higher power takes the form of an ideal synthesis which accounts for the genesis of sufficient reason by grounding it in the circulation of an aleatory point.[74] But even if the details are not fully present in *Nietzsche and Philosophy*, the general structure and sense of the movement is: what Deleuze sketches here is the way in which a principle determined in both its form and content can function as the necessary first principle of a system founded on a vanishing foundation.

This programme becomes apparent if we pursue a final question: from the perspective of the will, what is the difference between these two modes of positing? In a way, we have already encountered it in the distinction between the two directions of plasticity. Insofar as the will is modulated in relation to that which it modulates, it is determined in both its form and content. It is posited conditionally. But insofar as it becomes capable of self-determination, by virtue of this process of determination and the possibility of development and reflection it opens up, it raises itself to its highest power and becomes constitutive.

When Deleuze himself raises the distinction between hypothetical and absolute positing in the final pages of *Nietzsche and Philosophy*, he articulates the difference in a way that returns us to the problematic of constitutive finitude with which this essay began. From the perspective of the hypothetical positing of the principle, the will appears as 'the entanglement of causes or the connection of moments (*instants*), the synthetic relation of moments to each other'.[75] This perspective belongs to what he called, in *The Logic of Sense*, the primary order of the mixture of bodies, a corporeal field of forces whose synthesis necessarily implies a synthesis of time. Insofar as each instant is vanishing, the very act of gathering them together constitutes a present, and then a past and then a future. Time here appears in its dimensionality through the

---

[74] Deleuze, *Difference and Repetition*, p. 171.
[75] Deleuze, *Nietzsche and Philosophy*, p. 193.

synthetic process of the passive self (a process most thoroughly outlined in Chapter 2 of *Difference and Repetition*).

When the principle is posited absolutely, however, it becomes something altogether different. It is no longer a question of entangled instants determining one another from the outside. Rather, when the will is posited absolutely, it is the

> synthetic relation of the moment (*instant*) to itself, as past, present and to come, which absolutely determines its relations with all other moments. The return is not the passion of one moment pushed by others, but the activity of the moment which determines the others in determining itself (*se déterminant lui-même*) through what it affirms.[76]

Here the principle of synthesis, the will, is no longer conceived in its passivity, as determined by all other moments or bodies pushing on it and determining it. It is conceived in its activity as a pure self-positing or affirmation which takes the form of a process of self-determination.[77] It is thus grasped no longer as this or that dimension of time, but becomes time as a whole. Put differently, and in relation to Jean Wahl's account of repetition as a mode of transcendence, we could say that the will is conceived, finally, as substance in the sense of Aristotle's *to ti ên einai*: 'the individual must be what it was', as Wahl says. 'It is a question of "remaining what one was" and of reaffirming oneself as such.'[78] In the absolute positing of the principle, then, we rediscover the subject as ground through its movement of self-transcendence.

---

[76] Ibid.
[77] As Zöller notes, Fichte's term, 'positing' is derived from logic where it represents affirmation in judgement. In this sense, to posit is to affirm. Cf. Zöller, *Fichte's Transcendental Philosophy*, p. 29.
[78] Wahl, *Existence humaine et transcendance*, p. 48.

Chapter 8

# 'The magic formula we all seek': Spinoza + Fichte = x

*Frederick Amrine*

*Sed omnia praeclara tam difficilia, quam rara sunt.*

## THE REVOLUTIONARY RHIZOME

All eyes, it would seem, are on Spinoza at the moment.[1] Much of the credit for this remarkable renaissance is due to Gilles Deleuze, who wrote two books on Spinoza, and then went even further in his best-selling manifesto *What is Philosophy?*, anointing Spinoza both the 'prince' and the 'Christ' of philosophy.[2] And Deleuze is hardly alone in his attentions. Spinoza now looms large in our understanding of the entire Age of Goethe.[3] The controversy over Spinoza still figures as a minor flap in Beck's classic study, *Early German Philosophy*;[4] but it has become the defining intellectual controversy of the whole age since Beiser published *The Fate of Reason* in 1987.[5] And now Jonathan Israel has published three massive tomes in quick succession asserting

---

[1] This is a revised and condensed version of an essay originally published under the same title in Elisabeth Krimmer and Patricia Simpson (eds), *Religion, Reason and Culture in the Age of Goethe* (Rochester: Camden House, 2013), pp. 244–65, and it is reprinted with their kind permission.

[2] Gilles Deleuze and Félix Guattari, *What is Philosophy?* (New York: Columbia University Press, 1994), pp. 48 and 60. Deleuze's provocative claim is that, like Christ, the true and immaculate philosophy incarnated only once, in the person of Spinoza.

[3] See, for example, Eckart Förster and Yitzhak Y. Melamed (eds), *Spinoza and German Idealism* (Cambridge: Cambridge University Press, 2012).

[4] Lewis White Beck, *Early German Philosophy: Kant and His Predecessors* (Cambridge, MA: Harvard University Press, 1969).

[5] Frederick Beiser, *The Fate of Reason: German Philosophy from Kant to Fichte* (Cambridge, MA: Harvard University Press, 1987). By 1992, Manfred Walter had published an important volume of essays devoted to the topic, *Spinoza und der deutsche Idealismus*, Schriftenreihe der Spinoza-Gesellschaft, 1 (Würzburg: Königshausen & Neumann, 1992).

that, basically, every significant thinker of the Enlightenment was a closet Spinozist.[6] Scepticism may be in order: on Wall Street, this latest development would be read as a 'contrary indicator', signalling a market top. But the centrality of the *Spinozastreit* clearly means that we have to understand both the extent and the import of Spinoza's influence on the Age of Goethe. And the centrality of Spinoza to contemporary discourse is beyond doubt; somehow, he figures in everyone's equations.

Not so with Fichte. There has been some outstanding recent scholarship, but compared to the boom in Spinoza, Fichte studies remains a cottage industry. Fichte has long been the most neglected and the least understood of the great philosophers. Hegel wanted to be buried next to him, and he was, but Fichte rates only a few sentences in Bertrand Russell's 836-page *History of Western Philosophy*, which mentions only the *Addresses to the German Nation* and wonders aloud whether he was insane.[7] Deleuze seldom mentions Fichte by name, but I contend that it is Fichte who contributes the terms that ultimately allow Deleuze's philosophy to add up. Indeed I want to suggest that all three of these seminal thinkers – Spinoza, Fichte and Deleuze – are deeply connected by a Deleuzian rhizome stretching across four centuries.[8] Viewed in this light, both the *Spinozastreit* specifically and a range of larger issues within German Idealism can be situated within a much larger context, and those issues reveal a surprisingly direct relevance to the latest philosophical developments culminating in the work of Gilles Deleuze.

Ironically, it is Charles Taylor's book on *Hegel*, of all people, that provides the clue. In his magnificent first chapter, 'The Aims of a New Epoch', Taylor connects the failed Revolution of 1789 forward to the failed 'French' revolution of 1968, and back to Spinoza.[9] If not to the degree Israel asserts, Spinoza was omnipresent in the intellectual life of the German-speaking world at the turn of the nineteenth century. In response to the failure of their Revolution, the generation of the 1790s strove to attain a specific kind of philosophical breakthrough that was

---

[6] Jonathan Israel, *Radical Enlightenment: Philosophy and the Making of Modernity 1650–1750* (Oxford: Oxford University Press, 2002); Jonathan Israel, *Enlightenment Contested: Philosophy, Modernity, and the Emancipation of Man 1650–1752* (Oxford: Oxford University Press, 2009); and Jonathan Israel, *Democratic Enlightenment: Philosophy, Revolution, and Human Rights, 1750–1790* (Oxford: Oxford University Press, 2011).

[7] Bertrand Russell, *A History of Western Philosophy* (New York: Simon & Schuster, 1967), p. 718.

[8] Gilles Deleuze and Félix Guattari, *A Thousand Plateaus: Capitalism and Schizophrenia* (Minneapolis: University of Minnesota Press, 1987), chap. 1.

[9] Charles Taylor, *Hegel* (Cambridge: Cambridge University Press, 1975).

formulated variously as a union of Spinoza or the 'Spinozist' Goethe + Kant or Fichte; Hegel termed it a 'union of union and non-union' that would reconcile *Substanz* and *Subjekt*. Schelling began as a Fichtean, and then went on to complement Fichte with Spinoza. As early as 1795, Hölderlin, Schelling, and Hegel were exchanging letters in which they seem to equate Fichte's Absolute 'I' with Spinoza's 'God'.[10] In a famous letter to Jacobi of 9 June 1785, Goethe declared Spinoza's philosophical project to be his life's work.

## SPINOZA + FICHTE

Spinoza and Fichte might seem initially to have no common denominator. After all, they are the prime expressions of the very opposition that the generation of the 1790s laboured so mightily to synthesise. Moreover, Fichte had gone out of his way to criticise Spinoza as a 'dogmatist' in the earliest version of the *Science of Knowledge*,[11] and we know that Jacobi's accusation of 'Spinozism' (tantamount to atheism) was the charge that offended Fichte more than any other. But I shall argue that it is easier than one might imagine to reconcile Fichte and Spinoza, because Fichte's philosophy is suffused with Spinozist elements right from the beginning, and he moves even further in the direction of Spinoza in his later philosophy.

The strongest evidence of his Spinozist turn is contained in three remarkable diaries from the last year of Fichte's life, which were suppressed by Fichte's son, and have been published only very recently.[12] These will be discussed more fully below.[13] Even in versions of his

---

[10]   Richard Fincham, 'Schelling's Subversion of Fichtean Monism, 1794–1796', in Daniel Breazeale and Tom Rockmore (eds), *Fichte, German Idealism, and Early Romanticism* (Amsterdam: Rodopi, 2010), pp. 149–64; p. 155.

[11]   Johann Gottlieb Fichte, *The Science of Knowledge* (Cambridge: Cambridge University Press, 1982 [1794]).

[12]   These philosophical diaries have been designated as *Diarium I*, *Diarium II*, and *Diarium III*. *Diarium I* and *Diarium II* appeared in vols 15 and 16 (2009 and 2011) of Fichte's *Nachgelassene Schriften*, ed. Erich Fuchs et al. (Stuttgart-Bad Cannstatt: Frommann-holzboog). *Diarium III* was published in Reinhard Lauth (ed.), *Ultima Inquirenda: J. G. Fichtes letzte Bearbeitung der Wissenschaftslehre Ende 1813 / Anfang 1814: Textband* (Stuttgart-Bad Canstatt: Frommann-holzboog, 2001), pp. 131–45.

[13]   For an excellent discussion of these late diaries, to which I am much indebted, see Günter Zöller, 'Leben und Wissen: Der Stand der Wissenschaftslehre beim letzten Fichte', in Erich Fuchs, Marco Ivaldo and Giovanni Moretto (eds), *Der transzendental-philosophische Zugang zur Wirklichkeit: Beiträge aus der aktuellen Fichte-Forschung* (Stuttgart-Bad Cannstatt: Frommann-holzboog, 2001), pp. 307–30.

*Science of Knowledge* that date from the turn of the century, Fichte has begun to veer sharply towards Spinoza, abandoning his earlier, dialectical presentation and seeking to explain the nature of intellectual intuition through a systematic analogy to mathematical construction. In the so-called *Neue Bearbeitung* of 1800–1, Fichte begins each of eight sections with a *Lehrsatz* or proposition, followed by specific postulates and corollaries – i.e., he argues, like Spinoza himself, *more geometrico*, and asserts that his arguments are as rigorous as mathematics itself. In another text from the same period, Fichte describes the method of the *Science of Knowledge* as 'the *mathēsis* of reason itself'.[14] Moreover, the manuscript of the same late version ends with a series of disjointed speculations and notes, many of which are startlingly Spinozist: here Fichte clearly echoes Spinoza in speculating about the possibility of a 'pure intuition of God' that might serve as the 'band for connecting the entire intelligible world'.[15]

## EXPRESSION

Charles Taylor contends that what drew Herder, Goethe, and others of the next generation to Spinoza was 'a vision of the way in which the finite subject fitted into a universal current of life'.[16] In late versions of the *Science of Knowledge*, Fichte had begun articulating the same Spinozist vision of God as pure, self-unfolding and self-expressing life. In an extraordinary passage from the version of 1810, for example, Fichte follows Spinoza in defining God as the single substance: 'Only one thing exists absolutely through itself: God, and God is not the dead concept which we enunciated just now, but he is in himself pure life.'[17] Fichte then proceeds to an assertion that echoes perfectly Deleuze's interpretation of Spinoza: 'However, if there should be knowledge . . . then it can only be God himself, because there is nothing but God, but outside of God himself . . . his expression.' Taylor's insight is confirmed: what united the whole generation of the 1790s, drew them to Herder, and drew Herder to Spinoza, was a shared anthropology of *expression*.

---

[14] Daniel Breazeale, 'Toward a *Wissenschaftslehre more geometrico* (1800–1801)', in Daniel Breazeale and Tom Rockmore (eds), *After Jena: New Essays on Fichte's Later Philosophy* (Evanston, IL: Northwestern University Press, 2008), pp. 3–40; p. 10. Unless otherwise indicated, all translations are my own.

[15] Ibid. p. 21.

[16] Taylor, *Hegel*, p. 16.

[17] Quoted in Errol E. Harris, 'Fichte and Spinozism', in Klaus Hammacher (ed.), *Der transzendentale Gedanke: Die gegenwärtige Darstellung der Philosophie Fichtes* (Hamburg: Felix Meiner, 1981), pp. 407–20; pp. 416–17.

But what drew Deleuze and the late Fichte to Spinoza was a metaphysics and an ontology of expression that opened the door to a potent, non-reductive philosophical monism. Just as Spinoza fought to overcome Cartesian dualism, Deleuze strove to redeem the original sin of metaphysics, its perpetual construction of a transcendental 'other' to which concepts can only refer, by experiencing the expressive immanence of living concepts.[18]

The concept of expression is so central to Deleuze's interpretation of his arch-predecessor Spinoza that his translators featured the concept in their title of his major study of Spinoza, demoting Spinoza's name to the subtitle.[19] Deleuze's Introduction begins by quoting the sixth definition of Spinoza's *Ethics*, emphasising the word 'expresses' with added italics: 'By God I understand a being absolutely infinite, that is, a substance consisting of an infinity of attributes, of which each one *expresses* an eternal and infinite essence.'[20] The single substance that is God expresses itself initially in the two attributes that are God's essence, and then again at the level of the modes, which can be viewed as 'an expression, as it were, of expression itself'.[21] Hence, 'God expresses himself in himself "before" expressing himself in his effects: he expresses himself in himself constituting *natura naturans*, before expressing himself through producing within himself *natura naturata*.'[22] Important epistemological correlates follow directly from this ontology of expression, chiefly the privileging of intuition as the organ whereby expression is directly apprehended: it is just this aspect of Spinoza's epistemology that allows him to transcend Descartes' ultimate criteria of clarity and distinctness as embodied in discursive thought.[23] Indeed, it is what makes Spinoza the perfect cure for the ills incurred by Cartesian dualism.[24] What made Spinoza so

---

[18] Deleuze's philosophy was profoundly influenced in this regard by Neoplatonism, Hermeticism and the mathematical mysticism of Cusanus. See Joshua Ramey, *The Hermetic Deleuze: Philosophy and Hermetic Ordeal* (Durham, NC: Duke University Press, 2012).

[19] Gilles Deleuze, *Expressionism in Philosophy: Spinoza* (New York: Zone Books, 1990). The French original of 1968 gives them equal billing: *Spinoza et le problème de l'expression* (Paris: Minuit, 1968).

[20] Ibid. p. 13.

[21] Ibid. p. 14.

[22] Ibid. Spinoza's key terms *natura naturans* and *natura naturata* are difficult to translate (hence usually referred to in the Latin original). *Naturans* would be the present participle of an imagined verbal form of 'nature', and *naturata* would be the past participle of same, so a literal translation would be something like 'nature naturing' and 'nature having natured' respectively.

[23] Ibid. p. 15.

[24] Ibid. p. 17.

exciting to Herder, Goethe, and the post-Kantians, and led Deleuze to recuperate his philosophy yet again at the end of the twentieth century, is his epistemology of intellectual intuition framed for an ontology of unifying expression.

Taylor reminds us that the students' rallying cry in May 1968, 'décloisonnement', was likewise a call for unity. In the case of Deleuze, it was the failure of the 'French' revolution of May 1968, in which students took to the streets, rallying under the motto 'L'imagination au pouvoir!', that led to a desire for unity. Like their German ancestors, the generation of 1968 strove for a unifying philosophy as well, which Deleuze and Guattari famously termed 'the magic formula we all seek: PLURALISM = MONISM'.[25] My own contention is that, especially in his late writings, Deleuze hits upon the same magic formula by synthesising Spinoza and Fichte via a *Wechselwirkung* whereby all three of these intensely radical philosophers are mutually transformed, illuminated and renewed.

## FICHTE + DELEUZE

Spinoza's influence on Deleuze is patent, but Fichte participates as an omnipresent silent partner as well. On its face, this argument might seem implausible. In many places Deleuze seems hostile to German Idealism as such: he framed his entire project as anti-Hegelian, and he characterised Kant as an 'enemy'.[26] But there is no trace of the late Hegel's conservative apologetics in Fichte; indeed, Altman has written persuasively about Fichte's 'anti-Hegelian legacy'.[27] And in the same sentence in which he describes Kant as an enemy, Deleuze avers that he likes his own book on Kant very much, and, on close inspection, his reading of Kant reveals itself to be surprisingly sympathetic.

How is this possible? Because Deleuze neutralises Kant by reading him in the spirit of Fichte. I suspect Deleuze was not entirely conscious of the degree to which he was doing this, but if so, then my case is all the stronger: the deep connections he discovered without seeking them are real, not adventitious. For both Fichte and Deleuze, it was not Kant, but dualism that was the great enemy – as it had been for Spinoza, who strove to overcome the letter of Cartesian dualism in the spirit of Descartes.

[25] Deleuze and Guattari, *A Thousand Plateaus*, p. 20.
[26] Gilles Deleuze, *Kant's Critical Philosophy: The Doctrine of the Faculties* (Minneapolis: University of Minnesota Press, 1985), p. xv.
[27] Matthew C. Altman, 'Fichte's Anti-Hegelian Legacy', in Breazeale and Rockmore, *Fichte, German Idealism, and Early Romanticism*, pp. 275–86.

Although it never mentions Fichte by name, Deleuze's book on Kant is thoroughly Fichtean. Where Kant had insisted on the hegemony of the understanding in the production of knowledge, Deleuze follows Fichte in asserting the priority of the imagination. He reminds us that, for Kant, all knowledge is representation; that 'representation means the synthesis of that which is presented'; and that 'this synthesis, as both apprehension *and* reproduction, is always defined by Kant as an act of the imagination'.[28] What guarantees the objectivity of representation in both senses – both its universality and its relationship to the objects of experience – is for Deleuze *not*, as in Kant, the applicability of the underlying categories of the understanding. Deleuze's account of the transcendental deduction could be pages straight out of Fichte. Deleuze assigns the categories a distinctly minor role – indeed, they are barely mentioned, and they are not listed as a topic in the index of the book. What guarantees objectivity is rather the fact that '[the categories] are linked in the unity of a consciousness, in such a way that the "I think" accompanies them'.[29] 'Indeed, all use of the understanding is developed from the "I think"; moreover the unity of the "I think" "is the understanding itself"'.[30] This last phrase is a quote from the *Critique of Pure Reason* – but it is a point that Kant mentions only in passing, in a footnote.[31] It was Fichte who promoted Kant's footnotes on imagination (here and elsewhere) to the centre of the argument, and Deleuze follows him. *L'imagination au pouvoir!*

In the elegant and witty Preface to the English edition, which grew out of his seminars on Kant of 1978, Deleuze again follows Fichte without naming him, epitomising the *Critique of Pure Reason* entirely in terms of the self, the tension between the active, self-determining

---

[28] Deleuze, *Kant's Critical Philosophy*, pp. 14–15.
[29] Ibid. p. 15.
[30] Ibid.
[31] The passage to which Deleuze refers is in the crucial section 16 of the 'Transcendental Deduction' [B131–5], which Fichte took as the foundation of his own epistemology of imagination. Kant begins this section by asserting that 'it must be possible for the "I think" to accompany all my representations; for otherwise something would be represented in me which could not be thought at all, and that is equivalent to saying that the representation would be impossible, or at least would be nothing to me'. Kant then terms this spontaneous act of 'representation' (which Fichte will later call 'intellectual intuition') '*pure apperception*'. At the end of the following paragraph, continuing the same discussion, he adds a long footnote, which ends with the assertion: 'The synthetic unity of apperception is therefore that highest point, to which we must ascribe all employment of the understanding, even the whole of logic, and conformably therewith, transcendental philosophy. Indeed this faculty of apperception is the understanding itself.'

*je* and the 'phenomenal, receptive and changing' *moi*. The latter is constructed within time, but the former synthesises time itself. 'Thus time moves into the subject, in order to distinguish the Ego from the I in it ... [time as the] "form of interiority" means not only that time is internal to us, but that our interiority constantly divides us from ourselves, splits us in two: a splitting in two which never runs its course, since time has no end. A giddiness, an oscillation which constitutes time.'[32]

Deleuze's invocation of Fichtean *Schweben* to summarise the whole of Kant's first *Critique* in a single term is particularly noteworthy. The movements of the concept that Deleuze describes here simultaneously evoke Spinoza's unity of thought and extension in *scientia intuitiva*: 'The plane of immanence has two facets as Thought and as Nature, as *Nous* and as *Physis*. This is why there are always many infinite movements caught within each other, each folded in the others, so that the return of one instantaneously re-launches another in such a way that the plane of immanence is ceaselessly being woven, like a gigantic shuttle.'[33] Deleuze's descriptions in his later texts of the living concept moving inside its plane as a shuttle flying – elsewhere, 'the incessant to-ing and fro-ing of the plane'[34] – are another clear evocation of Fichtean *Schweben*.[35]

As Zöller has argued, 'Fichte takes up Spinoza's insight that all determination is by way of negation (*omnis determinatio est negatio*)',[36] arguing that thinking as active determination always necessarily calls forth its *Anstoß* or 'check', an irreducible, determinable *other*. But this central concept links Fichte forward within the trans-historical rhizome as well. It is but a short step from this aspect of Fichte to some

---

[32] Ibid. p. ix.

[33] Deleuze and Guattari, *What is Philosophy?*, p. 38.

[34] Ibid. p. 59.

[35] Another important register of metaphors that Deleuze favours is structurally homologous to Fichtean *Schweben*: topological transformations such as the Möbius band, on which the seeming dichotomy between inner and outer is overcome by a simple folding of an object that has *only one edge and one side*. For Deleuze (as for Spinoza and Fichte), the turning of truth towards thought and the turning of thought towards truth are a single, instantaneous motion that is executed with an infinite speed that bridges all gaps: 'this is not a fusion but a reversibility, an immediate, perpetual, instantaneous exchange – a lightning flash. Infinite movement is double, and there is only a fold from one to the other' (Deleuze and Guattari, *What is Philosophy*, p. 38). For his part, Fichte invokes the concept of 'immanence' repeatedly in his late philosophical diaries, for example on pp. 278–9 of *Diarium II*.

[36] Günter Zöller, *Fichte's Transcendental Philosophy: The Original Duplicity of Intelligence and Will* (Cambridge: Cambridge University Press, 1998), p. 77.

of the profoundest passages in Deleuze's masterpiece, *Difference and Repetition*, on the thinking that is pure difference:

> For it is not figures already mediated and related to representation that are capable of carrying the faculties to their respective limits but, on the contrary, free or untamed states of difference in itself; not qualitative opposition within the sensible, but an element which is in itself difference, and creates at once both the quality in the sensible and the transcendent exercise within sensibility ... every time it is a free form of difference which awakens the faculty, and awakens it as the different within that difference.[37]

'Difference' is Deleuze's name for the mobile, creative energy of thinking that resists – checks – reason's constant striving for totalising, tautologous identity. For Deleuze, as for Fichte, this limitation of referentiality is what frees thinking to intuit genesis of the living concept through introspection.

It is in Deleuze's own, later philosophy, however, that the deepest connections between Deleuze and Fichte reveal themselves. There he likewise recuperates central aspects of Spinoza's ontology, which Fichte had recuperated independently through the 'ontological turn' in his own late philosophy: here 'thinking and being are said to be one and the same. Or rather, movement is not the image of thought without being also the substance of being'.[38] The import of Fichte's late turn from an epistemology centred on the imaginative faculties of the individual self to an exploration of thinking as an immediate manifestation of the life of nature will be discussed further in the section on 'Immanence' below.

## TRANSCENDENTAL EMPIRICISM

Although their terminology is different, Deleuze, Fichte and Spinoza all share a number of key concepts. The most important of these is a privileging of intuition over both empirical sensation and discursive thinking. I follow Deleuze in calling this shared stance 'transcendental empiricism', as for example in his short essay 'Immanence: A Life': 'It may seem curious that the transcendental be defined by such immediate givens: we will speak of a transcendental empiricism in contrast to everything that makes up the world of the subject and the object.'[39]

---

[37] Gilles Deleuze, *Difference and Repetition* (New York: Columbia University Press, 1994), pp. 144–5.

[38] Deleuze and Guattari, *What is Philosophy?*, p. 38.

[39] Gilles Deleuze, 'Immanence: A Life', in *Pure Immanence: Essays on a Life* (New York:

What Deleuze is describing is 'of course not the element of sensation (simple empiricism), for sensation is only a break within the flow of absolute consciousness'.[40] This 'transcendental empiricism' cannot involve reference to external signs: understanding is a pure activity; ideas are not, as Spinoza puts it so derisively, 'mute pictures on a panel'.[41] 'Simple empiricism' breaks the 'flow' of a consciousness that, for Deleuze as for Spinoza and Fichte, is 'absolute' – a 'pure stream of a-subjective [pre-reflexive, hence pre-subjective] consciousness'.[42] Here we are inevitably reminded of Spinoza's central assertion that there is only one 'absolutely infinite' substance with only two attributes.[43] Fichte resolves *Tatsachen* into *Tathandlungen*;[44] Spinoza raises *naturata* up into the pure activity of *naturans*, apart from which there is no sign. For Deleuze, 'things' ultimately dissolve into processes, unfolding 'events'; in one interview, he even asserts flatly: 'I don't believe in things.'[45]

Deleuze makes it clear how little his 'transcendental empiricism' has to do with empiricism as understood more conventionally: 'When immanence is no longer immanent to something other than itself it is possible to speak of a plane of immanence. Such a plane is, perhaps, a radical empiricism: it does not present a flux of the lived that is immanent to a subject and individualized in that which belongs to a ["phenomenal"] self.'[46] After this thoroughly Fichtean description of the realm beyond subject and object accessed via intellectual intuition, Deleuze proceeds to credit not Fichte, but Spinoza, who 'knew full well that immanence

Zone Books, 2001), pp. 25–34; p. 25.
[40] Ibid. p. 25.
[41] Benedict de Spinoza, *A Spinoza Reader: The Ethics and Other Works*, ed. and trans. Edwin Curley (Princeton, NJ: Princeton University Press, 1994), p. 148. See also ibid. p. 142: 'For no one who has a true idea is unaware that a true idea involves the highest certainty. For to have a true idea means nothing other than knowing a thing perfectly, or in the best way. And of course no one can doubt this unless he thinks that an idea is something mute, like a picture on a tablet, and not a mode of thinking, namely, the very [act of] understanding.' Spinoza's thought (shared by Fichte and Deleuze) is that our sense of truth never arises out of correspondence to an object – even a mental object – but rather through direct participation in its genesis. Cf. Spinoza's 'dynamic' definition of a circle, discussed below.
[42] Deleuze, 'Immanence: A Life', p. 25.
[43] Baruch de Spinoza, *Ethics and On the Improvement of the Understanding* (New York: Hafner, 1949), pp. 47–8.
[44] Fichte's neologism, implying a mental activity that is simultaneously a fact of consciousness.
[45] Gilles Deleuze, *Negotiations 1972–1990* (New York: Columbia University Press, 1990), p. 160.
[46] Deleuze and Guattari, *What is Philosophy?*, p. 47.

was only immanent to itself'.[47] And again, surprisingly for the orthodox view of Spinoza but not at all in the new context we are creating
here, Spinoza is invoked in terms much more appropriate for Fichte,
as a philosopher of *freedom*: 'He [Spinoza] discovered that freedom
exists only within immanence.'[48] For all three thinkers mapped by our
rhizome, freedom flows only from a direct *participation* in meaning; we
are free only to the extent that we actively and transparently co-create
the processes determining our knowledge.[49]

Nor should 'transcendental empiricism' be confused with logic.
Deleuze quickly dismisses logic's 'infantile idea of philosophy',[50] and
his hostility is implacable: 'Logic is reductionist not accidentally but
essentially and necessarily: following the route marked out by Frege
and Russell, it wants to turn the concept into a function.'[51] In a rivalry
with philosophy inspired by 'real hatred', logic 'kills the concept twice
over'.[52] In the same vein, Fichte responded harshly to Reinhold and
others who wanted to reduce philosophy to logic: such a philosophy
can achieve only a purely analytic kind of necessity and universality,
and it can claim this only because it sacrifices all real content; hence it is
nothing but a 'desiccated conceptual game'.[53]

## INTUITION

For Deleuze, as for Spinoza and Fichte, the concept is reborn from its
own ashes by revealing itself to a faculty that corresponds exactly to
'intellectual intuition' and *scientia intuitiva*. Only intuition can appre-
hend this supersensible yet entirely real content:

> Instead of a string of linked propositions, it would be better to isolate the
> flow of interior monologue, or the strange forkings of the most ordinary
> conversation ... thought as such produces something *interesting* when
> it accedes to the infinite movement that frees it from truth as supposed
> paradigm and reconquers an immanent power of creation ... *It would be
> necessary to go back up the path that science descends*, and at the very end
> of which logic sets up its camp.[54]

---

[47] Ibid. pp. 48, 60.
[48] Ibid. p. 48.
[49] See also Rudolf Steiner, *The Philosophy of Freedom* (London: Rudolf Steiner Press, 1970 [1894]).
[50] Deleuze and Guattari, *What is Philosophy?*, p. 22.
[51] Ibid. p. 135.
[52] Ibid. p. 140.
[53] Breazeale, 'Toward a *Wissenschaftslehre more geometrico*', p. 16.
[54] Deleuze and Guattari, *What is Philosophy?*, pp. 139–40.

Deleuze does not use Fichte's terminology here, but rather Wittgenstein's: 'The concept shows itself and does nothing but show itself.'[55] Nevertheless, the methodological parallel to the 1794 version of Fichte's *Science of Knowledge* is striking: 'going back up the path that science descends' could stand as a one-sentence commentary on Fichte's text.[56] Again we see that, intentionally or unintentionally, Deleuze's relationship to Fichte has been strangely veiled. For his part, Deleuze has captured the distinction between discursive thought and intuition in a brilliant metaphor, comparing propositional thought-structures to the devices of Baroque emblems, which represent only an abstract schema of the living *event* that is 'shown' in the rich and dynamic iconography of the accompanying image.[57] Like Fichte, who argued that only intellectual intuition is able to fill thinking with a content that is *real*, Deleuze describes the experience of intuition as an encounter with substance: 'Something in the world forces us to think. This something is an object not of recognition but of fundamental *encounter* . . . its primary characteristic is that it can only be sensed.'[58]

Kicking away the ladder of propositional logic, we step into a realm that Deleuze calls 'virtual' and Fichte calls 'intellectual'. The *virtual* is a realm of pure 'consistency', the non-formal, non-discursive, synthetic activity that Fichte finds by stepping behind logic's first principle, the axiom of identity (A=A). Logic destroys the concept's 'inseparability of intensional components (zone of indiscernibility)', limits the infinite 'plane of consistency' by reducing it to finite, referential movements.[59] Logic is the enemy, because logic destroys immanence. Deleuze echoes Fichte's discovery of a higher, pure subjectivity (I=I) behind the formal axiom of identity: for Deleuze, the genuine philosophical concept 'requires a "belonging" to a subject'.[60]

---

[55] Ibid. p. 140.
[56] In a nutshell, Fichte is trying to find his way to that inaccessible thing-in-itself that Kant had called 'the transcendental unity of apperception'. Fichte's approach is thoroughly consonant with Kant's 'transcendental method': he attempts to step behind the structures of thinking and see what constitutive activities must necessarily be in place in order to account for the structures. Changing the metaphor, one can say that Fichte is climbing toward the top rung of a ladder, the most universal and fundamental and abstract and indubitable things we can think, which are the fundamental axioms of logic. Fichte says boldly, now let's step *behind* even those axioms.
[57] Deleuze, *Negotiations*, pp. 160, 201; this thought was first presented in Deleuze's late masterpiece *The Fold: Leibniz and the Baroque* (Minneapolis: University of Minnesota Press, 1993).
[58] Deleuze, *Difference and Repetition*, p. 139.
[59] Deleuze and Guattari, *What is Philosophy?*, p. 138.
[60] Ibid. p. 141.

For Spinoza, *scientia intuitiva* is the third and highest mode of knowledge; understanding things in light of intuition was for him 'the highest effort of the mind and its highest virtue'.[61] Its ultimate goal and promise is to reveal 'the knowledge of the union existing between the mind and the whole of Nature'.[62] Spinoza concedes that human thinking is still too weak to achieve this highest intuition, but then in a remarkable passage immediately following, he asserts that, because we can *imagine* such a degree of knowledge, we should strive to attain it.[63] It is a remarkable anticipation both of Fichte's notion of endless striving towards an unattainable limit, which Fichte views as the motive power driving all of the activities of mind, and of the centrality of imagination as the ultimate impetus to striving.

Spinoza's surprising example of *scientia intuitiva* is the 'fourth proportional', a : b : c : x, which exemplifies intuitive knowledge when it is apprehended immediately, rather than deduced discursively via an algebraic algorithm.[64] In words that Deleuze and Fichte could have written, Spinoza asserts that the truth needs no external sign; we are moved to a conviction of certainty because we find ourselves at every moment *inside* the pure activity of the truth's construction. Surprisingly, the arch-rationalist Spinoza has no interest in the discursive algorithm that allows one to deduce the fourth proportional logically: instead, he pushes mathematical demonstration in the direction of a Fichtean intuition – 'a pure activity into which an eye has been inserted'.[65] 'For an idea is in itself nothing else than a certain sensation.'[66]

Spinoza rejects any attempt to deduce the direct *expression* of substance that is God. Rather, he subsumes deduction within its '*direct manifestation*' to the faculty of intuition:

> It is now the object that expresses itself, the thing itself that explicates itself. All its properties then jointly 'fall within an infinite understanding'. So that there is no question of deducing Expression: rather it is expression that embeds deduction in the Absolute ... One cannot understand attributes

---

[61] Spinoza, *A Spinoza Reader*, p. 257. For a fuller discussion of Spinoza's two main accounts of *scientia intuitiva*, see my article 'Goethe's Intuitions', *The Goethe Yearbook* 18, (2011), pp. 35–50.

[62] Spinoza, *Ethics and On the Improvement*, p. 6.

[63] Ibid.

[64] Ibid. p. 9.

[65] See my discussion in 'The Metamorphosis of the Scientist', *The Goethe Yearbook* 5, (1990), pp. 187–212.

[66] Spinoza, *Ethics and On the Improvement*, p. 27.

without proof, which is the manifestation of the invisible, and the view within which falls what thus manifests itself. Thus demonstrations, says Spinoza, are the eyes through which the mind sees.[67]

Deleuze's explication of Spinoza here recalls vividly Fichte's method in *The Science of Knowledge* of 1794, where logic is the ladder one climbs to an intuition that can no longer be 'said' in propositional form, but only 'shown'. For Spinoza, the highest kind of knowledge is a knowing that is a seeing. Viewed in this light, Spinoza stands arm-in-arm with Deleuze when he asserts that 'reason is only a concept, and a very impoverished concept for defining the plane and the movements that pass through it'.[68]

Deleuze affirms 'the grandiose Leibnizian or Bergsonian perspective that every philosophy depends upon an intuition'.[69] Intuition is 'prephilosophical', which is to say the ground of all possible knowledge, in that it is the chaotic, infinitely mobile matrix out of which specific concepts are born: 'The concept is the beginning of philosophy, but the plane is its instituting.'[70] Intuition is the third kind of knowledge that sees immediately 'a plane of immanence that constitutes the absolute ground of philosophy, its earth or deterritorialisation, the foundation on which it creates its concepts'.[71]

Spinoza, Fichte, and Deleuze all found their philosophies upon intuition, and their founding intuition leads them all to the same fundamental insight: the ground of all knowledge is a synthetic, monistic activity that is immanent only to itself. Deleuze's descriptions of this immanence are filled with Fichtean and Spinozist resonances, as for example when he describes it as

> a state of survey without distance, at ground level, a self-survey that no chasm, fold, or hiatus escapes ... a *form in itself* that does not refer to any external point of view, any more than the retina or striated area of the cortex refers to another retina or cortical area; it is an absolute consistent form that surveys *itself* independently of any supplementary dimension.[72]

Here we are reminded immediately of a striking locution in Fichte's latest version of his *Science of Knowledge*, that of the recently published diaries from March 1813 to January 1814, where intellectual intuition

---

[67] Deleuze, *Expressionism*, p. 22.
[68] Deleuze and Guattari, *What is Philosophy?*, p. 43.
[69] Ibid. p. 40.
[70] Ibid. p. 41.
[71] Ibid.
[72] Ibid. p. 210.

is described as 'a seeing of seeing'.[73] As in Spinoza, this intuited immanence is 'an absolute consistent form', a pure substance that is also pure
subject, the 'I = I' that is the first precipitate of the self-positing Fichtean
self.

In an important passage that may be directly indebted to Spinoza,
Deleuze describes the concept (as opposed to the logical proposition,
the scientific function, and the referential prospect) as infinite, active
and creative. As in both Spinoza and Fichte, the philosopher's task is
to free thought from mere 'repetition', from referentiality, 'from truth
as supposed paradigm' by 'acceding to [thought's] infinite movement'
in a way that 'reconquers an immanent power of creation'.[74] Deleuze is
far from reviving speculative metaphysics: concepts are not read out of
some transcendent order. Rather, they must be created, because 'there
is no heaven for concepts',[75] and the first, grounding act of philosophical knowledge is bearing witness to the genesis of the concept: 'But the
concept is not given, it is created; it is to be created. It is not formed but
posits itself in itself – it is a self-positing ... The concept posits itself
to the same extent that it is created. What depends on a free creative
activity is also that which, independently and necessarily, posits itself in
itself: the most subjective will be the most objective.'[76] The language is
pure Fichte,[77] but then, strangely, Deleuze adds immediately: 'The post-
Kantians, and notably Schelling and Hegel, are the philosophers who
paid the most attention to the concept as philosophical reality in this
sense.'[78] Later in the same chapter, Deleuze again invokes Fichte without
naming him: 'What remains absolute, however, is the way in which the
created concept is posited in itself and with others. The relativity and
absoluteness of the concept are like its pedagogy and its ontology, its
creation and its self-positing, its ideality and its reality – the concept

[73] Of the many passages containing this insight that might be quoted, the most memora-
ble is Fichte's report at the very beginning of *Diarium II* of a dream to rival Decartes':
'In a dream, a task appeared to me, shining very brightly. [It was to show that] seeing
was an eye that sees itself' (ibid. p. 209). Elsewhere, Fichte refers to 'the eye [*Auge*] of
intuition' (Breazeale, 'Toward a *Wissenschaftslehre more geometrico*', p. 21). See also
*Diarium II*, pp. 220 and 235.

[74] Deleuze and Guattari, *What is Philosophy?*, p. 140.

[75] Ibid. p. 5.

[76] Ibid. p. 11.

[77] See, for example, the extraordinary passages at *Diarium II*, p. 221, 'It is thus throughout all of consciousness until the science of knowledge emerges and *uncovers* the
hidden *genesis*: / that *life bears its own concept* within itself' and again at *Diarium II*,
p. 223: '*Comprehension* means now thinking through the essence, as in *seeing*, and
now its *genesis*. These are one and the same. Seeing is *a reflex of life*; it is genesis itself.'

[78] Deleuze and Guattari, *What is Philosophy?*, p. 11.

is real without being actual, ideal without being abstract.'[79] Only at the very end of his life will Deleuze reveal Fichte as his second great Muse.

## CONCEPTUAL REALISM

All three of our thinkers are conceptual Realists. Deleuze's *event*, 'real without being actual', offers an uncanny parallel to the Scholastic notion of *universalia ante rem*, and both concepts help greatly in understanding Spinoza's challenging notion of *natura naturans*. As we have argued above, both thinkers are adamant that Spinoza's expression of divine substance, Deleuze's 'events', can be grasped by intellectual intuition, but never by discursive thought. The 'event' is what resists embodiment in any particular 'state of affairs'; it is 'the part that eludes its own actualization in everything that happens'.[80] Hence it cannot be grasped or expressed by *universalia in re*. What characterises the *event* is precisely what made it seem unreal to the Nominalists: it has 'a shadowy and secret part that is continually subtracted from or added to its actualization . . . it neither begins nor ends but has gained or kept the infinite movement to which it gives consistency . . . The event is immaterial, incorporeal, unlivable: pure *reserve*'.[81]

Spinoza's distinction between *natura naturans* and *natura naturata* maps neatly onto the Scholastic distinction between *universalia ante rem* and *universalia in re*. He warns against 'abstractions' from experience – that is, against dealing in *universalia post rem*: 'we shall be extremely careful not to confound that which is only in the understanding with that which is in the thing itself'.[82] Hence Spinoza's initially surprising insistence that a circle cannot be adequately understood as the set of points equidistant from any given point: that would be to define it from the outside, *post rem*, as static *naturata*.[83] The only way in which to understand the circle adequately is to witness its genesis, by intuiting a line with one endpoint fixed, and the other moving freely. In Fichtean terms, Spinoza is describing an intuition of the circle's positing, the intellectual movement out of which the structure of the circle precipitates. Spinoza, Fichte, and Deleuze all strive to find rigorous ways of describing the ineffable. Spinoza proceeds from his dynamic definition

---

[79] Ibid. p. 22.
[80] Ibid. p. 156.
[81] Ibid.
[82] Spinoza, *Ethics and On the Improvement*, p. 31.
[83] Ibid. p. 32.

of the circle to prescribe general 'rules for defining uncreated things'.[84] Another example would be Spinoza's remarkable assertion that the idea of a well-constructed building in the mind of an architect is fully real and true, even if the building is never built.[85] A more complicated instance is the extended discussion of Peter and Paul that recurs throughout both the treatise *On the Improvement of the Understanding* and the *Ethics*: 'the true idea of Peter', which is 'the reality of Peter represented subjectively' and 'in itself something real, and quite distinct from the actual Peter',[86] clearly must be a *universalium ante rem* as opposed to a *universalium in re*. Extending the same argument further in the *Ethics*, Spinoza distinguishes between 'the idea, for example, of Peter, which constitutes the essence of the mind itself of Peter [*ante rem*], and the idea of Peter himself which is in another man; for example, in Paul [*post rem*]'.[87]

For Spinoza, God has infinite attributes, which means that all possible states of affairs exist simultaneously *in potentia*, unrealised yet fully real. Deleuze's description of the temporality of the *event* helps us to understand how this can be so. For Deleuze, this temporality stands apart from clock-time; it is an infinite movement that takes place at infinite speed, hence has no duration; a *naturans* in which war is willed 'against past and future wars, the pangs of death against all deaths, and the wound against all scars'.[88] Like Fichte, Deleuze asserts that these *universalia ante rem* can be known only through 'the strange indifference of an intellectual intuition'.[89] In the 1814 version of his *Science of Knowledge*, Fichte describes the ultimate limit of Idealism as a self-grounding Realism.[90] As in Spinoza, this highest plane of philosophical knowledge can be accessed only by a science unique to philosophy, apart from propositional logic and scientific functions: it can be accessed only by a *scientia intuitiva*.

---

[84] Ibid. p. 33.
[85] Ibid. p. 23.
[86] Ibid. p. 12.
[87] Ibid. p. 97.
[88] Deleuze and Guattari, *What is Philosophy?*, p. 160.
[89] Ibid. p. 158. 'Strange' evokes the 'strange attractors' that feature so prominently in Gleick's book on chaos that Deleuze has just cited in his own text: James Gleick, *Chaos* (New York: Viking, 2008). And surely we are meant to hear Schelling's central concept of generative identity, *Indifferenz*, in the word 'indifference'.
[90] Zöller, 'Leben und Wissen', p. 325.

## LIVING THINKING

Explicitly in both late Deleuze and late Fichte, and implicitly in Spinoza, this pure, *ante rem* immanence that exists apart from particular states of affairs, and cannot be represented with reference to them, is described as *life itself*. 'Philosophical concepts will be functions of the lived, as scientific concepts are functions of states of affairs; but the order or the derivation now changes direction since these functions of the lived become primary.'[91] In the earliest versions of the *The Science of Knowledge*, Fichte had opposed 'speculation' to mere life as lived, which he viewed as the naïve 'other' of philosophy,[92] but in the late deliberations recorded above all in his philosophical diaries, Fichte's stance towards 'life' shifts radically. By the time of the final *Diarium*, written in the last months of his life, Fichte clearly has subordinated the 'I' to 'a life that *I* do not imagine, but rather that *imagines* me':[93] 'I tell you it is thus . . . it is not the I that *sees* itself, but rather life looks upon I: / that it [the I] speaks afterwards: it has seen itself, is the reflex of the perception [of life].'[94] Throughout his diaries, for example on page 214 of *Diarium II*, intuition is clearly identified as a 'reflex of life' and the 'I' is now viewed as the focal point of a *divine* 'seeing': 'this I is a lawful point within which the divine, as a life in itself and through itself, can appear'.[95] The 1814 version *of The Science of Knowledge* describes the Absolute as 'pure life through and through in itself and through itself',[96] and the understanding as form determined by life itself: '[The understanding] comes to know itself as the *form of a life*, and as something existing by virtue of Life's self-determination of the existence of this form.'[97] For Fichte, the highest intuition would be that of 'the genesis of the first act of seeing',[98] of the lawfulness of life revealing itself as 'visibility of visibility'.[99]

Spinoza asserts repeatedly that God's understanding *is* His will; when God thinks, *life* happens, because 'substance thinking and substance extended are one and the same substance, which is now comprehended

---

[91] Deleuze and Guattari, *What is Philosophy?*, p. 142.
[92] Zöller, *Fichte's Transcendental Philosophy*, p. 30.
[93] Zöller, 'Leben und Wissen', p. 322.
[94] Ibid.
[95] Fichte, *Diarium II*, p. 217.
[96] Zöller, 'Leben und Wissen', p. 327.
[97] Ibid. p. 325.
[98] Fichte, *Diarium II*, p. 235.
[99] Ibid. p. 233.

under this attribute and now under that'.[100] He claims this is 'a truth which some of the Hebrews appear to have seen as if through a cloud, since they say that God, the intellect of God, and the things which are the object of that intellect are one and the same thing'.[101] In his late philosophy, Fichte moves closer to Spinoza than he ever had dared before in identifying his philosophical Absolute not just with *life*, but with 'divine life':[102] Zöller may be right in speculating that Fichte's untimely death probably saved him from having to endure another round of the *Spinozastreit* with the attendant charges of atheism.[103]

If thought and extension are infinite attributes of a single divine substance, it follows that the highest thought, the pure activity that is God's self-understanding, must simultaneously express itself in extension as the genesis of actual states of affairs. *Natura naturans* is the '*Gott-Natur*'[104] from which the discrete, finished forms of *natura naturata* flow. Deleuze's 'plane of immanence' must be what Rudolf Steiner termed in his own late work a realm of 'living working', as opposed to the realm of 'finished work'.[105]

In his late writings, Deleuze follows and conjoins Fichte and Spinoza explicitly in calling for philosophy to create 'vital ideas':

> To reach the concept it is not even enough for phenomena to be subject to principles analogous to those that associate ideas or things, or to principles that order reasons ... what suffices for 'current ideas' does not suffice for 'vital ideas' – those that must be created. Ideas can only be associated as images and can only be ordered as abstractions; to arrive at the concept we must go beyond both of these and arrive *as quickly as possible* at mental objects determinable as real beings. This is what Fichte or Spinoza have already shown: we must make use of fictions and abstractions, but only so far as is necessary to get to a plane where we go from real being to real being and advance through the construction of concepts.[106]

[100] Spinoza, *Ethics and On the Improvement*, p. 84.
[101] Ibid.
[102] Zöller, 'Leben und Wissen', pp. 316–17.
[103] Ibid. p. 330.
[104] Goethe's neologism '*Gott-Natur*', clearly meant to recall Spinoza's famous dictum *deus sive natura*, is invoked in the final lines of Goethe's late poem 'Schillers Reliquien':

> What higher goal can anyone attain
> Than seeing God-in-Nature as it is revealed?
> How forms once fixed to Spirit she lets flow,
> How Spirit's firmly held in forms below?

[105] See Rudolf Steiner, *Anthroposophical Leading Thoughts* (London: Rudolf Steiner Press, 1999), which he composed on his deathbed in 1925.
[106] Deleuze and Guattari, *What is Philosophy?*, p. 207.

Tellingly, Deleuze footnotes this passage with a reference to Guéroult's two-volume study of Fichte.[107] Hence there is good evidence that Deleuze was at least reading *about* Fichte late in his career.

> The concept is neither denotation of states of affairs nor signification of the lived; it is the event as pure sense that immediately runs through the components. It has no number, either whole or fractional, for counting things that display its properties, but a combination that condenses and accumulates the components it traverses and surveys. The concept is a form or a force; in no possible sense is it ever a function.[108]

In his last deliberations, Fichte arrives at the same epiphany: '*[Life] itself*, that incomprehensible thing, *is, comes into being* . . . it *is* as an active verb, not as a *verbum neutrum*. That is indeed the main purpose of Idealism: to cancel out the *verbum neutrum* completely, so that everywhere only active verbs remain.'[109] Life is to the concept, and the concept is to the understanding, as *natura naturans* is to *natura naturata*. For all three thinkers, the concept reveals itself to be ultimately a formative force, a life force or living form.[110]

The import of Deleuze's passages, quoted above, in which he describes the plane of immanence 'rocking back and forth' as it is woven by a flying shuttle, is now revealed. His intuition recalls perfectly the epiphany of the Earth Spirit to Faust in the opening scene of Goethe's drama:

> In tides of living, in doing's storm,
> Up, down, I wave
> Waft to and fro,
> Birth and Grave,
> An endless flow,
> A changeful plaiting,
> Fiery begetting,
> Thus at Time's scurrying loom I weave and warp
> And broider at the Godhead's living garb.[111]

---

[107] Martial Guéroult, *L'Évolution et la structure de la Doctrine de la science chez Fichte* (Paris: Belles Lettres, 1982).

[108] Deleuze and Guattari, *What is Philosophy?*, pp. 143–4.

[109] Zöller, 'Leben und Wissen', p. 319.

[110] Cf. Zöller, *Fichte's Transcendental Philosophy*, p. 111 on Fichte's 'treatment of thinking as form, more specifically as formative activity'. Perhaps this is also what Deleuze meant in his many enigmatic descriptions of the living concept as a plane cutting through and organising chaos.

[111] Johann Wolfgang Goethe, *Faust*, Norton Critical Edition, trans. Walter Arndt (New York: Norton, 2001), lines 501–9.

It is a revelation of the Goddess Natura, an immediate intuition of life itself.[112] In such epiphanies, the infinitely remote goal of Spinoza's striving, union of the mind with the whole of nature, 'the magic formula that we all seek', seems within reach after all.

## IMMANENCE

All these threads come together in Deleuze's last published essay, 'Immanence: A Life'. In this intensely personal testimonial to his deepest beliefs, Deleuze begins with a purely Fichtean description of the positing of the finite self within a *Tathandlung* that transcends subject and object: 'Consciousness becomes a fact only when a subject is produced at the same time as its object, both being outside the field and appearing as "transcendents".'[113] Further, he argues that '[consciousness] is expressed, in fact, only when it is reflected upon a subject that refers it to objects'.[114] He then proceeds via Spinoza's concept of absolute immanence to a remarkable passage that includes a rare explicit reference to Fichte. The key concept shared by all three thinkers is the 'transcendental field':

> What is the transcendental field? It can be distinguished from experience in that it doesn't refer to an object or belong to an object (empirical representation). It appears therefore as a pure stream of a-subjective consciousness, a pre-reflexive impersonal consciousness, a qualitative duration of consciousness without a self . . . we will speak of a transcendental empiricism in contrast to everything that makes up the world of the subject and the object.[115]

In his earlier philosophy, Fichte had sought to ground cognition on a pure activity, a *Tathandlung*, which cannot be any *thing* or pre-existent *fact* (*Tatsache*), even within consciousness. But the early Fichte's subject as positing agent stops short of genuine immanence.[116] The Fichtean

---

[112] See my article 'The Unconscious of Nature: Analyzing Disenchantment in *Faust I*', *The Goethe Yearbook*, 17, (2010), pp. 117–32, where I argue that the Earth Spirit in Goethe's *Faust* should be understood as an epiphany of the Goddess Natura.

[113] Deleuze, 'Immanence: A Life', p. 26.

[114] Ibid.

[115] Ibid. p. 25.

[116] 'Immanence is not related to Some Thing as a unity superior to all things or to a Subject as an act that brings about a synthesis of things: it is only when immanence is no longer immanence to anything other than itself that we can speak of a plane of immanence' (Deleuze, 'Immanence: A Life', p. 27). Or, as Deleuze puts it even more gnomically in the same essay, 'The One is not the transcendent that might contain immanence but the immanent contained within a transcendental field' (ibid. p. 30).

subject and object reveal themselves in Deleuze's late philosophy as 'transcendent' rather than 'transcendental': both Deleuze and Fichte himself overcome the dangers of Fichte's early philosophy by situating the transcendental not within a *self* (not even an 'absolute' self), or even within Being (as though immanence could be immanent to something other than immanence itself, as in Spinoza), but rather within *life itself*.[117] Deleuze ends his final essay evoking Fichte by name at last:

> We will say of pure immanence that it is A LIFE, and nothing else. It is not immanence to life, but the immanent that is in nothing is itself a life. A life is the immanence of immanence, absolute immanence: it is complete power, complete bliss. It is to the degree that he goes beyond the aporias of the subject and the object that Johann Fichte, in his last philosophy, presents the transcendental field as a *life*, no longer dependent on a Being or submitted to an Act – it is an absolute immediate consciousness whose very activity no longer refers to a being but is ceaselessly posed in a life.[118]

And then he immediately evokes Spinoza: 'The transcendental field then becomes a genuine plane of immanence that reintroduces Spinozism into the heart of the philosophical process.'[119] In this exquisite final essay, Deleuze maps the rhizome with a single masterstroke. The magic formula is: Spinoza + Fichte = x. We solve for x, and x = Deleuze. Only Deleuze is equal to the radicality of his illustrious predecessors. His synthesis calls forth a new plane of consistency, with uncanny 'nondiscursive resonances' – an event that surveys *us* as it actualises revolutionary potentials.

[117] Ibid. pp. 26–7.
[118] Ibid. p. 27.
[119] Ibid. pp. 27–8.

# Chapter 9

# State Philosophy and the War Machine

*Nathan Widder*

## INTRODUCTION

This chapter puts Hegel's political philosophy into conversation with Deleuze and Guattari's war machine thesis along four axes: a shared understanding of political structure as an assemblage of desire; competing understandings of dialectical and non-dialectical becoming; how moments of semblance in the unfolding of Hegelian right offer points where the war machine can emerge from within State structures; and finally, Hegel's civil servant as the mediating figure within the State in relation to Deleuze and Guattari's metallurgist as the figure who disjunctively relates the State to the war machine. In establishing this exchange, I hope to demonstrate how Hegel's and Deleuze and Guattari's accounts present comparable structures and ambiguities, but with very different priorities surrounding them. While Hegel aims to contain the excessive contingencies and multivalent desires that mark the ideals and institutions of his State's Ethical Life, Deleuze and Guattari seek to use them to problematise the State's purported rationality, and whereas Hegel's political philosophy culminates with Ethical Life as the highpoint and precondition of politics, Deleuze and Guattari show that these same arrangements find their precondition in a fundamental exteriority. Recent scholarship on Deleuze and Hegel has moved beyond the simplistic viewpoint that Deleuze's philosophy of difference has no real relation to Hegel's dialectical thought, and has demonstrated clearly how Deleuze has significant affinities with Hegel even while breaking sharply with him, and, indeed, how Deleuze's and Hegel's projects share many philosophical aspirations.[1] With respect to their political thought, I

---

[1] See, for example: Henry Somers-Hall, *Hegel, Deleuze, and the Critique of Representation: Dialectics of Negation and Difference* (Albany: State University of

hope to show that the relation between Hegel and Deleuze and Guattari is that of a disjunctive synthesis, wherein they are intimately intertwined but incapable of full and final resolution. The stark antithesis to Hegel often appearing in Deleuze's and Deleuze and Guattari's rhetoric must be understood in light of this much more complex and subtle connection.

## THE STATE AS AN ASSEMBLAGE OF DESIRE

The Introduction to the *Philosophy of Right* contains a substantial discussion of human drives or impulses (*Trieb*). It follows Hegel's well-known derivation of the will's freedom, which is 'both the substance of right and its goal',[2] as the dialectical synthesis of the abstractly opposed moments of indeterminacy and determination. A will abstracted from all determining restriction is empty and self-negating, whereas determination denies the will its infinitude by particularising it; but this opposition is overcome through the notion of freedom as *self*-determination, the will being restricted by nothing but itself.[3] After deriving concrete freedom this way, Hegel outlines two forms of the will that parallel the moments of self-consciousness outlined in the *Phenomenology of Spirit* before the Dialectic of Lordship and Bondage. The first is that of a will whose 'determinate character lies in the abstract opposition of its subjectivity to the objectivity of external immediate existence', which characterises 'the formal will of mere self-consciousness which finds an external world confronting it' and 'constitutes only the *appearance* of the will'.[4] The second is that of a will determined not by separating itself from what it is not but by reflecting its particularisation into itself, whereby its content emerges as the purpose it gives itself in relation to itself or its world.[5] This second form expresses the genuine concept of the will, but in being immediately self-determining, the will is only implicitly free: 'It is not until it has itself as its object that the will is for *itself* what it is in itself.'[6] Only through mediation, which takes it outside itself in such a way that it finds itself again, can the free will transcend its

New York Press, 2012); Karen Houle and Jim Vernon (eds), *Hegel and Deleuze: Together Again for the First Time* (Evanston, IL: Northwestern University Press, 2013); Nathan Widder, 'Thought after Dialectics: Deleuze's Ontology of Sense', *Southern Journal of Philosophy* 41:3, (2003), pp. 451–76.

[2] G. W. F. Hegel, *Philosophy of Right*, trans. T. M. Knox (Oxford: Oxford University Press, 1967), §4.

[3] Ibid. §§5–7.

[4] Ibid. §8.

[5] Ibid. §9.

[6] Ibid. §10.

finitude, where its being-in-itself and its being-for-itself exist in distinct senses,[7] and become infinite and actual.[8]

The will that is only implicitly free 'is the immediate or natural will', whose content is 'the impulses [*Trieb*], desires, inclinations, whereby the will finds itself determined in the course of nature'.[9] This will's substance thereby comprises 'a medley and multiplicity of impulses, each of which is merely "my desire" but exists alongside other desires which are likewise all "mine", and each of which is at the same time something universal and indeterminate, aimed at all kinds of objects and satiable in all kinds of ways'.[10] The will does not stand above this multiplicity of impulses, but rather comes to exist by resolving its indeterminacy and identifying with a particular drive or desire directed towards a specific object.[11] However, this leaves the will 'infinite in form only',[12] its freedom expressed merely as arbitrariness.[13] Moreover, this arbitrary will is self-contradictory because in this 'dialectic of impulses and inclinations . . . each of them is in the way of every other – the satisfaction of one is unavoidably subordinated or sacrificed to the satisfaction of another, and so on',[14] and because 'an impulse is simply a uni-directional urge and thus has no measuring-rod in itself',[15] meaning no immanent principle exists to weigh conflicting impulses and resolve their struggle. All this is further complicated inasmuch as each specific

---

[7] Ibid. §10R. References with an 'R' refer to the Remark to that paragraph.

[8] Compare with the two moments of self-consciousness outlined in the *Phenomenology*: 'But in point of fact self-consciousness is the reflection out of the being of the world of sense and perception, and is essentially the return from *otherness*. As self-consciousness, it is movement; but since what it distinguishes from itself is *only itself as* itself, the difference, as an otherness, is *immediately superseded* for it; the difference *is not*, and *it* [self-consciousness] is only the motionless tautology of: "I am I"; but since for it the difference does not have the form of *being*, it is *not* self-consciousness. Hence otherness is for it in the form of *a being*, or as a *distinct moment*; but there is also for consciousness the unity of itself with this difference as a *second distinct moment*. With that first moment, self-consciousness is in the form of *consciousness*, and the whole expanse of the sensuous world is preserved for it, but at the same time only as connected with the second moment, the unity of self-consciousness with itself; and hence the sensuous world is for it an enduring existence which, however, is only *appearance*, or a difference which, *in itself,* is no difference' (G. W. F. Hegel, *Phenomenology of Spirit*, trans. Arnold V. Miller (Oxford: Oxford University Press, 1977), §167).

[9] Hegel, *Philosophy of Right*, §11.

[10] Ibid. §12.

[11] Ibid.

[12] Ibid. §14.

[13] Ibid. §15.

[14] Ibid. §17.

[15] Ibid.

content 'is only a possible one, i.e. it may be mine or it may not'.[16] The will can resolve itself differently, moving from impulse to impulse or object to object, but this merely engenders a spurious infinity that 'never enables it [the will] to get beyond its own finitude, because the content of every such choice is something other than the form of the will and therefore something finite'.[17] Moral theories calling 'for the *purification* of impulses' by raising them above their immediacy, naturalness, contingency, and subjectivity are really demanding that they be 'brought back to their substantial essence', which means that 'the impulses should become the rational system of the will's volitions. To grasp them like that, proceeding out of the concept of the will, is the content of the philosophical science of right.'[18] And, as Hegel states earlier in the Introduction, 'the system of right is the realm of freedom made actual, the world of mind brought forth out of itself like a second nature'.[19] The system of right thus mediates and organises the impulses into this rational system, raising the will from finite to infinite freedom.

Considered as this immanent organisation (mind coming forth out of itself, the will being 'practical mind in general')[20] of natural impulses into a rational second nature, Hegel's system of right exemplifies what Deleuze and Guattari call a social machine, an assemblage of desire at the molar level of rights, moral codes, and social institutions (for Hegel, these being Family, Civil Society, and the State) operating under a 'rule of double conditioning'[21] in relation to a molecular level of dispersed and forceful desiring-machines. This assemblage can unfold, for Hegel, because at the molecular level of multiple, competing drives, desire can desire this ethical structure: 'man has by nature the impulse towards right, also the impulse to property and morality, also the impulse of love between the sexes, the impulse to sociability, &c.'.[22] As these impulses, belonging 'to the immediate will and to instinctive feeling',

---

[16] Ibid. §14.
[17] Ibid. §16.
[18] Ibid. §19.
[19] Ibid. §4.
[20] Ibid. §4R.
[21] This is Foucault's term for the reciprocal relationship between microscopic and macroscopic domains of power relations (Michel Foucault, *The History of Sexuality*, vol. 1: *An Introduction*, trans. Robert Hurley (New York: Vintage Books, 1990), pp. 99–100). Deleuze and Guattari speak similarly when holding that 'everywhere there exist the molecular *and* the molar: their disjunction is a relation of included disjunction' (Gilles Deleuze and Félix Guattari, *Anti-Oedipus: Capitalism and Schizophrenia*, trans. Robert Hurley, Mark Seem and Helen R. Lane (Minneapolis: University of Minnesota Press, 1983), p. 340).
[22] Hegel, *Philosophy of Right*, §19R.

have 'not been developed to the point of becoming ethical',[23] it is further necessary that 'individuals are simply identified with the actual order',[24] so that the alignment of their impulses with Ethical Life conforms to freedom's self-determining character. In themselves, impulses remain immediate and merely implicit, appearing as simple givens and having 'the abstract reciprocal externality characteristic of nature'.[25] The Understanding grasps them as particulars subsumed under abstract universal categories – hence the way empirical psychology describes and classifies the impulses 'as it finds them, or presumes it finds them, in experience'.[26] But their true objective character is one that is 'stripped of the form of irrationality which it possesses as impulse'.[27] External reflection can estimate and compare impulses with a view to finding the resolution yielding the greatest happiness.[28] But this 'abstract universality' still separates the impulses' sensuousness and particularity from thought's universality,[29] and remains an arbitrary resolution for the reasons given above. Impulse becomes identical with duty only when will becomes thinking will, which is will formed through Ethical Life.

> When the will's potentialities have become fully explicit, then it has for its object the will itself as such, and so the will in its sheer universality – a universality which is what it is simply because it has absorbed in itself the immediacy of instinctive desire and the particularity which is produced by reflection and with which such desire *eo ipso* becomes imbued. But this process of absorption in or elevation to universality is what is called the activity of thought. The self-consciousness which purifies its object, content, and aim, and raises them to this universality effects this thinking getting its own way in the will. Here is the point at which it becomes clear that it is only as thinking intelligence that the will is genuinely a will and free.[30]

Hegel's task, then, is to demonstrate the dialectical necessity of this aligning of impulse with duty, whereby duty becomes the object of desire reflectively brought before the mind, so that the self is driven by its own impulses towards this ethical goal.[31] Rational free will raises

---

23 Ibid. §150R.
24 Ibid. §151.
25 Ibid. §10R
26 Ibid. §11R.
27 Ibid.
28 Ibid. §20.
29 Ibid. §21.
30 Ibid. §21R
31 'The will determines itself and this determination is in the first place something inward, because what I will I hold before my mind as an idea; it is the object of my thought. An

will from finite to infinite by unifying Ethical Life and thinking will in concrete actuality.

In principle, other social machines – alternative configurations of drives and desire – are possible, but for Hegel they would lack the internal mediation necessary to achieve the speculative unity of form and content and thus must appear as thoughtless, irrational, and sunk into the chaos of unreflective, contingent nature. And indeed, Hegel consistently treats the seemingly contingent and disorganised elements of his State as inevitable moments of irrationality within its otherwise rational structure. At one notable point, he declares it rational to acknowledge them as such: 'Reason itself requires us to recognise that contingency, contradiction, and show have a sphere and a right of their own, restricted though it be, and it is irrational to strive to resolve and rectify contradictions within that sphere.'[32] This admission, however, appears within a discussion of the point at which right becomes positive law, where the application of universal rules to particular cases, being a function of Understanding, cannot eliminate the discretion inherent to this procedure.[33] For Hegel, this difficulty simply demonstrates how, in addition to the philosophical grounding of right, which is decidedly unhistorical,[34] there is a further 'inescapable duty'[35] to study positive law's historical development, where these moments of discretion form part of a rational progress unfolding over time. This example cannot be made to stand for other moments where ethical structures engender contingencies that refute any mediation and higher unification of form and content, contesting and deterritorialising the State without serving its further development. Such moments are, on Deleuze and Guattari's terms, *nomadic*, and indicate a different kind of social machine emerging within Hegel's State, one that 'bears witness to another kind of justice ... another species, another nature, another origin than the State apparatus',[36] to 'another movement, another space-time'[37] and

---

animal acts on instinct, is driven by an inner impulse and so it too is practical, but it has no will, since it does not bring before its mind the object of its desire.' (Ibid. §4A. References with an 'A' refer to the Addition to that paragraph.)

[32] Ibid. §214R.

[33] Ibid. §§211–14. For this reason, Hegel maintains that the philosophical study of right cannot yield 'a code of positive law, i.e. a code like the one an actual state requires' (Ibid. §3R).

[34] This point is discussed further below.

[35] Ibid. §212R.

[36] Gilles Deleuze and Félix Guattari, *A Thousand Plateaus: Capitalism and Schizophrenia*, trans. Brian Massumi (Minneapolis: University of Minnesota Press, 1987), p. 352.

[37] Ibid. p. 353.

'another dynamism',[38] all of which are related to a 'form of exteriority of thought'.[39] This is the assemblage of the war machine, marked by its 'exteriority' to the State.

Deleuze and Guattari declare: 'We thought it possible to assign the invention of the war machine to the nomads. This was done only in the historical interest of demonstrating that the war machine as such was invented, even if it displayed from the beginning all of the ambiguity that caused it to enter into composition with the other pole, and swing toward it from the start. However, in conformity with the essence, the nomads do not hold the secret.'[40] Correlating the war machine's key features with historical nomadic peoples living at the borders of real states and empires has the advantage of making clear the coherence of the different way of thinking and living the war machine expresses. But it is also invites the criticism of ignoring the historical facts and controversies, such as there being no agreement on whether the stirrup was a nomad invention and clear agreement that the sabre was not.[41] But the war machine thesis does not turn on any question of historical origins,[42] and its exteriority is not one of physical geography. As much as the war machine may be associated with what lies beyond the State in that respect, it speaks to an 'exteriority' immanent to it, one that emerges because the State machine, like all desiring-machines, functions only by breaking down.[43] Ironically, Hegel's own account of the State highlights these moments of fracture.

## PURE CHANGE, PURE EXTERNALITY, PURE EXTERIORITY

If desire is a configuration of drives, one that tempers their vicissitudes by orienting them in a certain direction and perhaps towards a specific object, then Hegelian desire is clearly a configuration organising drives in conformity with an ideal of self-conscious subjectivity. Hegel defines self-consciousness as '*Desire* in general' because desire's move-

---

[38] Ibid. p. 366.

[39] Ibid. p. 377.

[40] Ibid. p. 422.

[41] Ibid. pp. 404–5.

[42] 'It may be objected that tools, weapons, signs, and jewelry in fact occur everywhere, in a common space. But that is not the problem, any more than it is to seek an origin in each case. It is a question of assigning assemblages, in other words, of determining the *differential traits* according to which an element formally belongs to one assemblage rather than to another.' (Ibid. p. 402).

[43] 'Desiring-machines work only when they break down, and by continually breaking down.' (Deleuze and Guattari, *Anti-Oedipus*, p. 8).

ment encompasses the distinct moments of self-consciousness and free will highlighted earlier: the first whereby self-consciousness or will remains distinct and negatively separated from its object, and the second whereby it negates this negation by taking itself as the object of a self-determining act.[44] But whereas a primitive realisation of desire would relate self-consciousness to itself by absorbing or negating its object – desire satisfied by consuming or destroying what self-consciousness is not – genuine desire negates but also preserves the otherness of its object, so that self-consciousness relates to itself precisely by relating to *another* independent but also identical self-consciousness. This relation between self-consciousnesses is, of course, one of mutual recognition, where desire is no longer the desire for an object but the desire to be desired as a valuable object by another. Here the conditions for self-consciousness' realisation discussed in the *Phenomenology* converge with those for the free will's realisation discussed in the *Philosophy of Right*. Self-consciousness is secured when recognition affirms the self-conscious subject as rationally free and moral, and this entails an ethical community where freedom is realised by aligning the individual with the universal. To recognise another is to identify a human interiority – a capacity to carry on a conversation with oneself, feel the depth of one's emotions, reflect on one's existence in the world, etc. – that persists no matter how different or alien the other might outwardly seem to me to be, while other's recognition of me in turn validates my own human subjectivity and interiority. Ethical Life provides the institutional structure in which the reciprocity satisfying this desire for recognition obtains.

The movement of desiring recognition is also one of 'pure change', exemplifying the form of dialectical movement as such. As an immanent and internal movement from identity to opposition and back, it goes beyond the Understanding, which grasps the separation and higher unification of opposites from an external perspective that spreads them over an indifferent space or medium.

---

[44] 'This antithesis of its appearance and its truth has, however, for its essence only the truth, viz. the unity of self-consciousness with itself; this unity must become essential to self-consciousness, i.e. self-consciousness is *Desire* in general. Consciousness, as self-consciousness, henceforth has a double object: one is the immediate object, that of sense-certainty and perception, which however *for self-consciousness* has the character of a *negative*; and the second, viz. *itself*, which is the true *essence*, and is present in the first instance only as opposed to the first object. In this sphere, self-consciousness exhibits itself as the movement in which this antithesis is removed, and the identity of itself with itself becomes explicit for it.' (Hegel, *Phenomenology of Spirit*, §167).

We must eliminate the sensuous idea of fixing the differences in a different sustaining element; and this absolute Notion of the difference must be
represented and understood purely as inner difference, a repulsion of the
selfsame, as selfsame, from itself, and likeness of the unlike as unlike. We
have to think pure change, or *think antithesis within the antithesis itself*,
or *contradiction*. For in the difference which is an inner difference, the
opposite is not merely *one of two* – if it were, it would simply *be*, without
being an opposite – but it is the opposite of an opposite, or the other is
itself immediately present in it. Certainly, I put the 'opposite' here, and the
'other' of which it is the opposite, there; the 'opposite', then, is on one side,
is in and for itself without the 'other'. But just because I have the 'opposite'
here in and for itself, it is the opposite of itself, or it has, in fact, the 'other'
immediately present in it.[45]

Through this movement, self-consciousness secures itself by recognising
itself in the other even as it separates itself from this other, rather than
simply representing the other as being in various respects distinct from
and identical to it in appearance only. The same process also occurs at
the level of the self-conscious State aware of its autonomy in relation to
other autonomous states,[46] and for this reason interstate relations must
take the form of relations between monarchs who embody their states'
individuality.[47] 'Pure change' contrasts with the 'pure externality'[48] of
merely material or un-self-conscious entities, which change perpetually
but lack self-consciousness' return-to-self. A material thing 'lacks subjectivity, [because] it is external not merely to the subject but to itself',[49]
and thus reflects a spurious infinity of extension that makes it rightfully
an object of possession and ownership by a subjective will whose infinite
freedom is actual.[50] A parallel logic applies to the nation dominant at a
particular moment in World History: in relation to it, 'the minds of the
other nations are without rights',[51] although even in conflict a moment
of recognition remains that ensures, for example, that norms of justice
apply even during war.[52]

   The war machine, however, is distinct from the State's war machin-
ery, even if it is appropriated by the latter. Lacking fully reflective self-
consciousness, the man of war's character appears 'from the standpoint

[45]  Ibid. §160.
[46]  Hegel, *Philosophy of Right*, §322.
[47]  Ibid. §329.
[48]  Ibid. §42R.
[49]  Ibid. §42A.
[50]  Ibid. §42, 44.
[51]  Ibid. §347.
[52]  Ibid. §338.

of the State . . . in a negative form: stupidity, deformity, madness, illegitimacy, usurpation, sin',[53] and seems at best 'outmoded, condemned, without a future, reduced to his own fury, which he turns against himself'.[54] But this comes from the war machine expressing a becoming that is neither the pure change of Hegelian subjectivity nor the pure externality of Hegelian thinghood. While the war machine's exteriority is a form 'that is always external to itself',[55] it is not comparable to the way thinghood is external to both subjectivity and itself – to the way that, in saying a thing is 'external' to me, I am saying both that it is not 'internal' to me the way my consciousness is and that it has no such internal consciousness itself: 'It is not enough to affirm that the war machine is external to the apparatus. It is necessary to reach the point of conceiving the war machine as itself a pure form of exteriority, whereas the State apparatus constitutes the form of interiority we habitually take as a model, or according to which we are in the habit of thinking.'[56] With the war machine, the emotional feelings associated with self-consciousness 'become uprooted from the interiority of a "subject", to be projected violently outward into a milieu of pure exteriority that lends them an incredible velocity, a catapulting force'.[57] This uprooting contests the self-conscious subject's internal/external distinction.

Now, as indicated by the passage on pure change quoted above, in being established through mediation, interiority depends on extension – on placing opposites 'here' and 'there' – which establishes a movement from self to other and back even if each opposite is also immediately present in the other and even if this spatialisation is part of the dialectical movement itself rather than an indifferent medium prior to it. Conversely, and despite the implication of the term 'nomadic', the war machine does not actually concern movement, but rather speed. The former is extensive and therefore relative, but the latter, understood

---

[53] Deleuze and Guattari, *A Thousand Plateaus*, pp. 353–4.

[54] Ibid. p. 355. Consider, in this regard, Hegel's treatment of heroes as an anachronism after the state's foundation (Hegel, *Philosophy of Right*, §93 and §93A), as having a self-consciousness that 'had not advanced out of its primitive simplicity either to reflection on the distinction between act and action, between the external event and the purpose and knowledge of the circumstances, or to the subdivision of consequences' (ibid. §118R), and, in his reply to Solger, as emerging only in the tragic clash of individuals embodying different stages of ethical life, which is thereby eliminated as ethical life becomes fully actual (ibid. §140R). Consider also his treatment of courage as a merely '*formal* virtue' whose intrinsic worth is found only when it is oriented towards 'the genuine, absolute, final end, the sovereignty of the state' (ibid. §§327–8).

[55] Deleuze and Guattari, *A Thousand Plateaus*, p. 356.

[56] Ibid. p. 354.

[57] Ibid. p. 356.

as infinite speed, is *intensive* and absolute. In this respect the war machine effects a 'false movement', only appearing to go from place to place: 'It is therefore not surprising that reference has been made to spiritual voyages effected without relative movement, but in intensity, in one place: these are part of nomadism.'[58] Or, put differently, the war machine's movement is akin to the atomic swerve or *clinamen* of Epicurean philosophy, which is infinite by virtue of going *beyond* the minimum difference between discrete points in extended space, making it no longer a movement from 'here' to 'there'.[59] The space of this swerve is 'smooth' as opposed to a 'striated' space divisible into identifiable and measurable components. Nomadism is defined not by movement as such, but rather by its distribution in and occupation of smooth space, whereby it remains 'exterior' to the State by virtue of its intensive becomings. Residing 'in between' the points of extended space or territory, 'the life of the nomad is the intermezzo'.[60]

This occupation of the smooth space of exteriority, undercutting dialectical opposition and interiorisation, correlates also with special forms of number and affect. Against the number that counts units and measures magnitudes, Deleuze and Guattari invoke the idea of numbering number, which 'relates only to conditions of possibility constituted by nomadism and to conditions of effectuation constituted by the war machine', and wherein 'number becomes a subject'.[61] In a smooth space lacking discrete points, number no longer measures lengths but instead

---

[58] Ibid. p. 381.

[59] See ibid. pp. 361–2, 371. See also Nathan Widder, *Genealogies of Difference* (Urbana, IL and Chicago, IL: University of Illinois Press, 2002), pp. 76–82.

[60] Deleuze and Guattari, *A Thousand Plateaus*, p. 380.

[61] Ibid. p. 389. Deleuze attributes the idea of numbering number to Bergson in an early essay but leaves it undeveloped there (see Gilles Deleuze, 'Bergson's Conception of Difference', trans. Melissa McMahon, in John Mullarkey (ed.), *The New Bergson* (Manchester: Manchester University Press, 1999), p. 44). The distinction between numbering number and numbered number in fact belongs to Aristotle, who defines the first as 'the counter that counts' and the second as 'the dimension that is counted' (Aristotle, *Physics*, trans. Philip H. Wicksteed and Francis M. Cornford, 2 vols (Cambridge, MA: Loeb Classics, 1933–57), pp. 220b and 219b). Twelve, for example, is a numbered number when referring to a collection of discrete things such as twelve horses, but is a numbering number when referring to a single magnitude. The numbering number twelve is in no way 'composed' of smaller numbers such as seven and five, let alone the number one taken twelve times, whereas the group of horses is comprised of separate units counted up to that total. But the act of counting discrete units depends on the numbering number taken as an indivisible whole. Deleuze and Guattari's conception similarly treats numbering number as an order of magnitude (as ordinal rather than cardinal number) and as distinct from any counting of units, but differs from Aristotle's conception in other respects, as will be seen.

expresses vectors, directions of force: 'it is a directional number, not a dimensional or metric one'.[62] It thus invokes a 'geometry of the trait',[63] where traits 'are "generated" as "forces of thrust"'[64] and 'constitute a matter of expression'.[65] Numbering number, then, expresses a quantum of drive or impulse – the power or propulsion that makes movement possible, including the extended dialectical movement constituting self-conscious interiority. A multiplicity of drives is always at play in the war machine – 'it is always complex . . . a complex of numbers every time' – and these heterogeneous drives or forces are assembled by way of a synthesis, forming 'a special numerical body' that 'implies the most variety and originality in nomad existence'.[66] The war machine is a composition, and the numbering number constitutes its spirit, its 'esprit de corps'.[67] But this spirit, rather than being that of a reflective self-consciousness, is what Nietzsche would call a will to power, expressing the sense of related or synthesised forces.[68]

The war machine's affects are those of weapons, rather than the tools of work associated with the State assemblage. Work, in Hegelian terms, 'is desire held in check',[69] and is the crucial experience that develops the self-consciousness of Hegel's bondsman in the Dialectic of Lordship and Bondage, disciplining his world and himself so that 'he acquires a mind of his own'.[70] Work's tools, for Deleuze and Guattari, are thus 'much more introceptive, introjective' than weapons, and correlate with 'a form of interiority' and a regime 'inseparable from an organization and a development of Form, corresponding to which is the formation of the subject'.[71] Although work checks desire, however, desire is not absent – on the contrary, the work assemblage, like the war machine, is an assemblage of desire, but the two assemblages 'fundamentally mobilize passions of different orders'.[72] While work mobilises passions for self-restraint and interiority, the passions Nietzsche associates with

[62] Deleuze and Guattari, *A Thousand Plateaus*, p. 390.
[63] Ibid. p. 389.
[64] Ibid. p. 364.
[65] Ibid. p. 369.
[66] Ibid. pp. 391 and 392. As Deleuze states in his work on Nietzsche, 'Any two forces, being unequal, constitute a body as soon as they enter into a relationship.' See Gilles Deleuze, *Nietzsche and Philosophy*, trans. Hugh Tomlinson (London: Athlone Press, 1983), p. 40.
[67] Deleuze and Guattari, *A Thousand Plateaus*, p. 390.
[68] See Deleuze, *Nietzsche and Philosophy*, p. 85.
[69] Hegel, *Phenomenology of Spirit*, §195.
[70] Ibid. §196.
[71] Deleuze and Guattari, *A Thousand Plateaus*, pp. 395, 399–400.
[72] Ibid. p. 399.

the man of *ressentiment*,[73] the war machine mobilises those associated with Nietzsche's noble: 'the active discharge of emotion, the counterattack' rather than the interiority of feeling, which 'is an always displaced, retarded, resisting emotion'; the release of a forceful vector of speed, whose effect is 'to undo things, and to undo oneself . . . the "not-doing" of the warrior, the undoing of the subject'.[74] This other assemblage implies another order: 'it is not the same justice or the same cruelty, the same pity, etc.'.[75]

The State can only secure itself by inverting these forces of exteriority: it must 'striate the space over which it reigns, or . . . utilize smooth spaces as a means of communication',[76] impose an 'imperial *spatium*' or 'modern *extensio*' that 'links the number to metric magnitudes',[77] reconstitute the special body 'in bureaucratic staff form, or in the technocratic form of very special bodies',[78] and convert the war machine into an army.[79] If impulses towards Ethical Life make this possible, a multitude of counter-tendencies also undermines it. Unsurprisingly, Hegel's state is, in Foucauldian terms, decidedly disciplinary,[80] its purportedly rational necessity remaining inadequate to the configuration of impulses it must achieve, leaving it struggling to ward off the war machine's immanent exteriority and forces of deterritorialisation.

## RIGHT AND ITS SEMBLANCES

Throughout the *Philosophy of Right*, key transitional moments meant to ground concrete freedom present a specific negation to be negated – that of show or semblance (*Schein*). Semblance is not appearance (*Erscheinung*), which presents the outward face of an essential reality, even if it is an abstract and one-sided face. It is instead 'a determinate

---

73   As Deleuze notes, from Nietzsche's perspective the lord and the bondsman in Hegel's dialectic are both slaves (Deleuze, *Nietzsche and Philosophy*, p. 10).
74   Deleuze and Guattari, *A Thousand Plateaus*, p. 400.
75   Ibid. p. 399.
76   Ibid. p. 385.
77   Ibid. p. 389.
78   Ibid. p. 393.
79   Ibid. p. 402.
80   This is particularly clear in Hegel's discussion of police surveillance of individuals and organisations (Hegel, *Philosophy of Right*, §§234–5), which precedes his account of civil society's impoverished rabble, implying that surveillance is at least in part required for them (thanks to Kimberly Hutchings for first drawing my attention to this connection). It appears also in Hegel's view of civil society pressing the individual to turn his life into a project and become a member of one of its organised groups (ibid. §207).

existence inadequate to the essence, the empty disjunction and positing of the essence, . . . the falsity which disappears in claiming independent existence'.[81] While a still abstract appearance may entail semblance, the latter's negation is not a mediation and reconciliation because it lacks the standing in reality to be one of the opposites the dialectic brings together. Because semblance nevertheless presents itself as having such standing, its negation must be its annulment, which then allows the dialectical mediation of abstract sides of reality to progress.

The path towards genuine freedom's concrete conditions begins with Abstract Right, where freedom appears as the will's power to negate its surroundings and establish its personality over the pure externality of things. This makes property the most basic individual right, as through the possession, use, and alienation of things, personality's supremacy becomes actual: 'I take possession of my personality, of my substantive essence, and make myself a responsible being, capable of possessing rights and with a moral and religious life.'[82] This situation is precarious, however, because property rights depend on recognition. 'Contract' is therefore needed to mediate among property owning wills, but as contracting parties share a common will only contingently, the arrangement is liable to being broken. The immediate appearance of universal right in particular will, via contract's mediation of separate wills, becomes 'a *show*'[83] through the various forms of Wrong it entails: Non-Malicious Wrong, where each party has a particular claim of right, the contract losing authority until the dispute is resolved;[84] Fraud, which presents a façade of right between parties engaged in a seemingly legitimate exchange;[85] and finally, Coercion and Crime, where Abstract Right as such devolves into charade, as criminal coercion must be negated by coercive punishment, but 'the annulling of crime in this sphere where right is immediate is principally revenge', and 'revenge, because it is a positive action of a particular will, becomes a new transgression'.[86] Abstract Right's mechanisms, leading back to Wrong, cannot raise it above this status as semblance. A negation of another order is therefore needed, one that answers to 'the demand for a justice freed from subjective interest and a subjective form and no longer contingent on might,

---

[81] Hegel, *Philosophy of Right*, §82A.
[82] Ibid. §66R.
[83] Ibid. §82.
[84] Ibid. §§84–6.
[85] Ibid. §§87–9.
[86] Ibid. §102.

i.e. it is the demand for justice not as revenge but as punishment'.[87]
Abstract Right thus transitions to Morality.

Presenting a more concrete notion of selfhood than that of a property
owner with abstract rights, Morality's subject is an agent who shapes
the world through its deeds, shoulders responsibility for the intended
and sometimes unintended consequences of its actions,[88] but who also
obtains the right to find satisfaction in these actions as the consumma-
tion of its freedom.[89] The moral subject's capacity to make universal
judgements of good and evil, as required to raise the annulment of crime
from subjective revenge to objective justice, entails also being judged by
these standards. However, there is only a qualified connection between
agency and morality, the moral law remaining an 'ought' that the subject
may or may not will. The vehicle of objective morality – subjective will
– remains inadequate to the task, and Morality's content is reduced 'to a
form and a show'[90] as it appeals to individual subjective conscience to
realise it, this attempt to ground morality in conscience entailing hypoc-
risy, evil will, morally dubious theories of probabilism, the assertion
of merely subjective opinion in which 'the very pretense of an ethical
objectivity has totally disappeared', and finally ironic detachment that
reduces moral law to a pure subjectivism and void.[91] Morality can rise
above this semblance of itself only through Ethical Life, which imparts
'the identity of the good with the subjective will'.[92] Ethical Life 'is a
subjective disposition, but one imbued with what is inherently right'.[93]

Yet Ethical Life's institutions too contain moments that threaten to
reveal that the mediated unity it promises is no more adequate to reality
than those promised by Abstract Right and Morality. The Family begins
the inculcation of Ethical Life by uniting its members in bonds of love,
but its foundation in marriage remains at the mercy of contingent subjective wills that may become estranged, and 'there is no merely legal or positive bond which can hold the parties together once their dispositions and
actions have become hostile and contrary'.[94] Though Hegel does not say
it directly, marriage would clearly become a sham in the easily imaginable
scenario where the couple has become estranged but divorce is not sought

---

87 Ibid. §103.
88 Ibid. §§118–20.
89 Ibid. §121.
90 Ibid. §137R.
91 Ibid. §140R.
92 Ibid. §141.
93 Ibid. §141R.
94 Ibid. §176.

or cannot be granted. Civil Society, turning subjectivity loose to seek satisfaction in the market, aligns the particular to the universal through the Invisible Hand, which ensures the satisfaction of diverse arbitrary wills. But this is only a 'show of rationality'[95] because it derives from the Understanding's extraction of abstract principles from a mass of individual details.[96] And while more explicit forms of mediation are achieved in the formal institutions of Civil Society and the State, these fail to resolve the problem of the free market producing an impoverished underclass that does not enjoy any of its economic benefits, thereby falling outside the influence of and potentially threatening Ethical Life.[97] Indeed, after considering and rejecting the options of welfare support and public jobs, Hegel famously concludes: 'It hence becomes apparent that despite an excess of wealth civil society is not rich enough, i.e. its own resources are insufficient to check excessive poverty and the creation of a penurious rabble.'[98] The State is meant to turn the particularity generated by Civil Society back to the universal, building on the unifying powers of patriotic sentiment[99] and the church[100] by demonstrating the rationality of its structure. Through a figurehead monarch embodying the state's individuality in his personhood, a bicameral legislature mediating between the crown and the people, and a bureaucracy of civil servants selected by objective standards and discharging executive duties dispassionately,[101] the State purports to unite concretely an objective good delivered through subjective agents. But Hegel himself indicates that this is mere show when he concludes his account of the State's constitutional structure with the admission that unification is not actually achieved.

> Subjectivity is manifested in its most external form as the undermining of the established life of the state by opinion and ratiocination when they endeavour to assert the authority of their own fortuitous character and so bring about their own destruction. But its true actuality is attained in the opposite of this, i.e. in the subjectivity identical with the substantial will of the state, the subjectivity which constitutes the concept of the power of the crown and which, as the ideality of the whole state, has not up to this point attained its right or its existence.[102]

[95] Ibid. §189 and 181.
[96] Ibid. §189R.
[97] Ibid. §§241–5.
[98] Ibid. §245.
[99] Ibid. §268.
[100] Ibid. §270.
[101] Ibid. §§291–7.
[102] Ibid. §320.

At this point Hegel turns to the State's external relations to consolidate it internally, holding that the threat of war makes the State's absolute priority over all particular claims manifest.[103] Ethical Life now seems left at the mercy of the contingencies of international anarchy. But Hegel responds – in a way notably different from the previous transitions where right, morality, and ethicality presented themselves as mere show – by holding the anarchy that would seem to negate Ethical Life to be only semblance, proclaiming: 'the point of view from which things seem pure accidents vanishes if we look at them in the light of the concept of philosophy, because philosophy knows accident for a show and sees in it its essence, necessity'.[104] Anarchy is annulled as the conflict between states, each embodying a national mind, engenders a universal mind that develops through history,[105] becoming progressively realised in a series of dominant historical states until Ethical Life is finally attained.[106] It is thus in World History that right's rational structure is finally secured.

This final appeal to World History, however, signals the failure to provide a philosophical foundation for right, as Hegel maintains from the start of the text that this is distinct from any historical foundation.

> By dint of obscuring the difference between the historical and the philo-
> sophical study of law, it becomes possible to shift the point of view and slip
> over from the problem of the true justification of a thing to a justification
> by appeal to circumstances, to deductions from presupposed conditions
> which in themselves may have no higher validity, and so forth [. . .]. When
> those who try to justify things on historical grounds confound an origin in
> external circumstances with one in the concept, they unconsciously achieve
> the very opposite of what they intend.[107]

The turn to history in the final paragraphs would not present an issue if, as Hegel seems to intend,[108] it simply followed a completed philosophical justification and showed how it unfolds in time and space. But its role in surmounting the final semblance in the realm of interstate relations indicates that it cannot be kept separate in this way, undermining the claim that right is grounded through its internal philosophical necessity. The consequences for Hegel's project are extreme. On the one hand, absent a philosophical justification showing international anarchy to be a façade concealing true rightfulness, Ethical Life as a whole cannot rise

---

[103] Ibid. §§323–5.
[104] Ibid. §324R.
[105] Ibid. §340.
[106] Ibid. §§348–60.
[107] Ibid. §3R.
[108] Ibid. §33.

above being a semblance of the unity of subjective and objective, which further entails that the universal character of Morality and the rightful character of Abstract Right are charades too. Hegelian right and mediation, in short, remain inadequate to reality, whereas irresolvable strife and conflict embody it. On the other hand, if war fought in the name of World History – each dominant nation having only one epoch when 'it can make its hour strike'[109] – is indeed the ultimate gambit the State plays to secure itself, then its true foundation lies in the appropriation of the war machine, both into a military institution of war and into history itself: 'One of the biggest questions from the point of view of universal history is: How will the State *appropriate* the war machine?'[110] Right is grounded neither in philosophical necessity nor historical circumstance, but in a striation and organisation that make (State) philosophy and history possible.

Inasmuch as the war machine appears wherever forces turn away from and contest the State apparatus – and the war machine, concerned with creating and occupying smooth space, only assumes a war posture when it collides with the State[111] – it can be glimpsed at each transition point in right's purported development. It appears, in other words, where right, morality, and ethicality become semblances, and there is every reason not to take them seriously and instead pursue different paths: Why affirm rights when revenge shows that might makes right? Why be moral when morality is a façade? Why idealise the market as the path to prosperity through personal effort when its reality generates undeserved poverty? Why feel loyalty to the 'rational state' when its bureaucrats treat everyone as numbers rather than people? Appropriation, in turn, takes place at these same moments, as the State seeks to turn revenge towards moral conscience, the impoverished rabble towards patriotic loyalty to its supposedly rational institutions, etc. From the appropriating State's perspective, these forces must be considered irrational, unethical, antisocial, and even sinful. But seen differently, the war machine's forces can struggle against the State '*only on the condition that they simultaneously create something else*, if only new nonorganic social

---

[109] Ibid. §347.

[110] Deleuze and Guattari, *A Thousand Plateaus*, p. 418. Although Deleuze and Guattari suggest that archaic States did not have war machines because their authority was grounded in a combination of mystique and religious law – 'the magician-king and the jurist-priest' (ibid. p. 351) – and only appropriated them after an extrinsic war machine counterattacked and destroyed them (ibid. pp. 417–18), they also hold that the two assemblages were bound up from the beginning (ibid. p. 422). Furthermore, mystique and religion can themselves be considered forms of appropriation.

[111] Ibid. p. 417.

relations'.[112] Their struggle speaks to another justice, another morality, and another way of being.

## CIVIL SERVANTS AND METALLURGISTS

If Hegel is an exemplary State philosopher, it is because he inaugurates 'a whole line of reflection on the relation of the modern State to Reason, both as rational-technical and as reasonable-human', in which 'the rational-reasonable cannot exist without a minimum of participation by everybody'.[113] In this reflection, the civil service plays the central role. Hegel explicitly identifies civil servants with 'the *universal* class'[114] that is tasked with securing 'the universal interests of the community'[115] in relation to the particular interests advanced by Civil Society's other two classes, the agricultural and the business class.[116] He further gives them a mediating role between civil life, which is 'governed in a concrete manner from below where it is concrete', and the specialist officials who administer the various sides of government business and who 'are directed on civil life from above, in the same way as they converge into a general supervision in the supreme executive'.[117] Finally, reminiscent of Aristotle's view that a stable polis requires a large and moderate middle class,[118] he maintains that they form 'the greater part of the middle class, the class in which the consciousness of right and the developed intelligence of the mass of the people is found'.[119] With their 'dispassionate, upright, and polite demeanour' resulting from 'direct education in thought and ethical conduct',[120] the civil service thus embodies both the technical rationality of the State's functioning and the reasonable consensus that gives it popular legitimacy.

But if the State achieves universal rationality in its mediation with the particularity of agricultural and business interests, it is because these interests, in their particularity, already conform to one side or another of the State's universal interests. In contrast to the civil service, which mediates the State in isolation with itself, Deleuze and Guattari present

[112] Ibid. p. 423.
[113] Ibid. p. 556, n. 42.
[114] Hegel, *Philosophy of Right*, §202.
[115] Ibid. §205.
[116] Ibid. §§203–4.
[117] Ibid. §290.
[118] Aristotle, *Politics*, trans. Benjamin Jowett (Cambridge: Cambridge University Press, 1988), Bk. 4, chap. 11.
[119] Hegel, *Philosophy of Right*, §297.
[120] Ibid. §296.

the figure of the metallurgist, who relates the State directly to the exterior war machine. Historians and archaeologists, assessing how nomads obtained the technological elements necessary for their weaponry, accept the prejudiced assumption that deserters from the State's army gave them the secret of metallurgy. This presumes 'that these metallurgists were necessarily controlled by a State apparatus; but they also had to enjoy a certain technological autonomy, and social clandestinity, so that, even controlled, they did not belong to the State any more than they were themselves nomads'.[121] Metallurgy, they maintain, entails a network of connections completely distinct from the State's: metallurgists 'depend on an imperial agricultural stockpile for their very sustenance', and also 'have relations with the forest dwellers, and … must establish their workshops near the forest in order to obtain the necessary charcoal'; but they also relate to the nomads, since 'there are no mines in the alluvial valleys of the empire-dominated farmers' and so 'the question of control over the mines always involves nomadic peoples'.[122] Unsurprisingly, 'archaeology and history remain strangely silent on this question of the control over the mines', whose remoteness 'implies a shifting politics, in which States confront an outside'.[123] This complex metallurgic network entails a space that is neither smooth nor striated but 'holey'.[124]

Metallurgy stands between the State and war machine assemblages, connecting them to each other even while their difference remains irreducible. The metallurgist resides in and communicates with both assemblages while being neither a warrior nor a worker but an artisan who follows flows and traits rather than imposes form on matter. Metal seems well suited to the hylomorphic model that dominates State science, yet the metallurgist's operations on it 'are always astride the thresholds, so that an energetic materiality overspills the prepared matter, and a qualitative deformation or transformation overspills the form'.[125] This energetic material's malleability – the option it presents to melt down and reuse it, etc. – in turn makes metallurgy a practice in which 'the succession of forms tends to be replaced by the form of a continuous development, and the variability of matters tends to be replaced by the matter of a continuous variation', so that metal becomes

---

[121] Deleuze and Guattari, *A Thousand Plateaus*, p. 405.
[122] Ibid. p. 412.
[123] Ibid.
[124] Ibid. pp. 412–13.
[125] Ibid. p. 410.

'neither a thing nor an organism, but a *body* without organs'[126] capable of entering into and structuring assemblages in divergent ways. But it remains always heterogeneous from these assemblages, as metallurgists 'are not nomadic among the nomads and sedentary among the sedentaries, nor half-nomadic among the nomads, half-sedentary among sedentaries'.[127] While metallurgy's holey space communicates with both smooth and striated, 'the two communications are not symmetrical . . . it is always *connected* to nomad space, whereas it *conjugates* with sedentary space'.[128] When relating to the war machine, metallurgy enhances and accelerates its rhizomatic deterritorialisations; when relating to the State, it advances the powers of appropriation and striation. But as the middle term disjoining the two, it also ensures a composition and resonance wherein each side swings back towards the other.[129]

Without any war machine, politics would be as Hegel's State outwardly presents itself: an organisation and unfolding in relation to a rational and ethical ideal. But with the war machine's inclusion, it becomes fundamentally a matter of strategy and logistics, plans of action and complex organisation: 'Every assemblage has this strategic aspect and this logistical aspect.'[130] Hegel's State displays these too whenever it must appropriate its immanent war machine. What is crucial to strategy is that it cannot be oppositional but must instead be creative: simple opposition is what the strategist wants to manipulate his opponent into pursuing to make the opponent predictable. But creation nevertheless comes by way of borrowing, which is ensured by the communication between State and war machine: 'We are constantly reminded that there is communication between these two lines or planes, that each takes nourishment from the other, borrows from the other: the worst of the world war machines reconstitutes a smooth space to surround and enclose the earth.'[131] In this respect the war machine, even while emerging from contingencies within the very apparatus seeking to appropriate it, cannot simply come into being spontaneously or accidentally, but depends on the strategic context and the possible resources it can borrow, as well as the logistics that can enable it to develop. The war machine's emergence is, on Foucauldian terms, 'intentional and nonsubjective', and is intelligible not because it results from any

126 Ibid. p. 411.
127 Ibid. p. 414.
128 Ibid. p. 415.
129 Ibid. p. 422.
130 Ibid. p. 391.
131 Ibid. p. 423.

choice or decision but because it is 'imbued, through and through, with calculation'.[132] It comes about not by way of the interiority of a subject, but by way of desire assembled in an exteriority. For as an assemblage, desire itself is always already strategic and logistical.

[132] Foucault, *The History of Sexuality*, vol. 1, pp. 94 and 95.

Chapter 10

# Tragedy and Agency in Hegel and Deleuze

*Sean Bowden*

INTRODUCTION

The aim of this chapter is to clarify Deleuze's thinking about agency and action in the context of the ontology of events advanced in *The Logic of Sense*.[1] In order to do this, I will examine several points of convergence and divergence between Deleuze's and Hegel's thinking about action and agency, particularly in connection with their respective references to Sophocles' *Oedipus Rex*. This is not at all to say that Deleuze's account of action and agency in *The Logic of Sense* is somehow derived from Hegel. My argument is rather that both Deleuze and Hegel share a certain understanding of action and agency – namely, an *expressivist* one – whose general features I outline in what follows. In particular, I will show that for both Deleuze and Hegel, *Oedipus* brings into focus three aspects of action and agency: retrospectivity, publicness, and heroism. Retrospectivity means that we only understand what we are doing and intending after the fact. Publicness refers to the way in which our understanding of what we do and intend is inseparable from how the content of our action is made sense of in a broader social space. Finally, the heroic character of action and agency refers to an agent's being responsible for doings which outstrip what she intends and can know. The main point of divergence between Deleuze's and Hegel's conceptions of agency will then be brought out with reference to the way in which the difference between the agent's perspective on her intentions-actions and the perspective of others on these intentions-actions (the difference

[1] I would like to thank James Williams, Martijn Boven and Jack Reynolds for their critical comments on an earlier version of this paper, presented at the 2013 Society for Phenomenology and Existential Philosophy annual conference, hosted by the University of Oregon.

constitutive of the heroic character of action and agency) is dealt with. In Hegel, this difference is understood to be overcome within a recognitive community structured by mutual 'confession' and 'forgiveness'. In Deleuze, by contrast, there is no dialectically necessary overcoming and reconciliation of perspectives.

In what follows, I will first of all give an account of Hegel's expressivist approach to action and agency, drawing on two recent studies by Allen Speight and Robert Brandom. This account will be structured around the three aspects of action and agency just mentioned: retrospectivity, publicness and heroism. I will then argue for the existence of an expressivist understanding of action and agency in Deleuze's *The Logic of Sense* and explore the points of convergence and divergence between this conception and Hegel's. Before turning to this task, however, two important qualifications should be made. Firstly, the expressivist approach to action and agency in *The Logic of Sense* remains largely implicit in the text and has yet to be explored in significant detail in the secondary literature.[2] As will be demonstrated, however, it is present in this work and, moreover, follows directly from the ontology of events and sense to be found therein. Secondly, I restrict my account of Deleuze's expressivist understanding of action and agency to *The Logic of Sense* and do not claim that Deleuze's œuvre as a whole exemplifies this approach. Indeed, the discontinuities between *The Logic of Sense* and Deleuze's later work with Guattari have often been noted, and it seems evident that the shift from an ontology of sense and events in *The Logic of Sense* to, for example, an ontology of assemblages in *A Thousand Plateaus*, entails a seismic shift in Deleuze's thinking about action and agency. However, it is beyond the scope of this article to explore this shift, and a full justification of this claim must be left to a subsequent work.

OEDIPUS AND HEGEL'S 'EXPRESSIVE METAPHYSICS OF AGENCY'

In 2001, Allen Speight published a very interesting study of Hegel's theory of action, titled *Hegel, Literature and the Problem of Agency*, which argues that Hegel's references in *The Phenomenology of Spirit* to various literary forms (tragedy, comedy and the romantic novel of the beautiful soul) are crucial in developing his account of action and agency. Speight begins by arguing that Hegel should be read as a

---

[2] See, however, Sean Bowden, '"Willing the Event": Expressive Agency in Deleuze's Logic of Sense', *Critical Horizons* 15:3, (2014), pp. 231–48.

post-Kantian thinker who rejects what Sellars called the 'myth of the given' in both theoretical and practical activity. In other words, Hegel rejects the idea that we have access to immediate and unrevisable empirical data which can function as the ground of knowledge claims. But he also rejects the 'voluntarist' conception of action and agency insofar as this depends on the givenness of a prior mental state such as an intention, to which an agent has unrevisable access, and which can be said to cause a given action.[3]

With respect to his philosophy of action, then, Hegel defends a 'corrigibilist' view of agency. He holds that an agent's intentions are not incorrigibly known by the agent and, correspondingly, are not artificially separable from the action itself such as this appears in public space. In other words, on this view of agency, what an agent intends becomes clear only in the course of the action that 'expresses' it, and more particularly, as this action is variously interpreted by the agent and the other members of his or her recognitive community. The practical identity of the agent which is 'expressed' in his or her action, then, will ultimately be a product of the recognitive mediation of these different, first- and third-person perspectives.[4]

The three crucial features of Hegel's corrigibilist conception of action and agency are thus, following Speight, *retrospectivity*, *theatricality* and *forgiveness*. *Retrospectivity*: because what an agent does cannot be decided by the privileging of an agent's (presumably unrevisable) prior intention, but must be determined after the fact.[5] *Theatricality*: because an agent cannot claim epistemic access to her own intentions except through the 'mirroring' relation between actor and spectator implicit in her social situation, which is to say, through the various 'masks' in which she is recognised (and recognises herself) in her social context.[6] *Forgiveness*: because what must be 'confessed', 'forgiven' and consequently 'sublated' in order to achieve a reconciliation between first- and third-person perspectives on action is both the fallibility of the agent's perspective, and the injustice of the community who judges particular actions according to universal standards. In other words, reciprocal confession and forgiveness acknowledges and reconciles both the agent's particular interest in an action and the community's demand for its justification.[7]

---

[3] Allen Speight, *Hegel, Literature and the Problem of Agency* (Cambridge: Cambridge University Press, 2001), pp. 2–4.
[4] Ibid. pp. 4–6.
[5] Ibid. p. 44.
[6] Ibid. p. 82.
[7] Ibid. pp. 105, 119–21.

Of interest to us in the present context is Speight's argument that Hegel arrives at and presents these features of agency in *The Phenomenology of Spirit* through a study of the sequential emergence of a number of literary genres: Greek tragedy, comedy (paradigmatically, Diderot's *Rameau's Nephew*) and the romantic novel. More specifically, as Speight writes:

> Tragedy, particularly ancient Greek tragedy in its presentation of fate, opens up the retrospective experience of agency; comedy is seen to involve a self-reflectiveness about the socially mediated or theatrical character of agency . . .; and the romantic novel of the beautiful soul, in its concern with resolving the paradoxes of conscience, articulates a notion of recognitive practical identity that is most fully achieved in certain novelistic moments of forgiveness.[8]

Now, we can recall that it is the contention of this chapter that, for Hegel and Deleuze, Sophocles' *Oedipus Rex* brings into focus three aspects of action and agency: retrospectivity, publicness, and heroism. There is much overlap between these categories and Speight's, particularly with respect to retrospectivity. However, what I am calling publicness is not equivalent to theatricality. For Speight, theatricality has to do with the 'masks' or social roles in which an agent is recognised, and through which the agent's intentions and motivations can be comprehended. By contrast, as will be seen when we turn our attention to Brandom's reading of Hegel, publicness has to do with the status of the action itself and its various descriptions. It concerns the way in which the determinable content of the action that is retrospectively attributed to the agent is the affair of everybody in the agent's community. Forgiveness is also not equivalent to what I am calling 'heroism', although as will be seen, forgiveness is an essential element of Hegel's 'post-modern' conception of heroism.

Given these divergences, I will leave to one side Speight's discussion of the genres of comedy and the romantic novel and focus instead on his contention that Greek tragedies such as *Oedipus Rex* revealed to Hegel the retrospective character of agency, such as he presents this in *The Phenomenology of Spirit*. Moreover, while it is true that Speight devotes more attention to Hegel's reading of *Antigone* in the *Phenomenology*, focusing on his remarks about Oedipus will allow us to connect the idea of the retrospectivity of agency with the heroic character of agency such as this is discussed with reference to Oedipus in Hegel's later work, *The*

---

[8] Ibid. pp. 7–8.

*Philosophy of Right*. Focusing on *Oedipus* will also allow us to explore and better understand Deleuze's references to Oedipus in his discussion of action, agency and intentions in *The Logic of Sense*.

Now, Speight argues that for Hegel, tragedy teaches us something essential about action in general. Tragedies begin with a willed action, but this action has consequences that could not have been foreseen by the agent – consequences that radically diverge from his or her original willing, but for which the agent is nevertheless recognisable as responsible.[9] In this respect, then, tragedies reveal with particular clarity something common to all action, namely, the potential for a discrepancy between an agent's prior deliberations in willing an action, and what the action that the agent is responsible for turns out to be in actuality. Such a tragic moment is represented in an extreme fashion by an agent like Oedipus, 'who does not know at all what his deeds involve, and will experience a necessity that is alien to him in his action',[10] recognising himself and being recognised as responsible for the crimes of parricide and incest. In other words, what *Oedipus Rex* demonstrates with tragic lucidity is that in order to understand an actual deed as the deed of a particular agent, it is not sufficient to simply make reference to this agent's *prior* intention in its isolated simplicity. We must attend to the action itself and to what it retrospectively reveals about the agent of that action. As Speight puts it: 'Something of what the deed *is* – and hence who the agent is to be taken to be – can only emerge for the agent's knowledge *in* the action itself.'[11] In other words, what the action turns out to be retrospectively reveals or expresses something – both to the agent and to others – about the nature of the agent responsible and what can be taken to be intentional. Or again, as Hegel writes in section 469 of the *Phenomenology*, alluding to Oedipus:

> Ethical self-consciousness now learns from its deed the developed nature of what it *actually* did . . . [T]he son does not recognize his father in the man who has wronged him and whom he slays, nor his mother in the queen whom he makes his wife . . . [T]he accomplished deed is the removal of the antithesis between the knowing self and the actuality confronting it. The doer cannot deny the crime or his guilt.[12]

Of course, and as Speight rightly notes, 'Hegel's account of the Oedipus play [in the *Phenomenology*] requires understanding that there is at

---

[9] Ibid. p. 48.
[10] Ibid. p. 36.
[11] Ibid. p. 54.
[12] G. W. F. Hegel, *Phenomenology of Spirit*, trans. A. V. Miller (New York: Oxford University Press, 1977), p. 283.

work in the play both a standard of responsibility and intentionality that is no longer valid in modern morality.'[13] Nevertheless, that action, agency and intentions properly understood have for Hegel this retrospective character is clear.[14] In order to appreciate this point, however, it will be useful to turn now to Robert Brandom's account of Hegel's 'expressive metaphysics of agency'.

In Chapter 7 of *A Spirit of Trust*, Brandom's as yet unpublished book on Hegel,[15] Brandom notes that Hegel's œuvre in fact offers us two contrasting views on the nature of action: 1) A pre-modern, externalist, consequentialist view, which identifies and individuates actions according to what is actually done; and 2) A modern, internalist, intentionalist view, which identifies and individuates actions by the agent's intention or purpose in acting.

The first, pre-modern and externalist view can be found primarily in the *Phenomenology of Spirit*, where, for example, Hegel writes in section 401 that:

> Consciousness must act merely in order that what it is *in itself* may become explicit *for it* . . . An individual cannot know what he is until he has made himself a reality through action . . . [The agent] only gets to know his original nature, which must be his End, from the deed.[16]

The idea here is that the content of the inner intention of an agent is only determined with reference to what is true of the external action that expresses that intention 'in actuality'. Or to put it another way, the intention only becomes epistemically available – to the agent as much as to others – *retrospectively*, as the action and its consequences unfold. But what is more, to say that the retrospectively attributed deed is 'actual' is to make reference to its *publicness* – to the fact that it is essentially 'available to all' and made sense of in a broader social space. As Hegel writes, actualisation is 'a display of what is one's own in the element of universality whereby it becomes, and should become, the

---

[13] Speight, *Hegel, Literature and the Problem of Agency*, p. 54, n. 25.

[14] Robert Pippin also argues for the retrospectivity of actions and intentions in Hegel. See, for example, Robert B. Pippin, 'Recognition and Reconciliation: Actualized Agency in Hegel's Jena Phenomenology', *International Yearbook of German Idealism*, vol. 2 (Berlin: Walter de Gruyter, 2004), p. 262; see also Robert B. Pippin, *Hegel's Practical Philosophy: Rational Agency as Ethical Life* (Cambridge: Cambridge University Press, 2008), p. 156.

[15] Available at <http://www.pitt.edu/~brandom/hegel/index.html> (last accessed 23 January 2014).

[16] Hegel, *Phenomenology of Spirit*, p. 240.

affair of everyone'.[17] Or again, as Brandom puts it in a more contemporary philosophical vocabulary:

> The truth of the performance, what it is in itself, is expressed in *all* of the descriptions of what is actually achieved, all the specifications of the content in terms of its consequences. These descriptions are available in principle to anyone in the community to recognize the performance . . . or to characterize its content.

Now, the story of Oedipus clearly exemplifies this externalist view of action. Indeed, we noted above how in section 469 of the *Phenomenology*, Hegel presents an externalist view of action through an implicit reference to *Oedipus Rex*: 'Ethical self-consciousness now learns from its deed the developed nature of what it *actually* did . . . [T]he accomplished deed is the removal of the antithesis between the knowing self and the actuality confronting it. The doer cannot deny the crime or his guilt.'[18] And we clearly see here in the figure of Oedipus action's retrospective and public character. Again, for action to have a retrospective character means that one only understands what one is doing and intending after the fact. For action to have a public character means that an understanding of what we do and intend is inseparable from how our actions and intentions appear or are actualised in the light of the external world and to others, as when Oedipus' crime and guilt were made manifest through his very public inquiries.

The modern, internalist view of action, by contrast, is much more prominent in Hegel's later work, the *Philosophy of Right*, particularly in the 'Purpose and Responsibility' section of Part 2 on 'Morality'. Here, Hegel argues that:

> It is . . . the right of the will to recognize as its *action* [Handlung], and to accept *responsibility* for, only those aspects of its *deed* [Tat] which it knew to be presupposed within its end, and which were present in its *purpose* [Vorsatz] – I can be made *accountable* for a deed only if *my will was responsible* for it – *the right of knowledge*.[19]

Following Brandom, Hegel understands this distinction within an action between what the agent is responsible for (by virtue of his 'purpose') and what he is not responsible for to be a distinctive achievement of *modernity*. Prior to this, the agent assumed responsibility for, not just

---

[17] Ibid. §417, p. 251.
[18] Ibid. p. 283.
[19] G. W. F. Hegel, *Elements of the Philosophy of Right*, trans. Hugh Barr Nisbet (Cambridge: Cambridge University Press, 2003), §117, p. 144.

what he was initially aware of intending, but for the deed in its entirety. Such was, we've just seen, the case of Oedipus, whom Hegel mentions once again in the *Philosophy of Right*, and this time explicitly. Indeed, Oedipus regarded himself as a criminal responsible for murdering his father and marrying his mother, despite the fact that he had not originally intended to commit parricide and incest. And for Hegel, to take responsibility for an action which outstrips what is originally intended or can be known is to possess a '*heroic* self-consciousness'. As he writes in the *Philosophy of Right*:

> The *heroic* self-consciousness (as in ancient tragedies like that of Oedipus) has not yet progressed from its unalloyed simplicity to reflect on the distinction between *deed* [Tat] and *action* [Handlung], between the external event and the purpose and knowledge of the circumstances, or to analyse the consequences minutely, but accepts responsibility for the deed in its entirety.[20]

I'll return to this notion of heroism in connection with action and agency. For now, let us ask what the relation is between these two different views of action – the intentionalist/internalist and the externalist/consequentialist. For Brandom, the relation and, indeed, tension between these seemingly opposing views is in fact fundamental to Hegel's 'expressive metaphysics of agency'. He proposes that we understand Hegel as saying that an adequate conception of action must involve both views, and hence a certain 'identity-in-difference'. Brandom proposes that we understand Hegel as saying that one and the same action can fall under different descriptions – namely, *intentional* and *consequential* descriptions – and that these different descriptions amount to a distinction between the agent's perspective on his or her action and the community's perspective on that action. The content of an action will then be what is *both* acknowledged by the agent and attributed by the community, which is to say, a product of a process of reciprocal specific recognition.

In order to explain the synthesis of two divergent perspectives on one content, Brandom appeals to Frege's distinction between sense and reference. Following this distinction, the action 'in-itself', the referent, must be distinguished from its different senses or 'modes of presentation', that is: from what it is *for* the agent at different stages in the unfolding of the agent's overall 'plan', as well as what it is *for* the community as the consequences of the action ripple outwards. The action in-itself can then be conceived as the product of the recognitive mediation of these different

[20] Ibid. §118Z, p. 146.

perspectives, that is to say, whereby the different senses appear as cognitively presenting and semantically determining the action in-itself, but only insofar as these senses are able to form part of a story or 'recollection', told by both the agent and the community, in which these different senses feature as better or worse attempts to present the action in-itself.

In Chapter 8 of *A Spirit of Trust*, Brandom then argues that the concluding eleven paragraphs of the *Phenomenology*'s 'Spirit' chapter sketches the way in which we can understand the different perspectives on action – the agent's and the community's – to be mediated by reciprocal recognition. The concepts we must understand are *confession* and *forgiveness*.

*Confession*, on Brandom's interpretation, involves acknowledging a disparity between sense and reference. In other words, both the agent and the community must confess the particularity and contingency of their attitudes, and acknowledge that what the action is *for* them, subjectively, is not what the action objectively is *in itself*, that is to say, *apart from any particular subjective perspective*. In Brandom's terms, mutual confession means that both the agent and her community treat their intentions and beliefs as *normative statuses*, which is to say, as commitments to which they are *entitled* only insofar as these are acknowledged by one's peers as standing in legitimate inferential relations with other accepted commitments within a shared 'space of reasons'.

But as well as confession, what is required is *forgiveness*. On Brandom's interpretation, forgiving overcomes the confessed disparity between sense and reference, between what the action is *for* the agent and *for* the community, and what the action is in-itself, apart from these subjective perspectives. Forgiving, then, is the 'recollective' labour of finding a concept for the action that is being expressed (now less, now more fully and faithfully) by the subjective conceptions endorsed by the agent and her community. In other words, the task of forgiving is to reveal the confessed disparity between sense and reference as a retrospectively necessary phase of a process of more adequately expressing what the action is in-itself. Through mutual confession and forgiveness, then, both the agent and the community acknowledge that what is recollectively determined as the action in-itself has authority over what were their merely subjective perspectives on it.

For Brandom, this new understanding of action and agency, couched in terms of confession and forgiveness, also represents a new, *post*-modern stage of the development of Spirit. Moreover, this new stage recovers an element of the older, pre-modern, *heroic* conception of action and agency which was lost to modernity with its emphasis on the subjective rights of intention and knowledge. As we saw, the pre-modern, heroic conception of agency was most visible in tragedies such as *Oedipus Rex*. Indeed, the tragic dimension of heroic agency was precisely that the agent assumed responsibility for happenings (in the case of Oedipus, parricide and incest) which were completely alien to what they originally intended and could foresee. In the new, post-modern conception of agency, however, this tragic dimension of agency disappears, even though the heroism is maintained. The heroism is maintained insofar as, in Brandom's words, agents still 'identify themselves as the seats of responsibilities that outrun their own capacity to fulfil'.[21] But the tragic dimension is lost insofar as the agent recognises, and is recognised by, a community who forgives the particularity of the agent's subjective perspective by making it a fundamental, albeit partial, progressively expressive contribution to a larger process of determining the action in-itself.

## SENSE AND ACTION-EVENTS IN DELEUZE'S *LOGIC OF SENSE*

In *The Logic of Sense*, Deleuze can be understood as putting forward an account of action and agency that displays the characteristics of retrospectivity, publicness and heroism. Moreover, as will be seen, this 'expressive' account of agency is also tied to references to Oedipus. Before coming to the argument for this thesis, however, it will be helpful to pre-empt three likely objections. Firstly, it will no doubt be said that given Deleuze's well-known hostility to Hegel, Deleuze's philosophy of action and agency can in no way be derived from Hegel. But this is not at all my position. I am not claiming that Deleuze was influenced by Hegel, or owes Hegel a conceptual debt in this regard. I rather wish to argue that there is an account of action and agency implicit in *The Logic of Sense* that can be explicated by showing how it instantiates in a certain way some of the structural features of action and agency that thinkers such as Speight, Brandom and Pippin have recently identified in Hegel.

Secondly, it may well be objected that a Deleuzian understanding of action and agency could not depend on those notions which form the core of the expressive account of action and agency just presented – notions such as the will, intentions, 'the social', and so on. It will be said that Deleuze's theory of action and agency rather depends on notions such as force relations, complex relations of affect, machinic assemblages of bodies, collective assemblages of enunciation, and so

---

[21] Robert B. Brandom, *A Spirit of Trust*, available at <http://www.pitt.edu/~brandom/hegel/index.html> (last accessed 23 January 2014), chap. 8.

on. This may well be true of Deleuze's other works, including those co-authored with Guattari, but it is not true of *The Logic of Sense*. We should take seriously Deleuze's observation that the concepts that are mobilised in *The Logic of Sense* diverge in many ways from those mobilised in his previous and subsequent works.[22] Indeed, Deleuze explicitly employs the notions of intentions and willing in a number of key series in *The Logic of Sense*, including in the 29th Series – Good Intentions are Inevitably Punished; and in the 20th Series on the Moral Problem in Stoic Philosophy and the 21st Series of the Event, where he presents his conception of the 'actor' who 'wills the event'. Moreover, it should be borne in mind that the idea of 'the social' – understood in psychoanalytic fashion as the structural-symbolic dimension of language and culture – plays a crucial role in the second 'half' of *The Logic of Sense*, which deals with the 'dynamic genesis' of sense and the event.[23]

Finally, it will be said that in any case, in *The Logic of Sense*, Deleuze situates actions on the side of bodies, and distinguishes them from events, which are incorporeal.[24] Thus, when Deleuze discusses the actor's willing of the event in *The Logic of Sense*, he is not talking about the willing of actions. He is rather talking about how we make the incorporeal event – which is something we *undergo* on the expressive surface of sense rather than something we physically *do* – our own. But it cannot be correct to say that no action is an event in this respect. When Deleuze writes that 'action is itself produced by the offspring of the event', he cannot be arguing that an incorporeal event produces something capable of corporeal activity.[25] As he makes clear elsewhere, incorporeal events have no such causal power.[26] What we must rather understand, then, is that actions are indeed events – we can call them action-events – and that in a certain way we undergo our actions because they are connected to a larger event, namely, an ongoing process of sense-making or 'sense-event'. In other words, as I will now argue for in more detail, in Deleuze's *The Logic of Sense*, actions and their corresponding intentions are thought of as having a *retrospective* character, and cannot be isolated from the *public* or social production of sense.

---

[22] See Gilles Deleuze, 'Note for the Italian Edition of *The Logic of Sense*', in *Two Regimes of Madness: Texts and Interviews 1975–1995*, trans. Ames Hodges and Mike Taormina, ed. David Lapoujade (New York: Semiotext(e), 2007).

[23] For a detailed account of this, see Sean Bowden, *The Priority of Events: Deleuze's Logic of Sense* (Edinburgh: Edinburgh University Press, 2011), chap. 5.

[24] I owe this objection to Martijn Boven.

[25] Gilles Deleuze, *The Logic of Sense*, trans. Mark Lester with Charles Stivale, ed. Constantin V. Boundas (New York: Columbia University Press, 1990), p. 150.

[26] Ibid. p. 7.

Turning firstly, then, to the notion of *retrospectivity*, if we understand this as the idea that an agent's intention does not directly cause her action so much as come to be revealed or expressed in the unfolding of the action itself, then it is clear that Deleuze defends a version of this idea in *The Logic of Sense*. Two points can be noted in this regard. First of all, in the 2nd Series of Paradoxes of Surface Effects, Deleuze follows the Stoics in making a strict ontological distinction between the realm of bodies and causes, and the realm of events.[27] The net effect of this division is that actions, insofar as we agree that they must be a type of event, never belong to the same ontological register as psychological causes or the physical states of brains on which psychological causes are often said to supervene. Insofar as they do not belong to the same ontological register, for Deleuze, actions will never be said to be caused by intentions or desires or any other kind of psychological cause.

The second point to be noted is that Deleuze nevertheless continues to speak of 'willing the event', particularly in the 21st Series of the Event. But how can we understand this if willing the event, willing an action, cannot be understood as 'causing' an action to take place? It appears that we must retain the category of willing, intentions, and so on, in order to distinguish between somebody actively 'doing' something, and something merely 'happening'. To paraphrase Wittgenstein, intentions or willings are what are left over if we subtract the fact of my arm going up from the fact of my actively raising my arm.[28] But this willing or intention must be understood as inseparable from the event which expresses it. It is in this sense that Deleuze writes that the corporeal or 'organic will' must be exchanged for a 'spiritual will', and that the event itself creates in us this spiritual will.[29] We are not the direct causes of our actions, it seems. The action-event rather reveals something about the agent, such that, as Deleuze puts it, 'action is produced by the off-spring of the event'.[30] In short, then, for Deleuze, we must understand the will, or our intentions, to be inseparable from the action-event, and to become clear only retrospectively, as the action-event unfolds in the incorporeal dimension that is proper to it.

With respect to *publicness*, if we understand this as the idea that an agent's action is not isolatable from its appearance and interpretation in

---

[27] Ibid. pp. 4–11.
[28] Ludwig Wittgenstein, *Philosophical Investigations*, trans. Gertrude Elizabeth Margaret Anscombe, ed. Gertrude Elizabeth Margaret Anscombe and Rush Rhees (Oxford: Blackwell, 1953), §621.
[29] Deleuze, *The Logic of Sense*, pp. 148–9.
[30] Ibid. p. 150.

social space, then Deleuze implicitly defends a version of this idea in *The Logic of Sense*. Three points can be made in this regard. The first is that, as Deleuze argues in the 3rd Series of the Proposition, the 5th Series of Sense and elsewhere, events in general are inseparable from expressed or expressible sense.[31] In other words, the action-event, for Deleuze, only exists as the sense of propositions bearing on what happens. But not only this, the action-event also only exists as the sense of the propositions bearing on the propositions bearing on what happens. This is the crux of Deleuze's reference in the 5th Series to Frege's work on the sense and reference of propositions (and we can recall that Frege is also a key reference in Brandom's reading of Hegel).[32] As Deleuze makes clear, the proposition which expresses an event is internally divided. On the one hand, it denotes a body or bodies; on the other, it expresses a sense which is, in Frege's terms, the 'mode of presentation' of the referent.[33] But the sense expressed by a proposition is not identical with the actual words used. As Deleuze argues, alluding to Frege's discussion of sense and reference in indirect contexts, the sense of a declarative sentence, while not identical with the words used, can always be denoted by a second sentence uttered by another speaker. Moreover, since this utterance expresses a sense that is not identical with the words used, its sense can always be taken as the object of a third sentence uttered by a further speaker. The third utterance, in turn, expresses a sense that is not identical with the words used . . . and so on.[34] Deleuze thus appears to be arguing here that, if a first speaker's declarative sentence expresses a sense which is a 'mode of presentation' of its referent, when a second speaker's sentence takes the sense of the first sentence as its object, it expresses a sense which is a 'mode of presentation' both of the sense of the first speaker's sentence and of the referent of the first speaker's sentence. In other words, if the action-event exists as the sense of propositions bearing on what happens, it also exists as the sense of the propositions bearing on the propositions bearing on what happens. The action-event, in short, cannot be isolated from an ongoing and open-ended process of making sense both of what happens and what is said about what happens in an intersubjective or public space.

The second point to be made about publicness in *Logic of Sense* is that, in the 20th Series on Stoic Philosophy and, more particularly, in

[31] See, for example, ibid. pp. 12, 21, 22 and 181.
[32] Ibid. p. 29.
[33] On this point, see ibid. p. 25.
[34] See ibid. pp. 28–31. For Frege's discussion of these issues, see 'On *Sinn* and *Bedeutung*', in *The Frege Reader*, ed. Michael Beaney (Oxford: Blackwell, 1997), pp. 151–71.

the 21st Series of the Event, Deleuze explicitly talks about the 'actor' or agent in theatrical terms, that is, as the one who acts before an audience. The upshot of Deleuze's discussion of the actor here consists of two points. First of all, action-events have a public character, which is to say, once again, that they cannot be isolated from their multiple 'modes of presentation' in a complex process of sense-making. Secondly, while an actor has his or her being as a determined agent *in* the action-event such as this is made sense of, the sense that is made of the action-event depends on the way it 'communicates' with an entire series of other events.[35] Although Deleuze does not state this explicitly, it is plausible to think that these other communicating events must include the numerous events making up the life of the agent, since the sense of one's actions must be considered in the light of what else one does and undergoes. But they will also include the actions of sense-making by the members of the actor's community – actions which must similarly be considered in light of what these other individuals do and undergo. In short, we can say that an actor or agent is not so much behind her actions in a causal sense as 'out there' *in* her actions; but actions are always 'out there' as well, insofar as they can be made sense of in perspectivally multiple ways depending on the actions and other events with which they are brought into communication.[36]

The third point to be made about publicness is the one already mentioned: from the 27th series of Orality onwards, Deleuze is clear that the dynamic genesis of sense and the event is inseparable from what Lacanians would call the structural-symbolic dimension of language and culture. All the 'steps' of the dynamic genesis as outlined by Deleuze both presuppose and produce the public surface of sense on which the events composing our lives are progressively determined.[37]

Now, these two characteristics of action and agency – retrospectivity and publicness – come together in Deleuze's discussion of action in the 29th Series – Good Intentions are Inevitably Punished. This is also where Deleuze's reference to Oedipus comes in. Deleuze's focus here, it will be noted, is the Freudian conception of the 'Oedipus complex'. But we should also recall Deleuze's argument that it is the story of Oedipus that

---

[35] Deleuze, *The Logic of Sense*, p. 150. See also pp. 178–9.

[36] This is a paraphrase of Robert Pippin's helpful formulation of this element of action and agency in Hegel and Nietzsche. See Pippin, *Hegel's Practical Philosophy*, p. 159; see also Robert B. Pippin, *Nietzsche, Psychology, and First Philosophy* (Chicago and London: University of Chicago Press, 2010), p. 82.

[37] The full argument for this cannot be given here, and I would humbly refer the reader to Chapter 5 of Bowden, *The Priority of Events*.

teaches us about the complex, not the complex that tells us something about Oedipus.[38] With reference to Oedipus, then, Deleuze argues in this series that all actions are always-already divided in two: into a willed image of action, and into an action projected on the incorporeal surface of sense. He writes:

> On one hand, the entire image of action is projected on a physical surface, where it appears as willed . . .; on the other, the entire result of the action is projected on a metaphysical surface, where the action appears as produced and not willed . . . The famous mechanism of 'denegation' (that's not what I wanted . . .), with all its importance with respect to the formation of *thought*, must be interpreted as expressing the passage from one surface to the other.[39]

On the one hand, then, we have the agent's 'image of action', that is, his image of what he is purposefully doing (so, Oedipus' killing of a stranger and marriage to the queen of Thebes). On the other hand, we have the action such as this is made sense of in the structural-symbolic dimension of language and culture (thus, Oedipus' parricide and incest, such as this is revealed through his public investigations). In other words, we have the agent and his intentions on the one hand, as the element necessary for even talking about an action (as opposed to a mere happening); and on the other hand, we have the actualisation of that action in public space, and the retrospective attribution of responsibility for *that* action to the agent.

But now, as the reference to Oedipus makes clear, Deleuze also appears here to understand action and agency as involving a certain *heroism*, insofar as this is understood as the agent's being held to be responsible for deeds that outstrip what he intends and can know. However, this heroism takes a slightly different form to the pre-modern, tragic heroism identified by Hegel, as well as to Hegel's post-modern heroism without tragedy, mediated by reciprocal confession and for-giveness. Indeed, while for Brandom's Hegel it is important to overcome the disparity between the referent and its different senses, between the action-in-itself and what the action is *for* the agent and *for* the agent's community, for Deleuze, as is well known, this desire to overcome difference is simply to display a non-necessary preference for identity over difference, for peace and conformity over struggle and novelty. Instead, Deleuze would want to say here that the community's attribu-tion of responsibility to an agent for an action that outstrips what the

---

[38] See Deleuze, *The Logic of Sense*, p. 237.
[39] Ibid. pp. 207–8.

agent intends and can know, first and foremost confronts the agent as a *problem* ('that's not what I wanted!'). It is then up to the agent how to deal with this problem. The agent could assume responsibility for the alien action in its entirety (this is pre-modern, tragic heroism). She could also enter into a process of reciprocal confession and forgiveness with her community, provided, of course, that the power-relations constitutive of the agent's community allow for this type of relationship (postmodern heroism without tragedy). Finally, she could treat the problem as involving all kinds of social and conceptual conditions which can themselves be creatively engaged with. To treat the problem in this way is to transform the difference between first- and third-person perspectives on action into what Deleuze calls in the 29th Series the 'crack of thought': a crack which provokes the agent to respond creatively to her concrete situation, and a crack through which new self-understandings have the potential to emerge.[40] My suggestion is that we also call this last response 'heroism', for it involves the agent holding herself responsible, not for the alien action attributed to her by her community, nor for the 'identity-in-difference' of the action such as this appears in a community structured by reciprocal confession and forgiveness, but for the 'counter-actualization' of the action-event. This heroism and this responsibility is, as Deleuze puts it, precisely that of the 'free man, who grasps the event, and does not allow it to be actualized as such without enacting, the actor, its counter-actualization'.[41] The free man who, for Deleuze, avoids bitterness and *ressentiment* when faced with an action-event that turned out differently to what he intended or foresaw.

By way of conclusion, then, let us say a few brief words about how we might heroically take responsibility for – by counter-actualising – those of one's actions that outstrip what one intends and can know. We must, it seems, engage with our action-events in their publicness and expressivity or, as Deleuze puts it, employ a certain 'usage of representations'.[42] In other words, we must creatively intervene in our shared expressive medium in order to reorient how we and how others think about what we are doing. As has been argued, the elements of the language that express the sense of what happens and what is said are not given once and for all. The sense of any particular proposition bearing on what happens is not compresent with that proposition, but must rather be determined by subsequent expressive activity. What this implies is that

---

[40] On the 'crack of thought', see ibid. p. 208.
[41] Ibid. p. 152.
[42] Ibid. pp. 144–7.

the expression of sense is open to future, and indeed novel, language-events. Moreover, insofar as sense is understood as, in Frege's terms, the 'mode of presentation' of the referent of our propositions, such novel language-events will come to transform what we are talking about using language.[43] It is in this way, I would argue, that we ought to understand Deleuze's claim that 'language ... is endlessly born, in the future direction of the Aion where it is established and, somehow, anticipated', that is, insofar as its expressible sense is concerned; and what this language talks about is 'the past of states of affairs which go on appearing and disappearing in the other direction'.[44] Understood in this way, as Paul Patton has put it in a different context, 'language use is not primarily the communication of information but a matter of acting in or upon the world: event attributions do not simply describe or report pre-existing events, they help to actualize particular events in the social field'.[45] The heroic element of agency, then, involves recognising our responsibility for our own action-events and directing their counter-actualisation through a creative and public use of representations. It is through this activity that, for Deleuze, we become *worthy* of the action-events that 'happen' to us.[46]

[43] Frege, 'On *Sinn* and *Bedeutung*', p. 152.
[44] Deleuze, *The Logic of Sense*, p. 167.
[45] Paul Patton, 'The World Seen from Within: Deleuze and the Philosophy of Events', *Theory and Event* 1:1, (1997), §7.
[46] On becoming worthy of the event, see Deleuze, *The Logic of Sense*, pp. 148–50.

# Part III
## Deleuzian Lines of Post-Kantian Thought

# Chapter 11

# Schopenhauer and Deleuze

*Alistair Welchman*

Deleuze does not mention Schopenhauer very frequently. Certainly Schopenhauer does not appear to be in the counter-canon of life-affirming philosophers that Deleuze so values – indeed, far from it. Nor does he appear to be even a favoured 'enemy' as he describes Kant,[1] or as he sometimes appears to view Hegel.[2] In Jones and Roffe's collection on Deleuze's historical antecedents, *Deleuze's Philosophical Lineage*, Schopenhauer is mentioned exactly once (in the chapter on Hume) and certainly not in the dignified role of one of the twenty leading influences on Deleuze.[3]

Nevertheless, I think Schopenhauer's break from Kant is crucial for understanding not only Deleuze's account of Nietzsche, but also for a proper grasp of the core Deleuzian distinction between the actual and the virtual, at least in its guise as the distinction between desiring-production and social production in *Anti-Oedipus*.

## SCHOPENHAUER

The general contours of Schopenhauer's development of Kant's transcendental philosophy are fairly well known, but bear examination. Schopenhauer was not quite in the first wave of post-Kantian excitement

---

[1] Gilles Deleuze, 'Letter to a Harsh Critic', in *Negotiations*, trans. Martin Joughin (New York: Columbia University Press, 1995 [1973]), p. 6/*110*. [Note on the citations: the first page number refers to the English translation, the second, italicised, number to the French original.]

[2] Christian Kerslake, 'The Vertigo of Philosophy: Deleuze and the Problem of Immanence', *Radical Philosophy* 113, (May/June 2002), pp. 10–23. Henry Somers-Hall, *Hegel, Deleuze and the Critique of Representation: Dialectics of Negation and Difference* (Albany: State University of New York Press, 2012).

[3] Graham Jones and Jon Roffe (eds), *Deleuze's Philosophical Lineage* (Edinburgh: Edinburgh University Press, 2009).

that produced Maimon, Fichte, Schelling, and the young Hegel. The early texts of these figures date from around 1790 to perhaps 1809 (the date of publication of Schelling's *Freiheitsschrift*). Schopenhauer was already writing by then, but did not develop his signature doctrine, that the world is representation *and* will, until the publication of his main work in 1819. He was of course also intellectually and socially isolated from the ferment of the early idealist movement, and treated its prominent thinkers (with the occasional exception of Schelling) with polemical contempt.

The world is will and representation. Considered as representation, Schopenhauer's conception of the world is similar to Kant's, although Schopenhauer simplifies Kant's system of categories and collapses the Kantian understanding, the faculty of concepts, into sensibility – the faculty of intuition-perceptions or *Anschauungen*. At the end of this process Schopenhauer retains only space, time and causality as transcendental conditions of the world as representation. Even in this simplification, however, he makes a clear advance (in a Deleuzian direction) on Kant by displacing and exacerbating the concept/intuition distinction.

Early in *Difference and Repetition* Deleuze tables his slogan for repetition, 'difference without a concept'[4] and immediately relates the way in which repetition's form of difference escapes conceptuality by appealing to the 'peculiar power of the existent, a stubbornness of the existent in intuition, which resists every specification by concepts, no matter how far this is taken'.[5]

Some of the difficulty of Deleuze's work is due to the fact that what interests him is what resists intelligibility or conceptual understanding and accountability. The (albeit ambiguous) draw of Kant for Deleuze shows the way in which the Kantian concept/intuition distinction lies at the crossroads of modern thought. For Kant intelligibility can indeed be achieved, but its victory is neither easy nor guaranteed: witness the way the problematic of the ultimate intelligibility of nature emerges anew in the third *Critique* of the 1790s. For the absolute idealist tradition culminating in Hegel, intelligibility is presupposed at the outset and the labour of the negative a sham. But there is a counter-tradition running through Nietzsche, in which theoretical attention is directed towards what resists intelligibility, the 'indivisible remainder' in Schelling's words. Such resistance is manifest first of all in the stubbornness of

---

⁴ Gilles Deleuze, *Difference and Repetition*, trans. Paul Patton (New York: Columbia University Press, 1994 [1968]), p. 13/23.
⁵ Ibid. pp. 13–14/23.

intuition, but also in Deleuze's subtle reprioritisation of problem over solution.[6]

Kantian intuition marks the first philosophical site of this resistance in modernity. And for Schopenhauer, intuitive knowledge is absolutely primary, so that animals perceive causal connections, and have an experience of objects quite similar to human experience.[7] None of this requires concepts. Schopenhauer's account of human reason and conceptuality (he identifies the faculties, in contrast to Kant) is strikingly modest, not least in comparison with the other thinkers of the classical German idealist movement: reason is a merely passive storehouse for perceptual knowledge. The latter is the 'direct light of the sun' while the former is the 'borrowed light of the moon'.[8] While this has some uses – not least in widening the range of factors that motivate human action – it is at best a discrete approximation to the intrinsic continuity of intuitive perceptual experience:

> abstract knowledge is to such [intuitive] nuances as a mosaic is to a *van der Werft* or a *Denner*: however fine the mosaic may be, there always remain borders between the stones, and so a continuous transition of one colour into another is impossible; in just the same way, however much the rigid and sharp boundaries between concepts are divided through increasingly minute definition, they will never be able to reach the fine modifications of the intuitive.[9]

Something always 'escapes' coding, of whatever type it is.

But these are minor modifications of Kant's thought in comparison with the major innovation Schopenhauer introduces: the will. Schopenhauer's rethinking of the notion of will is deep and remarkable. A clear understanding of its nature is a prerequisite for any grasp of his signature claim that the Kantian thing-in-itself is will. Although it is almost a badge of membership of the post-Kantian idealist band to maintain that, despite Kant's strictures, knowledge of some kind of things as they are in themselves is possible, Schopenhauer's claim that the thing-in-itself is will has nevertheless often been regarded as naïve. In

---

[6] Ibid. chap. 4.

[7] Arthur Schopenhauer, *The World as Will and Representation*, trans. and ed. Judith Norman, Alistair Welchman and Christopher Janaway (Cambridge: Cambridge University Press, 2010), vol. 1, §6, pp. 42–3/2:24–5. [Note on the citations: the second italicised reference refers to the volume and page number of the German edition, *Sämtliche Werke*, ed. Arthur Hübscher, 4th edn (Wiesbaden: Brockhaus, 1988), 7 vols.]

[8] Ibid. vol. 1, §8, pp. 57–8/2:41.

[9] Ibid. vol. 1, §12, p. 81–2/2:67.

fact, Schopenhauer is a lot less methodologically naïve than for instance Schelling with his postulation of an active human faculty of intellectual intuition (contempt for Schelling's view is one of the few things that Schopenhauer and Hegel have in common). The reason for this is that the proposition 'the thing-in-itself is will' can be interpreted in such a way that even Kant could subscribe to it. So, far from naively extending cognition there, just where Kant's critique of metaphysics says it cannot go, Schopenhauer is, in contradistinction to almost all the other post-Kantian idealists, sustaining a certain kind of Kantian position.

In what way could Kant agree with this proposition that the thing-in-itself is will? Will [*Wille*] is the faculty acting not just 'according to law', but according to a 'representation' of a law[10] or according to 'concepts' or 'the representation of a purpose'.[11] Kant is clear that empirical concepts will not suffice: after all, if the concept that determines the will is itself a causal product, then the will is itself merely causal. It is therefore only spontaneously generated rational representations that can ground a will: the will is free, or it is not a will.

The overall structure of the critical works, as Kant makes clear, is not to show that the claims of transcendent metaphysics are *false*, but that they are merely 'problematic': since such claims transcend the possibility of any experience, there is necessarily no evidence that can decide such statements. Thus, in the case that is most crucial for the second *Critique*, while the Second Analogy has proven that human beings are empirically determined by exceptionless causal laws, the solution Kant tables is that it remains merely problematic whether human beings *in themselves* might not yet be free: perhaps, perhaps not.

Kant defends the possibility of this kind of transcendental compatibilism in the Third Antinomy. The Antinomy starts out curiously however. The thesis argues that causal explanations are insufficient, because an individual causal explanation of *x* by *y* does not explain the *cause* of *y*. Since causes regress back without limit, causal explanation is always insufficient. And therefore there must be another kind of causation, causation by freedom. The argument has a suspiciously theological ring to it, and closely resembles the First Antinomy, which address the question whether the world has a beginning in time. The freedom at issue looks like the freedom god might have to initiate the causal series

[10] Immanuel Kant, *Groundwork of the Metaphysics of Morals*, trans. Mary J. Gregor (Cambridge: Cambridge University Press, 1998), AA 4:412.
[11] Immanuel Kant, *Critique of the Power of Judgment*, trans. Paul Guyer and Eric Matthews, ed. Paul Guyer (Cambridge: Cambridge University Press, 2000), §10, p. 105/AA 5:220.

that comprises the world, to 'begin a series of occurrences *entirely from itself*'.[12]

How does Kant negotiate between this theological problematic and the free will that he seeks at least to register the possibility of? By arguing that the in-itself of a human being may (for all we know) be akin to god in its ability freely to initiate causal series. This is an argument whose promiscuity anticipates Schopenhauer: if my in-itself may be transcendentally free (for all anyone knows), then so may the in-itself of *anything*.

The last phase in Kant's argument is to allow that although nothing can be strictly *known* about things-in-themselves, we may nevertheless *rationally believe* certain claims about them, if such claims are (a) not impossible and (b) are necessary conditions of practical agency. Of the three claims Kant endorses, the first (that I have a soul) is really indistinguishable from the second (that I am in-myself a will). Since the soul cannot be a Cartesian substance (as the Paralogisms have shown), the only content the notion of 'soul' therefore has is that of 'will'. Of course, the soul must survive empirical death; but so does the will, since it is, as we have seen, atemporal. And the third is that god exists; to the extent that this is not already made true by the frankly divine dimension of the human will, then this claim shows that we may rationally believe that *another* will exists. But it does not say that (we may rationally believe) in-itself I am anything other than will. Taken in conjunction with the promiscuousness of the Third Antinomy argument, then the result is that Kant thinks we may rationally believe that things-in-themselves are will (or if we may not, then we may believe nothing about them). Schopenhauer is not that distant from Kant.

This structural similarity, however, masks a deep shift in the nature of the will. The shift is a consequence of Schopenhauer's revaluation of reason and concomitant privileging of intuitive/perceptual cognition. In a long appendix to the first volume of *The World as Will and Representation*, Schopenhauer focuses his critique of Kant here on what he regards as problematic misuse of the terms 'phenomenon' and 'noumenon'. Correctly understood, Schopenhauer argues, these terms apply to just his distinction between intuitive/perceptual cognition and rational/conceptual i.e. abstract cognition.[13] Kant however reapplies these terms so that they become synonymous with the distinction

---

[12] Immanuel Kant, *Critique of Pure Reason*, trans. and ed. Paul Guyer and Allen W. Wood (Cambridge: Cambridge University Press, 1998), A534/B562.

[13] Schopenhauer, *The World as Will and Representation*, vol. 1, Appendix, p. 506/2:566.

between appearances and things-in-themselves. This is a serious mistake, because it presupposes that things-in-themselves are essentially intelligible. And applied to the view he shares with Kant that 'will' is the only way we have of viewing things-in-themselves, this presupposition entails that the will comprising things as they are in themselves (what we might call the transcendental or Big Will) must have an intentional structure: rational willing is purposive action, action governed by a concept.[14] Thus the definitions of the Kantian will quoted above represent an assumption that stands in need of justification.

Schopenhauer thinks no such justification can be provided, and (partly as a result) studiously avoids the term 'noumenon', sticking rigorously to 'thing-in-itself'.[15] This drives a crucial wedge between thing-in-itself (as source of pathological stimulation) and its intelligibility. But Schopenhauer's argument is more specific than this: it is not just that the intelligibility of the thing-in-itself is an unwarranted presupposition; in fact Schopenhauer has a positive argument that the presupposition is false. And this has even more specific consequences for the notion of will.

In broad outline, Schopenhauer argues in this way. There are three levels of transcendental condition that make possible the world as representation. At the most basic level is the bare distinction between subject and object.[16] At the next level is Schopenhauer's generalisation of Kant's account of causality. He widens the scope of Kant's reasoning by trying to show that Kant's mechanical conception of causation is only a special case of ground/consequent relations, which Schopenhauer brings together under the general rubric of the principle of sufficient reason. Using this idea he generalises Kant's Second Analogy, arguing that ground/consequent relations jointly comprise the conditions of possibility of experience in general. In the *Freedom* essay he gives a particularly clear version of this argument that stands as an emblem of clarity for a transcendental

---

[14] Kant's interest of course is in showing the possibility of *purely* rational action, i.e. action governed *only* by a concept or law (the two are identical for Kant), something that Kant equates with moral action.

[15] With one indirect exception: Schopenhauer takes over Kant's distinction between empirical and intelligible character ('On the Basis of Morality', in *The Two Fundamental Problems of Ethics*, ed. and trans. Christopher Janaway (Cambridge: Cambridge University Press, 2009), §10, p. 172/4:174). The distinction is important. But to retain the claim that the nature of anyone's in-itself is 'intelligible' is obviously to regard it as still fundamentally a 'thought thing', a *noumenon*. And exactly Schopenhauer's point is that this is not the case.

[16] Schopenhauer, *The World as Will and Representation*, vol. 1, §1.

argument.[17] Perceptual experience of objects is only possible because, on the basis of pre-objective sensory affections, we project objects in exterior space as the causes of our perceptual experience of them. This projection presupposes the concept of causation. But since the projection is what first constitutes experience this concept cannot be derived from experience. Therefore it must be *a priori*. This argument is the basis of a general argument showing that the principle of sufficient reason is the most general condition of possibility of experience. Lastly, at the bottom-most level come space and time. Schopenhauer describes these two taken together as the 'principle of individuation', i.e. the condition of distinction between different objects.[18] The *relational* nature of the principle of sufficient reason at the second level therefore essentially presupposes the principle of individuation at the third level because there must be individuated things to have 'sufficient reason' relations *between*.[19]

The thing-in-itself is therefore in the first instance negatively drawn:[20] as that which is 'expressed' in representation, the ultimate source of the content of representation, it must be non-temporal, non-spatial and 'beyond' the principle of sufficient reason. It shares its non-temporality and non-spatiality with Kant's thing-in-itself; but the subtraction of Schopenhauer's thing-in-itself from the general form of object-relatedness, the principle of sufficient reason, deprives it of any 'ground'[21] and clearly distinguishes it from the Kantian *noumenon*, which is all intelligibility but without the possibility of confirmation by experience.

This subtraction is the basis of Schopenhauer's account of the 'freedom' of the will, which is really the freedom of the thing-in-itself from its transcendental forms. No individual can be empirically free, i.e. free at the level of representation, for every event has a 'ground'. This is no less true for human beings, who act on 'motives' or on the basis of abstract representations, as it is for inanimate objects operating under strictly mechanical causation. These are only different 'shapes' the principle of sufficient reason may take. So the whole notion of freedom must

[17] Arthur Schopenhauer, 'On the Freedom of the Will', in *The Two Fundamental Problems of Ethics*, ed. and trans. Christopher Janaway (Cambridge: Cambridge University Press, 2009), III, p. 50/4:27.

[18] Schopenhauer, *The World as Will and Representation*, vol. 1, §23.

[19] One might think that the subject/object distinction would guarantee a plurality of things. But this is not so, as the subject is not a cognitive object and has no causal interaction with objects, only the body, itself a representation has causal interaction with (other) objects.

[20] Schopenhauer, *The World as Will and Representation*, vol. 1, §23, p. 137/2:134.

[21] Ibid. §20, p. 131/2:127.

be radically shifted: it no longer signals the freedom of an event from an empirical cause (which is impossible), but is the freedom of things as they are in themselves from transcendental governance. Schopenhauer is quick to derive from this the following entailment: since science in its general conception seeks various kinds of causal relations, or, for Schopenhauer, the lawful relations between ground and consequent in various mutually irreducible shapes of the principle of sufficient reason, it follows that

> no science in the proper sense of the term (I mean: systematic cognition guided by the principle of sufficient reason) will ever reach its final goal or be able to achieve a fully satisfactory explanation.[22]

Explanations have to stop somewhere. And where they stop is the thing-in-itself which is *by its nature* inexplicable because it lies by definition outside of the most general principle of explanation: the principle of sufficient reason. Note that Schopenhauer's argument is similar to, but reverses, Kant's. For Kant, approximately, the given failure of explanation to be sufficient motivates the introduction of another form of causality (intentional willing) and starts the search for a way of reconciling this with empirical determinism. For Schopenhauer on the other hand, it is the excess of thing-in-itself over explanation that motivates the *a priori* claim that science can never be complete. Nevertheless, this negative construal of the will as (merely) the groundless is something Deleuze clearly understands about Schopenhauer, and most of his references to Schopenhauer (along with Schelling) outside of the crucial *Nietzsche* text relate, not particularly sympathetically, to the groundlessness of the will. Deleuze's reading is however insufficient, even if not completely askew (see section 'The 1960s' in this chapter).

One way of starting to see why this is so, why the will is not just blank groundlessness, is to see how Schopenhauer derives the identification of thing-in-itself with will, and what consequences his de-rationalisation of the thing-in-itself has specifically for this will.

First, why does Schopenhauer identify thing-in-itself with will? His argument is in part phenomenological. First, negatively, we experience a kind of dissatisfaction with explanations that proceed merely in accordance with the principle of sufficient reason: such explanations relate objects (including our bodies, considered as objects) to each other, but

> [w]e want to know the *sense* [*Bedeutung*] of those representations: we ask if this world is nothing more than representation; in which case it would

have to pass over us like an insubstantial dream or a ghostly phantasm not worth our notice.[23]

This is an acute observation that pre-empts both Heidegger's conception of being-in-the-world and the related trend towards an emphasis on the irreducibility of embodiment in cognitive science: the hypervalorisation of the intellect neglects the basic fact that things, even their representations, have a *significance* for us.

But Schopenhauer does not think that embodiment is sufficient to account for the sense of things, for the body is in part an object among objects. But the body is not just an object, it is rather the privileged representation of which we are phenomenologically aware in two distinct ways: as objective representation among others; but also from the 'inside'. For Schopenhauer, the question is what aspect of our phenomenological – i.e. interior – experience both explains the sense of (objective) things and can be successfully subtracted from the governance of transcendental forms, especially the principle of sufficient reason. Will is the answer to this question.

But why? Certainly willing has a phenomenological profile. On the one hand, we have an 'inside' view of the actions of our own bodies that is based (actively) on the experience of intentional action; on the other, things grab us by affecting our wills. Intentional action however takes us back to the Kantian conception of willing as causation by means of concepts (intentions). This is where the second criterion comes in: it is only willing that can be fully subtracted from representation. Every episode of actual willing is inserted into a framework of representation governed by the principle of sufficient reason: in Schopenhauer's vocabulary, I can explain why I willed something to occur on the basis of the representation that forms my motive. But, as with other representational explanations, I cannot explain why I will at all.[24] There might simply be a limit to thinking here: just because we experience a lack of sense, doesn't mean sense-making must be accessible. But willing *can* be so subtracted: there is a core of conative activity in every episode of willing, a not-yet directed striving or surging, that does not require a transitive object, and hence escapes the most general form of representational structure, the division into subject and object. In doing so, of course, it is also independent of the principle of sufficient reason, since causes (of any kind) are relational; but without the transitivity of subject/object division, the pure core of willing is non-relational. Consider two other cases that will not

[23] Ibid. vol. 1, §17, p. 123/2:*118* (translation modified, AW).
[24] Ibid. vol. 1, §29, p. 199/2:*194–5*.

survive this subtraction: any representation, or 'thing', including rational representations are completely bound up with the principle of sufficient reason, and hence leave no precipitate when it is subtracted.[25] Similarly, passion or affect, on its own (i.e. independent of the active notion of will) is also inherently transitive, since both terms imply an 'undergoing at the hands of something else' and hence imply an object.[26]

This completes Schopenhauer's reconceptualisation of the notion of will: he makes it undergo a crucial reversal from Kant's view. Will as such is no longer the locus of responsible free human action. Rather it is a fundamentally intransitive form of activity of production:

> [T]he absence of all goals, of all boundaries, belongs to the essence of the will in itself, which is an endless striving.[27]

Similarly, 'freedom' as a problematic has also been radically displaced: no longer concentrated in individuated human beings, it is only the will as such that is 'free', a term that therefore no longer implies arbitrary choice, but rather escape from grounding.

This account, from the pivotal Book II of *The World as Will and Representation*, is the centrepiece of Schopenhauer's philosophical novelty. The rest of the work fills out Schopenhauer's system-philosophical ambitions. Most of these are negative: he deduces an *a priori* argument for pessimism from these premises, and argues that the highest practical human goals are to minimise the suffering of others through a compassion-based morality, but ultimately to renounce willing altogether, as the saintly ascetic does.

But before he gets to this, Schopenhauer offers an account of art that only partly shares this pessimism. It is true that Schopenhauer regards the disinterested contemplation of beautiful forms as the most accessible path to at least temporary release from the sufferings of the will:

> for that moment we are freed from the terrible pressure of the will, we celebrate the Sabbath of the penal servitude of willing, the wheel of Ixion stands still.[28]

But the freedom of the will in Schopenhauer's sense also makes the will the ultimate originator of those forms that are copied by the artist: the

---

[25] Of course this means that Schopenhauer's retention of the term 'thing' in 'thing-in-itself' is unhelpful. But it can be regarded as a mere placeholder, to be filled only by the notion of will.

[26] Dale Jacquette, 'Schopenhauer's Proof that the Thing-in-Itself is Will', *Kantian Review* 12:2, (2007), pp. 76–108.

[27] Schopenhauer, *The World as Will and Representation*, vol. 1, §29, p. 188/2:195.

[28] Ibid. vol. 1, §38, p. 220/2:231.

will produces the world as representation, in a series of 'grades of objec-tivation' that push creatively forward.[29] The problematic of freedom is no longer that of the undetermined individual human action, but the space for nature's creativity in the production of arbitrary new forms.

What is trickiest is Schopenhauer's subtraction of the will from temporality and spatiality. Two aspects in particular make this move implausible. First, some commentators find the very notion of an atem-poral act implausible,[30] although it has long been part of a theological tradition and its possibility has been vigorously defended.[31] Second, if Schopenhauer is right that space and time together form the principle of individuation, then it follows that the will as such is incapable of individuation.

And this notion of the identity or oneness of the will is not a free wheel, but appears to play a significant role in the rest of his philosophi-cal system. To pick up the thread: the intransitive nature of the pro-duction embodied by the will is the most important of Schopenhauer's arguments for his signature pessimism. I *am* will; although each episode of willing has a rationale, my willing as such has no such rationale. Although I *appear* to will specific things, the will that I am is in fact intransitive, just a willing and not a willing of something. This manifests itself phenomenally in the fact that after achieving one object, I start to will some further object. There is no object that will yield lasting satis-faction because the will that I am cannot be satisfied because it actually *has* no object. With the standard assumption that to will something is to lack it, then the intransitivity of the transcendental will implies the necessity of suffering at the phenomenal level: I keep on willing *stuff*, none of which can possibly satisfy the will at the transcendental level.

Schopenhauer's pessimism about the ultimate value of existence drives both his moral philosophy and his account of religion. And both his arguments appear to make significant use of the claim that the will is ultimately one. Schopenhauer's moral philosophy, for instance, is predicated on a corollary of the unity of the will: the will is the ultimate agent of its own suffering. As Schopenhauer picturesquely puts it, each of us is 'the perpetrator and the victim'.[32] In a way, evil is the result of what Kant would have called a transcendental subreption, a confusion of transcendental and empirical levels: I experience the will as mine

[29] Ibid. vol. 1, §45, p. 246/2:260.
[30] Christopher Janaway, 'Necessity, Responsibility and Character: Schopenhauer on Freedom of the Will', *Kantian Review* 17:3, (2012), pp. 431–57; p. 450.
[31] Brian Leftow, *Time and Eternity* (Ithaca, NY: Cornell University Press, 1991).
[32] Schopenhauer, *The World as Will and Representation*, vol. 1, §63, p. 367/2:402.

because of its individuation within the empirical; but when I act on my own interests to the detriment of others I forget that it is the same (transcendental) will that suffers. The remedy is compassion [*Mitleid*] in which I suffer along with the other, a state that Schopenhauer argues can be achieved by recognition of my metaphysical identity with others, 'seeing through' the 'veil of [representational] Maya'.[33]

Perhaps compassion enables the individual to act so as to reduce the overall level of suffering, but it is at best a Band-Aid on the basic wound that comprises existence. Thus Schopenhauer proposes a deeper value than moral value: asceticism, or denial of the will. Denial of the will is based on an extension of compassionate motivation: where the compassionate person distinguishes 'less' between self and other, the ascetic completely obliterates the distinction between self and other. This insight precipitates a dramatic change: it acts as a 'tranquilliser' on the individual will, 'turning' it away from life in 'renunciation', 'resignation' and ultimately 'complete will-lessness',[34] a state that Schopenhauer describes in religious terms as both saintly and akin to Buddhist nirvana.[35]

It is uncontroversial that these views had a great impact on Nietzsche, who vehemently rejects Schopenhauer's pessimism, compassion and asceticism, all the while retaining the basic framework of a philosophy of will, in the Schopenhauerian sense of intransitive production. Deleuze's proximity to – or at least favourable relation to – Nietzsche makes him reproduce this attitude to Schopenhauer. But in so doing, Deleuze's attitude to Schopenhauer is more dictated by tactical considerations of intellectual positioning than by a proper appreciation of the importance of Schopenhauer's reinterpretation of the notion of will.

## NIETZSCHE

Overwhelmingly, Deleuze's most extensive discussion of Schopenhauer is in the context of Nietzsche at the outset of the 1962 text *Nietzsche et la philosophie*. But Deleuze's engagement with Schopenhauer in this text is determined mostly by a need to position Schopenhauer with respect to Nietzsche but also with respect to Hegel. Deleuze must make it clear what an advance Nietzsche has made on Schopenhauer, while also marking the importance of Schopenhauer for Nietzsche; at

---

[33] Ibid. vol. 1, §66, p. 397/2:439.
[34] Ibid. vol. 1, §68, p. 406/2:448.
[35] Ibid. vol. 1, §63, p. 383/2:421.

the same time, Deleuze seeks to differentiate both the Nietzsche and Schopenhauer traditions from the Hegelian dialectic.

The dialectic is the main enemy in the book: 'There is no possible compromise between Hegel and Nietzsche.'[36] What Deleuze wants to do above all is distinguish Nietzsche's account of the master/slave encounter in *The Genealogy of Morality* from Hegel's master/slave dialectic.[37] Broadly speaking, on the Hegelian account, the master can only even pretend to be master by negating the slave; and this negation embroils the master in a dialectic of negation motorised by the slave. On Nietzsche's account, the master is distinguished 'positively' from the slave. Only in this way, Deleuze argues, can difference be affirmed as such, as difference, rather than reduced to its dialectical forms of negation and contradiction.

Resisting a Hegelian account is a standard procedure, in some ways that of Nietzsche himself, whose 1888 account of *The Birth of Tragedy* describes it as 'offensively Hegelian'.[38] But the procedure leaves Schopenhauer in an ambiguous position: Nietzsche himself claims that the problem with the *Birth of Tragedy* was Hegel and that it was not (despite all appearances) Schopenhauerian.[39] But Deleuze claims the opposite, that the *Birth* is not dialectical but Schopenhauerian.[40] Since Schopenhauer was of course infamously anti-Hegelian, studding his works with sometimes unreadably hyperbolic polemics against Hegel, the distinction between Schopenhauer and Nietzsche must be itself distinct from Deleuze's account of the way Nietzsche resists the dialectic.

The fundamental problem of the dialectical account of the will lies in its 'representational' character, according to Deleuze:[41] the Hegelian master is really a slave because 'will' is filtered through 'representation' in the form of 'recognition' (*Anerkennung* in German, derived from the same root, *Erkennen*, as the term Schopenhauer uses for representational knowledge or cognition). Later Deleuze argues that Nietzsche's concept of will-to-power is radically misunderstood if it is treated as a will that

---

[36] Gilles Deleuze, *Nietzsche and Philosophy*, trans. Hugh Tomlinson (London: Athlone Press, 1983 [1962]), p. 195/223.

[37] Friedrich Nietzsche, *On the Genealogy of Morality*, ed. Keith Ansell-Pearson, trans. Carol Diethe (Cambridge: Cambridge University Press, 2006 [1887]).

[38] Friedrich Nietzsche, *The Anti-Christ, Ecce Homo, Twilight of the Idols and other Writings*, ed. Aaron Ridley and Judith Norman, trans. Judith Norman (Cambridge: Cambridge University Press, 2005 [1888]), p. 108.

[39] Ibid.

[40] Deleuze, *Nietzsche and Philosophy*, p. 11/12.

[41] Ibid. p. 10/11.

'wants . . . desires or seeks out power as an end'.[42] Will-to-power is not, in other words, a transitive will for some particular end. For it to be so would presuppose a representation, since the 'end' would be represented. We would be back to Kant's conception of will. But as we have seen, this is exactly what Schopenhauer rejects: the (transcendental) will is precisely subtracted from representation and wills without having any particular telos. Schopenhauer inaugurates a critique of representation just as powerful as either Nietzsche's or Deleuze's. This therefore cannot be the point at which Deleuze's Nietzsche departs from Schopenhauer.

What is that point? Deleuze argues that the break is quite specific:

> Nietzsche's break with Schopenhauer rests on one precise point; it is a matter of knowing whether the will is unitary or multiple. Everything else flows from this. Indeed, if Schopenhauer is led to deny the will it is primarily because he believes in the unity of willing. Because the will, according to Schopenhauer, is essentially unitary, the executioner comes to understand that he is one with his own victim. The consciousness of the identity of the will in all its manifestations leads the will to deny itself, to suppress itself in pity, morality and ascetism (Schopenhauer *The World* as *Will and Representation*, Book 4). Nietzsche discovers what seems to him the authentically Schopenhauerian mystification; when we posit the unity, the identity, of the will, we must necessarily repudiate the will itself.[43]

We have seen that Schopenhauer does indeed argue that the will cannot be individuated. And the standard story that he tells about compassion and ascetism, morality and religion, depends crucially in individuated human beings achieving a kind of insight into the 'unity' with others.

But Schopenhauer is guilty of ambiguous formulation at just the point of this claim for the 'unity' of the will. For, on the one hand, he argues that the transcendental will is 'free of all *multiplicity*', but then he tries to infer from this what does not follow, that '[i]t is itself one'. Indeed he knows that it does not follow, for he immediately adds 'but not in the manner of an object, since an object's unity is known in contrast to a possible multiplicity'.[44] Strictly, the will is free from both unity *and* multiplicity; but Schopenhauer often talks as if the will in itself were thereby one. This of course makes him seem to be a philosopher of identity and not difference, and hence on the face of it, not one with affinity for Deleuze.

But Deleuze himself (with Guattari) suggest that there *is* such an affin-

---

[42] Ibid. p. 79/90.
[43] Ibid. p. 7/8 (translation modified, AW).
[44] Schopenhauer, *The World as Will and Representation*, vol. 1, §23, pp. 137–8/2:134.

ity. For the notion of multiplicity (as a noun) is precisely distinguished from the Platonic dialectical relation of the one and the many. When Schopenhauer argues that the transcendental will is not multiple, he is using the term as a correlative of the one, as a synonym for the many. One might make a comparison here with Kant. The thing-in-itself in Kant is coded proximally into sensations [*Empfindungen*] which are described as 'manifold [*mannigfaltig*]'. The way in which sensations are manifold cannot be the way in which individuated objects are many since sensations are prior to individuation. Schopenhauer is committed to a similar manifoldness transcending either unity or manyness.

This can seem a rather technical move. Yes, Schopenhauer may be committed to such a notion as a matter of (transcendental) logic. But Schopenhauer in fact thinks of the will as 'one' and deploys this notion to generate the 'extremely unfortunate "tone" or emotional tonality' in the philosophy of the will characterised by pessimism, compassion and asceticism.[45] There's no doubt that Schopenhauer was a pessimist and valued asceticism. But it is not obvious that these really derive, as Deleuze argues, compactly, from any putative postulation of the unity of the transcendental will or from consciousness of that unity. Indeed in the case Schopenhauer's analysis of compassion, despite Nietzsche's hostility to the notion, and despite some of what Schopenhauer says, I think Schopenhauer makes rather a Deleuzian case for the undoing of the representational subject.

The standard view of Schopenhauer's defence of compassion is that one can achieve a compassionate outlook by coming to a conscious-ness of the metaphysical identity of one's self with others, or at least making 'less of a distinction than is usually made' between one's self and others,[46] as described above. In his 1839 text *On the Basis of Morality*, Schopenhauer argues that it is indeed compassion that is the basis: only compassion motivates us to set aside the interests of our (empirically) individuated wills. Schopenhauer distinguishes tradition-ally between acts of justice and those of philanthropy or loving kind-ness [*Menschenliebe*]. In the *Basis* he clearly articulates the dependence of both kinds of moral acts on the motivation of compassion and the dependence of compassion on consciousness or recognition of meta-physical identity.[47] But in the earlier *World as Will and Representation* (1819) compassion is conspicuous by its absence from his account of

---

[45] Deleuze, *Nietzsche and Philosophy*, p. 82/94.
[46] Schopenhauer, *The World as Will and Representation*, vol. 1, §66, p. 398/2:439.
[47] Schopenhauer, 'On the Basis of Morality', §14.

justice (section 62). Although the metaphysical identity thesis is mentioned in both cases, compassion comes up only some sections later in the account of the virtue of loving kindness (section 67). This suggests that Schopenhauer is drawing some conceptual distinction between compassion and the identity thesis.

What might this be? Schopenhauer is really reversing the order of priority of the metaphysical identity thesis and the experience of compassion. Rather than consciousness of identity leading to compassion it is the 'everyday phenomenon of *compassion*' that explains the otherwise mysterious 'process' whereby I can be motivated by the suffering of another.[48] His argument is phenomenological: the experience of compassion should not be *equated* with the thesis of metaphysical identity; rather the experience of compassion is the mechanism by means of which the metaphysical identity claim is able actually to operate upon us as an incentive: compassion is our phenomenological mode of access to metaphysical identity, 'the empirical emerging of the will's metaphysical identity'.[49]

But now why should one retain the metaphysical underpinning of identity? The phenomenology of compassion is that of the partial breakdown of the numerical identity of the cognitive subject. The experience of compassion breaks the subject down and marks a non-representational irruption of the other in the subject: it is a contagion or infection that promises no necessary re-unificatory identity at the end.

Everyone agrees that Deleuze's term 'transcendental empiricism' gets at something important about what he is doing. But it is quite unclear what that is. One popular view is that it has to do with specifying the conditions of real rather than possible experience.[50] This view can itself be divided: perhaps it is the conditions themselves that must change, in which case transcendental empiricism describes a certain kind of transcendental condition, the 'plastic' ones of the *Nietzsche* text that are not bigger than what they condition.[51] But another view is that it is not about conditioning at all, but de-conditioning. On this view the 'transcendental' of transcendental empiricism concerns not the various conditioning procedures that do in fact go to comprise representation, but rather concerns the constitution of what resists representation: in

[48] Ibid. p. 200/4:209.

[49] Arthur Schopenhauer, *The World as Will and Representation*, trans. E. J. F. Payne (New York: Dover, 1969), vol. 2, chap. 47, p. 602/3:691 (my own translation, AW).

[50] Levi Bryant, *Difference and Givenness: Deleuze's Transcendental Empiricism and the Ontology of Immanence* (Evanston, IL: Northwestern University Press, 2008), p. 3.

[51] Deleuze, *Nietzsche and Philosophy*, p. 50/57.

Kant's and Schopenhauer's vocabulary, the thing-in-itself. There is a sense in which Schopenhauer's argument for the claim that the thing-in-itself is will already comprises a form of transcendental empiricism: from an *experience* of willing in intentional actions within the sphere of representation, he argues to a *transcendental* notion of willing subtracted from that representation. The (phenomenological) experience of compassion extends this process of transcendental empiricism by pointing to a paradoxical (though nevertheless familiar) experience of the other invading or infecting the self, that tends to destabilise the very conditions of representational experience.

There is much debate about how to understand the numerous occasions in his texts in which Deleuze appears to inhabit a frankly phenomenological register. He himself describes phenomenology in highly negative terms, terming it 'our modern scholasticism' in the *Nietzsche* book.[52] But it is hard to see how 'empiricism' can be completely divorced from experience. And a solution may be found in the idea that Deleuze is interested primarily in experiences that defeat the conditions of representation and threaten to dissolve the subject in a becoming.[53] Here Deleuze's peculiar relation to phenomenology might actually help Schopenhauer scholarship, which often becomes entangled in issues of epistemic integrity concerning the possibility of a cognitive relation with what, in strict Kantian form, we can have no cognitive relation with: the thing-in-itself.

So Schopenhauer's arguments neither require the will to be thought of as identical (even if he talks that way sometimes), nor do they require anything like *consciousness* of such identity to generate compassion. Rather compassion is itself the experience of the breakdown of (representational) experience in the direction of the impersonality of the will.

Deleuze's accounts of Schopenhauer's two flaws with respect to Nietzsche therefore both fail: Schopenhauer offers a clear critique of representation; and it is not true that either identity or consciousness, i.e. a representation of identity, are required for compassion. Still it is clearly true that Schopenhauer is a pessimist and at the same time as he identifies a form of intransitive production in the transcendental will he also seeks to deny it. And these mark a great difference at least of 'tone' from Nietzsche and Deleuze.

---

[52] Ibid. p. 195/223.

[53] Christian Kerslake, 'Insects and Incest: From Bergson and Jung to Deleuze', *Multitudes* 25, (summer 2006), available at <http://www.multitudes.net/Insects-and-Incest-From-Bergson/> (last accessed 10 October 2014).

## THE 1960s

It seems hard to imagine a positive Deleuzian account of asceticism. Yet Peter Hallward's *Out of this World: Deleuze and the Philosophy of Creation* outlines an understanding of 'asceticism', at least of a certain kind, as opening up the space for a critique of representation. Hallward views Deleuze's philosophy as guided fundamentally by a movement out of the (actual) world, and it would be easy to interpret this as involving a certain form of asceticism, albeit of a 'positive and affirmative' kind.[54] In an explanatory comparison, Hallward argues that Deleuze privileges the still figural art of Francis Bacon over the backwater of abstraction for much the same reason:[55] in Bacon the figure is de-formed, in transition, becoming something else (like an embryo); while in abstraction, like negative theology or 'mystical extinction'[56] or the abyss of the undifferentiated, sees the only alternative to the phenomenon as blank absence of individuation.

Hallward's interpretation of Deleuze has not been popular among Deleuzians. But the distinction he tables between a movement out of the actual world (the world as representation) that is deforming rather than blankly abstract raises another of Deleuze's own criticisms of Schopenhauer. This criticism comes from Deleuze's middle period texts, *The Logic of Sense* and *Difference and Repetition*. Whereas in the *Nietzsche* text, Deleuze identified Schopenhauer's problem as presupposing or asserting the unity or identity of the will; in these texts Deleuze criticises Schopenhauer for making the will 'a completely undifferenciated abyss, a universal lack of difference, an indifferent black nothingness'.[57] These two complaints are similar, but by no means the same: for the 'abyss' (French: *sans-fond*, following the German *Abgrund*, i.e. the groundless) may lack unity while being entirely undifferentiated.[58]

---

[54] Peter Hallward, *Out of this World: Deleuze and the Philosophy of Creation* (London: Verso, 2006), p. 86.

[55] Ibid. p. 85.

[56] Ibid. p. 84.

[57] Deleuze, *Difference and Repetition*, p. 276/354; see also Gilles Deleuze, *The Logic of Sense*, trans. Mark Lester (London: Athlone, 1990 [1969]), pp. 106–7/130. In *Difference and Repetition*, Nietzsche's *Birth of Tragedy* is now included on the list with Schelling and Schopenhauer.

[58] Deleuze distinguishes between differentiation (which is the process of the production of difference as such at the level of the virtual ideas) and differenciation (which is the process of production of empirical differences at the level of the actual). If the abyss lacks differenciation, then it also lacks differentiation, since the latter is the condition of the former.

Indeed that would appear to be the upshot of the argument so far: Schopenhauer's will is indeed subtracted from representation (with its attendant conditions of empirical individuation); it follows that it is neither individuated nor fails to be individuated. This is the very problem of the groundless.

According to Henry Somers-Hall, what the undifferenciated (and undifferentiated) abyss lacks is precisely the resources for an account of the 'production' of the formed matters of the world as representation.[59] This is a plausible view of the deficit. But it is surely inappropriate to single out Schopenhauer. For Schopenhauer's 'deduction' of the will as thing-in-itself subtracts precisely (the experience of) intentional action from the forms of representation. It is thus not a formless *nothing*, but formless *will*. The twin risks of Schopenhauer's philosophy are anthropomorphism (i.e. interpreting the claim 'everything is will' as the claim that 'everything is intentional action') and mystical negation (i.e. interpreting the claim that 'the will is subtracted from the forms of representation' as the claim that 'the will is nothing'). But Schopenhauer is clear that it is will that is subtracted from representation, and the result is not formless nothing but a conception – arguably the first in Western philosophy – of non-teleological becoming or intransitive production. And what gets produced is precisely the world as representation.

It must nevertheless be said that Schopenhauer's system of production is less well worked out than Deleuze's. At the same time, it should also be noted that it took Deleuze a while to work this out too. In the works of the 1960s, Deleuze develops a systematic account of the mechanisms (in the broadest sense) of production of the actual that cannot be themselves regarded as actual. But he locates them topographically outside of the abyss. Often these productive mechanisms are described as 'syntheses', referring to but radically displacing Kant's use of the term. Deleuze treats the abyss as a kind of trap, locating the syntheses of production in *The Logic of Sense* on the surface of sense and making it hard to give an account of the processes of dynamic genesis of sense out of the schizophrenic abyss of the body. But such a dynamic account is surely crucial. In the 1970s this changed, and Deleuze, now in cahoots with Guattari, relocated the mechanisms of synthetic production precisely to what he had previously characterised as the abyss: the transcendental unconscious.[60]

---

[59] Somers-Hall, *Hegel, Deleuze and the Critique of Representation*, pp. 36, 88–9.

[60] See Alistair Welchman, 'Deleuze: Into the Abyss', in Simon Glendinning (ed.), *The Edinburgh Encyclopaedia of Continental Philosophy* (Edinburgh: Edinburgh

## ANTI-OEDIPUS

*Anti-Oedipus* is a clearly Schopenhauerian text; and it helps to read the text through the lens of Schopenhauer. Deleuze and Guattari take a lot of trouble trying to pull Freud back to his original energeticism and away from the structuralising interpretations of Lacan and his school. But this is the very Freud who 'fetched up unwittingly' himself, in the course of *Beyond the Pleasure Principle*, in the midst of Schopenhauer's philosophy.[61] And they spend an equal amount of effort trying to pull Freud back away from the notion of an unconscious that is individuated empirically and personally. But just such an unconscious is the Schopenhauerian will, which Freud had to personalise and psychologise for his own purposes.

The idea that *Anti-Oedipus* is a Schopenhauerian text is not new, it is suggested in Frank[62] and by François.[63] Frank's text is characteristically uncharitable towards Deleuze and Guattari, and he performs his own kind of subreption, persistently mistaking desiring-machines and desiring-production (which operate at the level of primary process or will) for technical machines (which operate at the level of secondary social processes or representation). As a result he regards Deleuze and Guattari as giving a kind of systems-theoretic account of the real that proceeds with automaticity and excludes any form of subjectivity, which, for Frank, necessitates reflection and representation.[64]

But this interpretation is quite incorrect. Deleuze and Guattari's cri-

---

University Press, 1999), pp. 615–27; and the idea is tabled independently by Daniel Smith, 'From the Surface to the Depths: On the Transition from Logic of Sense to Anti-Oedipus', in Constantin V. Boundas (ed.), *Deleuze: The Intensive Reduction* (London: Continuum, 2009), pp. 82–100.

61 Sigmund Freud, *Beyond the Pleasure Principle and Other Writings*, trans. John Reddick, with an Introduction by Mark Edmundson (London: Penguin, 2003), p. 226.

62 Manfred Frank, 'Die Welt als Wunsch und Repräsentation oder gegen ein anarchostrukturalistisches Zeitalter (Besprechung des "Anti-Ödipus" von G. Deleuze und F. Guattari)', in *FUGEN, Deutsch-Französisches Jahrbuch für Text-Analytik* (Olten and Freiburg: Walter-Verlag, 1980), pp. 269–78. Translated as 'The World as Will and Representation: Deleuze and Guattari's Critique of Capitalism as Schizo-Analysis and Schizo-Discourse', *Telos* 21:9, (1983), pp. 166–76.

63 Arnaud François, 'De la volonté comme pathos au désir comme production. Schopenhauer, Nietzsche, Deleuze', in Nicolas Cornibert and Jean-Christophe Goddard (eds), *L'Anti-Œdipe de Deleuze et Guattari* (Milan and Geneva: Mimesis/MétisPresses, 2008), pp. 27–36.

64 The German translation that Frank is reviewing does not help here. It translates Deleuze and Guattari's French 'désir' with German 'Wunsch', i.e. wish rather than 'Wille', making it sound as if Deleuze and Guattari's conception of primary process should still be identified with the transitive properties of wish-fulfilment.

tique of 'desire' tracks Schopenhauer's deduction of the will closely and critically, as well as illuminating the subreption that Schopenhauer performs and that underlies his fallacious argument from his account of the transcendental will to a pessimistic conclusion. The tradition, Deleuze and Guattari argue,[65] has regarded desire as lack: to desire x is precisely not to possess x, for all x. This conception of desire as lack is internally connected to Kant's conception of desire (*Wille* in German) as transitive and representational: it is because we do not have x that desire can only take the form of desiring in relation to a representation, a representation, namely of the missing x. But the concept of desiring-production is precisely the intransitivisation of desire – desire becomes productive at the point where it is no longer tied to representation through lack.

Isn't Schopenhauer here, however, the arch theorist of lack? Yes. But this is the result of *his own subreption*. In itself the will lacks nothing, because *it does not and cannot* represent anything as missing. The will simply wills, intransitively. It is only at the level of individuated representation that the will can be understood as lacking anything. But the problem is not then the will, but the representation. And this is exactly Deleuze and Guattari's argument. They filter it back through a Kantian vocabulary of legitimate versus illegitimate synthesis. But legitimate means only immanent to desiring-production, i.e. to the will. If the reading of Schopenhauer's account of compassion above is correct, then Schopenhauer also shares with Deleuze and Guattari an account of experiences (experiments) that pull us back from representation into a will that cannot be said to lack anything.

It likely that Deleuze and Guattari would have nothing good to say about the vocabulary within which such a breaking-apart of the cognitive subject takes place in Schopenhauer: Deleuze at least has taken Nietzsche's critique of the morality of compassion too seriously for that. Nevertheless, the *form* of that break casts a revealing light on what Deleuze and Guattari mean by the 'vagabond, nomad subject',[66]

> where the reality [*réel*] of matter has abandoned all extension, just as the interior voyage has abandoned all form and quality, henceforth causing pure intensities – coupled together, almost unbearable – to radiate within and without, intensities through which a nomadic subject passes.[67]

---

[65] Gilles Deleuze and Félix Guattari, *Anti-Oedipus: Capitalism and Schizophrenia*, trans. Robert Hurley, Mark Seem and Helen R. Lane (London: Athlone, 1984 [1972]), p. 25/32.

[66] Deleuze and Guattari, *Anti-Oedipus*, p. 26/34.

[67] Ibid. p. 84/100.

An *interior* – i.e. in some sense phenomenological journey beyond the representational conditions of materiality – yields an experience that is no longer bound to the sedentary individuality of the cognitive subject, but moves through that of others and ultimately broadens out into the intensive matter of the world as will/desire. Schopenhauer's philosophy anticipates the major contours of Deleuze's in very basic ways that go far beyond the mere privileging of intuition over concept.

Doubtless too much can be made of this – and clearly Schopenhauer has a less worked out understanding of the processes of intransitive production. Nevertheless, he was the first to break through representation and find something there on the order of a transcendental conception of materiality that Deleuze (especially with Guattari) then takes up with such force.

# Chapter 12

# Feuerbach and the Image of Thought

*Henry Somers-Hall*

## INTRODUCTION

'The Image of Thought' could be considered to be the most important piece of writing in the entire Deleuzian corpus.[1] This is the chapter of *Difference and Repetition* that several decades later, Deleuze claims is the 'most necessary and the most concrete'[2] section of the book, and the one that provides a basis for his later work with Guattari. Here, Deleuze engages with two basic issues. First, he separates out his conception of thinking, and with it, philosophy, from prior philosophical approaches, explaining why the difference of his philosophy from prior systems itself differs from the traditional relationship between philosophical positions. Second, he raises the question of how one should begin to philosophise. As we will see, a philosopher often begins by refuting the implicit presuppositions that they recognise in prior thinkers. Descartes, for instance, criticises Aristotle for presupposing the transparency of categories such as rational and animal. Kant, in turn, criticises Descartes for presupposing the determinability of his own foundational moment, the *cogito*. If we see the development of philosophy as the unmasking and critique of presuppositions of prior systems, then the endpoint of philosophy will be a system entirely without presuppositions. This is the goal Hegel aims at with his system of absolute idealism. Deleuze's claim is that such a model of the progress of philosophy itself operates within one overarching assumption: the good will of thinking.

In this essay, I want to relate these questions of thinking and

---

[1] This essay presents an expanded analysis of material originally published in Henry Somers-Hall, *Deleuze's* Difference and Repetition: *An Edinburgh Philosophical Guide* (Edinburgh: Edinburgh University Press, 2013).

[2] Gilles Deleuze, *Difference and Repetition*, trans. Paul Patton (New York: Columbia University Press, 1994), p. xvii.

beginnings to the work of one of Deleuze's predecessors. Deleuze writes of Ludwig Feuerbach that 'Feuerbach is among those who have pursued farthest the problem of where to begin.'[3] As we shall see, prefiguring Deleuze, Feuerbach accuses Hegel of operating within 'an image of Reason'. While Feuerbach is famous as a precursor of Marx, and for his critique of traditional accounts of religion, I want to here focus on an early piece by Feuerbach, his *Critique of Hegelian Philosophy*. Here Feuerbach sets out the limitations of traditional philosophical accounts, and provides the groundwork for his own later materialism. Deleuze discovered Feuerbach through his friend Althusser's translation of this work, published in 1960. While many of the intuitions behind Deleuze's critique of the image of thought can be found within a broader pantheon of thinkers, including Nietzsche, Bergson, and Foucault, the specific mechanics of Deleuze's criticism bear a striking resemblance to the formulation of the critique of philosophy in Feuerbach's earlier thought. I want to explore this connection, first by looking at the dialectical interrelation of two thinkers, Descartes and Hegel, to get a sense for how criticism in philosophy typically operates. I then want to move on to look at Feuerbach's critique of Hegel and philosophy more generally, drawing out several aspects that will be taken up by Deleuze himself. I will then look at some of the ways in which Deleuze goes beyond Feuerbach by recognising some of the limitations that persist in Feuerbach's own analysis. I will conclude by showing how Deleuze's desire to think the two common acceptations of aesthetics together (the artistic and the sensible) bring Feuerbach into relation with an unexpected figure: the playwright and poet, Antonin Artaud.

### DESCARTES' CRITIQUE OF ARISTOTLE

In this first section, I want to look at the question of how one begins philosophising. I want to take up Descartes' own characterisation of the problem of beginnings. As Hegel notes, Descartes' revolution in philosophy originates in his development of a 'new and absolute beginning' for philosophy: 'thinking as such'.[4] Both Hegel and Deleuze also note that the central concern of Descartes' *Meditations* is to find some way to avoid making unwarranted presuppositions about the world, since

---

[3] Ibid. p. 319.
[4] G. W. F. Hegel, *Lectures on the History of Philosophy 1825–1826*, vol. III, ed. Robert F. Brown, trans. R. F. Brown and J. M. Stewart (Los Angeles: University of California Press, 1990), p. 137.

these could lead us into error. Deleuze himself introduces the question of where to begin in terms of the approaches of Epistemon and Eudoxus,[5] two characters representing the key differences between the Aristotelian and Cartesian approaches to philosophising. In doing so, Deleuze is alluding to a dialogue written by Descartes, entitled *The Search for Truth by means of the Natural Light*. The *Search for Truth* presents a dialogue between Eudoxus, who represents Descartes, and a scholastic named Epistemon. Descartes presents the situation as follows:

> Let us imagine that Eudoxus, a man of moderate intellect but possessing a judgement which is not corrupted by any false beliefs and a reason which retains all the purity of its nature, is visited in his country home by two friends whose minds are among the most outstanding and inquiring of our time. One of them, Polyander ['everyman'], has never studied at all, while the other, Epistemon, has a detailed knowledge of everything that can be learned in the schools.[6]

Epistemon, the scholastic, declares that 'desire for knowledge ... is an illness that cannot be cured'.[7] In making this assertion, Epistemon is putting forward the implicit belief that philosophical inquiry involves an investigation of the world, and hence requires us to make a series of assumptions about the nature of things. As he notes, 'there are so many things to be known which seem to us to be possible and which are not only good and pleasant but also very necessary for the conduct of our actions'.[8] The implications of this statement are that philosophical enquiry is not something purely internal to reason, as it involves some kind of investigation of the external world. It is also the case that it is not inherently systematic. That is, different domains of knowledge may not have any connections in terms of the truths to be discovered, or the methods of enquiry to be employed. In putting forward this model of philosophy, Descartes is alluding to the approach of a thinker such as Aristotle, who develops an essentially empirical approach to philosophy. Eudoxus instead declares that '[his] mind, having at its disposal all the truths it comes across, does not dream there are others to discover'.[9] Eudoxus' statement carries with it the implication that for a

---

[5] Deleuze, *Difference and Repetition*, p. 130.

[6] René Descartes, 'The Search for Truth', in *The Philosophical Writings of Descartes*, vol. II, trans. Robert Stoothoff and Dugald Murdoch, ed. John Cottingham, Robert Stoothoff and Dugald Murdoch (Cambridge: Cambridge University Press, 1984), p. 401.

[7] Ibid. p. 402.

[8] Ibid.

[9] Ibid.

well-ordered mode of thinking, there is no difference between thinking, and thinking what is true. That is, reason is able to conduct a philosophical inquiry simply by using its own internal resources. This has two further implications. First, that the inferences made by reason, when it is operating correctly, are certain, and second that the meaning of terms which reason uses to think through problems is transparent to reason without further need for investigation.

The difference between these two methods can be seen in that for Epistemon, the role of reason is to act as a corrective to the beliefs given to us by the senses and the imagination. It therefore operates on pre-existing beliefs. For Eudoxus, on the contrary, 'as soon as a man reaches what we call the age of discretion, he should resolve once and for all to remove from his imagination all traces of the imperfect ideas which have been engraved there up till that time'.[10] In order to demonstrate this method, Descartes has Eudoxus propose that Polyander attempt the method of doubt. By doubting everything given by the senses and the imagination, we realise that the only thing that cannot be doubted is one's own existence as a doubting thing. Thus, the self as a thinking substance becomes the foundation for philosophical enquiry. Here, we have arrived at the most famous result of Cartesian philosophy – Descartes' *cogito* argument. As Descartes notes in the *Search for Truth*, however, as well as the existence of the self, we also have a question to answer about what we mean by the *cogito*. The key question is how we might characterise this doubting thing – what kind of being is it? For the Aristotelian, the nature of man is defined by his species, in much the same way that the nature of any other natural kind might be. Man belongs to the genus, animal, and is distinguished from other animals by his rationality. Thus, for Aristotle, the nature of man is ultimately reliant on a series of categories that we discover through empirical enquiry. Eudoxus here explicitly criticises such an approach on the grounds that it relies on terms that are not given by reason alone, and hence are not transparent to it:

> First, what is an *animal*? Second, what is *rational*? If, in order to explain what an animal is, he were to reply that it is a 'living and sentient being', that a living being is an 'animate body', and that a body is a 'corporeal substance', you see immediately that these questions would be pure verbiage, which would elucidate nothing and leave us in our original state of ignorance.[11]

[10] Ibid. p. 406.
[11] Ibid. p. 410.

A term such as 'corporeal substance' does not tell us anything more about the world than a term such as 'body', because if we cannot conceive of the terms corporeal and substance clearly, then conjoining them will not help us to conceive of the term 'body' clearly. So how do we determine the meaning of the 'I' of the *cogito*? Once Polyander has concluded his exercise in Cartesian doubt, he realises that 'of all the attributes I once claimed as my own there is only one left worth examining, and that is thought'.[12] That is, the I is determined according to an attribute that is clearly conceived by reason itself. What allows us to determine the essence of man, therefore, is a property that is transparent to thinking itself, and therefore readily comprehensible by any thinking being.

We can now see how Descartes attempts to solve the problem of philosophical beginnings. Descartes rejects the scholastic approach to philosophy because it presupposes a whole nexus of terms which are not given by reason, and which cannot be determined through their systematic relations to one another. To determine what a man is in the Aristotelian manner, not only do we have to rely on determinations which are given to us by the senses, but as we proceed in analysing the term, 'man', our enquiry brings in more unknown terms, rather than reducing the number. Descartes therefore rejects the approach of Epistemon in favour of that of Eudoxus. We can already state here a number of the key claims which Descartes makes about the true method of philosophy. First, it accords a 'natural light' to reason whereby it is the arbiter of truth and falsity. Second, as a consequence of this, it operates internally to reason, excluding the effects of the other faculties on it, as it takes these to be capable of misleading reason. Third, it does not presuppose anything, apart from reason itself. We can also note that Descartes makes Polyander, the 'everyman' conduct the method of doubt, suggesting, as Deleuze notes, that Descartes believes that 'good sense is of all things in the world the most evenly distributed'.[13] A corollary of this is that Descartes' aim is not to teach metaphysics, but rather to provide an example which, when followed by others, given the universality of reason and the certainty of the deduction, will lead each individual to come to the same conclusion by their own active enquiry ('My present aim, then, is not to teach the method which everyone must

---

[12] Ibid. p. 415.
[13] Deleuze, *Difference and Repetition*, p. 131 and René Descartes, 'Discourse on Method and Essays', in *The Philosophical Writings of Descartes*, vol. 1, trans. Robert Stoothoff, ed. John Cottingham, Robert Stoothoff and Dugald Murdoch (Cambridge: Cambridge University Press, 1985), opening line.

follow in order to direct his own reason correctly, but only to reveal how I have tried to direct my own.'[14]). By following a deductive method, Descartes therefore believes he has avoided the difficulty of the kinds of presuppositions at play in Aristotle's method.

## HEGEL'S CRITIQUE OF DESCARTES

In presenting his own reading of Descartes, Hegel's account clearly frames the question of Descartes' method in terms that see him as a predecessor of Hegel's own thought. What is central to Descartes' project is 'his requirement . . . that thinking should proceed from itself and that therefore no presupposition may be made, since every presupposition is something found already there that thinking has not posited, something other than thinking'.[15] In this respect, Descartes prefigures Hegel's assertion, for instance, that 'science should be preceded by universal doubt, i.e., by total presuppositionlessness'.[16] Nonetheless, Hegel argues that Descartes' foundation of the Cartesian *cogito* is illegitimate for this purpose. The reason is that while Polyander clearly is a subject who is capable of thinking, Descartes illegitimately equivocates between a common sense notion of thinking, and a philosophical conception of thinking. Thinking is in fact always related to a world, and run through with a multiplicity of differences and contingencies. What Descartes in fact requires, however, is what he takes to be the pure substance of thinking that lies behind this contingent surface structure. As such, Hegel reiterates something like Kant's claim that Descartes' *cogito* rests on a paralogism:

> But inasmuch as this pure ego must be essential, pure knowing, and pure knowing is not immediately present in the individual consciousness but only as posited through the absolute act of the ego in raising itself to that standpoint, we lose the very advantage which is supposed to come from this beginning of philosophy, namely that it is something thoroughly familiar, something everyone finds in himself which can form the starting point for further reflection; that pure ego, on the contrary, in its abstract, essential nature, is something unknown to the ordinary consciousness, something it does not find therein. Instead, such a beginning brings with it the disadvantage of the illusion that whereas the thing under discussion is supposed to

[14] Descartes, 'Discourse on Method and Essays', p. 112.
[15] Hegel, *Lectures on the History of Philosophy*, vol. III, pp. 138–9.
[16] G. W. F. Hegel, *The Encyclopaedia Logic, with the Zusätze*, trans. Theodore F. Geraets, Wallis Arthur Suchting and Henry Silton Harris (Indianapolis: Hackett, 1991), §78.

be something familiar, the ego of empirical self-consciousness, it is in fact something far removed from it.[17]

As Deleuze notes, therefore, Hegel claims that there is still an illegitimate presupposition in Descartes' work: one could hold to the claim that one should begin with consciousness, but still deny the 'abstract unity'[18] of the *cogito*. What is Hegel's own solution to this difficulty?

Descartes' assumption can be seen as the claim that implicit in our concrete, empirical conception of thinking is the pure, philosophical category of thinking. Hegel's claim is that we cannot begin by assuming the primacy of a philosophical perspective, as to do so is to do violence to our everyday relationship to the world: 'When natural consciousness entrusts itself straightaway to Science, it makes an attempt, induced by it knows not what, to walk on its head too.'[19] Similarly, it cannot declare that consciousness will find within itself intimations of a philosophical view, as such an approach still privileges the assumption of philosophical truth over natural consciousness. It is only a legitimate approach if we have already asserted the superiority of what is intimated over what is already present. Instead, Hegel provides what he calls a 'ladder'[20] whereby natural consciousness can develop into a properly philosophical perspective on the world. That is, rather than assuming that notions such as thinking are transparent to consciousness, Hegel attempts to show how our natural consciousness develops its categories of thought through a process of immanent dialectic. It is through the recognition of inherent problems within consciousness' view of the world that we gradually develop an appropriate relationship to the world, by the rejection of ways of relating to the world that are inadequate in favour of those that do not have the same limitations. For Hegel therefore, the process of the development of consciousness to a properly philosophical point of view does not involve the privileging of a philosophical mode of thinking, but rather a process whereby the problems inherent within consciousness lead it to develop a series of more and more adequate interpretations of the world. As such, philosophy need begin neither with the kind of empiricism Descartes criticises Aristotle for, nor with the presupposition of an understanding of philosophical cognition that Descartes takes

---

[17] G. W. F. Hegel, *Science of Logic*, trans. A. V. Miller (Amherst, NY: Humanity Books, 1999), §118.

[18] Hegel, *Lectures on the History of Philosophy*, vol. III, p. 142.

[19] G. W. F. Hegel, *Hegel's Phenomenology of Spirit*, trans. A. W. Miller (Oxford: Oxford University Press, 1977), §26.

[20] Ibid.

for granted. Rather, it can begin with a simple model of consciousness that contains no assumptions with which anyone would argue. This is the model of sense-certainty, which holds that consciousness at the least knows *that* it is confronted by something, even if it does not consider the nature of what it relates to. As such, we begin with the least determinate formulation of natural consciousness we can come up with. Hegel's claim will therefore be that such a simple mode of consciousness in the end turns out to be incoherent according to its own criteria of knowledge, and through a series of more adequate forms that each in turn show themselves to be problematic, we eventually develop a set of categories of thought adequate to philosophical enquiry immanently.

Despite the differences between Hegel and Descartes, we can see a number of commonalities in their approaches. Both attempt to develop a philosophical position that does not make any presuppositions. In both cases, there is also the implicit assumption that the justification of a philosophical position involves developing an account which can be held with certainty by natural consciousness. As Deleuze puts it, 'postulates in philosophy are not propositions the acceptance of which the philosopher demands; but, on the contrary, propositional themes which remain implicit and are understood in a pre-philosophical manner. In this sense, conceptual philosophical thought has as its implicit presupposition a pre-philosophical or natural Image of thought, borrowed from the pure element of common sense.'[21] While there is an attempt to eliminate *philosophical* assumptions, therefore, the common sense structure of thinking itself is something that isn't questioned, at least at the outset. Within the thought of Descartes and Hegel, therefore, there are subjective presuppositions about the nature of reason. These presuppositions are also present in Aristotle's thought. Even there, where we begin with objective presuppositions, we still require the assumption of a shared structure of thought according to which we can analyse and relate these different *endoxa* to one another:

> As in other cases, we must set out the appearances and run through all the puzzles regarding them. In this way we must prove the credible opinions about these sorts of experiences – ideally, all the credible opinions, but if not all, then most of them, those which are the most important. For if the objections are answered and the credible opinions remain, we shall have an adequate proof.[22]

---

[21] Deleuze, *Difference and Repetition*, p. 131.
[22] Aristotle, *Nicomachean Ethics*, 2nd edn, ed. and trans. Terence Irwin (Indianapolis: Hackett, 1999), 1145b2–7.

In the next section, I want to take up Feuerbach's analysis of these subjective presuppositions in order to shed some light on Deleuze's own account of beginnings.

## FEUERBACH'S CRITIQUE OF HEGEL

Deleuze's criticism of Descartes and Hegel isn't of the particular assumptions that they make, but rather of 'the form of representation or recognition in general'.[23] It is at this point in his analysis that Deleuze turns to Feuerbach. Ludwig Feuerbach was, leaving aside Marx and Engels, the most influential member of the philosophical movement called the young Hegelians, which emerged in the years following Hegel's death. This movement sought to develop the implications of Hegel's philosophy, and Feuerbach himself began his philosophical career as a thoroughgoing supporter of Hegel. The essay that Deleuze refers to, *Towards a Critique of Hegel's Philosophy* (1839), represents a radical break on Feuerbach's part from Hegel. In this work, Feuerbach sets out a series of criticisms of Hegel's philosophy, revolving around the claims that the work begins with an abstraction from the singularity of real experience, and that it focuses on only those aspects of the subject that are shared by other subjects belonging to the same species. Feuerbach presents three interrelated criticisms of Hegel in this essay, all of which are taken up by Deleuze, and applied to the use of reason in philosophy as a whole. These are that presuppositionlessness usually simply means that the presuppositions of prior philosophies have been removed, that rather than presenting a philosophy of reason, we only attain an image of reason, and that reason emerges through an abstraction from its conditions. I want to go through what Feuerbach's criticisms are, and how they tie into Deleuze's notion of an image of thought, before turning to Deleuze's criticisms of Feuerbach's view.

To understand Feuerbach's criticism of traditional philosophy, we need to look at what Feuerbach thinks philosophy is attempting to do. We can begin by noting that thinking is an activity: 'Plato is meaningless and non-existent for someone who lacks understanding; he is a blank sheet for one who cannot link ideas that correspond with his words.'[24] Feuerbach's point is that a philosophical argument is not of value in

---

[23] Deleuze, *Difference and Repetition*, p. 131.
[24] Ludwig Feuerbach, 'Towards a Critique of Hegelian Philosophy', in Lawrence S. Stepelevich (ed.), *The Young Hegelians: An Anthology* (Amherst, NY: Humanities Press, 1997), p. 102.

itself, but only insofar as it is taken up by the understanding of the person to whom it is addressed. That is why in Descartes' *Search for Truth*, Eudoxus does not present an argument for the *cogito*, but rather leads Polyander to discover the conclusion through his own reasoning. Similarly, in the *Discourse on the Method*, Descartes claims that his aim is not 'to teach the method which everyone must follow in order to direct his reason correctly, but only to reveal how I have tried to direct my own'.[25] Implicit in this is the view that philosophy is not about demonstration, but rather about communication, with the aim to simply show that the ideas presented are in keeping with my own thought. Feuerbach describes the situation as follows:

> For this very reason, what the person demonstrating communicates is not the *subject matter itself*, but only the medium; for he does not instil his thoughts into me like drops of medicine, nor does he preach to deaf fishes like Saint Francis; rather, he addresses himself to *thinking* beings. The main thing – the understanding of the thing involved – he does not give me; he *gives* nothing at all – otherwise the philosopher could really produce philosophers, something which so far no one has succeeded in achieving. Rather he presupposes the faculty of understanding; he shows me – i.e. to the other person as such – my understanding only in a mirror.[26]

If a philosophical text is primarily a means of communication, rather than a demonstration in its own right, then the question arises, under what conditions is thought able to be communicated?

In order to make my thinking comprehensible to another, the first point is that I need to 'strip my thought of the form of "mine-ness" so that the other person may recognise it as his own'.[27] In effect, in putting thinking into language, we eliminate the thinker's 'individual separateness', and present a form of thinking which is 'nothing other than the *realization of the species*'.[28] That is, philosophical thought abstracts from the particularity of my thinking, and operates by presupposing that which is universal to all thinkers. As Deleuze puts it, '*Everybody knows, no one can deny*, is the form of representation and the discourse of the representative.'[29] The second point is that in order to present our thoughts, they must be reformulated in a form that is capable of presentation:

[25] Descartes, 'Discourse on Method and Essays', p. 112.
[26] Feuerbach, 'Towards a Critique of Hegelian Philosophy', p. 105.
[27] Ibid. p. 104.
[28] Ibid. p. 103.
[29] Deleuze, *Difference and Repetition*, p. 130.

And yet, systematic thought is by no means the same as *thought as such*, or *essential* thought; it is only self-*presenting* thought. To the extent that I present my thoughts, I place them in time; an insight that contains all its successive elements within a simultaneity within my mind now becomes a sequence.[30]

As it stands, Feuerbach has simply noted that there is a fundamental distinction between thought and the presentation of thought. This in itself is not a criticism of prior philosophy, but the difficulties emerge when philosophers succumb to a form of paralogism whereby they mistake the successive, abstract presentation of thinking for thinking itself. For Kant, the term paralogism applies to Descartes' mistaken inference that we can move from the consciousness of thinking to the existence of a thinking substance. Descartes arrives at the existence of a thinking substance by not recognising the fact that a category such as substance can only be applied to something that is given to me in intuition, that is, in time. In applying the category of substance to a subject as it is in itself (the *cogito*), Descartes applies the category of substance to a domain in which its application is illegitimate, and, therefore, falls into error. The same error occurs in our formulation of philosophical thought. The mistake that Hegel and Descartes make, according to Feuerbach, is failing to recognise that in order for thought to be presented, it needs to be presented in a systematic manner (and under the form of time), and in terms of determinate, shared, concepts. In developing a systematic philosophy, therefore, we are, in effect, developing an account of this necessary structure of presentation and communication, rather than presenting thinking itself. To equate thinking with the systematic presentation of thought is therefore to fall into the same kind of paralogistic reasoning that renders Descartes' *cogito* illegitimate. While the inference is illegitimate, it is nonetheless quite natural, since the way in which we present thinking in a systematic manner is not arbitrary, since 'the presentation of philosophy must itself be philosophical'.[31] There is thus a tendency to make 'form into essence, the being of thought for others into being itself, the *relative goal* into the final goal'.[32] This is the reason why Deleuze writes that Hegel 'remains in the reflected element of "representation", within simple generality'.[33] Deleuze supplements this paralogism with an argument that there is a moral element to systems

[30] Feuerbach, 'Towards a Critique of Hegelian Philosophy', p. 101.
[31] Ibid. p. 106.
[32] Ibid. p. 107.
[33] Deleuze, *Difference and Repetition*, p. 10.

that mistake the presentation of thought for thought itself, in that to trust in the structure of thinking as communicative implies a fundamental accord between man and the world, and presupposes the belief that 'thought has a good nature and the thinker a good will'.[34]

Feuerbach's claim that 'every system is only an expression or image of reason'[35] can be seen as a forerunner of Deleuze's own claim that representational thinking rests on an 'image of thought', and the aim of Chapter 3 of *Difference and Repetition* is to explore in more detail what this image consists in, and how it is possible to think outside of it. I now want to explore a number of implications of the image of thought before looking at how Deleuze differs from Feuerbach.

The first implication is that even projects such as those of Descartes and Hegel that attempt to remove all objective presuppositions still make a number of presuppositions in order to operate. As Deleuze notes, the same criticism that Hegel raised against Descartes, the equivocation of the empirical and abstract egos, can also be raised against Hegel himself: both begin with an abstraction.[36] While the notion of pure, indeterminate being that Hegel begins with in the *Science of Logic* is communicable, this is only because communication removes the 'mine-ness' of my relation to the world. In actual fact, 'sensible, concrete, empirical being'[37] is prior to the abstraction which Hegel takes as a beginning. As well as presupposing empirical reality, philosophy which operates according to the image of thought also presupposes the structure of presentation itself. That is, 'we presuppose the form of representation or recognition in general'.[38] As Feuerbach puts it, 'the artist presupposes a sense of beauty – he cannot bestow it upon a person – for in order that we take his words to be beautiful, in order that we accept and countenance them at all, he must presuppose in us a sense of art . . . [Similarly] in order that we recognise [the philosopher's] thoughts as true, in order that we understand them at all, he presupposes reason, as a common principle and measure in us as well as himself.'[39] The history of philosophy can from this perspective be seen, not as a progressive extension of our knowledge of the world, but rather as series of more and more accurate ways of systematically providing an image of the presentation of reason. In this respect, Feuerbach considers Hegel not to

[34] Ibid. p. 132.
[35] Feuerbach, 'Towards a Critique of Hegelian Philosophy', p. 106.
[36] Deleuze, *Difference and Repetition*, p. 129.
[37] Ibid.
[38] Ibid. p. 131.
[39] Feuerbach, 'Towards a Critique of Hegelian Philosophy', p. 103.

have provided the final, presuppositionless, metaphysics, but rather the most accomplished image of reason:

> The systematiser is an artist – the history of philosophical system is the picture gallery of reason. Hegel is the most accomplished philosophical artist, and his presentations, at least in part, *are unsurpassed models of scientific art sense.*[40]

What this means is that Feuerbach's critique of prior philosophers isn't a criticism of particular philosophies, but of a whole tradition founded on a faulty conception of reason. Feuerbach sums up this claim as follows: 'Do we not thus come to those general questions that touch upon the truth and reality not only of Hegel's *Logic* but also of philosophy altogether?'[41] This notion that there is 'a single Image in general which constitutes the subjective presupposition of philosophy as a whole'[42] is one that is fundamental to the project of *Difference and Repetition*, which begins with the need to develop a new philosophical style or mode of presentation that escapes from the paralogism of the image of thought.

The second implication is that if philosophy simply maps out the image of thought in systematic terms, then it will be incapable of novelty. As Feuerbach puts it, 'the *creation* of concepts on the basis of a particular kind of philosophy is not a real but only a formal creation; it is not creation out of nothing, but only the development, as it were, of a spiritual matter lying within me'.[43] As we are just dealing with the presentation of what was already implicated in the structure of pre-philosophical thinking, then we have a philosophical thought that '"rediscovers" the State, rediscovers "the Church"'[44] during its development.

The third implication is that philosophy must begin with something that is outside of thought. In *The Search for Truth*, Descartes tries to show that if one thinks through the structure of everyday reason, then one arrives at philosophy. Hegel's *Phenomenology of Spirit* likewise tries to show that speculative philosophy develops immanently from a common sense worldview. 'Anyone who can countenance being at the beginning of the *Logic* will also countenance the Idea; if this being has been accepted and proved by someone, then he must also accept the

---

[40] Ibid. p. 106.
[41] Ibid. p. 109.
[42] Deleuze, *Difference and Repetition*, p. 132.
[43] Feuerbach, 'Towards a Critique of Hegelian Philosophy', p. 102.
[44] Deleuze, *Difference and Repetition*, p. 136.

Idea as proved.'[45] In contrast, if systematic philosophy is simply an expression of pre-philosophical reason, Deleuze argues that philosophy must 'find its difference or its true beginning, not in an agreement with a *pre-philosophical* Image but in a rigorous struggle against this Image, which it would denounce as *non-philosophical*'.[46] Here, Deleuze is referring directly to Feuerbach's rejection of reason as a foundation for philosophy, and arguing for the importance of an outside to reason. For Descartes, while it appears that philosophy relates to the world outside of the subject, we instead find, in his famous wax example, for instance, that perception is always already a form of reasoning, where we use reason to infer the existence of unified substances behind the diverse properties of the things we find around us. Similarly, Feuerbach complains of Hegel that 'the whole first chapter of the *Phenomenology* is . . . nothing but a verbal game in which thought is already certain of itself as truth plays with natural consciousness'.[47] In contrast to the Cartesian account, philosophy must begin with a radical encounter with something outside of it:

> Demonstrating would be senseless if it were not also *communicating*. However, communication of thoughts is not material or *real* communication. For example, a push, a sound that shocks my ears, or light is real communication. I am only passively receptive to that which is material; but I become aware of that which is mental only through myself, only through self-activity.[48]

As we shall see, a similar claim can also be made for Deleuze's philosophy, which calls for a 'shock to thought' in order to open it to an outside:

> Do not count upon thought to ensure the relative necessity of what it thinks. Rather, count upon the contingency of an encounter with that which forces thought to raise up and educate the absolute necessity of an act of thought or a passion to think. The conditions of a true critique and a true creation are the same: the destruction of an image of thought which presupposes itself and the genesis of the act of thinking in thought itself.[49]

[45] Feuerbach, 'Towards a Critique of Hegelian Philosophy', p. 109.
[46] Deleuze, *Difference and Repetition*, p. 132.
[47] Feuerbach, 'Towards a Critique of Hegelian Philosophy', pp. 114–15.
[48] Ibid. p. 105.
[49] Deleuze, *Difference and Repetition*, p. 139.

## DELEUZE'S CRITIQUE OF FEUERBACH

The claim that philosophy operates according to a paralogism, or a 'transcendental illusion'[50] is therefore one that is shared by both Deleuze and Feuerbach. In both cases, it is the form of presentation of thinking that is mistaken for thinking itself, and in both cases, this mistake covers over the possibility of the encounter which would form the basis for a proper philosophical approach to the world. As such, Feuerbach forms one of the most important hidden reference points in deciphering Deleuze's project. Nonetheless, while Feuerbach makes explicit some of the key moves in Deleuze's rejection of classical philosophy, Deleuze is still not a Feuerbachian. What, therefore, is the difference between Deleuze and Feuerbach?

The key moment of difference between Deleuze and Feuerbach emerges in their account of the encounter that provides the opening onto truly philosophical thought. For Feuerbach, true thinking begins through an encounter with sensuous intuition, which is prior to the abstractions that generate the 'mediating activity of thought for others'.[51] As such, Feuerbach reinstates something like the Kantian distinction between intuition and understanding. It is for this reason that when he criticises Hegel, for instance, he does so for failing to recognise that the incommensurability of thought and the senses merely shows that the sensible cannot be captured by reason, rather than that it is invalid. In privileging the rational categories over the inherent structure of intuition, and using those categories as a criterion to judge sense experience as empty, Feuerbach claims that 'the *Phenomenology* is nothing but a phenomenological Logic'.[52] The encounter, for Feuerbach, therefore means returning to the sensuous nature of experience prior to its abstraction into the categories of systematic reason. It is here that we find a difficulty in Feuerbach's account that mirrors the one found in Kant's own philosophy. While the recognition of the difference between intuition and understanding is for Deleuze a revolutionary moment in the history of philosophy, it relies on an illegitimate characterisation of the opposition between activity and passivity, one that inadvertently carries over into Feuerbach's thought. For Kant, the faculty of the understanding was responsible for active synthesis, and therefore organised the world according to its own categories. The active, synthetic

[50] Ibid. p. 265.
[51] Feuerbach, 'Towards a Critique of Hegelian Philosophy', p. 102.
[52] Ibid. p. 115.

nature of the understanding meant that it rediscovered on an empirical level what it had previously put into the world on a transcendental level. In this sense, we can note that for Kant too, the understanding is incapable of the discovery of genuine novelty. Sensibility provided the material that was organised by the understanding.

For Deleuze, Kant's error was to assume that all synthesis was active synthesis, and hence that all synthesis operated on an inert sensibility. We can see that a similar assumption is being made here by Feuerbach. In rejecting the active element of reason as unable to provide a genuinely novel beginning to philosophy, he is forced to resort to a purely passive notion of sensibility for his alternative beginning. Therefore, we move from reason to that which is materially and passively given to us. As Deleuze puts it, 'he supposes that this exigency of the true beginning is sufficiently met by beginning with empirical, perceptible and concrete being'.[53]

Once we have recognised the possibility of a passive synthesis, however, we open the possibility that what is given in sensibility is not the sensible itself, but that which gives rise to the sensible. It is this transcendental which is prior to the sensible that will be the site of an encounter for Deleuze. It is in order to explore this realm of the genesis of the sensible that Deleuze calls for the reunification of the two meanings of aesthetics:

> Everything changes once we determine the conditions of real experience, which are not larger than the conditioned and which differ in kind from the categories: the two senses of the aesthetic become one, to the point where the being of the sensible reveals itself in the work of art, while at the same time the work of art appears as experimentation.[54]

I want to conclude this chapter by introducing a paradigm case of the encounter with the aesthetic that opens the way to thinking, namely, Deleuze's analysis of Artaud.

## CONCLUSION: ARTAUD AND THE ENCOUNTER

As we saw when we looked at the notion of the encounter, Feuerbach dismisses reason as a true medium of encounter, since with reason, what is taken up is that which is already present in the understanding of the subject. He instead favoured a more physical form of encounter ('a push,

---

[53] Deleuze, *Difference and Repetition*, p. 319.
[54] Ibid. p. 68.

a sound that shocks my ears, or light'), where an object directly impacts on a subject. In the theatre of the poet, playwright and theorist, Antonin Artaud, we find an attempt to develop such a model of the encounter through the use of disturbing lighting, sound and music, and by the elimination of a clear boundary between the audience and the stage. He emphasises the importance of this move from a theatre of the mind to a theatre of the nervous system in his manifesto for a theatre of cruelty:

> Without an element of cruelty at the foundation of every spectacle, the theatre is not possible. In the state of degeneracy, in which we live, it is through the skin that metaphysics will be made to re-enter our minds.[55]

To see what the encounter might consist in for Deleuze, we can turn to the analysis he provides of the correspondence between Jacques Rivière, editor of the avant-garde literary journal *Nouvelle Revue Française*, and Artaud. The correspondence concerned a collection of poems that Artaud submitted for publication in the journal. While the poems themselves were rejected, the subsequent correspondence with Artaud over the process of writing itself was published. In it, we find Rivière misunderstanding the aim of Artaud's poetry. Rivière rejects the poems because Artaud has 'not yet achieved a sufficiently unified impression', and suggests that 'with a little patience, even if this simply means cutting out some of the divergent imagery or traits, you will be able to write perfectly coherent, harmonious poems'.[56] For Artaud, however, these difficulties in presenting a harmonious image of thought are not contingent failures to properly organise his thought that could be overcome with patience, but rather an attempt to explore the emergence of thinking itself. That is, Artaud's project is precisely to reject the kind of unity that for Rivière would characterise the successful production of a work of art.

In order to escape from the image of thought, therefore, Deleuze follows Artaud in proposing an effort to prevent the presentation of thinking from overcoming the real nature of thought that runs beneath its expression. For Deleuze, this involves a stuttering, or in his own words, a deterritorialisation of language that prevents the kind of reliance on ready-made categories of thought that inhibits true philosophical engagement. In this respect, it is the poetry of Artaud, rather than the

---

[55] Antonin Artaud, 'The Theatre of Cruelty: First Manifesto (1932)', in Susan Sontag (ed.), *Antonin Artaud: Selected Writings* (New York: Farrar, Straus and Giroux, 1976), p. 251.

[56] Antonin Artaud, 'Correspondence with Jacques Rivière', in Victor Corti (ed.), *Collected Works of Antonin Artaud*, vol. 1 (London: John Calder, 1968), p. 29.

sensible itself, that provides the archetype of the encounter. As Artaud writes:

> This diffusion in my poems, these defective forms, this constant falling off of my ideas, must not be set down to lack of practice or control of the instrument I was manipulating, of intellectual development. Rather to a focal collapse of my soul, a kind of essential and fugitive erosion in thought, to a transitory non-possession of physical gain to my development, to the abnormal separation of elements of thought (the impulse to think at every stratifying endpoint of thought, by way of every condition, through all the branching in thought and form).[57]

Rather than straightforwardly rejecting language, as Feuerbach does, in favour of intuition as the starting point for philosophy, Artaud instead attempts to subvert the traditional structures of thinking. Deleuze writes that his early letters show 'an awareness that his case brings him into contact with a generalised thought process which can no longer be covered by the reassuring dogmatic image but which, on the contrary, amounts to the complete destruction of that image'.[58] As such, in Artaud, we don't find the kind of rejection of 'mineness' that Feuerbach took to be a prerequisite for the image of thought. Rather, Artaud's writing maintains the singularity of his thinking, even while recognising that this singularity does not preclude it from relating to objective conditions, even if these conditions fall outside of our normal modes of representation.

In this sense, Artaud's poetry is first, according to Deleuze at least, not the attempt to present the difficulties in thinking that are peculiar to Artaud, but the difficulties in genuinely thinking outside of representation for all thought. Artaud's poetry is the model of a transcendental exercise of a faculty. It becomes transcendental because it operates at the limits of language. Artaud's project mirrors Descartes', but rather than seeking those ideas which cannot be doubted, the innate ideas that are the first principles of knowledge (and of the image of thought), Artaud is interested in the principles that give rise to the structure of thought itself. When Deleuze therefore claims that 'Artaud opposes *genitality* to innateness in thought',[59] the point he is making is that the image of thought rests on conditions that themselves are non-representational (the thinking in thought). Descartes' principles are themselves a part of the image of thought, and are those features of the image of thought that

---

[57] Ibid. pp. 30–1.
[58] Deleuze, *Difference and Repetition*, p. 147.
[59] Ibid.

are necessary features of a representation of thought. What Artaud discovers is different in kind from the image of thought, and the apparent weaknesses in his poetry signify this difference in kind of thinking to the 'coherent, harmonious' nature of the image of thought itself.

The encounter is not, therefore, with the sensible itself, but rather with the conditions which give rise to the sensible. As we saw, the difficulty with the traditional image of thought was that it relied on a paralogism. Feuerbach's claim was that we needed to return to a moment of intuition outside of the image of thought in order to properly begin to philosophise. I want to conclude by returning to this point. In what sense is the aesthetics of Artaud related to the classical Kantian (and Feuerbachian) notion of aesthetics as the domain of the sensible? In a short piece entitled 'Man against Destiny', Artaud himself clarifies this relation. He says the following:

> You all know that one cannot grasp thought. In order to think, we have images, we have words for these images, we have representations of objects. We separate consciousness into states of consciousness. But this is merely a way of speaking. All this has no real value except insofar as it enables us to think. In order to consider our consciousness we are obliged to divide it, otherwise the rational faculty which enables us to see our thoughts could never be used. But in reality, consciousness is a whole, what the philosopher Bergson calls *pure duration*. There is no stopping the motion of thought. That which we place before us so that the reason of the mind can consider it is in reality already past; and that which reason holds is merely a form, more or less empty of real thought.[60]

Here we find Artaud recognising the structure of the necessary illusion in the image of thought, and the recognition that the aim of his aesthetics of theatre is to open us up to a moment of that other acceptation of aesthetics: time itself. This moment prior to the genesis of the image of thought is not the time of Feuerbach, however, with its already constituted diversity of things and properties. Rather, thinking moves upstream to a point prior to this, to Bergson's pure process of duration, before the moment of reflection that constitutes for us a world of objects.

---

[60] Antonin Artaud, 'Man Against Destiny', in Susan Sontag (ed.), *Antonin Artaud: Selected Writings* (New York: Farrar, Straus and Giroux, 1976), pp. 357–8.

# Chapter 13

# Deleuze's 'Power of Decision', Kant's =X and Husserl's Noema

*Jay Lampert*

This chapter has two agendas. First, I am interested in how decisions refer to the future. This is an issue of temporal ontology, temporal predication, and temporal ethics. I use Deleuze's spin on Kant's formula of the object=X in order to show how a decision diverges into a plurality of possible timelines. The second agenda for this chapter is to follow the trajectories of Kant's object=X, with its post-Kantian variations in Fichte, Hegel, and Husserl, through to Deleuze.

When Deleuze speaks of the 'power of decision',[1] he means something like commitment to a serial problem. A decision is not 'decisive' in the sense that an argument or a battle is. It is not a state of mind, a set of reasons, or an outcome, but a divergence-point and all its possible branches, both fulfilled and unfulfilled. A decision with unknown consequences and continuations may be well defined. Even so, decision is neither about the present nor the future, but in-between. A true in-between is not between actual times, like waiting for an outcome, but is its own kind of time-structure. A decision is inside an assemblage of possible time-worlds, the only kind of time in which we might be morally responsible.

I will call on a number of resources. Husserl describes decision as a 'volitional noema'. Deleuze explains sense in terms of Husserl's noema. Husserl defines a noema by its open horizon, and following Kant, as an object=X. Kant's =X sounds like a formula for identity, but not once it is read through Fichte and Hegel. Deleuze too describes sense as an object=X, citing Kant and Husserl. Deleuze describes decisions as singularities emitting diverging lines into the future. Deleuze calls the future

---

[1] Gilles Deleuze, *Difference and Repetition*, trans. Paul Patton (New York: Columbia University Press, 1994), pp. 197, 199.

an =X, and says the 'future is the proper place of decision'.[2] The single decision encounters diverging timelines, and affirms many possible worlds, like throwing dice, which Deleuze calls an =X. Deleuze calls Adam's decision to sin a 'pure game'[3]: but more like Go than dice.[4]

At the time a decision is made, its outcomes are open. If I decide, for example, to wake up at 6am tomorrow, there is no temporal puzzle. But if I decide to get more politically engaged, what sequence of which events, under which unexpected branches and delays, do I intend? What does the future of serial divergences look like when it begins? What is the temporal noema of a decision?

## DECISION

Deleuze does not use the word 'decision' often, since it sounds like 'judgement': Where a voluntary subject rationally assesses evidence, cuts off deliberation, and imposes an allegedly knowable future on others. But 'decision' does not have to mean that; a decision can be involuntary, collective, or rambling. In the essay, 'To Have Done with Judgment', Deleuze says: 'A decision is not a judgment . . .: it springs vitally from a whirlwind of forces that leads us into combat'.[5]

Similarly, in *Difference and Repetition*, Deleuze distinguishes two senses of 'decision'. The bad kind, like judgement, 'imposes limits'. The good kind is like questioning, expressing 'excessive systems which link . . . the multiple with the multiple, the fortuitous with the fortuitous . . .'. Although a decision occurs at a point, it is a dark precursor of sequences by 'adjunction and condensation'.[6]

## TURNING POINTS

A decision, like any singular 'object of affirmation', is 'prolonged in a line of ordinary points' and then 'begins again in another singularity'.[7]

---

[2] Ibid. p. 296.

[3] Gilles Deleuze, *The Logic of Sense*, trans. Mark Lester and Charles Stivale (New York: Columbian University Press, 1989), p. 172.

[4] Gilles Deleuze, *The Fold: Leibniz and the Baroque*, trans. Tom Conley (Minneapolis: University of Minnesota Press, 1993), pp. 67–8.

[5] Gilles Deleuze, 'To Have Done with Judgment', in *Essays Critical and Clinical*, trans. Daniel W. Smith and Michael A. Greco (Minneapolis: University of Minnesota Press, 1997), p. 134. Deleuze cites D. H. Lawrence.

[6] Deleuze, *Difference and Repetition*, p. 115.

[7] Deleuze, *The Logic of Sense*, p. 53. And further, a 'singularity [. . .] is the source of a series extending in a determined direction right up to the vicinity of another singularity'.

A problem is a diagram of such 'turning points',[8] a field of selection with diverging pathways.[9] Futuricity is carried by relays, shaped by direction and vicinity, density and distance, and time to arrival at destinations by different routes. Deleuze offers an example drawn from mathematical series, but a better paradigm of turning points is found in decision.

In a decision's pathway, new decisions interrupt and communicate.[10] One decision may be disguised as another. A decision may stabilise, but may diverge so far as no longer to seem the same decision. For example, when somebody decides to emigrate, which may already be disguised by politics or intersect with disease control or some other trajectory, this has some ordinary continuations – bureaucratic, rational and utilitarian – but may in time generate another decision topos regarding vocation, with its own series of ordinary jobs, then other not-so-ordinary divergences around love, justice, or frivolity. 'Their transformations form a history';[11] or better, each is caused by, 'a fragment of a future event'.[12] The future is not just the outcome of a decision; it is inside the decision-content. If the future branches or goes off track, then each decision is *about* that branching and anticipates it from the start. Since we cannot know when or how it will get enacted, the time-space coordinates of a decisional future are virtual. Turning towards a particular end, then, also points to the whole set of alternatives in the time-multiple, all but one of which remains in-actual. Just as irrational numbers constitute the vast majority of number, so virtual time is the vast majority of time. The present, a point on infinitely many timelines, is 'the empty square [though saturated] or the mobile element'.[13]

It lays out a 'positive distance of different elements' (ibid. pp. 52–3). Decisions, and actions generally, have regular consequences as they affect neighbouring objects and events, but they can diverge into situations that redefine it and the events around it. 'Points of inflection' (ibid. p. 52) are 'crisis points, boiling points, knots, and foyers' (ibid. p. 55). A field is a 'jet of singularities' (ibid. p. 53). An 'element . . . is defined as the locus of a question' or of a 'sense' (ibid. p. 56). A turning-point 'spreads out in a determined direction over a line of ordinary points'. It is 'renewed locally for the sake of new articulations and extensions' (ibid. p. 110). A series of events is 'surrounded by a cloud of ordinaries', and emits a singular point that 'can be made to move anywhere' (Deleuze, *The Fold*, p. 60). In these ways, a decision 'communicates' with its possible enactments (Deleuze, *The Logic of Sense*, p. 172). A decision is relayed through points, and can only '*begin* again' at the very next point.

[8] Deleuze, *The Logic of Sense*, p. 55.
[9] Ibid. p. 172.
[10] Ibid. p. 53.
[11] Ibid.
[12] Ibid. Deleuze cites Péguy. It is not that a decision introduces the future; the future introduces the decision.
[13] Ibid. p. 55.

Deleuze here quotes Borges saying, 'No decision (*décision*) is final, all diverge into others.'[14] Many Borges stories say that all forks of a decision get actualised; but Borges writes fiction. Where, if anywhere, does this happen in life? For Deleuze, only one thing can force time to branch into 'elongated pasts and futures': thought.[15] Thought contains the only true singularities. Or in other words, thought is the medium of decision. This is because a thought-object is an object=X.

## KANT'S OBJECT=X

The 'transcendental object=x' originates in Kant's *Critique of Pure Reason*, in the A version of the Transcendental Deduction. Kant names two very different kinds of X: 'X (the object)', and the 'object=X'.[16]

It is clear that, since we have to deal only with the manifold of our representations, and since that x (the object) which corresponds to them is nothing to us—being, as it is, something that has to be distinct from all our representations—the unity which the object makes necessary can be nothing else than the formal unity of consciousness in the synthesis of the manifold of representations. It is only when we have thus produced synthetic unity in the manifold of intuition that we are in a position to say that we know the object ... This *unity of rule* determines all the manifold, and limits it to conditions which make unity of apperception

14   Ibid. p. 61. The Borges story that Deleuze cites here is 'The Lottery of Babylon'. A person wins a lottery; the prize is death, but before he gets it, a large but unknown number of further decisions will get made, which might alter the prize entirely. The moral is that the distance from a decision to its effects is increased by subdivisions. Borges' story 'The Garden of the Forking Paths', which Deleuze refers to elsewhere, has a more direct conceit that all possible decisions are made and enacted in parallel. Jorge Luis Borges, *Labyrinths*, trans. John M. Fein and Donald A. Yates (New York: New Directions, 1962), pp. 19–35.

15   Deleuze, *The Logic of Sense*, p. 62. Only thought can devote itself to what will happen, and yet remain 'neutral' to how much time passes. A decision takes off from actual psychic moments and 'becomes autonomous in the act of disinvesting itself from its matter and flees in both directions at once, toward the future and toward the past'.

16   Deleuze makes a similar distinction: the simple X refers to an unspecified object as an identity. The =X is 'the unformed paradoxical element which ... misses its own identity' (Deleuze, *The Logic of Sense*, p. 119, see also p. 145). Deleuze's vocabulary is not consistent. In one passage, he distinguishes the object=X from the thing=X (ibid. p. 145). Here he defines object=X as a self-identity, also known as the phallus (ibid. p. 228). This is more like Kant's 'object X'. In this passage, Deleuze defines 'thing=X' as the paradoxical constellation without identity, which is more like what he calls the object=X in other passages.

possible. The concept of this unity is the representation of the object=x, which I think through the predicates.[17]

The first, 'X (the object)', 'is nothing to us'. This is the thing-in-itself distinct from representations: simple identity. There is no such thing. The second is the 'object=X', the synthesis of apperception directed towards a singular object. There *is* such a thing, even when the rule of synthesis is 'imperfect or obscure'.[18] The synthesis is not itself a representation, but a '*transcendental* object=X'.[19] Transcendental apperception (Deleuze calls it the 'zone'[20]) makes =X's out of anything. If experience were limited to apperceptions alone, its objects would consist of unordered sensible contents. If experience were unlimited, its objects might include things in themselves. But experience extends to something between these two extremes. By synthesising apperceptions according to rules, its objects consist of complex empirical things. The sides of a figure, or the shapes and sounds of a thing, do not attach to things in themselves; but the transcendental act of synthesis makes these properties cluster around a common target. The act of synthesis constructs an intentional object; it generates a convergence point so that we can predicate qualities in the various representations of the same referent. And since there is nothing to define the object other than the procedures and materials for constructing it, nothing prevents further properties from being added to the object. In short, synthesis constitutes the empirical object as a divergence point at the same time that it constitutes its convergence.

Some commentaries on Kant focus on other points to interpret the object=X. For Longuenesse, for example, =X emphasises rules.[21] For Rudisill, it means objects are 'mentally supplied'.[22]

Some commentaries on Deleuze connect him to Kantian issues other than the nature of objects. Simont, for example, connects Deleuze and Kant on the issue of schemata;[23] Beaulieu in terms of epoché.[24]

---

[17] Immanuel Kant, *Critique of Pure Reason*, trans. Norman Kemp Smith (New York: St Martin's Press, 1965), p. 105.

[18] Ibid. p. 106.

[19] Ibid. p. 109.

[20] Gilles Deleuze, *Kant's Critical Philosophy*, trans. Hugh Tomlinson and Barbara Habberjam (Minneapolis: University of Minnesota Press, 1996), p. 15.

[21] Béatrice Longuenesse, *Kant and the Capacity to Judge*, trans. Charles T. Wolfe (Princeton: Princeton University Press, 1998), pp. 48–9.

[22] Philip McPherson Rudisill, 'Circles in the Air: Pantomimics and the Transcendental Object=X', *Kant-Studien* 87:2, (1996), pp. 132–48.

[23] Juliette Simont, *Essai sur la quantité, la qualité, la relation chez Kant, Hegel, Deleuze* (Paris: L'Harmattan, 1997).

[24] Alain Beaulieu, *Gilles Deleuze et la phénoménologie* (Mons: Sils Maria, 2004).

As I see it, Deleuze draws from Kant a theory of objects, and interprets Kant in the best way. For Deleuze, the =X formula appeals to the genesis of synthetic objects in a way that is both connective and unbounded. Deleuze cites four =X functions. (1) =X lets attributes resonate.[25] (2) =X accommodates disguises.[26] (3) =X synthesis is motivated by desire.[27] (4) =X makes the future present.[28]

Deleuze extrapolates from the perceptual object=X in cognition to a symbolic object=X in the unconscious; to a portmanteau word=X in language;[29] and to an action=X in history.[30] My project extrapolates to a decision=X in ethics.

In his 1978 course at Vincennes, Deleuze interprets Kant as saying that synthesis is the contraction of parts in space and time, grasping simultaneous and successive parts in a single object: 'It's from this level of the analysis of the synthesis of perception that Kant can be considered as the founder of phenomenology.'[31] In one sense, the presupposed form of synthesis 'refers' to Nothing. But it produces =X, so it is not simply nothing; it is an 'any-object-whatever'. A perceiver can only find determinate objects [object=lion, for example], if she first has the object=X form to put that determinacy into, and can reproduce possible continuations in imagination. She also has to recognise what determination this =X should convert into, namely what predicates to describe it with.[32] =X is never the final description of the object. It exists only to have some determinate content substituted for the X. Yet the object's form remains indeterminately =X even after it is determined =lion.

The object=X thus anticipates catastrophes: we will 'not be able to stop' adding parts to the object. We might not be able to reproduce preceding phases of its genesis or recognise the increasing whole. This dizziness is the original sublime. Deleuze in this text treats the aesthetic consequence of =X,[33] but not the ethical.

---

[25] Deleuze, *Difference and Repetition*, pp. 122, 291, 117, 124.

[26] Ibid. pp. 105, 291.

[27] Ibid. p. 110.

[28] Ibid. pp. 119, 291–2.

[29] Deleuze, *The Logic of Sense*, p. 234; Deleuze, *Difference and Repetition*, p. 123.

[30] Deleuze, *Difference and Repetition*, p. 299.

[31] Deleuze, Cours Vincennes: 28 March 1978, at <www.webdeleuze.com>.

[32] See Elhanan Yakira, 'From Kant to Leibniz? Salomon Maimon and the Question of Predication', in Gideon Freudenthal (ed.), *Salomon Maimon: Rational Dogmatist, Empirical Skeptic: Critical Assessments* (Dordrecht: Kluwer, 2003), pp. 54–79.

[33] Daniel Smith applies this point from Deleuze's lecture to Bacon. Daniel W. Smith, 'Deleuze on Bacon: Three Conceptual Trajectories in "The Logic of Sensation"', in *Essays on Deleuze* (Edinburgh: Edinburgh University Press, 2012), pp. 222–34 (esp. p. 227).

FICHTE'S =X

Hegel would (rightly) oppose the simple =X as a bad infinite, a mere 'also', the bland assumption that we can add any definition we like to an object, or fulfill a decision with any action at all.[34] But the Kant-Fichte-Hegel-Deleuze trajectory is complicated.

Kant discusses the object=X only in the A version of the Transcendental Deduction. Perhaps because that version was printed in few copies, and most of his contemporaries read the B deduction, the object=X did not have much direct effect on philosophers of the day. The post-Kantian philosopher with the most X is Fichte.[35] Depending on the stage of Fichte's analysis, we see the Kant-Fichte-Deleuze object=X lineage through different facets.

On the surface, Fichte's A=A is the opposite of Kant's object=X. The former seems to be a dialectic of identity, whereas the latter is a collector function on a field of encounter. But beneath the surface, identity for Fichte is already a kind of overreaching, an encounter with difference.

Fichte's starting point is any act of consciousness whatsoever that affirms some A, and just that. Affirming a thing takes the form A=A. This already takes up two positions towards A: the first posits A as itself; the second posits A as the predicate of itself, as its own self-reflection. A=A is thus like an object=X, in that the object =itself. The difference is that for Fichte, what does the equalising, and so contains the =X, is the subject.[36]

On this score, Fichte's subjective idealism is quite opposed to Kant and Deleuze's transcendental empiricism. For Fichte, the self has to recognise the identity of the object with X (i.e., the identity of the object with its identity), so ultimately it is the self that is, and contains the ground of, self-identity. For Kant, the subject has to go look for the object, so the object is not identical merely with itself, but must be combined with the determinations that limit it, determinations which are not contained in the self alone. This implies for Kant that the self's consciousness is not merely identical with itself, but is determinable by another over time. The self's unity is not given, but transcendental. On this picture, Deleuze would fit into the Kantian mode of thought, but not the post-Kantian mode that starts with Fichte.

---

[34] Perhaps a formula like object=dx/dy might express divergences better.

[35] Johann Gottlieb Fichte, *Science of Knowledge*, trans. Peter Heath and John Lachs (New York: Appleton-Century-Crofts, 1970).

[36] Ibid. pp. 97–8.

Yet it is too simple to say that Fichte's object is self-identical and Kant's is synthetic. It might seem that Fichte posits the pure identity of X=X, but Fichte makes the second X in X=X, the reflection, into the precursor of the ~X, an obstacle to the object's identity within the object itself. Now Fichte starts to sound more like Kant. Conversely, it might seem that Kant makes the object=X depend on independent predicates, but Kant posits =X as the repetition of the object, an immanence found out in the world. On this picture, Deleuze's =X develops out of both Kant and Fichte.

But there is another layer that separates Deleuze and Fichte. At stake is not just identity, but also how objects can have determinate predicates. For Fichte, the subject knows that the second X, the predicates, the scope of ~X, is related to the first X, the X to be defined. But Fichte's subject does not know *what* ~X is, so the object it apprehends is only ever a generalised object. For Kant, since the subject anticipates what the next X is, objects have particular, contingent shapes.

For Fichte, in short, an object presents as X, but the object cannot incorporate the X into itself objectively (only the subject can do that). For Kant, the object itself engages with X-predicates. The transcendental object is not a general substrate that might or might not get determined; it is the construction of determinations *in medias res*. This is phenomenology: objects do not appear *in* the subject, but appear *to* the subject. If we divide theories of =X according to whether the object's identity is general or particular, the former include Fichte, Heidegger, and Badiou; the latter include Kant, Hegel, Husserl, and Deleuze.

On its most developed version (the 'third principle'), Fichte's =X is not a list of positive predicates, but rather a limit. It distributes degrees of reality and negation in the object, determining what the object has in it and what it does not: which elements in the object the subject is free to determine, and which not. Only by its limit, is either a subject or an object 'something'.[37] The =X structure progressively undergoes all the Kantian categorical expansions, first representing quantitative and qualitative predicates, then causal and relational predicates. That categories are produced dynamically from a first principle all the way to fully organised phenomenological structure is of course the key to the lineage of Kant, Fichte, and Hegel. The result might not look like Kant's =X any more, since '=' is no longer a single predicate-collection relation, but has a different meaning for each way that predicates are organised under an object. But Kant himself undertakes this expansion

[37] Ibid. pp. 108–9.

in the schematism chapters of the *Critique of Pure Reason*. Deleuze, in his turn, uses Kant's =X in order to say that objects assemble predicates across categorical boundaries. The post-Kantian lineage is all about sedimenting the categorical divisibility of the =X.

HEGEL'S =X

Hegel can either be seen to reject the =X formula, or to expand on its hidden complications.

In the 'Perception' chapter of the *Phenomenology of Spirit*, Hegel criticises the =X approach for describing objects by naming one predicate, then another predicate 'also', and another 'also'. . ..[38] It is easy for Hegel to show that predicates do not simply accumulate by addition, but combine under many forms of tension. Colour predicates may exclude one another; colour predicates require shape predicates; one object's active predicate (an eagle's claws) correlates with nearby objects' receptive predicates (a rabbit's skin); diachronic predicates are negated later. This is not to dismiss the object=X formula altogether, since an object does hold many predicates. But '=' is not simple identity; it is the genesis and structure of predicate interrelations.

Hegel's twist on 'The Thing and its Properties' (*Science of Logic*) challenges the separation between Kant's two senses of X.[39] Kant, as we saw, distinguished the thing-in-itself and the synthetic empirical object. Hegel argues that since the empirical object is flexible enough to contain several properties, it divorces itself from any particular set of properties, presents itself as an empty substrate, and so becomes thing-in-itself-like. And from the side of the property, since a property is free to get instantiated of a plurality of things, the property is as independent of phenomena as the thing is, and so becomes a property-in-itself. The thing-in-itself status proliferates to the point where every phenomenal difference is a micro-thing-in-itself. For Hegel, the upshot is of course not to confirm the thing-in-itself model, but to show the absurd consequences of the very ontology of things and properties.

The ultimate consequence of the fact that things are neutral with respect to which properties they can absorb, and properties are neutral with respect to which things have them, is that things can have the prop-

[38] G. W. F. Hegel, *Phenomenology of Spirit*, trans. Arnold V. Miller (Oxford: Oxford University Press, 1977), p. 73.
[39] G. W. F. Hegel, *Science of Logic*, trans. Arnold V. Miller (Atlantic Highlands: Humanities Press, 1989), pp. 484–96.

erties of *other* things as easily as they can have their own. ('It is through property that the thing is continuous with other things.'[40]) It is not just that a stem and a leaf can both be green, but also that the greenness of the stem is transferred to the leaf. Causality is the distribution of properties from one thing to another. Hegel concludes that instead of the category of properties, we should use the category of 'free matters', like pigments and electrical forces (and, we might add, *petit a* desires, and ideational memes). 'Matters circulate freely out of or into "this" thing.'[41] This gives a very different model for the object=X. The object here is as much a distributor as an individuator for properties. On this interpretation, the formula =X is a field for the circulation of properties across space, time, and substance. =X represents a turning point, where individuals turn universal, and things turn into other things.

Hegel gives two main arguments to show that identity implies difference, or that if A=A, then A= some other X also. First, identifying A requires isolating it from a manifold.[42] Therefore A has relational predicates prior to self-identity. Second, while the *linguistic* proposition A=A seems to say nothing new in the predicate, the *thought* proposition has a cognitive sequence, namely A . . . =A. The thought 'sets out to say something more', and is disappointed (it 'contradicts itself') when it ends up saying nothing else.[43] Therefore, again, there is a place for predications different than A in the form A=A. As a static predication, it is true that identity takes the essentialist form of A=A; but as a genetic predication, identity takes the synthetic form, which we have called object=X.

That a predicate other than A is found in the object =A, requires immanent development, which Hegel calls the 'concept'. In its naïve form, Kant's =X judgement seemed to collect a conjunction of predicates. Interestingly, Hegel does not have a separate heading for judgements of conjunction. (In fact, neither does Kant's list of judgements.)[44] For Hegel, conjunction appears as a subspecies of disjunction.

This sounds like Deleuze, but what is the reasoning? A predicative judgement, A is B, implies the conditional judgement, If this is A then it is B.[45] This in turn implies that, If an object has all the properties involved in A then it gains all the properties involved in B. Therefore, the more we know about how A is B, the more we know a series of

[40] Ibid. p. 493.
[41] Ibid. p. 494.
[42] Ibid. pp. 414–15.
[43] Ibid. p. 415.
[44] Kant, *Critique of Pure Reason*, A70/B95.
[45] Hegel, *Science of Logic*, p. 654.

conditionals, articulating the gradual unfolding of A into B. Insofar as predications are hypothetical, several hypotheticals are needed to define A by its various disjunctive possibilities. A may hypothetically turn out to coincide with B, C, D, or many other things. Only once the object (or our knowledge of it) is actualised to a certain extent, does the inclusively disjunctive definition of the object take the form of a conjunctive judgement. Activated hypotheticals compile the results achieved so far, in the object=X form: A is B and C. To the extent that the object's determination is not complete (and its completeness, Hegel says, is never more than contingent), the final judgement regarding the object remains disjunctive. Only relative =X judgements can be conjunctive. Disjunctive =X judgements are more correct, expressing as they do that an object's ever widening conjunctions of predicates are built out of particulars that at various points virtualise, transform, and exclude one another. The object, in short, is equated with a self-expanding and self-limiting (inclusively and exclusively disjunctive) set of predications.

Different judgement forms express fluctuating subject-predicate relations by means of the sense they give to the copula. In cases of near tautologous predication, subject and predicate are so close in meaning that the judgement S is P is tantamount to simply naming S(P), and the copula recedes to insignificance. In predications that express essential transformations, S is P expresses a history of difference; in this case, both S and P are accidental, so the copula itself is effectively the subject of the sentence. The genesis of predication, in short, consists in the expanding and contracting scope of the copula, as objects take on determination. In the final analysis, we might say, predication is found not in the vicissitudes of the S 'is' P form, but in the object=X form.

I have lingered on the ontology of =X so that when we return to Deleuze's account of decision as a turning-point whose future has an =X relation, we have a subtle logic of '=' to work with, reducing neither to identity or additive conjunction, but capturing and releasing flows and interruptions of predicate series over time. The first step in connecting =X to the topic of decision is to apply the object=X model to acts of will, a step Fichte takes in his *Science of Rights*. Freedom means controlling a series of future possibilities.[46] The unity and impact of an agent over time is hypothetical:[47] decisional, not factual. Yet her will must get

[46] Johann Gottlieb Fichte, *The Science of Rights*, trans. Adolph Ernst Kroeger (New York: J. J. Harper, 1970), p. 77.
[47] Ibid. p. 140.

instantiated somewhere and in some way – the end must be equated with some X, which ought in turn to secure rights for the future.[48]

Deleuze calls the future an =X,[49] to the extent that it remains virtual even once actualised.[50] 'The object=X is the immanent limit of the series of virtuals.'[51] We could call the =X function 'pre-sense', 'nonsense', or 'co-sense' (*co-sens*).[52] Either way, the point is that when contemplating a decision, we are in a co-time between times; 'we temporarily abandon life',[53] since we are not just choosing one set of results among others, but get involved in a range of conditionals built on further conditions. As I will put it, as an object=X, a decision commits to events on non-existing time-lines. So what is the temporal meaning, the temporal noema, of a decision?

## NOEMA

Deleuze introduces his own concept of sense through Husserl's noema,[54] and Husserl introduces noema with Kant's object=X. In Husserl's

---

[48] Ibid. p. 170.

[49] Deleuze, *Difference and Repetition*, p. 103.

[50] The future is the territory where plans are fulfilled otherwise than intended, as an 'action=X' (Deleuze, *Difference and Repetition*, p. 110).

[51] Ibid. p. 109. When Deleuze associates the 'object=X' with the phallus (Deleuze, *The Logic of Sense*, p. 233), he calls it a 'floating signifier and floated signified' (p. 228). What 'happens' on one series 'insists' on the other (ibid. p. 228). The X is 'displaced', because its meaning spreads out over virtual time. In his essay 'How Do We Recognize Structuralism?' (in *Desert Islands and Other Texts: 1953–1974*, trans. M. Taormina (New York: Semiotext(e), 2004)), Deleuze brings together many definitions of =X, ending with a loose connection between =X and decision:

> (1) The =X is the 'empty square' on all series at once, like the handkerchief in *Othello* (pp. 258–9).
> (2) In games, Lacan says, =X is like the *place du mort*, the dummy hand in bridge.
> (3) =X is an object of exchange, like the phallus (p. 263).
> (4) =X is a *perpetuum mobile* (p. 262).
> (5) _X is 'perfectly determinable, even in its displacements' (p. 264). It permits a social system to find 'a certain number of possible choices', and to find, 'at each of their points of choice [or 'at each moment in history'], a certain number of possible individuals' (p. 265).

Edward Willatt connects the empty square =X in this text with the 'strange object'. In structuralism, =X stands for the genesis of structure, the way objects are outcomes of open processes. See Edward Willatt, 'The Genesis of Cognition: Deleuze as a Reader of Kant', in Edward Willatt and Matt Lee (eds), *Thinking Between Deleuze and Kant* (London: Continuum Books, 2009), pp. 67–85.

[52] Deleuze, *The Logic of Sense*, p. 233.

[53] Gilles Deleuze, *Nietzsche and Philosophy*, trans. Hugh Tomlinson (New York: Columbia University Press, 1983), p. 25.

[54] Deleuze, *The Logic of Sense*, pp. 20–1. Deleuze describes Husserl's noema favourably as 'the ideational objective unity as the correlate of the act of perception'.

terminology, a subjective experience is a 'noesis'; the object meant is the 'determinable X in the noematic sense'.[55] The noema is 'the pure X in abstraction from all predicates'.[56] The noema must remain an 'empty X',[57] to be open to new perceptions.[58] A 'plurality of rays' of meaning 'go to the X with the highest synthetic unity'.[59] Sense is thus future tensed, or genetic. Deleuze complains that Husserl's noema ought to, but cannot, describe both a meaning, and its future genesis. Deleuze says – perhaps wrongly – that the kinds of predicates that Husserl thinks define meaning cannot prefigure which subsequent events will confirm them.[60] For a meaning to engage as yet unknown objects, the noema would have to be a hybrid of meaning and effect.[61] Deleuze thinks this reduces Husserl's framework to nonsense. But for Deleuze, =X articulates just this necessary nonsense.

In fact, Husserl has a place for a meaning that projects its own future options. He calls it a noematic 'modification', expressing an intentional 'perhaps', a modal meaning: 'a volition-meaning', a 'noema belonging peculiarly to the willing', a decision-noema.[62] It seems like Deleuze ought to agree to the 'perhaps'-intention, and the decisional noema. I will come back to this line of development later. But first, we need to take a detour through a different, and in my view less successful, line that Deleuze sometimes takes on decisional futures, in which he describes decision less like noematic genesis, and more like throwing dice.

[55] Edmund Husserl, *Ideas Pertaining to a Pure Phenomenology and to a Phenomenological Philosophy*, vol. 1, trans. Fred Kersten (Dordrecht: Kluwer Academic Publishers, 1982), p. 313.

[56] Ibid. p. 313/271.

[57] Ibid. p. 315/272.

[58] Husserl says: 'in no noema ... can the pure determinable X be missing' (Ibid. p. 315/272). Deleuze says it is missing, but even for Deleuze, the missing X is never missing. Following Aristotle's view that the mind must be neutral in order to be formable by every object, Husserl says that the empty X is 'the possibility of harmonious combination to make sense-unities of any level whatever' (Ibid. p. 315/272). If we leave out the constraint of harmony, Deleuze can agree. Husserl says the 'substrate X' describes 'how' a horizon of an object's determinability follows an 'unceasingly changing sense'. Paradoxically, openness confers determinacy. See Edmund Husserl, *Analyses Concerning Passive and Active Synthesis*, trans. Anthony J. Steinbock (Dordrecht: Kluwer Academic Publishers, 2001), p. 58.

[59] Husserl, *Ideas*, vol. 1, p. 316/273.

[60] Deleuze, *The Logic of Sense*, p. 97.

[61] Ibid. pp. 98–9.

[62] Husserl, *Ideas*, vol. 1, p. 233/199.

## DICETHROW

Deleuze calls the dicethrow an action =X. He says the pure gamer throws without preferring any outcome. 'It is not a matter of several dicethrows', holding out for the right result.[63] Those who gamble on the number play an impure game.[64] The game is to preserve chance; just throw, that's it. An impure game exhibits (1) pre-existing rules, (2) statistical probabilities and if/then options evaluated by skill and effort, (3) distinct sequences of plays, and (4) calculated gain/loss. Game theory deals with such decisions. Pure games,[65] in contrast: (1) invent rules, (2) ramify chance without results, (3) play out in simultaneous constellations, (4) are nonsensical, and (5) have no winners or losers. The purest game, Deleuze says again, is Thought.

In my view, the dicethrow model of decision overplays chance and underplays time. Deleuze says that a dicethrow affirms chance 'every time',[66] and that 'the whole of chance is . . . there in a single time'.[67] To be sure, for every decision there is a vertiginous instant before it narrows down, but why should chance have so little future or seriality? When Deleuze says, 'The future is the proper place of decision',[68] his main idea is that decisions separate from the past, from prototypes and obligations. It is true that a dicethrow is independent of past throws, but the downside is that it has no effect on the next throw; it has virtually no effect; worse, it has no virtual effect. After all, we cannot throw, in 'a single time', anything like a philosophy, a child, or any interesting noema.

Why insist a thought-throw is singular and indivisible, since it emits loose ends? Of course, I can start a project and see where it goes; as one life contains many events. But these are classical one–many relations. Why insist that the dicethrow, or destiny, is decided just once? Whether it is a question of accepting fate, or creating the world by playing at drafts, why insist on a single throw?

Of course, singularity is complicated, since it is distributed through

---

[63] A 'bad player counts on many throws of the dice'. Deleuze, *Nietzsche and Philosophy*, pp. 24–31.

[64] Deleuze, *The Logic of Sense*, pp. 58–9. Raúl Ruiz suggests that decisions are made by herds of cunning and fearful dice. Raúl Ruiz, *Poetics of Cinema 1*, trans. Brian Holmes (Paris: Éditions Dis Voir, 2005), pp. 19–20.

[65] Deleuze, *The Logic of Sense*, pp. 59–60.

[66] Deleuze, *Difference and Repetition*, p. 198.

[67] Many thoughts 'communicate in one long thought . . . linking the "once and for all" to "each time" for the sake of "all time"' (Deleuze, *Nietzsche and Philosophy*, p. 60).

[68] Deleuze, *Difference and Repetition*, p. 296.

a field into destination-objects, subdividing and reassembling.[69] The throw is a multiple all at once: 'unity affirmed of multiplicity', 'multiple affirmation'.[70] In fact, Deleuze uses two different terms in *Logic of Sense*: there is one 'toss' (*lancer*) of the dice, but many 'plays' (*coups*).[71] Still, why just one toss? Why should the thrower, the third term in the dicethrow (in addition to the way up and the way down), who is after all more than thrownness, whether gambler or schizo-nomad, be content with one roll per assemblage?

And what is the role of the dice landing?[72] Deleuze says throwing the dice is a becoming, and the fall is the return: 'the being of that which becomes'.[73] While throwing affirms chance, 'the combination which they form on falling affirms necessity'.[74] Of course, a single throw yields a single number.[75] But why does Deleuze say that, 'there is only a single way of combining all the parts of chance, only one number of chance as such'?[76] Certainly, he is not talking of the number of dots on the die face, but perhaps a numbering number. But why call this necessity?

Perhaps Deleuze does not really mean that the dicethrow decision yields a single result. Perhaps he means that there is just one dicethrow decision but that it affords many interpretations. Speaking of Nietzsche's aphorisms, Deleuze says, 'The interpretation of the eternal return begins with the dicethrow but it has only just begun. We must still interpret the dicethrow itself at the same time as it returns.'[77] But interpretation sounds like a second decision, another dicethrow.

Another reading arises when Deleuze moves from the dicethrow model to a model of decision based on a field of forces. Chance and force might seem opposites, but Deleuze says, 'By affirming chance, we affirm the relation of all forces.'[78] The emphasis here is no longer on the flight of the dice, but on the uncontrollable vectors in the hand that throws. The chance in question is no longer a human throwing dice and seeing a number. That is now treated as a forced occurrence. The issue now is that 'the will to power is never separable from particular determined

---

[69] Deleuze, *The Logic of Sense*, pp. 113–14.
[70] Deleuze, *Nietzsche and Philosophy*, p. 29.
[71] Deleuze, *The Logic of Sense*, p. 113.
[72] Deleuze, *Nietzsche and Philosophy*, p. 25.
[73] Ibid. p. 24.
[74] Ibid. p. 26.
[75] Ibid. p. 28.
[76] Ibid. p. 26.
[77] Ibid. p. 31.
[78] Ibid. p. 48.

forces, from their quantities, qualities, and directions'.[79] In *Cinema 2*, Deleuze cites the casino scene in the abysmal Jerry Lewis movie, *Hollywood or Bust*; Jerry's body 'is shaken by spasms and various currents . . . when he is going to throw the dice'.[80] The chance-effect is now located earlier than the throw, in the pre-existing forces that mess it up. Perhaps the claim that there is only one throw is more palatable if it was already plural beforehand. In any case, the decisional throw may appear in one shot but is in truth made of a 'diversity of co-existing cycles'.[81] When Deleuze says of dice that 'the number of the combination produce repetition',[82] perhaps he does not mean we repeat one decision; perhaps he means 'repetition for itself' in the sense of *Difference and Repetition*, namely multi-levelled temporality. This trajectory returns us to what I think is Deleuze's better model of decision, the futural =X model. How, then, is a decision made up of co-existing temporal cycles?

Deleuze's case study for this is Adam's decision to sin.

## ADAM'S DECISION AND INCOMPOSSIBLE WORLD-CYCLES

Deleuze never quite says that Adam decides or chooses to sin, as the pre-Kantian Leibniz does. But they agree that when Adam sins, he branches into a possible world. Possible worlds could provide a semantics for =X, and have in fact been used to interpret Husserl's noema.[83]

All Adams start in the Garden, then diverge.[84] When an object=X like Adam splits, 'another world begins'.[85] Since it is not the individual object but its fragmentation into versions that begins worlds, it follows that 'all possible situations occur'.[86] Similar versions of an object are compossible in the same world, but an Adam who sins is incompossible with one who does not. Yet this irreducible difference between options is just what makes Adam's decision into a real divergence-point at the

---

[79] Ibid. p. 50.

[80] Gilles Deleuze, *Cinema 2: The Time Image*, trans. Hugh Tomlinson and Robert Galeta (Minneapolis: University of Minnesota Press, 1997), p. 65. Jerry wins money in this scene, but his jerky movements are out of all proportion with moving the dice around. It is not that the throw has no continuations, but that it is continued by the wave of energy that propagates through a whole situation rather than by any one particular result.

[81] Deleuze, *Nietzsche and Philosophy*, p. 49.

[82] Ibid. p. 26.

[83] David Woodruff Smith and Ronald McIntyre, *Husserl and Intentionality* (Dordrecht: Reidel Publishing Company, 1982), pp. 292–5.

[84] Deleuze, *The Logic of Sense*, p. 114.

[85] Ibid. p. 111.

[86] Ibid. p. 114.

moment it occurs in the real world. Incompossible worlds do not all exist in the same actual world, that is still impossible; and they are not in different worlds, since that would leave each Adam no choice; but incompossible worlds co-exist in the same virtual world. In Deleuzian modal realism, all worlds virtually occur.

We can compare this thesis with David Lewis' modal realism, which also holds that all possible worlds are real. For Lewis, only one possible world is actual, in the sense that only one world is indexed to a given person's life. Lewis says, 'I cannot think of a single philosopher who favours trans-world identity', namely the view that a given person 'leads double lives'.[87] But Deleuze favours it. For Deleuze, the same Adam is projected into different worlds, whereas the way Lewis puts it is that Adam counterparts in different worlds are almost exact duplicates up to a certain time; when they diverge, it is not the same Adam splitting but the counterpart Adams becoming more discernable.[88] Lewis' best hope for an argument against branching worlds is that 'it conflicts with our ordinary presupposition that we have a single future'.[89] What planet does he come from?

But Lewis says one Deleuzian thing, premised on the idea that individuals know which world they are in by knowing truths about their world. But since the truths a person knows might hold for many worlds, she cannot know which world she is in. Furthermore, each person has a counterpart in those other worlds, so she cannot know which, of many individuals, is her. If, as Deleuze thinks but Lewis does not, decisions branch, then at the moment of decision, we are pre-individual. For related reasons, we cannot know how far along we have gone on a decision's timeline, which makes us, we could say, pre-chronic.

In *The Fold*, Deleuze analyses incompossibility as a relation between Adam the sinner and the world in which Adam the non-sinner exists.[90] Incompossibility is not quite a relation between two versions of one person, or between two worlds, but between a person and his other possible world. It occurs – no surprise – when 'series diverge in the neighborhood of singularities'.[91]

---

[87] David Lewis, *On the Plurality of Worlds* (Malden, MA: Blackwell Publishing, 1986), p. 198.

[88] Lewis uses the term 'branching' for the idea that the same world has different futures; he uses the term 'diverging' for worlds that become increasingly different (ibid. p. 206). In Lewis' terminology, Deleuze's theory is about 'branching', though Deleuze calls it 'divergence'.

[89] Ibid. p. 207.

[90] Deleuze, *The Fold*, p. 59.

[91] Ibid. p. 60. It is partly to conform to Leibniz's theory that monads do not evolve

Entry into incompossible worlds is a 'divine game'; not dice this time, but a 'calculus of infinite series ruled by convergences and divergences'.[92] The first move decides the rules of the new world; as it were, on an empty board. In *The Fold*, Deleuze names Go as if it were Adam's game.[93] (There is speculation that Leibniz knew of Go.) Of course, Go has rules, but where chess begins with situated and determinate pieces, Go begins with an empty grid. Go strategy is to build groups whose meanings can be shifted. The goal in Go is to surround territory, but paradoxically you cannot get enough territory with the strategy of taking territory. Takemiya's 'moyo' strategy, for example, is to claim an impossibly large territory, sacrifice it as soon as his opponent invades, surround the invader at a distance, redirect power elsewhere, converting that power to territory only at the last minute.[94] Deleuze says that in Go, 'you encircle your adversary's presence to neutralize him, to make him incompossible, to impose divergence upon him'.[95] I think it would be better to say you make your opponent's stones inflexible, merely compossible, deprived of divergence. In fact, Go has many resources for a theory of decision. Usually, a result is judged good if each move leading to it was optimal, i.e. if we chose the divergence with the best outcome. But in 'tewari' analysis, we imagine a different sequence that could have led to the same outcome. If each move in that unplayed series was not optimal, then neither was the played series, even though *its* every move was. Good plays are hidden in those other possible game-worlds. Criteria are not inside a series, but inside its counterparts. To say a player considers many hypothetical games while actualising just one, is not the half of it. A 15 teraflop computer (a trillion floating point operations per second) is strong at chess but weak at Go; there are too many possible worlds on a 19x19 board (though programmers can eliminate sure losers by using the mathematics of surreal numbers,[96] co-incidentally Badiou's favoured number theory). The moral of Adam's incompossibility game is that decisions activate alternate temporal

---

that Deleuze's descriptions of divergence do not sound like projections into the future.

[92] Ibid. p. 61.

[93] Deleuze says that 'The ideal player of the game is Aion', as if time is the player. '[The game] plays ... at the border of two tables' (Deleuze, *The Logic of Sense*, p. 64), with an 'impenetrable window' connecting them. This sounds like Duchamps' 'Large Glass', played as a board game.

[94] Masaki Takemiya, *Le go cosmique* (Villers-le-Bel: Éditions Algo, 1997).

[95] Deleuze, *The Fold*, p. 68.

[96] 'Computer Go', Wikipedia, available at <http://en.wikipedia.org/wiki/Computer_Go> (last accessed December 2014).

cycles that run contemporaneously in the various possible worlds they initiate.

Now, co-existing hypothetical series make interesting decisional noemata, but a bad move in a game is no sin. The motive to play has no ethical value, so games do not ultimately suit Leibniz's concern, which, Deleuze says, is to provide 'the first great phenomenology of motives'.[97] In fact, Leibniz says little of Adam's motives, and in the event, the Biblical Adam shows little imagination for the future consequences of his choices. The Scripture's entire account of Adam's decision reads, 'She gave her husband some and he ate it' (*Genesis* 3:6). Nevertheless, Deleuze's view is that decisions are motivated, indeed motivated 'in *every* direction',[98] since motives are images of possible futures.[99] To put it bluntly, we have images of many incompossible futures, therefore we are motivated to make many incompossible choices, therefore we make many incompossible choices, therefore we bring about an incompossible object=X.

Deleuze here compares Adam's decision with one of his own. 'For example, I hesitate between staying home and working, or going out to a nightclub.'[100] We do not usually picture Deleuze at a nightclub, but he does. As the images of 'the hum of the word processor', or the drink in the bar, vary in intensity, inclination swings back and forth. (This sounds like William James.) Sometimes, the motive is determined merely by 'where my region goes the furthest', as if we incline to whichever image projects the longest future.[101] It may not be rational, but a motive is just a futural noema.

At each moment, a decision-image projects all the perceptions one has, and in that sense is autonomous and voluntary. A decision is on the one hand momentary, since at the next moment, the balance of perceptions might incline the same agent in a different direction. To persist, the decision would have to be 'renewed' at the next moment.[102] Yet the moment is the divergence-point, so deciding in the moment, the subject enters all his possible futures at once.

Controversial ontological theses like this one need arguments, so here is one: if we lived only one of our decisional options, then the present would have to be the moment *before* divergence; in that case, we *would*

[97] Deleuze, *The Fold*, p. 69.
[98] Ibid. p. 69.
[99] Ibid. p. 70.
[100] Ibid.
[101] Ibid. p. 73.
[102] Ibid. p. 71.

take one diverging path and never get on the other. But that would mean we are never inside the point of divergence; indeed, divergence could never occur. Lewis would be right, and we would never make a decision. In contrast, if the present *contains* the divergence into two paths, the decision-maker at the instant of decision is already on both paths. This does not prove that we make decisions; but it proves that if we make one decision, we make them all. This is the being of the becoming: the second synthesis of time *in which* the present passes. And it is the same present on different levels: the third synthesis of time, sheets of past. And once we are on both paths, how could we believe we follow one all the way and the others only a short way? We may live some futures with lower intensity than others, but we live them.

What did Deleuze decide? We know he finished the book on Leibniz. We know he took the occasional drink. We do not know which at that moment, but he did both over time. Can each of us say that while we made certain decisions, we made the other ones too, that there need be no anxiety or despair since we live all the lives we cut off? There are several ways to say this: we make all possible decisions; or, the paths we decided against, we lived out anyhow; or, minimally, we actually make one decision but the others still affect us virtually; or, we never actually decide, since decisions exist in virtual time only.

Obviously there are challenges to such a theory. For one thing, even if thought makes multiple decisions, don't bodies act one way at a time? To be sure, bodies too have virtual and ambiguous modes, but they seem not to display all their possibilities at once. Decisions resulting in somebody's death, for example, seem to limit variation (though the finality of death is not heavily marked in Deleuzian chronology). In any case, we should not expect the virtualities of thought and body to be parallel. The difference in temporal structure between noema and behaviour is genuine, but counts as just another level of poly-linear decision-making in three syntheses of time.

Finally, it might seem ethically problematic to restrict decision to virtual time: the best such decision will commit to no particular behaviour, but to endless timeline fantasies. Such a decision might seem both too casual and too burdensome to be ethically responsible. But it stands a better ethical chance than the theory of decision's two other extremes: namely, Sartre's view that decisions have no future, and game-theory's view that decisions have nothing but. For Sartre, a decision to stop gambling has no future, since the will cannot limit future will; the volitional noema cannot endure new situations. For game-theory, in reverse, decision calculates exclusively by backward induction from a future value.

But desiring the best future leads, in the Prisoner's Dilemma, to betrayal, which gives the worst future. Players do better when they do not know how many sub-decisions remain before the outcome will be settled, and so have time to negotiate; decisions are more rational when future branches are underdetermined.

Deleuze's account of the multiple futures of a decisional noema can be seen as working through the lineage of the Kantian object=X, following the Fichtean-Hegelian-Husserlian post-Kantian sense of '=' as a pathway along which objects trade off predications and futures. If this world is also Leibnizian, perhaps it is not surprising, given the second synthesis of time, that the post-Kantian and the pre-Kantian worlds operate in the same object=X.

## Chapter 14

# Kant's Bastards: Deleuze and Lyotard

*Gregg Lambert*

### WHO IS A 'BASTARD', PROPERLY SPEAKING?

In most cases, in order to be legitimate, a child must be born from and be recognised by proper parents.[1] Bastards, the illegitimate, are said to be absent of one these conditions. A bastard, usually male in gender, is born from illegitimate circumstances (legally defined), but more importantly, does not legally possess or have the right to claim the recognition of a parent, and therefore, cannot legally inherit. As Deleuze once remarked, in the genre of philosophy most commentaries also make a claim to inherit, to be recognised as proper and legitimate offspring of their philosophical parents. Thus, he writes, 'the history of philosophy plays a patently repressive role in philosophy, it's philosophy's own version of the Oedipus complex'.[2] This is because a fundamental rule of the genre is that the commentator must become depersonalised or subordinate his or her own identity in the reproduction of the legitimate host or proper parent. As Deleuze remarks, '[m]any members of my generation never broke free of this; others did, by inventing their own particular methods and new rules, a new approach'.[3]

Consequently, in his early work on the history of philosophy, Deleuze demonstrates an especially strong resistance to the subordination remarked above by inventing a unique approach to the exposition of another philosopher's system – a method he describes as the creation of slippages and dislocations in the system he examines in order to insert his own 'problematique'. This is the case of his earliest works on Hume

---

[1] This essay was originally published under the same title in *Philosophical Forum* 43:3, (2012), pp. 345–56 and it is reprinted with the journal editor's kind permission.

[2] Gilles Deleuze, *Negotiations*, trans. Martin Joughin (New York: Columbia University Press, 1995), p. 5.

[3] Ibid.

(1953) and Bergson (1966), but especially true in the case of his exposition of *Kant's Critical Philosophy* published in 1964, which in some sense inaugurates what could very loosely be described as a distinctively French postmodern reading of Kant. The influence of this work, however, is not owed to any systematic and thorough exposition offered on Deleuze's part, but rather the influence that this sly little volume to Kant's entire philosophy had on a generation of students in the French academy in preparing for their doctoral examinations. In fact, I would argue that it is partly from this pedagogical strategy, in the most positive of terms, or in more realistic and psychological terms, from this 'anxiety of influence', that Deleuze was first motivated to write what he has most famously defined as 'a book about an enemy'.[4]

Since the form of obligation in the history of philosophy is so close to patrimony, therefore we must imagine that there would be, as in the case of Deleuze, properly philosophical bastards as well! These are not just bad readers, who are like bad children and remain children of their parents nonetheless, but a species of reader or a particular 'phrase family' that are more monstrous. This method of doing commentary is given its most infamous description in an interview later published in *Negotiations*:

> But the main way I suppose I coped with it at that time was to see the history of philosophy as a kind of buggery or (it comes to the same thing) Immaculate Conception. I saw myself taking the author from behind and giving him a child that would be his offspring, but monstrous. It was really important that he be recognized as his own child, because the author had to say all that I had him saying. But the child was bound to be monstrous too, because it resulted from all sorts of shifting, slipping, dislocations, and hidden emissions that I really enjoyed.[5]

In his seminars on Kant conducted during the same period, Deleuze frequently employs two descriptions in reference to the German philosopher, both of which are equally comical and reveal both an enmity as well as a secret admiration for the Kantian system: at one point, Deleuze refers to Kant's system as a great fog that comes rolling in from the north and settles over Paris around the turn of the century; in another, he simply refers to Kant as 'the old Chinaman from Königsberg' – a description I am particularly fond of for its implicit comparison of the patriarchal role of the Kantian system in the Western tradition to Confucianism in the East.

---

[4]  Ibid. p. 6.
[5]  Ibid.

Returning to Deleuze's statement concerning 'others of his generation' who broke free of a certain history of philosophy by inventing 'new rules' and a 'new approach' to the genre itself, one might immediately locate the figure of Lyotard as well, particularly since both Deleuze and Lyotard were classmates at the Sorbonne and shared the same teachers, influences, and academic culture in the immediate post-war years, and by logical extension, would also be prone to share some of the same critical tastes and resistances. Stepping back from this partly psychological observation, we might ask what factors would cause such a strong urge that is expressed in Deleuze's earlier remark to break free from a certain history of philosophy? In other words, what is the source of the urge to liberate philosophy from its 'Oedipal straightjacket', as Deleuze calls it, a phrase which already betrays a severe psychological reaction or threat to personal or cultural identity? Of course, one explanation would be the infusion of either a strong national sentiment among philosophers of the immediate post-war generation in the French academy, what Derrida has commented on under the name of 'philosophical nationalism', or perhaps more accurately the opposite which is just as much (if not more) a psychological characteristic of nationalism: the weakening of a national spirit or culture of French philosophy caused by the dominance of another national tradition around the same time, specifically the Germanic tradition of Kant, Hegel, Husserl and Heidegger.

Would these factors be enough to explain the desire to become a pure bastard? Here, I must come back the psychological and legal condition of a subject defined as a bastard. Juridically, a bastard is defined simply as a person who cannot legally inherit. Psychologically, however, the typical reaction of a subject who is determined in this way is a super-added tendency to refuse what he cannot already legitimately possess, a refusal to inherit that is remarked most strongly in the creation of a new approach to the tradition of the parent and particularly in the sphere of *culture* (a word I will return to below). I would argue that Deleuze and Lyotard are pure bastards in two distinct senses having to do, first of all, with an inability to align themselves with a past culture of philosophy owing to some specific circumstances of their generation; and second, with an added political and psychological tension that is expressed as a refusal to inherit. In other words, first, we find in both contemporary philosophies a refusal of the French-Catholic traditions of Pascal and Montaigne, or the rationalist tradition of Voltaire or the Romanticism of Rousseau (of course, this is only partly true of Lyotard, and of the early works in particular, before his later return to the themes of ethical philosophy from the 1980s onward, though by way of Wittgenstein and Kant rather than Catholic philosophy). Nevertheless, both works strongly exhibit a certain 'becoming bastard', which Deleuze himself famously labels a 'bachelor desire' – that is to say, either an outright refusal, or at least a strong resistance, to two philosophical parents that came to dominate the French academic culture from the 1920s onward: Hegel and Husserl.

Here, I would argue that the French academic tradition bears some hereditary responsibility for breeding Deleuze and Lyotard as Kant's bastard children, beginning in the early twenties, with the influx of two German philosophical traditions that will come to dominate the French academy and even supplant the French traditions of Pascal and Montaigne, although this is not necessarily true in either the case of Descartes or Rousseau. On the one hand, there is the early influence of Husserl and phenomenology (in some ways, as the modern tradition of the Cartesian science of the cogito), which was actually introduced to the French by Russian *émigré* Alexandre Koyré in 1919, but more importantly and less well known, by Lithuanian born Emmanuel Levinas who first translated Husserl and published the first article in French in 1930 on the philosophy of Martin Heidegger. On the other hand, the Hegelian tradition was introduced ten years later by another Russian *émigré*, Alexandre Kojève, whose seminars influenced a whole line of thinkers including Bataille, Blanchot, Lacan, Hyppolite, Sartre, and several others. As superbly chronicled by the Continental philosopher Alan Schrift, along with Sartre and Jean Hyppolite these 'Russian Masters' (for lack of a better term) probably had the most lasting and transformative impact on the French establishment that set the stage for both Existentialism and Marxist philosophy of the immediate post-War years, as well as preparing the ground for the emergence of structuralism under Lévi-Strauss and Roland Barthes following the 1950s.[6]

I have provided only a snapshot of the 'academic culture', in the sense of what happens in a petri dish, that could be said to be formative of the strident and volatile manner of the new methods and approaches that Deleuze and Lyotard create, each in their own respects, from the 1960s onward. Of course, it is the singular decisions that a student of philosophy makes early on in his or her academic career that can have the most long-lasting consequences. In the case of Deleuze, I would highlight in particular his public distance from Husserlian phenomenology

---

[6] Alan Schrift, *Twentieth-Century French Philosophy: Key Themes and Thinkers* (London: Blackwell Publishing, 2006). Most of the facts and dates discussed have been derived from this important study.

and his somewhat cryptic stance toward the philosophy of Heidegger, but more importantly his continued championing of the philosophy of Bergson, which had been gradually rejected by the French academy under the name of 'spiritualism' (what is now called 'vitalism'), as well as a complimentary alliance with the philosophy of 'immanentism' (i.e., Spinozism and empiricism). I think it is also significant to note that in his tutelage under Hyppolite, the Hegelian and pre-structuralist, Deleuze chooses as his topic for his thesis Hume, which becomes his first book in 1953, *Empiricism and Subjectivity*. Of course, this will have some implications for his reading of Kant published ten years later in 1964, as I will return to discuss in more detail below.

As for Lyotard, his first major study, submitted for the *Doctorat d'État* in 1971, is primarily derived from structuralism and psychoanalysis applied to the fields of language and the plastic arts, but his earliest work is the theoretical study of *Phenomenology*, in 1954, which is described later on as a 'phenomenological episode'. Consequently, his reactions to both phenomenology and to Heidegger will be very distinctive from Deleuze, and what could be said to distinguish their projects is Lyotard's constant attention to ethical questions and to the notion of History and the 'Life world' [*Lebenswelt*] that particularly marks his reading of Kant in the pages of his 'philosophy book', *Le Differend*, but most significantly, the later emphasis on the concept of enthusiasm in both aesthetic and political phenomena. This later becomes the exclusive focus of his reading of the *Critique of Judgment*, especially concerning the question of what he will call the translatability [*analogia*] of idioms, or phrase regimens, between moral and aesthetic categories, which is the primary topic of the second part of Kant's thesis concerning the possibility of a systematically unified philosophy.

And yet, I would argue that there is yet another 'culture' that the generation of Deleuze and Lyotard shared in their formative years, which is not at all a tradition of philosophy, but rather specifically a culture of modernist art, and which can be signaled by the proper names of Nietzsche and Rimbaud, both of whom can first be identified with the statement: 'I am a bastard'.

## THE 'GROTESQUE LIMB' IN THE EXPOSITION OF THE THIRD CRITIQUE

To illustrate the above thesis, I will examine the importation of a certain concept of taste drawn from modernist art, which in the case of both Deleuze and Lyotard, influences their reading of the Third Critique. In this regard, I find it interesting that 'bastard' is also the technical name that French viniculture gives to a 'second rate wine', which results from grafting an impure or hybrid stem onto the trunk of the original vine. Likewise, I would argue that Deleuze and Lyotard's readings of the Third Critique are also bastards in the sense that they have grafted a stem from modernist art onto the appendage of the Kantian system. That appendage, of course, is the section that Kant himself calls a 'mere appendage' [*einen blossen Anhang*], where he introduces a 'divergence of method' for treating the analytic of the beautiful (in section 24) – one which, moreover, requires a subdivision between the mathematical and dynamically sublime. At this point, Kant introduces what he calls a 'theory' of the sublime as a 'mere appendage' [*einen blossen Anhang*], because it gives on the whole no indication of finality in nature, but only the possible employment [*Gebrauch*] of our intuitions by inducing a feeling [*fühlbar*] of finality in ourselves that is independent of the concept of finality in nature (hence, the departure from the First Critique).

Briefly turning to Deleuze's introductory work on Kant, the main body of the original volume contains a systematic and didactic exposition of the three critiques and a definition of the major terms of the Kantian system, which appears more like an examination of a machine to understand its various parts and how they work together to produce a system (as a prelude to the work of dismantling the Kantian framework that becomes the explicit goal of *Difference and Repetition*). The originality of Deleuze's interpretation, however, appears in the emphasis placed on the Third Critique rather than on the First, especially concerning the concept of the sublime in its 'dynamic representation'. The English translation, published in 1984, contains a new Preface, 'On Four Poetic Formulas which Might Summarize Kantian Philosophy', and it is here that we find the most succinct formulation of the meaning of the Kantian 'event' in modern philosophy (i.e., 'the Copernican turn').

Most importantly, it is significant to note that all the major tenants are summarised by literary statements (e.g., Hamlet's 'Time is out of joint', Rimbaud's 'Je est un autre', Kafka's 'the Good is what the law says', and again Rimbaud's poetic phrase 'a disorder of all the senses'). It is in the last formula that Deleuze finds in Kant's theory of the sublime the possibility of an 'unregulated free-play or discordant accord of the faculties', which is later on compared to the role that dissonance plays in modern music, and thus, the basis for a principle of experimentation in both aesthetics, politics, and moral philosophy, a thesis that was later applied in works written with Guattari post-1968. As he writes of this fourth moment:

Thus we have the *Critique of Judgment* as the foundation of Romanticism. It is an aesthetic of the beautiful and sublime in which the sensible is valid in itself and unfolds a pathos beyond all logic, which will grasp time in its surging forth, in its very origin of its thread and its giddiness. It is no longer the Affect of the *Critique of Pure Reason*, which related the Ego to the I in a relationship that was ever regulated by the order of time; it is a Pathos that leaves them to evolve freely in order to form strange combinations as sources of time; 'arbitrary forms of possible intuitions'.[7]

In commentating on this passage, my first observation is that it may not be completely accurate to ascribe this moment to Romanticism – at least, not in the sense that it is immediately described in the sentences that follow – since 'Nature' is not revealed as the causality of this 'discordant accord of the faculties'. In fact, as I will return to later on in reference to Lyotard's reading, it is strictly the discovery of a feeling of finality without Nature, and of the 'pathological' quality of this intuition that is aligned more closely with a major tenant of the modernist artwork as an autonomous (or, at least, 'exceptional') sphere of experience that 'evolves freely' in order to produce 'arbitrary forms of possible intuitions'. In other words, this is not the garden-variety sublime of Wordsworth and Coleridge, but rather the pathological feeling of Rimbaud, 'a disorder of all the senses', and especially of the one figure nowhere named, but everywhere present in the description of a pathos of pure time 'in its surging forth, in its thread and its giddiness' – Marcel Proust.

Let us recall that in the same year Deleuze published the first edition of *Proust and Signs* (1964), which concludes with the chapter on 'the Image of Thought' where we also find – almost in exactly the same terms as described above – an order of the sensible that is 'valid in itself and unfolds a pathos beyond all logic'; although here, this sensible order is produced by the work of art and not by nature, thus even approaching a 'disorder of the senses', or a violent encounter that wrests thought from its natural stupor and complacency. As Deleuze writes, 'the *Leitmotif* of Time regained is the word *force*: impressions that force us to look, encounters that force us to interpret, expressions that force us to think'.[8] Moreover, '[w]hat forces us to think is a sign', which is the impression of an arbitrary encounter that causes violence to the previous arrangement

---

[7] Gilles Deleuze, 'On Four Poetic Formulas that might Summarize Kantian Philosophy', in *Essays Critical and Clinical*, trans. Daniel W. Smith and Michael Greco (Minneapolis: University of Minnesota Press, 1997), p. 32.

[8] Gilles Deleuze, *Proust and Signs*, trans. Richard Howard (London: Athlone Press, 2000), p. 95.

of the faculties, which cause them 'to struggle against one another like wrestlers, with one faculty pushing another to its maximum or limit, forcing each to go beyond their previous limits' (that is, exactly in the same terms that Deleuze later describes the nature of the force that appears in the struggle between the faculties of reason and imagination in the encounter of the sublime).[9] Here, I think we have discovered the specific source of the pathos that is later on ascribed (or actually 're-discovered') in Kant's Third Critique: it is the specific 'Affect' that belongs to the Proustian intuition of time as the source of the 'arbitrary forms of possible intuitions' that is grafted onto what was already for Kant, a mere appendage. It would not be an exaggeration to state that it is upon this 'monstrous appendage', which has now grown to encompass the entire trajectory of the *Critique of Judgment*, that the emphasis on the pathological character of the sublime in subsequent postmodern readings is launched. One might even argue, on the basis of the success of this reversal or inversion, that it now appears to readers who have inherited this tradition of reading Kant's Third Critique that the analytic of the beautiful is in fact only a bastard appendage grafted onto the theory of the sublime!

Of course, the above observations only serve to identify the origin and nature of what Deleuze himself will later describe as 'the monstrous and bastard child' that he gave to Kant as his own offspring. The question for us to resolve, however, will not be whether we might call this child legitimate, but rather in what ways our 'feeling' for the sublime has changed as well, and how the specific pathos that now corresponds to the force of the sublime, 'as a feeling of finality in ourselves that is independent of the concept of finality in nature', has evolved in relation to the work of art through the period of modernism and postmodernism. As is well known from Adorno's interpretation of the modernist artwork written around the same period as Deleuze's own account, the emphasis on the sublime, rather than on the analytic of the beautiful, appears as a historical progression because the Kantian theory of sublime is most consistent with the psychology that determines the experience of artwork in the modernist period, and which explicitly commences with the figure of Rimbaud. As he writes, 'the modern . . . is not a chronological concept but a Rimbaudian postulate of an art of the most advanced consciousness, an art in which the most progressive and differentiated technical procedures are saturated with the most progres-

---

[9] Gilles Deleuze, *Essays Critical and Clinical*, p. 34.

sive and differentiated experiences'.[10] Here, let us also recall that the inquiry into the origin of the ideas of the beautiful and the sublime are placed in the Third Critique under the rubric of psychology or empirical psychology. In one sense, the historical exaggeration of the feeling of the sublime, both with respect to a lack of imagination and the power to find a corresponding form of nature in the presentation of an aesthetic judgement (i.e., negative quantities), partly corresponds to the evolution (or, rather, the de-evolution) of the idea of finality of the artwork in modernism, which is more concerned with negativity, lack, deformation, and increasing 'abstraction'. In other words, the exaggeration has to do with the changing psychological conditions of the artwork historically, and it is seemingly as simple as that. According to this thesis, the exaggeration placed on this moment in the Kantian exposition is akin to an evolutionary leap in the field of culture, whereby the original state of exception is converted into a normative rule that can be actually deduced from the experience of the modern artwork. Consequently, what in the Kantian exposition was originally phrased in a purely speculative or theoretical form becomes in the postmodern phrasing merely deduced from the actual aesthetic experience, and thus an analytical phrase that now belongs to the concept of modern art.

## LIABILITY, OR THE MORAL FEELING OF THE SUBLIME

At this point, let me return to Lyotard's passage above to underline three associations or presuppositions that might already represent an interpretation of the historical or dialectical meaning accorded to the sublime, almost in the sense of begging the question 'why is the sublime a modern feeling par excellence?' This is most consistently argued in the following passage from *Lessons on the Analytic of the Sublime*:

> The analytic of the sublime is negative because it introduces an aesthetic without nature. We call it modern in the same way we call Rabelais or Hamlet modern. I would even venture to say that, in view of this analytic and everything in Western thought that had been building toward it . . . the aesthetic in general, which is the modern thought of art (which takes the place of the poetics of natural order that had become impossible), contains from the moment of its appearance the promise of its disappearance. Despite the efforts of speculative thought and Romanticism, at the end of the nineteenth century, confidence in natural forms was shaken, and

---

[10] Theodore Adorno, *Aesthetic Theory*, trans. Robert Hullot-Kentor (Minneapolis: University of Minnesota Press, 1997), p. 33.

beyond forms or in their very depth, thought was made liable, *empfänglich*, for something that did not speak to it in good and proper form.[11]

In commenting on this passage, my first observation concerns the casual and somewhat remarkable statement that the sublime is modern 'in the same way we call Rabelais or Hamlet modern'. One should immediately ask who is the 'we' here and in what way have Rabelais or Hamlet been established as modern in the same way as the sublime? This is an analogy that cannot be naturally deduced, but must be understood as a dominant aesthetic judgement. (Moreover, we might wonder if this statement expresses a certain influence by Deleuze's famous interpretation of Hamlet's statement 'time is out of bounds'.) My second observation concerns the implicit teleology that Lyotard is evoking in the statement that the appearance of the sublime is the final appearance (which is to say the disappearance of the concept of the work of art in correspondence with nature or natural forms) that 'everything in Western thought has been building toward it' (even since Longinus' treatise) and culminates in the nineteenth century with the end of the art. In order words, how is this inner teleology deduced from the appearance of the sublime in the Kantian moment, which makes no reference to the history of the artwork?

My third observation, and potential criticism, concerns the use of the term 'liable for' (*assujettissement*, a term also frequently employed by Foucault) for the German *empfänglich* to depict the relationship between thinking and sensible nature (or natural forms). It would seem accidental or arbitrary that the French terms '*être susceptible*', '*responsabilité*', '*assujettissement*', allow for an aesthetic sensitivity (or physiological susceptibility of the human senses) to be translated immediately into a moral idea. We might ask whether this idea belongs to Kant's own analysis or is interpolated in order to express what is, after all, a very modern feeling concerning the question of aesthetic judgement. In other words, how does thinking become responsible or liable for its images? Or rather, how does the form-making power of thought become potentially libellous? Of course, even in Kant, thinking (served by the imagination or the faculty of presentation) would be potentially libellous if it were to appeal to its own form-making powers to represent the experience. It would be lying, or worse, producing a transcendental illusion.

As Lyotard defines this aspect in simpler terms, 'the sublime denies the imagination the power of forms, just as it denies nature the power

---

[11] Jean-François Lyotard, *Lessons on the Analytic of the Sublime*, trans. Elizabeth Rottenberg (Palo Alto: Stanford University Press, 1994), p. 54.

to immediately affect thinking with forms', thus, introducing a feeling of negativity, a lack of form, passivity, and susceptibility to formlessness.[12] Here, however, Lyotard employs a technical and legal term to translate what in the German is merely a 'receptivity, or susceptibility', concerning a physiological-psychological inclination, but which could in some cases also be used to designate a weakness or moral failing, even 'concupiscence' to use a Levinasian term for this same moment in Kant's treatment of the passivity felt by the imagination to the idea. Thus, in the presentation of the sublime, thinking is receptive or susceptible to 'that which does not speak to it in good or proper form'. In this sense, one could also say that thinking is susceptible to what is pathological, obscene, even monstrous, and thus is drawn to potentially libellous forms of social experience. Recalling Kant's own example of the prohibition of images in the Jewish religion as the most sublime of expressions, one cannot help but to feel that this 'denial of form', and particularly the denial to natural psychology of its own cognitive powers, has something of a moral probation that is translated into the aesthetic experience from that moment onward, historically speaking. Henceforth, the concept of the modern artwork becomes, after Baudelaire at least, a play with the limits of the *unpresentable* as both an aesthetic and sociable faculty of the imagination. The concept of art as a faculty of presentation is of an idea of 'negativity', that is, a critique of the sensible appearance that no longer finds its lawful and form-giving powers in nature and often appears in opposition to forms of social interest. Thus, modern art becomes the expression *sine qua non* of man's unsocial sociability, a sentiment also shared by Adorno when he writes, 'artworks organized by a subject are capable *tant bien que mal* of what a society organized by social subjects does not allow [. . .]'.[13]

Returning to the paradoxical example of the moral prohibition against images in reference to the Jewish religion, we find that *something is presented*, nevertheless. In the case of the commandment, 'Thou shall not make any image', it is not simply a command or a prohibition, but rather the expression of a divine enthusiasm that inspires the Jewish religion to restrain itself from making an image, or in the Kantian understanding, to become 'unbounded' (*unbegrenzt*) from any sensuous presentation, which produces an enthusiasm that sometimes borders on fanaticism (*Schwärmerei*), but nevertheless remains sublime in its strict observation and religious zeal. Ironically, it is the prohibition that

---

[12] Ibid.
[13] Adorno, *Aesthetic Theory*, p. 33.

'releases' or 'liberates' the imagination – it does not constrain the imagination onto another presentation – even though it provides nothing sensuous to take the place of the sensuous presentation, except that is, a pure feeling of an infinite that is without comparison. In the famous passage that concludes section 27, Kant writes:

> There need be no anxiety that the feeling of the sublime will lose anything through such an abstract presentation, which becomes entirely negative in regard to the sensible; for the imagination, although it certainly finds nothing beyond the sensible to which it can attach itself, nevertheless feels itself to be unbounded because of this elimination of the limits of sensibility; and that separation is thus a presentation of the infinite, which for that reason can never be anything other than a merely negative presentation, which nevertheless expands the soul.[14]

Here, the negative term does not only refer to the absence of an outward sensuous presentation, but rather to an expression of a subjective intensity that is the cause of enthusiasm. However, Lyotard gives to this moment a definition of the impulse for abstraction [*Abstraktion*] that is subsequently linked to this moment of modern art, since 'what is required for this abstract presentation, which presents nothingness, is the imagination be "unbounded" [*unbegrenzt*]'. Thus, as he goes on to speculate, 'this would be a good point of departure for a philosophy of abstract art. If the aesthetics of Romanticism is certainly linked to a philosophy of the sublime, so called abstract art would be at its most radical emanation and perhaps its exit route [. . .]'.[15]

Following Lyotard's explicit comparison of the inner teleology of the sublime to the historical appearance of abstract art, in its general repulsion from the figure (from representation), the abstract presentation is also felt as an 'unbounded' liberation from the figure and potentially an infinite possibility of presentation. At the same time, perhaps in analogy to the sublime prohibition against images, this aesthetic enthusiasm becomes socially instituted in the concept of taste and communicated as a prohibition of the figure itself, at least, its demotion to the rank of an outmoded and plebian art form, and sometimes even appears as a historical judgement against all forms of figural art. Deleuze, for his part, will also return to underscore the logic of figuration and abstraction in relation to the painter Francis Bacon in the *Logic of Sensation* (1981).

[14] Immanuel Kant, *Critique of the Power of Judgment*, trans. Paul Guyer and Eric Matthews (Cambridge: Cambridge University Press, 2000), p. 156.

[15] Jean-François Lyotard, *Enthusiasm: The Kantian Critique of History*, trans. Georges van den Abbeele (Palo Alto: Stanford University Press, 2009), p. 31.

However, unlike other modern painters who have broken with figuration (either through symbolism or abstraction), Deleuze underscores the aspect of Bacon's strategy to break with figuration by isolating the figure itself within a field of sensation and by creating a system of coloration that Deleuze defines in terms of 'rhythm' (also recalling the importance of this concept in his other works, including *A Thousand Plateaus*).[16] In both examples, we find the condition of the passage to the 'critical' which refers to a form of judgement as well as the subjective quality of enthusiasm that results from being 'unbounded' from the figure as a particular sensuous source of representation, or in the faculty of desire, from a form of interest. The critical enthusiasm would not therefore be merely negative, resulting from a prohibition, but primarily affirmative and resulting from a state of being unbounded, even though this critical enthusiasm sometimes communicated in the form of a severe and critical sociability. In other words, its outward form is negative, a prohibition against all form, but its condition and inner form is positive.

In conclusion, perhaps what is at stake here is what Kant calls 'an awakening' of 'a purely intellectual feeling' [*Geistesgefühl*], and it is this feeling alone that is worthy of the name 'sublime'. But here, we return to the nature of what makes this possible in the first place, which is not to be found in nature, but rather in a moment where the object of nature is inadequate or missing. Subjectively, what makes us susceptible to ideas? As Kant stresses, 'the disposition of the mind to the feeling of the sublime requires its receptivity [*eine Empfänglichkeit*] to ideas'.[17] Here again, let us recall the term 'liability' was used to translate what is technically, susceptibility. Liability can also be translated by the terms obligation, responsibility – even indicating negatively the breach of responsibility or obligation. In the above discussion of 'negative feeling' as actually an expression of being unbounded from a presentation, we might now understand this passage, particularly in the sense that the obligation becomes communicated as a social form in the aesthetic judgement. The human being as such is liable to become aroused by ideas, to find them the source of a greater enthusiasm and pleasure than in sensuous representations or forms of mere enjoyment, to be pushed to a greater extreme, even dangerous extremes by ideas. It is in this sense that what is at first a susceptibility or receptivity becomes the occasion for libel or scandal, even fanaticism. As Kant says, it is culture that produces in the

---

[16] Gilles Deleuze, *Francis Bacon: The Logic of Sensation*, trans. Daniel W. Smith (London: Continuum, 2003), pp. 34–43.

[17] Kant, *Critique of the Power of Judgment*, p. 148.

rational being an aptitude for any ends that may please him, because it is culture alone that makes people 'more susceptible to ideas'; however, in another passage, he also argues 'the judgement of the sublime in nature requires a certain culture'.[18] But what culture produces such an aptitude, a critical susceptibility? Would this not be the spirit of the culture of modernist art?

[18] Ibid.

Chapter 15

# Chronos is Sick: Deleuze, Antonioni and the Kantian Lineage of Modern Cinema

*Gregory Flaxman*

> My aim is to arrive at a fabulous conception of time.
>
> Gilles Deleuze, *Lecture on Kant*[1]

### KINO-KANT

This essay begins with what is, arguably, the signatory stroke of Gilles Deleuze's engagement with the cinema. In *The Movement-Image* and, especially, *The Time-Image*, Deleuze suggests that the cinema repeats, on its own terms and under its own conditions, the 'revolution' that shaped modern philosophy. Prior to their respective upheavals, the history of philosophy and the history of film were characterised by a kind of *classicism* that consigned time to the order of number, space and movement. Where classical philosophy determined time by bringing it 'into line with laws which saved movement, extensive movement of the world or intensive movement of the soul',[2] classical cinema organised time by bringing it into line with the laws of continuity editing and the sensory-motor schematisation of movements. On this basis, Deleuze argues, philosophy and cinema undergo corresponding transformations: in both cases, the regime of enumerated, conserved and indirect time eventually gives way to a direct confrontation with time. 'Over several centuries, from the Greeks to Kant, a revolution took place in philosophy, the subordination of time to movement was reversed', Deleuze writes, but what does it really mean to say that a 'similar story appears in the cinema'?[3]

---

[1] Gilles Deleuze, 'Seminar on Kant: 14/03/1978', trans. Melissa McMahon, available at <http://www.webdeleuze.com/php/texte.php?cle=66&groupe=Kant&langue=2> (last accessed 10 October 2014).

[2] Gilles Deleuze, *Cinema 2: The Time-Image*, trans. Hugh Tomlinson and Robert Galeta (Minneapolis: University of Minnesota Press, 1989), p. 39.

[3] Ibid.

This question lies at the heart of Deleuze's philosophy of cinema, but I suspect that some version of it – some articulation of the relationship between moving image and thought – defines the fundamental premise of what we have come to call 'film-philosophy'. Before it circumscribes a field or determines a discipline, film-philosophy insists on the more than merely arbitrary connection of its terms. This affirmation has grown ever more confident in recent years, but perhaps the unwitting cost of this evolution is that we gloss the most fundamental of questions. What makes the cinema a *necessary* subject for philosophy, a provocation or encounter that induces us to think? The question has a long history in classical film criticism, and Deleuze runs through an extensive lineage, but perhaps more than any of his predecessors, he elaborates the moving image as an intrinsically philosophical problem. Cinema introduces not only real movement but, also, a new 'form of time'[4] into thought, and this insight underwrites a history of modern film that redoubles that of modern philosophy. Indeed, Deleuze regards the 'form of time' as an unmistakably Kantian invention, and I suggest that, per the cinema, he devises a properly Kantian concept, the time-image. Above all, the essay to follow concerns the unsuspected proximity of Kant's critical philosophy and modern cinema: on the basis of Deleuze's return to Kant in the late 1970s, I argue that what critical philosophy inaugurates, the time-image consummates – the formation of a Kino-Kant.

Despite its notoriety, the pairing of Kant's critical philosophy and modern cinema is seldom subject to serious scrutiny. For this reason, we might begin by sketching the two histories, or revolutions, that compose this curious formulation. On the one hand, Deleuze argues that Kant marks a decisive shift in the history of philosophy: by introducing time into thought, the transcendental method irrevocably breaks with a longstanding philosophical tradition. Plato famously reduced time to the 'moving image of eternity',[5] and the transcendent sphere of Ideas or Essences endures in the definition of time as cardinal (reduced to number) and modal (reduced to attributes). What changes? Doubtless, the revolution of critical philosophy is inseparable from 'a very long scientific evolution',[6] and the *Critique of Pure Reason* duly makes Copernicus' method its precursor and Newton's physics its corollary. But Deleuze's

---

[4]  Ibid. p. 130.

[5]  Plato, *Complete Works*, ed. John M. Cooper and D. S. Hutchinson (Indianapolis, IN: Hackett Publishing, 1997), p. 1241 (37d).

[6]  Gilles Deleuze, 'Seminar on Kant: 21/03/1978', trans. Melissa McMahon, available at <http://www.webdeleuze.com/php/texte.php?cle=67&groupe=Kant&langue=2> (last accessed 10 October 2014).

point is that, philosophically speaking, we 'have to wait for Kant to carry out the great reversal'[7] – the *insubordination* of time – because the first *Critique* makes this reversal a matter of the philosophy itself. Time 'takes on a philosophical status' that is not only original but originary; as Deleuze says, 'Everything happens as if time "deployed itself" [*se déployait*].'[8] Where ancient and even classical philosophy conceived of time in relation to predetermined circles and cycles, critical philosophy unravels time in the transcendental line of a new consciousness, as if by losing its circular route the line eventuates a wholly new existence. No longer anticipated in ideal forms, nor bound by spatial determinations, nor even attached to measurable movements, time is sprung from the cosmic wheel. Time is uncoiled in the 'labyrinth' (Borges) of a straight line,[9] provided that straight does not mean predictable or teleological but, on the contrary, *unhinged*.

On the other hand, Deleuze argues that the history of cinema undergoes a transformation of its own whereby the regime of conserved and represented movement gives way to a direct image of time. Having outlined the Kantian revolution, Deleuze suggests that, *mutatis mutandis*, the cinema repeats 'the same experience, the same reversal, in more fast-moving circumstances'.[10] To this end, *The Time-Image* develops an account of cinematic evolution on the basis of a break in the sensory-motor linkages that had dominated classical cinema. Broadly construed, Deleuze argues that the history of classical cinema (above all, classical Hollywood cinema) bears witness to the development of the means of organising images – a 'system of continuity' – based on linking perception and action. Like Bergson, Deleuze regards received perception and executed action, the sensory and the motor, in relation to provisional centres of indetermination that anchor images and distribute movement. What changes? The system of sensory-motor continuity is disrupted, detoured, even destroyed. The reasons for this collapse are at once complex and obscure; Deleuze mentions the Second World War, economic turmoil, decolonisation, as well as the global proliferation of images, advertisements and clichés. In this context, *The Time-Image* elaborates its eponymous concept on the basis of a series of post-war (and, to be sure, largely European) cinematic traditions. From the

---

[7] Ibid.

[8] Ibid.

[9] Ibid. In Borges' 'Death and the Compass', the labyrinth 'is a single straight line'. Jorge Luis Borges, *Ficciones*, trans. Anthony Kerrigan (New York: Grove Press, 1994), p. 141.

[10] Deleuze, *The Time-Image*, p. xi.

efflorescence of Italian Neorealism to the subsequent New Waves that
swept across a number of European cinemas in the 60s and 70s, Deleuze
traces the development of a new idea of cinema based on 'aberrant
movement' and the 'irrational cut'.[11] An eye-line is mismatched with
a perception (Bresson); the unfolding of a drama precipitates a hiatus
of pure duration (Ozu); a graphic match displaces the same character,
without justification, from one place and time to another (Resnais): in
each case, the invention of erratic or false continuity creates images
without measure, irreducible to number, space and movement, so that
time 'rises up to the surface of the screen'.[12]

If this claim remains (after thirty years!) still so difficult to grasp,
perhaps the reason is that we have not yet come to understand what it
means to say that the cinema becomes Kantian. As Deleuze writes, 'the
time-image is no longer empirical, nor metaphysical; it is "transcendental", in the sense that Kant gives this word: time is out of joint and presents itself in the pure state'.[13] Naturally, this assertion raises significant
questions, but the audacity of the claim ought to provoke a measure of
incomprehension. How can we read philosophy, much less Kant's philosophical revolution, in relation to the cinematic image? How can we
read the cinema, much less the emergence of a modern cinema, in light
of what 'happened a very long time ago in philosophy'?[14] Published
roughly a hundred years before the first successful experiments with
the kinetoscope and cinematograph, Kant's first *Critique* initially seems
to have little in common with the mechanical production of moving
images. Even if we overlooked the sheer anachronism, there's little
reason to think that critical philosophy and modern cinema (or any
cinema, for that matter) demand to be brought together. Given as much,
and a great deal more we could add, readers may suspect me of having
doubled down on the most fragile of suggestions. Notwithstanding
Deleuze's perverse sense of commentary – 'One imagines a *philosophically* bearded Hegel, a *philosophically* clean-shaven Marx'[15] – the
project to create a Kino-Kant would seem to be no more than 'an
analogy in thought'.[16]

[11] These terms appear throughout *The Time-Image*. For 'aberrant movement' see, especially, ibid. pp. 36–41, 128–9; for 'irrational cut' see ibid. pp. 182–3, 214–15, 278–9.
[12] Ibid. p. xi.
[13] Ibid. p. 271.
[14] Ibid. p. ix.
[15] Gilles Deleuze, *Difference and Repetition*, trans. Paul Patton (New York: Columbia
University Press, 1995), p. xxii.
[16] Deleuze, *The Time-Image*, p. 39.

In this light, consider for a moment the network of relations, resonances, affinities and intersections with which Deleuze binds critical
philosophy and cinema. While Kant assumes an important if circum-
scribed role in *The Movement-Image*,[17] he plays a crucial part in the
second cinema book, appearing 'on-screen' in the analyses of post-war
European cinema and informing extensive discussions about reflective
judgement,[18] the 'heautonomy' of the audio-visual image,[19] and the
'transcendental' status of time itself.[20] The relation between cinema and
critical philosophy doesn't suffer from a dearth of evidence but, rather,
from its excess. Where and how to begin? For the purpose of this discussion, I want to consider the line that leads from critical qua transcendental philosophy to the 'transcendental representation' of time in modern
cinema (i.e., the time-image). My discussion leads from Deleuze's return
to Kant's critical philosophy, to Hölderlin's tragic interpretation of
Kantianism, to the emblematically modern cinema of Michelangelo
Antonioni, and while this seems an idiosyncratic itinerary, I think it
unfolds a vital line of philosophical development. Not only does this
trajectory disclose the formulations of time that Deleuze associates (via
Hölderlin) with critical philosophy, but it recasts those formulations (via
Antonioni) in terms of the time-image. Ultimately, as I hope will become
clear, nothing could be further from the model of analogy, which invariably subjects differences to a common measure, than the measureless-
ness of the time-image.

## TIME IS TRANSCENDENTAL

While *The Time-Image* naturally consummates the development of a
Kino-Kant, this conjunction is catalysed by a series of lectures Deleuze
gave on Kant almost ten years earlier (1978). These lectures mark a
crucial transformation in the long arc of his encounters with critical philosophy. Heretofore, Deleuze regarded Kantianism as both indispensible
and regrettable. Precisely because critique 'seemed equipped to overturn'
the model of thought that had dominated western philosophy,[21] Deleuze
cast Kant's 'respectful' exercise of critique as a betrayal, a capitulation

---

[17] Gilles Deleuze, *Cinema 1: The Movement-Image*, trans. Hugh Tomlinson and Barbara
Habberjam (Minneapolis: University of Minnesota Press, 1986), pp. 46–55.
[18] Deleuze, *The Time-Image*, pp. 186–7.
[19] Ibid. pp. 251ff.
[20] Ibid. p. 271.
[21] Deleuze, *Difference and Repetition*, p. 136.

to 'recognition or representation'.[22] Readers are likely to point out that this is precisely why Deleuze is compelled to go beyond (*dépasser*) Kant's transcendental idealism and, especially in *Difference and Repetition*, to invent his own 'transcendental empiricism'.[23] But inasmuch as this explanation makes sense of the early writings, it doesn't jibe with Deleuze's later work, when the Kantian subject reveals a delirious and revolutionary line of time leading beyond representation.[24] This line leads, finally, to the time-image itself, and one could justly argue that this concept owes as much to Kant as to any other philosopher – and perhaps more.

Having said almost nothing about Kant since *Difference and Repetition* (1968), Deleuze devoted a month of his 1978 seminar at Vincennes to critical philosophy. Elsewhere, I've described in greater detail the subtle but decisive revisions these lectures devise, but in the present context we can only afford to summarise this transformation.[25] Consider the fundamental project of the first *Critique*, namely, to give philosophy, based as it is in pure qua speculative reason, the 'secure course of a science'.[26] In order to vanquish error, opinion and illusion, Kant proposes to turn to *a priori* concepts: independent of the contingencies and vicissitudes of experience, such concepts are the 'standard and example of all apodictic (philosophical) certainty'.[27] Nevertheless, when Kant describes the failures of all previous exercises of speculative reason, he insists that the downfall of philosophy consists in having abandoned 'any touchstone of experience'.[28] Indeed, the danger of idealism is that, without experience, it carries us off into illusions: quite literally, metaphysics becomes too metaphysical. Hence, the *Critique of Pure Reason* derives from a problem, namely, how to make experience the

---

[22] Ibid. When he asks if it is 'really Kant's prestigious contribution to have introduced time into thought' (ibid. p. 87), Deleuze equivocates. In *Difference and Repetition*, Hölderlin, Kierkegaard, Péguy and Klossowski are more truly the 'culmination' of the Kantian problem – the 'third synthesis of time' or what I call transcendental status of time (ibid. p. 95) – than Kant himself.

[23] Ibid. pp. 56–7.

[24] The one great exception to this characterisation would have to be Deleuze's essay 'To Have Done with Judgment' (included in *Essays Critical and Clinical*, trans. Daniel W. Smith and Michael A. Greco (Minneapolis: University of Minnesota Press, 1992)), which once again envisions Kant as the architect of judgement.

[25] My essay on this subject, 'The Transcendental Line: Deleuze and the Transformation of Kant's Critical Philosophy', is forthcoming in *Deleuze Studies*.

[26] Immanuel Kant, *Critique of Pure Reason*, trans. Paul Guyer and Allen W. Wood (Cambridge: Cambridge University Press, 1999), Bvii.

[27] Ibid. Axv.

[28] Ibid. A711.

'checkup' on that which, by definition, cannot contain any shred of empiricism.[29]

For Deleuze, the fundamental problem here, the relation of thought and time, characterises the first *Critique* from end to end. While the task of determining the domain of understanding and the uses of reason defines Kant's profoundly conservative project, this project is contingent on a revolutionary pursuit: the imposition of the limit is achieved by introducing time itself directly into thought. The forms of space and time circumscribe the use of our faculties and the rights of our judgement: they inflict the very finitude on knowledge that defines the subject as such. Thus, it's precisely because appearances claim a phenomenal existence, because they are experienced in space and time, that Kant says we can never know 'things in themselves' (*noumena*). The limits of the subject are inscribed by the form of time, the result of which is that time 'acquire[s] a constitutive power [*pouvoir*] which will be the constitutive power of all possible experience'.[30] In other words, time becomes the genetic element, the groundless ground that underwrites even *a priori* concepts; with this suggestion, the axis of critical philosophy shifts. Where Deleuze formerly described the condition of possibility as Kant's crude means of capturing experience ('the net is so loose that the largest fish pass through'),[31] now he affirms time itself as 'the form under which an existence is determinable'.[32] The very sense of a limit changes with Kant: no longer that which 'limits the world' or 'an operation which limits something' in the world, the limit derives from the line of time that traverses the subject, carves out our interiority and orients thought.[33]

In the lectures, Deleuze tells his audience, 'I would simply like you to begin to feel the importance of this time which becomes a straight line':[34] this does not mean a 'simplification of the figure of time' but, rather, 'an intense complication'.[35] In fact, Deleuze elaborates the Kantian figure of time on the basis of three formulas: (1) Hamlet's phrase 'the time is out of joint', (2) Kant's own phrase, 'self-affection', and (3) Rimbaud's phrase, 'I is an Other'. The discussion to follow adumbrates these formulas as the basis for a Kino-Kant, but in order to flash forward to the

[29] Ibid. Bxx.
[30] Deleuze, 'Seminar on Kant: 14/03/1978'.
[31] Deleuze, *Difference and Repetition*, p. 68.
[32] Deleuze, 'Seminar on Kant: 21/03/1978'.
[33] Ibid.
[34] Ibid.
[35] Ibid.

cinema, I want to follow Deleuze's flashback, in these lectures, to Greek tragedy. This might seem a curiously dated basis on which to understand modern philosophy, much less modern cinema, but the incongruity dissolves when we understand that the recourse to the ancients is conducted under the auspices of Friedrich Hölderlin. The romantic poet and critic was deeply influenced by critical philosophy, and Deleuze calls him 'one of Kant's best disciples'.[36] More specifically, Deleuze argues that Hölderlin's poetic accounts of Greek tragedy unfold nothing less than Kant's figures of time: the disjointed line of time, the intervallic time of the caesura, and the borderline traversing the subject.

We have already said that the Kantian revolution consists in breaking the circle of time, at once natural and divine, that held sway over the ancient world, and this forms our point of departure. In the *Timaeus*, Deleuze recalls, Plato describes how the demiurge created the cosmos by bending time into the circular orbits of planets that can be plotted in the repetition of days and nights, lunar cycles and tides, months and seasons, years and other circles we cannot see.[37] Bending time means making it conform to spatial, numerical and cosmological constants, and in effect Deleuze will follow Hölderlin's analysis of the tragedy to both adumbrate and break this circle. Among the Greeks, the circle is given its tragic form by Aeschylus: the arc of the *Oresteia* is shaped according to the limits of justice, which will be exceeded or broken, only to be bent back by the swift imposition of atonement.[38] Deleuze explains:

> The tragic cycle of time is, broadly, like three unequal arcs of a circle; there is the moment of limitation; limitation is nothing other than justice, it's the lot assigned to each. And then there is the transgression of the limitation, the act which transgresses. The moment of the limit is the great Agamemnon; it's the beauty of royal limitation. Then there is the transgression of the limit, which is to say the excessive act [*l'acte de la démesure*]: it's Clytemnestra assassinating Agamemnon. Then there is the long atonement, and the tragic cycle of time is the cycle of limitation, of transgression and of atonement. The atonement is Orestes who will avenge Agamemnon. There will be the re-establishment of the equilibrium of the limit which for a moment was overstepped.[39]

---

[36] Deleuze, 'Seminar on Kant: 14/03/1978'. This exposition is to some extent anticipated in *Difference and Repetition* (pp. 91–2), but what Deleuze has to say about Hölderlin in the lectures goes much further.

[37] Plato, *Complete Works*, pp. 1249–50 (47a).

[38] Aeschylus, *The Oresteia: Agamemnon; The Libation Bearers; The Eumenides*, reprint edn (New York: Penguin Classics, 1984).

[39] Deleuze, 'Seminar on Kant: 21/03/1978'.

Inasmuch as we speak of a straight line, then, the circle must be severed, and this is precisely what happens in Sophocles: 'the circle is ruptured, the line of time irrevocably unravelled'. This, Deleuze adds, is 'the time of Oedipus'.[40] While this affirmation is surprising coming from the co-author of *Anti-Oedipus*, Deleuze subjects the tragedy to a kind of counter-appropriation whereby the hero becomes not only the great Kantian but, as we will see, the avatar of the time-image. In Aeschylus, tragedy had revolved around that which transgresses or 'eludes the limit',[41] but with Sophocles we can no longer speak of transgression or evasion. 'In the case of Oedipus', Deleuze says, 'it's the limit which is elusive. Where is it? It's the limit which becomes passage to the limit.'[42] Deleuze seizes on an expression of Hölderlin's – in so many words, *time ceases to rhyme* – to convey this transformation. Take the *Oresteia*: 'the arc of the time' was bent in such a way as to make the end rhyme with the beginning. Because the transgression of the circle of time was subject to 'atonement', the arc was bent back on itself, returned to the regularity of justice, distributed once more according to the cycles of time. By contrast, in both *Oedipus Rex* and *Oedipus at Colonus*, the circle is broken and the line sprung loose: 'the beginning and the end no longer rhyme'.[43] And how could they? In relation to Oedipus' 'crime', to what justice can one appeal? What atonement could there be? What action could be commensurate to what has transpired? The circle is broken because no return is possible: precisely because the line is disjointed, is straightened, it ceases to be normal, regular and predictable. The subject consists in living this line, but this line provides no spatial coordinates: in the absence of the rhyme that would curve it – in the absence of expectations that could link past and future – the line constitutes the 'zero instant'[44] of a pure present. Following Hölderlin, then, Deleuze calls this line the caesura, and we should take this cut (*écart*) to heart. Before and after exist on either side of this cut, but because they do not rhyme, because they are asymmetrical, the caesura marks both an 'ineffable interval' and an incommensurability.[45] 'Man is no longer anything but the caesura which prevents the before and after from rhyming

[40] Ibid.
[41] Ibid.
[42] Ibid. 'The same word "limit" radically changes in sense', and at this juncture, Deleuze is describing his reading as much as Kant's philosophy.
[43] Ibid.
[44] Ibid.
[45] Ibid.

together, which distributes a before and an after which do not rhyme together'.[46]

For Deleuze, as for Kant, such a line is neither emplotted nor composed of points, since this would only subordinate time to measure and space; in other words, this would leave time to be determined by 'something which happens in it'.[47] In fact, whenever it is represented, the line relegates 'time to a content which measures it'.[48] By contrast, when Kant elaborates 'the pure form of time detached from a movement to measure', Deleuze says, 'it's everything else which is subordinated to time'.[49] By divesting philosophy of Descartes' mechanism, Spinoza's modalism and Leibniz's monadism, Kant forecloses the constellation of fixed Ideas that had ordained the 'classical or ancient consciousness of time'.[50] Detached from essence, from space, and (as we will see) even from movement, the transcendental hero, Oedipus, is no longer 'encircled in a sort of harmony with God': instead, he is consigned to the 'perpetual suspension'[51] of a straight line. This is why Oedipus is called '*atheos*' – not an atheist but one 'who is separated from God'.[52] For Deleuze, the real 'crime' of Oedipus is neither patricide nor incest; instead, the crime is to have severed the circle of time. And as we know, this is also his punishment: Oedipus is henceforth condemned to walk a tightrope of time. The line is perilous because it is not composed of an 'order of possible successions',[53] because it cannot be given reduced to determination or mode, cannot be drawn or represented; rather, time is the form of determination, modality and even movement. For Kant, time is 'the form of everything that changes or moves'.[54]

The significance of this definition emerges when we consider this form in relation to the form of space. As opposed to the categories, which he defined as *a priori* concepts of understanding, Kant defines space and time as *a priori* forms of sensibility (intuition).[55] On the one hand,

[46] Ibid.
[47] Ibid.
[48] Deleuze, 'Seminar on Kant: 14/03/1978'.
[49] Deleuze, 'Seminar on Kant: 21/03/1978'.
[50] Deleuze, 'Seminar on Kant: 14/03/1978'.
[51] Deleuze, 'Seminar on Kant: 21/03/1978'.
[52] Ibid.
[53] Deleuze, 'Seminar on Kant: 14/03/1978'.
[54] Gilles Deleuze, *Kant's Critical Philosophy: The Doctrine of the Faculties*, trans. Hugh Tomlinson and Barbara Habberjam (Minneapolis: University of Minnesota Press, 1985), p. viii.
[55] Kant's elaboration of these forms comprises in the remarkable 'exposition' of the 'Transcendental Aesthetic' which forms the first part of *The Critique of Pure Reason*. See my earlier essay, 'Transcendental Aesthetics: Gilles Deleuze and the Philosophy

Kant defines space as the 'form of exteriority' or 'outer sense'.[56] 'That doesn't mean that it comes from outside', Deleuze says, 'but it means that everything which appears in space appears as exterior to whoever grasps it, and exterior from one thing to another.'[57] Thus, space is the form of appearances, and so absolutely are space and appearance bound that, Kant says, we cannot imagine the absence of space – i.e., even that absence would be envisioned in space. But what of time? This is where things get interesting for Deleuze, since Kant is compelled to follow reason to a remarkable conclusion: if space is 'outer sense', then time must be the 'form of interiority' or 'inner sense'. While the form of space cannot be eradicated, the form of time cannot be substantialised. Precisely because it accommodates everything that changes and moves, time is as an empty form. Without content, irreducible to appearance, the transcendental form of time introduces a kind of caesura into the subject, an interval within which we experience and affect ourselves. In his *Opus Postumum*, Kant returns at length to 'the affection of self by self', and in so doing provides the constituents of the second formula/figure. Self-affection is defined as both time and thought: it is a matter, Deleuze says, of 'thinking time'.[58]

To return once more to Oedipus: the real crime is 'time itself'[59] because this time costs him, so to speak, both divine and natural time: 'God himself is no longer anything but empty time. Man is no longer anything but a caesura in time.'[60] Oedipus describes a cut (*écart*) in the time of the cosmos, but the gap is no less the line of time that traverses the subject. Precisely because the subject is irreducibly divided, thought is compelled to affect or think itself as an Other. In this respect, Deleuze returns once more to Hölderlin's reflections on Oedipus in order to define the third figure of time, whereby the line becomes a borderline, that is, 'something which separates'.[61] Hölderlin writes:

> man forgets himself and the god and turns around like a traitor ... At the most extreme limit of suffering [*Leiden*], there exists nothing but the

---

of Space', in Ian Buchanan and Gregg Lambert (eds), *Deleuze and Space* (Edinburgh: University of Edinburgh Press, 2005), pp. 176–88.

[56] Deleuze, 'Seminar on Kant: 14/03/1978'.

[57] Ibid.

[58] Ibid. In the *Opus Postumum*, Kant writes that all appearances 'relate to the object of intuition insofar as [the subject] is affected by it, and are the subjective element of the subject's self-affection (formally)'. Immanuel Kant, *Opus Postumum*, ed. Eckart Förster and Michael Rosen (Cambridge: Cambridge University Press, 1995), p. 174.

[59] Deleuze, *The Time-Image*, p. 37.

[60] Deleuze, 'Seminar on Kant: 21/03/1978'.

[61] Deleuze, 'Seminar on Kant: 14/03/1978'.

conditions of time and space. At this limit, man forgets himself because he exists entirely within the moment, the God [forgets himself] because he is nothing but time; and either one is unfaithful, time because it is categorically turned away at such a moment, no longer fitting beginning and end; man because at this moment of categorical turning-away he has to follow and thus can no longer resemble the beginning in what follows.[62]

In Aeschylus, of course, the relationship that persisted between God and man had sustained the cyclical time of tragedy as a matter of fate: 'in so far as time is cyclical, there is a sort of God-man relationship which is one with destiny in Greek tragedy'.[63] By contrast, linear time indicates a 'double deviation' whereby both God and man turn away from each other. As Oedipus says, 'Time obliterates, crushes all to nothing. . .'[64]

At the 'limit' of the rift separating God and man, 'nothing in fact remains any more except the conditions of time or of space', and while Deleuze attributes this radical insight to Hölderlin, he adds that 'here Hölderlin is speaking like a Kantian'.[65] Indeed, this reading of ancient tragedy becomes modern, and truly Kantian, when we understand that in the *Critique of Pure Reason* the 'double turning away [*détournement*]'[66] of the human and the divine consists in the division of the subject itself. We have already touched on the origins of this division in the necessity to ground reason in experience, but the ingenuity of Kant's solution constitutes the 'fantastic architecture'[67] of the first *Critique* – the organisation of faculties, the distribution of *a priori* concepts (the categories) in relation to *a priori* forms of experience (space and time), the remarkable pursuit of the means to make these irreducible elements commensurable. Indeed, the fact that space and time are not included as categories, nor even considered concepts, means that the subject is organised around a kind of dehiscence that will precipitate a new sense of philosophy. Whence the third figure of time, 'I in an Other', which Deleuze borrows from Rimbaud to describe how time divides the subject from itself: 'Kant's problem is how the same subject, or self, can have two forms which are irreducible to each', Deleuze says. And there can be no doubt about what's at stake. The Kantian subject is split into two heterogene-

---

[62] Friedrich Hölderlin, *Friedrich Hölderlin: Essays and Letters on Theory*, trans. Thomas Pfau (Albany: State University of New York Press, 1987), pp. 107–8.
[63] Deleuze, 'Seminar on Kant: 21/03/1978'.
[64] Sophocles, *The Three Theban Plays: Antigone; Oedipus the King; Oedipus at Colonus* (New York: Penguin Classics, 1984), p. 322.
[65] Deleuze, 'Seminar on Kant: 21/03/1978'.
[66] Ibid.
[67] Deleuze, 'Seminar on Kant: 14/03/1978'.

ous elements, the forms and the categories, or what Deleuze simply calls *'the form of time and the form of thought'*.[68]

Thus, we return once more to the problem with which we began: how can we 'think time'? To this point, we have suggested that Deleuze's claim, coming out of his reading of Hölderlin, is that critical philosophy presages the encounter that culminates with the time-image. At first glance, however, it's hard to imagine Kant endorsing this conclusion. Inasmuch as the form of space refers to 'outer sense', Kant insists that the form of time refers to inner sense, and this means that time cannot be spatialised or reduced to what appears in space. Precisely because the form of time accommodates the endless variety and variability of appearances, because it conditions the distinct modes of temporal determination (succession, durations, simultaneity), Kant insists that this form must be *empty*: without appearance, image, or even content. How can we affirm a Kantian dimension of the time-image when the philosophy suggests that no image of time can exist? Of course, this paradox lies at the heart of Deleuze's second cinema book, but for this very reason I want to turn, in the remainder of this essay, to a particular filmmaker, Michelangelo Antonioni, whose work cashes out the consequences of this argument and consummates what I have called the Kino-Kant.

THE TIME-IMAGE

My hope is that, by virtue of the digression through Hölderlin, one can appreciate how Deleuze's lectures on critical philosophy inflect the development of the time-image. What Deleuze discovers, particularly in Oedipus, is the expression of the Kantian problem of time – but there's nothing especially theatrical about his analysis. On the contrary, when Deleuze describes Sophocles' tragic hero, dragged along a line of time in *Oedipus Rex* or forced to wander the line *in Oedipus at Colonus*, he envisions a 'perpetual suspension' that is explicitly renewed in his account of a modern cinema. Indeed, this account turns on a paralysis that grips characters and disrupts dramatic action: modern cinema, Deleuze says, produces a 'new race'[69] of 'seers' (*voyants*) whose powers of vision outstrip anything like a capacity to act. 'Sensory-motor situations have given way to pure optical and sound situations to which characters, who have become seers, cannot or will not react, so great is

---

[68] Deleuze, 'Seminar on Kant: 21/03/1978'.
[69] Deleuze, *The Time-Image*, p. xi.

their need to "see" properly what there is in the situation.'[70] No longer prolonged in coherent and contiguous space (extensity), the seers exist solely 'in the interval of movement' (intensity). Thus, we could say that in the absence of action, without spatiological determination, perception gives rise to images of feeling and thinking, affection-images. Inasmuch as we associate this kind of image with the close-up, this image is traditionally tied to that which is seen: for instance, an eye-line match connects the seer to the world, and in turn the world can be construed as the cause of a particular facial expression or the spatial effect of a particular way of seeing. But what happens when the image of seeing does not give rise to an 'eye-line match', or when it gives rise to an irrational cut, or introduces false movement? The answer, I think, can be posed in terms of the three figures of time we have described per Kant and via Hölderlin, and for Deleuze, we might say, these lines reach their apotheosis in *The Time-Image*.

The time-image remains one of Deleuze's most elusive concepts, but based on our prior discussion, we should be able to understand how the cinema resumes the problem at the heart of critical philosophy. Its predecessors (Renoir, Welles, etc.) notwithstanding, modern cinema emerges with the derangement of sensory-motor coordinates that had formerly organised movement, action and causation. Deleuze defines the predominant presupposition of classical cinema as 'organic', insofar as the 'composition of movement-images [montage]' is determined by 'the laws of a sensory-motor schema'[71] in accordance with the idea of a coherent and unified whole. Insofar as it disjoints time, modern cinema embarks on a timeline that deviates from the synthetic 'health' of organic images, and as we have already seen, Deleuze previews this argument in his discussion of Hölderlin. But perhaps we can go a step further, for the challenge that confronts us, in the remainder of this essay, is to demonstrate how the transcendental Oedipus is recast in *The Time-Image*.

In this respect, the decision to turn to Antonioni reflects the particular trajectory that we have traced to this point, especially insofar as the elaboration of critical philosophy carries us to the threshold of pathological images to which Antonioni was so deeply devoted. The director's incomparable depictions of boredom, malaise, and finally enervation seem not only to expend the vitality of his characters but to exhaust the meaning (representation) of the image. The filmmaker's

[70] Ibid. p. 128.
[71] Ibid. p. 128.

body of work – above all, the remarkable quarter century that begins with *Story of a Love Affair* (1950)[72] and ends with *The Passenger* (1975)[73] – rests on the rigorous depletion of representation, and it's in this regard that he invents tastes, techniques and images commensurate, I think, to the problem of critical philosophy. My contention is that the three figures of time that we have already elaborated are resumed and expressed in Antonioni's works of the 60s and 70s. By this point in his career, the director had shed his nominal link to Italian Neorealism in order to focus, as he said, on the fate of the individual. In relation to this transformation, which we might call 'the end of man',[74] Antonioni alludes to many of the same historical factors ('the war, the immediate postwar situation. . .'[75]) with which Deleuze explains the breakdown of the sensory-motor schema. But far from documenting this eventuality by virtue of causes it depicts, Antonioni's films concern the effects or symptoms of what has happened – what 'remains' [sic] of the individual.[76] More than merely critical, the filmmaker's most remarkable works are *diagnostic*, and Deleuze duly treats Antonioni as a 'physician of culture' – 'the only contemporary author [*auteur*] to have taken up the Nietzschean project of a real critique of morality'.[77]

Rather than debate this point, I want to affirm it on the basis of a crucial insight, namely, that the diagnostic project is inseparable from his temporal one. 'Eros is sick',[78] Antonioni says, but so is Chronos. What happens? Capturing the boredom, aimlessness, superficiality and self-consciousness of a leisured class, Antonioni pursues a kind of serial analysis of the sickness of the passions. In his most astonishing films, the director subjects this 'malady of feeling'[79] to remarkable analyses.[80]

[72] *Story of a Love Affair*, film, directed by Michelangelo Antonioni, Italy: Villani, 1950.

[73] *The Passenger*, film, directed by Michelangelo Antonioni, Italy: Compagnia Cinematographia Champion, 1975.

[74] We duly associate this phrase with Michel Foucault, and while Deleuze says that Foucault traced the death of man back to the classical and modern age (Gilles Deleuze, *Foucault*, trans. Sean Hand (Minneapolis: University of Minnesota Press, 1988), pp. 73ff.), he might have said that Antonioni's films belong to, and even consummate, this lineage.

[75] Michelangelo Antonioni, *The Architecture of Vision: Writings and Interviews on Cinema* (Chicago, IL: University of Chicago Press, 2007), p. 22.

[76] Ibid. p. 23.

[77] Deleuze, *The Time-Image*, p. 8.

[78] Antonioni, *The Architecture of Vision*, pp. 33–4.

[79] Ibid. p. 21.

[80] This phrase (in Italian, 'La malattia dei sentimenti') was the original title of an interview that Antonioni gave in 1962. Translated, the piece appears as 'A Talk with Michelangelo Antonioni on His Work' (Antonioni, *The Architecture of Vision*, pp. 21–46).

Hence, in a statement delivered upon the screening of *L'Avventura* at Cannes,[81] he characterised the film as a 'story told in images whereby, I hope, it may be possible to perceive not the birth of a mistaken attitude but the manner in which attitudes and feelings are misunderstood today'.[82] Antonioni continues: 'Why do you think eroticism is so prevalent today in our literature, our theatrical shows, and elsewhere? It is a symptom of the emotional sickness of our time.'[83] Again and again, Antonioni reveals the necrosis of libido, the decay of affects that (perhaps?) once bound us to each other and bound us all to the world: 'what has love become that a man or a woman should emerge from it so disabled, pitiful and suffering, and act and react as badly at the beginning as at the end, in a corrupt society?'[84]

Deleuze invokes Antonioni's symptomatology on several occasions, but we would do well to understand the gesture in light of his earlier meditations on Oedipus. After all, to which texts could 'Eros is sick' be more aptly applied than Sophocles' Theban trilogy? More to the point, Oedipus augurs what we discover in modern cinema: the immanence of erotic afflictions and the malady of temporality. Detached from the circle of time, Oedipus wanders the Kantian line, and Deleuze picks up this thread in *The Time-Image* – especially in the 'bal(l)ade', the meandering story stroll, with which a kind of 'schizo' becomes the protagonist of modern cinema.[85] 'Bicycle-less neo-realism', Deleuze says, 'replaces the last quest involving movement (the trip) with a specific weight of time operating inside characters and excavating them from within (the chronicle).'[86] Where characters of classical cinema had been confident centres of perception and action, regulating movement and indirectly representing time, Antonioni introduces a pathology that corrupts the dramatic action and introduces the malady of temporality. For Antonioni, Deleuze writes, 'there is no other sickness than the chronic, Chronos is sickness'.[87]

For Deleuze, then, the importance of Antonioni consists in having realised the pathology of time, not simply in the context of the cinema but *on the basis of the cinema*. What does this mean? Modern cinema

---

[81] *L'Avventura*, film, directed by Michelangelo Antonioni, Italy: Cinco del Duca, 1960.

[82] See 'A Talk with Michelangelo Antonioni on His Work', where the director reads the statement in response to an interviewer's question (Antonioni, *The Architecture of Vision*, pp. 32–4).

[83] Ibid. p. 33.

[84] Deleuze, *The Time-Image*, p. 6.

[85] Ibid. pp. 9–11, 185.

[86] Ibid. p. 23.

[87] Ibid. p. 25.

invents the means to outstrip movement itself and, thereby, to introduce time into the image – not by virtue of representation but as a consequence of its breakdown. In Deleuze words, 'the aberration of movement specific to the cinematographic image sets time free from any linkage'.[88] What we discovered of Kant ought to be born in mind here: *time is a priori*. To elucidate this 'anteriority of time' in the cinema,[89] Deleuze alludes to *L'Homme ordinaire du cinéma*, Jean-Louis Schefer's prose-poem of cinematic experience.[90] Notwithstanding his enormous respect for Schefer, Deleuze suggests that *L'Homme ordinaire du cinéma* explains cinematic time by virtue of 'a primordial crime with an essential link to this condition of cinema'.[91] In other words, there must be 'a birth of the world that is not completely restricted to the experience of our motivity':[92] of Schefer, Deleuze says, 'the most distant recollection of images must be separated from all movement of bodies'.[93] Deleuze calls this primordial myth of cinema an 'homage to psychoanalysis', and the reason is that the myth consists in a crime that explains, retroactively, a prelapsarian and unattainable state outside of time.

Psychoanalysis has provided the study of cinema with no more than 'one sole object, one single refrain, the so-called primitive scene', he writes. In truth, what's at stake in the 'primordial crime' is a myth of cinema commensurate to *Oedipus Rex* – or, better still, *Totem and Taboo*. To put it another way, the malady of cinematic time is referred to a first cause, a primordial crime, a modern myth to explain and thereby replace our broken idols – but this is precisely the logic against which Deleuze strives in both his lectures on Kant and his books on cinema. Why does he return to Sophocles if not to displace the Oedipal myth, which psychoanalysis created, by demonstrating that the Oedipal tragedies (even *Antigone*) concern the *crumbling of myth* – when man and God, divided by a line of time, turn away from each other?

Thus, while Deleuze rejects the pretence of a primordial crime, he is quick to add that 'there is no other crime than time itself'. We cannot explain time on the basis of a previous, or mythic crime, a crime before time, because in the cinema time is 'anterior to the controlled flow of every action'.[94] The 'anteriority of time' constitutes the transcendental

[88] Ibid. p. 37.
[89] Ibid.
[90] Jean-Louis Schefer, *L'Homme ordinaire du cinéma* (Paris: Cahiers du Cinéma, 1997).
[91] Deleuze, *The Time-Image*, p. 37.
[92] Ibid.
[93] Ibid.
[94] Ibid.

condition of the movement-image, the form of 'everything that changes and moves', but in the time-image we confront this form directly – not represented but realised. Antonioni's films of the 1960s and early 1970s can be situated along these quasi-Kantian lines. Antonioni undertakes an 'objective critique' of the individual, but at the bottom of his symptomatology, he discovers the malady of temporality. In *L'Eclisse*,[95] to take a notable example, the course of an aimless affair exposes images to a kind of perversion that precipitates endless tracking shots and abrupt cuts, distorted continuity and deformed movement. In Deleuze's words, Eros is sick 'not just because he is old and worn out in his content, but because he is caught in the pure form of a time which is torn between an already determined past and a dead-end future'.[96] With respect to Antonioni, we can identify three distinct, if related, predilections of the time-image, and by way of conclusion I want to suggest that these images resume and extend the three lines of Kantian time we have already elaborated – the straight and disjointed line ('time out of joint'), the invisible line and empty form of the caesura ('the affection of oneself by oneself'), and the line that divides the subject from itself ('I is an Other').

Antonioni's films do not explain Kant's three figures of time or provide their representational analogues: his images express relations and produce affects that renew the Kantian lines we have adumbrated. With Antonioni, the cinema renews critical philosophy, and Deleuze elaborates the first and second figures of time in view of what he calls an 'any-space-whatever' (the third figure we will educe on our own). Broadly construed, this concept of any-space-whatever describes a topos torn from continuous and contiguous coordinates, and so the any-space-whatever ought to be opposed at every level to the common sense of extended space. For Deleuze, modern cinema develops fragments of space in the absence of sensory-motor centres: the overarching pretence of organic space gives way to anomalous and anonymous milieu and, thence, to direct presentations of time.

> Antonioni's art will continue to evolve in two directions: an astonishing development of the idle periods of everyday banality; then, starting with *The Eclipse,* a treatment of limit-situations which pushes them to the point of dehumanized landscapes, of emptied spaces that might be seen as having absorbed characters and actions, retaining only a geophysical description, an abstract inventory of them.[97]

---

[95] *L'Eclisse*, film, directed by Michelangelo Antonioni, Italy: Cineriz, 1962.
[96] Deleuze, *The Time-Image*, p. 24.
[97] Ibid. p. 5.

In effect, Deleuze describes two distinct, yet intimately related, operations of the image, which we might call disconnection and deframing. In the first place, Antonioni opens up vast 'idle periods of everyday banality', and perhaps no director has gone further in the depiction of '[t]iredness and waiting'. The filmmaker's method is to convey 'the interior *through* behavior'[98] – not the event or the experience so much as its aftermath, when all that remains is a posture, gesture, or attitude. As Deleuze writes, 'the idle periods in Antonioni do not merely show the banalities of daily life, they reap the consequences or the effect of a remarkable event which is reported only through itself without being explained (the break-up of a couple, the sudden disappearance of a woman. . .)'.[99] Like Bresson, whom he greatly admired, Antonioni tends to elide or occlude what we would normally conceive of as the 'event' in favour of analysing its effects: 'When everything has been said, when the main scene seems over, there is what comes afterwards. . .'[100] This tendency characterises the first of Antonioni's three types of time-image, but more precisely, we should say that this image corresponds to the first figure/formula, 'the time is out of joint'. In Antonioni's film, scenes begin too late and shots go on too long (the director was known to keep the camera rolling even after saying cut in order to capture 'certain spontaneous movements in their gestures and facial expressions that perhaps could not have been gotten in any other way').[101] For all their durations, though, the director's notorious long takes are rarely obvious or simply synthetic. In the great trilogy of *La Notte*,[102] *L'Avventura* and *L'Eclisse*, the predominance of *plans séquences* do not consolidate space as such, but induce fragmentation, as if a kind of incoherence blossomed at the heart of images. 'The connection of the parts of space is not given',[103] and as a result, the line of time unfolds according to new and disjointed chrono-logic.

The second tendency is just as striking as the first, though it seems to operate in an entirely different direction. Where the first kind of image dwells in banality and boredom, Deleuze says that the second presses the image towards a 'limit-situation'.[104] No doubt the limit of this limit,

[98] Ibid. p. 9.
[99] Ibid. p. 7.
[100] Ibid.
[101] Antonioni, *The Architecture of Vision*, p. 25.
[102] *La Notte*, film, directed by Michelangelo Antonioni, Italy: Nepi Films, 1961.
[103] Deleuze, *The Time-Image*, p. 8.
[104] Ibid. pp. 5–7.

so to speak, can be found in the literal deserts of *Zabriskie Point*[105] and *The Passenger*, but as the industrial landscape of *Red Desert*[106] already indicates, a wasteland can be made as easily as it can be found. Hence, the second kind of time-image refers to the evacuation of determinate content qua space. From one film to the next, Antonioni undertakes a depopulation; even characters themselves are 'objectively emptied: they are suffering less from the absence of another than from their absence from themselves'.[107] In fact, the filmmaker evacuates the image in two dimensions. On the one hand, he does so by virtue of what Pascal Bonitzer famously called '*décadrage*' (deframing), namely, removing the constituents of the frame or moving the frame so as to leave well-nigh all constituents behind.[108] This practice grows increasingly prominent in Antonioni's films of the 60s and 70s, perhaps nowhere more astonishingly that in the conclusion of *L'Eclisse*, where the exhaustion of the melodrama gives way to a sequence of deframed and depopulated images of the Roman suburbs.

On the other hand, Antonioni also experiments with 'the subjective point of view of a character', which would otherwise stabilise movement and montage, by revising and even resisting attribution. Shots that seem relatively neutral, unattached to any one character, are subsequently assigned to a particular perspective. Still, Antonioni's more profound practice inverts this logic: the initial suggestion that a shot is identified with particular character is at turns unconfirmed, problematised and subverted. The character is 'absent, or has even disappeared, not simply out of frame, but passed into the void'.[109] Antonioni experiments with this operation to ingenious effect in *L'Avventura*: when the passengers disembark from the boat to scour the small crag of an island for the missing member of their party, the search inspires an orchestration of perspectives wherein both those seen and those seeing seem on the brink of being disappearing. In this light, perhaps Antonioni allows us to return the problem that we have already rehearsed with respect to Kant: if time is an empty form, if it cannot be represented in space or given content, how can we speak of a time-image? I've sought to answer this question more generally, but Antonioni provides a specific and altogether Kantian response. It should now be clear that, even as he analyses

[105] *Zabriskie Point*, film, directed by Michelangelo Antonioni, USA: Metro-Goldwyn-Mayer, 1970.
[106] *Red Desert*, film, directed by Michelangelo Antonioni, Italy: Film Duemila, 1965.
[107] Deleuze, *The Time-Image*, p. 9.
[108] Pascal Bonitzer, *Decadrages: Peinture et Cinema* (Paris: Diffusion, Seuil, 1985).
[109] Deleuze, *The Time-Image*, p. 8.

the fate of the individual, Antonioni presses the cinema to the point of evacuating the image. Exhausted of virtually all content, it becomes an any-spaces-whatever commensurate to the empty form of time. In this caesura, the cinema revokes its traditional coordinates of space-time: caught between an indeterminate perception and an impossible action, this image suspends recognition and representation in a pure and paralysed becoming of thought. 'The situation no longer extends into action through the intermediary of affections. It is cut off from all its extensions, it is now important only for itself, having absorbed all its affective intensities, all its active extensions.'[110] In other words, the unfolding of images expresses 'the affection of self by self',[111] and inasmuch as this is Kant's formula for both time and thought, the time-image opens up the domain of thinking or 'mental-images'.

Deleuze says that Antonioni's films oscillate between these two types of time-images – between disconnection (time out of joint) and defaming (self-affection) – and on the basis of this confrontation, we can now speak of a third kind of time-image, specifically, an image of doubling qua division. This image appears across the director's work, but in *The Passenger* (1975), his enigmatic film about a man who tries to 'lose himself', Antonioni fashions a consummate example. The story follows David Locke (Jack Nicholson), a respected reporter who has come to Saharan Africa to finish a documentary. When he fails to meet with the rebels involved in Chad's civil war, he returns to his hotel, exhausted and demoralised. Locke knocks on a neighbour's door, looking for a drink, only to discover the man, Robertson, dead in his bed. Locke turns over the body, surveys the room and then pauses to consider the dead man's pallid face: the two bear a passing resemblance. The intimation of an idea begins to take hold – could Locke pass for Robertson and vice versa?

The sequence that follows constitutes one of the most remarkable and complex in Antonioni's oeuvre. Once he's decided to switch places with Robertson, using the body to stage his own death, Locke retreats to his room to doctor the two passports. As he looks up, we hear a knock on the door, then a voice (Robertson's), then another (Locke's), even though the film frames Locke, in a medium shot, silent and alone. It soon becomes clear that what audibly transpires is their meeting from the day before, and eventually Antonioni cuts to the reporter's reel-to-reel tape player: we have been listening to a recording. Nevertheless, this

---

[110] Ibid. p. 272.
[111] Ibid. p. 83.

mundane explanation for the dehiscence of what is seen and what is said will condition an even more 'fabulous conception of time'.[112] From the tape player, the camera pans right to Locke, who pauses in the midst of his forgery to look off-screen; without a cut, the camera pans left to follow his gaze, past the tape player, to an open pair of glass doors leading onto a veranda; there, in the same shot, we see a man appear on the balcony (Robertson), and then another (Locke), embroiled in the very conversation we have been hearing. What has happened?

Of course, this is a trick shot, but the technical contrivances that made the shot possible are of no interest here: the mystery that Antonioni expresses is time itself – or, more specifically, the line of time that traverses the subject and divides thought from itself. In other words, this is the last of the three Kantian formulas ('I is an Other'), and Antonioni creates it by playing on a convention of continuity editing, an eye-line or eye-line match, with which a camera movement or even a cut can convey a character's perception. In this case, Locke's eye-line motivates a pan and thereby frames the image of the balcony, but the suggestion of his perspective is met with the image of Locke himself in the past of a recorded conversation rendered incarnate. Thus, in the duration of a single shot, the line of time bifurcates, propelling us in two directions – a past in which Locke complains of the force of habit, repetition, and conventions which determine ('It's we who are the same, who have the same codes. . .'), and a future in which Locke will dare to risk losing himself in order to try to discover a different mode of life. The past has become uninhabitable, but what happens when he resolves to divagate his future? Already on the way to becoming Robertson in the present, Locke catches sight of himself in the past as both the past he was and the future he will become, the other whose identity he will assume. In this vertiginous moment, Locke is no longer himself at all because he is (at least) two: 'I is an Other.'

With this image, Antonioni consummates the argument that has shaped this essay. 'Over several centuries, from the Greeks to Kant, a revolution took place in philosophy, the subordination of time to movement was reversed', Deleuze writes, and I began by asking how we can understand his suggestion that a 'similar story appears in the cinema'.[113] In relation to critical philosophy, and by way of Hölderlin, Deleuze formulates three formulas or figures for Kantian time; while these formulas can be found in various guises throughout *The Time-Image*,

---

[112] Deleuze, 'Seminar on Kant: 14/03/1978'.
[113] Deleuze, *The Time-Image*, p. 39.

I've argued that, for Deleuze, Antonioni in particular realises the three figures – 'time out of joint', 'the affection of self by oneself', and 'I is an Other' – in the expression of three types of time-image. These figures compose what I have called the Kino-Kant, and if this assemblage is inspired by a revolution that characterises both modern philosophy and modern cinema, I've suggested that this conjunction cannot be reduced to analogy or even pedagogy. For Deleuze, the task of film-philosophy is not to bring philosophy to bear on the cinema but, rather, to make the cinematic image a generative and genetic principle of philosophy, which is to say, the creation of concepts. Almost thirty years after the publication of *The Time-Image*, the endeavour to think images, to think time, has only just begun.

# Index

Kafka, F., 105, 298
Kant, I., 1–2, 5, 7, 8, 15, 17, 25–30,
    34, 36–43, 45–8, 50–1, 60–5,
    67, 68–9, 70n, 71–5, 77, 78,
    81, 85–95, 98, 100–2, 106–10,
    111–12, 114–16, 122, 128, 135,
    136, 137, 138, 140, 149, 151, 152,
    157, 160, 173–5, 179n, 231–8,
    245, 251, 253, 263, 268, 272, 275,
    276–81, 283, 294, 297–8, 300,
    303, 304, 305, 307–14, 316–20,
    323, 326
Kerslake, C., 4, 152
Kierkegaard, S., 156–7, 312n
Kleist, H., 19–20, 105–6, 108–10,
    111–12, 113, 114, 115–22, 125
knowledge, 5, 16, 29, 32, 34, 39, 56,
    72, 75, 88, 89–90, 115, 117, 174,
    180, 181, 182, 184, 218, 233, 255,
    260, 270, 313
    intuitive knowledge, 180, 233
Kohlhaas, 117–19, 122
Koyré, A., 296

Lacan, J., 54, 250, 283n, 296
Lacoue-Labarthe, P., 130, 132, 133,
    135, 140
Lautman, A., 1, 9, 44, 50, 53, 54–5,
    56, 57
Leibniz, G. W., 5, 14, 30, 31–2, 37, 43,
    46, 62, 63, 66, 68, 72, 75–6, 77,
    79–80, 83, 138, 140, 143n, 155,
    287, 290, 316
Levinas, E., 296
Lévi-Strauss, C., 54, 296
Lewis, D., 288, 291
life, 13, 20, 41, 132, 146, 162, 171,
    182n, 185–6, 187, 189, 205, 208,
    242
    Ethical Life (in Hegel), 190, 194–5,
    197, 199n, 202, 204, 206
    pure life, 20, 171, 185
limit, 42, 50, 51, 52, 54, 80–1, 83, 99,
    127, 130, 162, 176, 180, 279, 283,
    300, 303, 304, 313, 314, 315, 318,
    325
limitation, 34, 52, 60, 63, 67, 151, 314
lines of flight, 42, 113
logic, 5, 16, 40, 56, 71, 134, 144, 167n,
    174n, 178, 179, 181, 267, 299
Lucretius, 35
Lyotard, J.-F., 22, 295, 296, 297, 298,
    301, 302, 303, 304

machine, 1, 193, 195, 250, 298
    desiring-machines, 193, 196, 250; see
    also desire
    war machine, 19, 42, 105–6,
    110–15, 116, 118, 119, 120,
    122, 190, 196, 198–202, 207,
    209, 210
Maimon, S., 3, 5, 6–7, 9, 12, 18, 19,
    27, 28–31, 33, 36, 37, 43, 44–7,
    48, 50–2, 55, 56, 57, 60–1, 62–6,
    67n, 68, 69–78, 80, 81, 83, 84, 95,
    96, 98, 146, 158, 159, 232
Maimonides, M., 74–5
manifold, 61, 64, 65, 69–70, 86, 90,
    130, 131, 141, 143, 160, 245, 275;
    see also multiplicity
Marx, K., 254, 261, 296, 310
Mendelssohn, M., 74
metallurgist/metallurgy, 190, 209–10
method, 3, 6, 7–9, 19, 20, 27, 30,
    67n, 76, 83, 116, 117, 152, 157–9,
    164, 171, 181, 256, 257–8, 262,
    293, 294, 298, 325
    method of conditioning, 19, 27
    method of dramatisation, 9, 44, 52,
    53
    method of genesis/genetic method, 9,
    19, 27, 29, 30, 35
    more geometrico, 7, 171
    synthetic and constructive method,
    5, 6, 7, 9
    transcendental method, 44, 48, 53,
    73, 179n, 308
molar, 111, 120, 193
molecular, 111, 193
monism, 172, 173
Montaigne, M., 295, 296
multiplicity, 37–8, 54, 56, 57, 58, 67,
    130, 131, 136, 192, 244–5, 286
    differential multiplicity, 39, 58
    virtual multiplicity, 52, 55, 57
    see also manifold

nature, 15, 16, 18, 37, 86, 91–3, 97,
    98, 151, 172n, 175, 180, 188,
    193–4, 195, 241, 298, 299, 300,
    301, 302, 303, 305
    natura naturans, 172, 183, 186, 187
    natura naturata, 172, 183, 186
    state of nature, 91, 92, 96, 97
necessity, 129, 130, 131, 134, 136,
    178, 194, 206, 216, 266, 286
Newton, I., 66, 139, 142, 308